Author Chronologies

General Editor: Norman Page, Emeritus Professor of Modern English Literature, University of Nottingham

Published titles include:

J.L Bradley
A RUSKIN CHRONOLOGY

Michael G. Brennan and Noel J. Kinnamon
A SIDNEY CHRONOLOGY 1554–1654

Gordon Campbell
A MILTON CHRONOLOGY

Edward Chitham
A BRONTË FAMILY CHRONOLOGY

Martin Garrett
A BROWNING CHRONOLOGY:
ELIZABETH BARRETT BROWNING AND ROBERT BROWNING

A MARY SHELLEY CHRONOLOGY

A. M. Gibbs
A BERNARD SHAW CHRONOLOGY

Graham Handley
AN ELIZABETH GASKELL CHRONOLOGY

J. R. Hammond
A ROBERT LOUIS STEVENSON CHRONOLOGY
AN EDGAR ALLAN POE CHRONOLOGY
AN H.G. WELLS CHRONOLOGY
A GEORGE ORWELL CHRONOLOGY

Edgar F. Harden
A WILLIAM MAKEPEACE THACKERAY CHRONOLOGY
A HENRY JAMES CHRONOLOGY

John Kelly
A. W. B. YEATS CHRONOLOGY

John McDermott
A HOPKINS CHRONOLOGY

Roger Norburn
A JAMES JOYCE CHRONOLOGY

Norman Page
AN EVELYN WAUGH CHRONOLOGY
AN OSCAR WILDE CHRONOLOGY

Peter Preston
A D. H. LAWRENCE CHRONOLOGY

Nicholas von Maltzahn
AN ANDREW MARVELL CHRONOLOGY

Author Chronologies Series
Series Standing Order ISBN 0–333–71484–9
(*outside North America only*)

You can receive future titles in this series as they are published by placing a standing order. Please contact your bookseller or, in case of difficulty, write to us at the address below with your name and address, the title of the series and the ISBN quoted above.

Customer Services Department, Macmillan Distribution Ltd, Houndmills, Basingstoke, Hampshire RG21 6XS, England

AN ANDREW MARVELL
CHRONOLOGY

Nicholas von Maltzahn

First published 2005 by
PALGRAVE MACMILLAN
Houndmills, Basingstoke, Hampshire RG21 6XS and
175 Fifth Avenue, New York, N. Y. 10010
Companies and representatives throughout the world

PALGRAVE MACMILLAN is the global academic imprint of the Palgrave Macmillan division of St. Martin's Press, LLC and of Palgrave Macmillan Ltd. Macmillan® is a registered trademark in the United States, United Kingdom and other countries. Palgrave is a registered trademark in the European Union and other countries.

ISBN-13: 978–0–333–92888–2 hardback
ISBN-10: 0–333–92888–1   hardback

This book is printed on paper suitable for recycling and made from fully managed and sustained forest sources.

A catalogue record for this book is available from the British Library.

Library of Congress Cataloging-in-Publication Data
Von Maltzahn, Nicholas.
An Andrew Marvell chronology / Nicholas von Maltzahn
     p. cm. – (Author chronologies)
  Includes bibliographical references (p.) and index.
  ISBN 0–333–92888–1
     1. Marvell, Andrew, 1621–1678–Chronology. 2. Poets, English–Early modern, 1500–1700–Chronology. I. Title. II. Author chronologies (Palgrave Macmillan (Firm))

PR3546.V66 2005
824'.4–dc22   2004063665

10   9   8   7   6   5   4   3   2   1
14 13 12 11 10 09 08 07 06 05
Transferred to digital printing 2005

Contents

6760

113385

General Editor's Preface

Most biographies are ill adapted to serve as works of reference – not surprisingly so, since the biographer is likely to regard his function as the devising of a continuous and readable narrative, with excursions into interpretation and speculation, rather than a bald recital of facts. There are times, however, when anyone reading for business or pleasure needs to check a point quickly or to obtain a rapid overview of part of an author's life or career; and at such moments turning over the pages of a biography can be time-consuming and frustrating occupation. The present series of volumes aims at providing a means whereby the chronological facts of an author's life and career, rather than needing to be prised out of the narrative in which they are (if they appear at all) securely embedded, can be seen at a glance. Moreover whereas biographies are often, and quite understandably, vague over matters of fact (since it makes for tediousness to be forever enumerating details of dates and places), a chronology can be precise whenever it is possible to be precise.

Thanks to the survival, sometimes in very large quantities, of letters, diaries, notebooks and other documents, as well as to thoroughly researched biographies and bibliographies, this material now exists in abundance for many major authors. In the case of, for example, Dickens, we can often ascertain what he was doing in each month and week, and almost on each day, of his prodigiously active working life; and the student of, say, *David Copperfield* is likely to find it fascinating as well as useful to know just when Dickens was at work in each part of that novel, what other literary enterprises he was engaged in at the same time, whom he was meeting, what places he was visiting, and what were the relevant circumstances of his personal and professional life. Such a chronology is not, of course, a substitute for a biography; but its arrangement, in combination with its index, makes it a much more convenient tool for this kind of purpose; and it may be acceptable as a form of 'alternative' biography, with its own distinctive advantages as well as its obvious limitations.

Since information relating to an author's early years is usually scanty and chronologically imprecise, the opening section of some volumes in this series groups together the years of childhood and adolescence. Thereafter each year, and usually each month, is dealt with separately. Information not readily assignable to a specific month or day is given as a general note under the relevant year or month. Each volume also contains a bibliography or the principal sources of information. In the chronology itself, the sources of many of the more specific items, including quotations, are identified, in order that the reader who wishes to do so may consult the original contexts.

NORMAN PAGE

Acknowledgements

A chronology is especially dependent on previous labours in the field, here those of some notable modern students of Andrew Marvell and his works. The vital contribution of the successive Oxford editions of *The Poems and Letters of Andrew Marvell*, the work first of H.M. Margoliouth (1927) and then also Pierre Legouis and Elsie Duncan-Jones (1971), was matched by Legouis's extraordinary biography, *André Marvell* (Paris, 1928). That legacy has now been enriched by Hilton Kelliher's fine catalogue for the tercentenary exhibition, *Andrew Marvell: Poet and Politician* (1978); by Peter Beal's index to Marvell manuscripts as well as those more loosely Marvellian (1993); by Nigel Smith's imposing edition of *The Poems of Andrew Marvell* (2003); and by the ground-breaking work of Annabel Patterson, Martin Dzelzainis, and Neil Keeble, my fellow-editors of *The Prose Works of Andrew Marvell* (2003). Marvell has been the subject of much careful and ingenious investigation by these and other scholars, with some close studies of very disparate materials. Contributions from many skilful hands are gratefully credited in the documentation below. Such has been their achievement that any life-records and allusions hitherto unrecorded now seem to their discoverer to have a special lustre.

The present undertaking has also occasioned the kind assistance of Christina Alt, Claire Cross, Frans De Bruyn, Martin Dzelzainis, Sean Hawkins, Edward Holberton, Elena Ilina, Hilton Kelliher, Paul Mathole, Steven Pincus, Timothy Raylor, David Scott, Nigel Smith, Maria Unkovskaya, the Board of Hull Trinity House and its archivist Donald Woodward. I have been helped by many librarians and archivists and am thankful for their responsiveness and their welcome. I owe a special debt to the staff at the Bodleian Library, who have long borne the brunt of my many demands and have done so with exemplary professionalism and good nature.

Marvell was the first Renaissance poet I discovered for myself, that as a schoolboy in Nova Scotia encountering some anthology pieces, first of all 'The Bermudas'. I soon found a paperback *Poems of Andrew Marvell*, in Hugh Macdonald's edition for 'The Muses Library'. From that beginning it has sometimes seemed too much of a remove to later work of mine on the Whig Marvell and my edition of his *Account of the Growth of Popery and Arbitrary Government*. The chance further to read, teach and write about Marvell's poetry and prose has been a privilege for which I am greatly indebted to my students and colleagues at the University of Ottawa.

In completing this book, I have often had cause to be thankful for the friendship and hospitality of Rachel Pantin, Rachel Langdale and Simeon Maskrey. My personal and scholarly debts to Blair Worden are too little acknowledged in the pages that follow but his has been a major contribution. Clara and Poppy von Maltzahn have helped in many ways. To Ann Pantin and above all to Sarah Pantin my gratitude is beyond words. It is to them the book is dedicated, in memory of John Pantin.

Abbreviations and Conventions

The appended bibliography supplies fuller references for works cited in brief in this Chronology. With abbreviations, I have followed the archivists' lead with documents held in the Hull City Archives (BRB etc.) and in the Trinity House, Hull, the latter records distributed between ATH (administration), FTH (finances) and NTH (navigation).

1681	Andrew Marvell, *Miscellaneous Poems*. 1681
Account	Andrew Marvell, *An Account of the Growth of Popery and Arbitrary Government*
AM	Andrew Marvell
AM Letters	Hull City Archives, Andrew Marvell Letters, 2 vols (see also LHC below)
ATH	Hull, Trinity House, administration files
BL	British Library
Bodl.	Bodleian Library, Oxford
BRB	Hull City Archives, Borough Records, Bench Book
BRD	Hull City Archives, Borough Records, Deeds
BRF	Hull City Archives, Borough Records, Finances
BRL	Hull City Archives, Borough Records, Letters
BRM	Hull City Archives, Borough Records, Miscellaneous
Cash Book	Corporation of the Trinity House, Deptford (= London Trinity House), Cash Book 1661–95. London, Guildhall Library, MS 30032, vol. 2
CJ	*Journal of the House of Commons*
Cooke	Thomas Cooke, ed., *The Works of Andrew Marvell Esq.* 1726
Court Minutes	Corporation of the Trinity House, Deptford (= London Trinity House), Court Minutes. London, Guildhall Library, MSS 30004, vols 4 (1670–76) and 5 (1676–81)
CPW	*Complete Prose Works of John Milton*. Gen. ed. D.M. Wolfe. 8 vols. New Haven, 1953–82
CSPD	*Calendar of State Papers, Domestic*
FTH	Hull, Trinity House, finance files
Henning	Basil Duke Henning, *The House of Commons 1660–1690*. 3 vols. 1983
HMC	*Historical Manuscripts Commission, Reports*
Hull CA	Hull City Archives
LHC	Letter(s) to Hull Corporation. Almost all of Marvell's constituency correspondence is held at Hull City Archives, bound separately in the two volumes of 'Andrew Marvell

	Letters', as summarized in *The Poems and Letters of Andrew Marvell*, ed. H.M. Margoliouth, Pierre Legouis and Elsie Duncan-Jones (Oxford, 1971), vol. 2, p. 358
Luttrell	Parks, Stephen. *The Luttrell File: Narcissus Luttrell's Dates On Contemporary Pamphlets 1678–1730*. New Haven, 1999
MPW	Marvell Prose Works: *The Prose Works of Andrew Marvell*. Ed. Annabel Patterson, Martin Dzelzainis, Nicholas von Maltzahn and Neil Keeble. 2 vols. New Haven, 2003
Mr. Smirke	Andrew Marvell, *Mr. Smirke. Or, the Divine in Mode*
NTH	Hull, Trinity House, Navigation: 52/1 lights file Hull, Trinity House, Navigation: 57/1 duties file
PL	*The Poems and Letters of Andrew Marvell*. H.M. Margoliouth revised by Pierre Legouis with E.E. Duncan-Jones. 3rd edn Oxford, 1971
POAS	*Poems on Affairs of State*: further specified as either the 1697 or other late seventeenth- or early eighteenth-century publications with this title, or George deForest Lord, gen. ed. *Poems on Affairs of State: Augustan Satirical Verse 1660–1714*. 7 vols. New Haven, 1963–75
PRO	Public Record Office, London
Remarks	Andrew Marvell, *Remarks Upon a Late Disingenuous Discourse*
RO	Record Office
RT	Andrew Marvell, *The Rehearsal Transpros'd*
RT2	Andrew Marvell, *The Rehearsall Transpros'd: The Second Part*
Smith	*Poems of Andrew Marvell*, ed. Nigel Smith. 2003
Stats Co.	Stationers' Company (with further specification whether Wardens' Accounts, Court Books, or Waste Books)
SR	Stationers' Register: *A Transcript of the Registers of the Worshipful Company of Stationers. 1640–1708*. Ed. G.E. Briscoe Eyre. 3 vols. 1913–14
t.-p.	title-page
TC	*The Term Catalogues, 1668–1709*. Ed. Edward Arber. 3 vols. 1903
TH	Trinity House (specified as that of Hull or that of London, Deptford [the latter records now in London, Guildhall])
Thomason	Thomason Collection, British Library
Thompson	*The Works of Andrew Marvell, Esq. Poetical, Controversial, and Political...* Ed. Edward Thompson. 3 vols. 1776
Thurloe	*A Collection of the State Papers of John Thurloe*. Ed. Thomas Birch. 7 vols. 1742
W	Westminster

Conventions

Place of publication is London unless otherwise specified. Abbreviations in original documents have usually been expanded. Italic font, u/v, i/j and foul case I have usually conformed to modern practice. I have supplied sigla where pagination is too irregular; with manuscripts I have followed foliation or pagination as found. Square brackets are used for editorial interpolations and for inferences that seem plausible; square brackets with a question mark for interpolations or inferences where there is more doubt. There are numerous records for which some Marvellian dimension might be imagined – for example, disbursements from the Stationers' Company for press searches in 1672–73, in May–June 1676, and in the winter and spring of 1678 – but only the more evident connections have been listed here. Also included in square brackets are some letters cited in Marvell's correspondence that are no longer extant or remain to be discovered.

With Marvell's constituency correspondence, the entries here have been pared to a minimum for each of the almost 300 letters surviving. This calendar for the most part refers the reader to the full texts available (with persons index) in the second volume of Margoliouth's *Poems and Letters*. I have been unable to determine the present location of the few letters Margoliouth cited as in the Wilberforce House Museum. From the two great volumes of Marvell's constituency correspondence in the Hull City Archives, the following letters have gone missing, with the manner of their excision giving grounds for concern: *Poems and Letters*, no. 5 (29 November 1660), no. 67 (26 October 1667), no. 182 (13 May 1675), and no. 284 (4 June 1678). In the listings below, the distinction is sometimes blurry between news and business, but by the latter is meant Marvell's services in parliament (or London) to Hull and to its Trinity House. In referring to those corporations, I often use what may be styled the corporate plural, since Marvell usually addresses respectively the mayor and aldermen or the wardens.

The dates provided are old style but with the year taken to begin on 1 January. With letters from or events in that greater part of continental Europe that had adopted the Gregorian calendar, I have also supplied the date new style (ten days 'later') to avoid confusion. The chief run of dates from outside England are those arising from Marvell's part in Carlisle's embassy to Russia, and these are old style, since Russian suspicions of papal innovation delayed the adoption of the Gregorian calendar until the twentieth century. For events or documents dating from the first months in the year (through to 24 March), I have, as occasion invites, cited the year using both seventeenth-century English and modern practice: in this style, the date of Marvell's father's drowning is 23 January 1640/1 (or 1641 as we would have it), the date of Charles I's execution is 30 January 1648/9 (thus 1649). Often cited in the listings below are four major sources for dating publications within a given calendar year: 1) the bookseller George Thomason's notes on the thousands of publications from the 1640s and 1650s that he collected (at the British Library; see also Campbell, 6); 2) the book collector Narcissus Luttrell's dates on copies of publications in his collection, ca. 1679 to the early eighteenth century (widely dispersed, but see Stephen Parks, *The Luttrell File*); 3) the Term Catalogues advertising books after 1668–1709 (a more approximate index); and 4) the register of books entered to the Stationers' Company (a still more erratic guide to publication dates).

Introduction

This Chronology had its inception in a file I kept to organize information about Andrew Marvell's works and life, to record allusions to him and his writings, and to assist in finding fresh facts about him. Since Pierre Legouis's compendious *André Marvell* (Paris, 1928; revised and much abbreviated in English translation, 1968), there has been no comprehensive biography or allusion-list to compare with those afforded other authors, most conspicuously Marvell's more famous friend, John Milton. The lack is only partly compensated for by the excellence of the two-volume *Poems and Letters of Andrew Marvell*, of which the third edition appeared over 30 years ago (Oxford, 1971), edited by H.M. Margoliouth and revised by Pierre Legouis with the collaboration of Elsie Duncan-Jones. Rich as those volumes are and handsome in their presentation of the texts, they are selective in what they present of Marvell's life-records and of course contain little information about his prose works. Subsequent scholarship has added considerably to our store of knowledge about his life and works. The only counterparts to this Chronology are George deForest Lord's chronology in the Everyman edition of Marvell's *Complete Poems* (1984) and Hilton Kelliher's informative and richly illustrated *Andrew Marvell: Poet and Politician* (1978), the catalogue of the tercentenary exhibition at the British Library. There are many further life-records, however, and much related evidence for consideration by the student of Marvell. There is some consensus that Marvell is an enigma. That he may remain – it may be characteristic of a great poet to be so in some part and few persons are without their secrets – but it is hoped that this summary of his life-records may encourage wider reference to the rich store of information about him.

Another benefit of such a Chronology is its potential for encouraging further discoveries. My experience with a previous work in this series, Gordon Campbell's *A Milton Chronology*, is that such handbooks can greatly help the scholar, not least with fieldwork. It should be no melancholy fact for the chronologist that fresh finds will come to date his work increasingly. Marvell's open and regular handwriting makes documents from his hand peculiarly recognizable. Few literary figures of this date have left so much manuscript material behind. His energies as a correspondent and the sometimes secretarial dimension of his career ensure that more letters and state papers from his hand will continue to come to light. The canon of Marvell's poetry is still in some doubt – and not only the famously vexed problem of which Restoration satires to attribute to him – so the identification of more of his work in verse and prose may follow. New perspectives on Marvell have also been opened by Nigel Smith's edition of *The Poems of Andrew Marvell* (2003) and by the critical edition of *The Prose Works of Andrew Marvell* (2003) under the general editorship of Annabel Patterson.

A further reason for such a Chronology and new scholarship is that we are overcoming the legacy of Modernism and the degree to which New Criticism forced a separation between Marvell the politician and man of business and Marvell the poet. With Marvell the problem was aggravated by T.S. Eliot's influence on his twentieth-century reputation, drawing on a Kantian aesthetic inheritance. But there is much of interest in the intersections of the parts of Marvell's life and the different institutions and discourses in which he participated. Marvell's parliamentary career, which has been too much scanted, deserves fuller notice, in part because of its immediate relation to his satires and prose-works and in part because it was so central to his reputation in the century after his death and thus to the reception of his works in prose and poetry alike. That eighteenth-century afterlife I have gone some way to recording in the listings below. I regret not being able to give some account of the nineteenth and early twentieth-century reception of Marvell, but this would have much enlarged this volume and taken me further out of my competence, making me still more dependent on the work of other scholars. There are other sources of help in this quarter, the best being Legouis's durable *André Marvell*, Elizabeth Story Donno's *Marvell: The Critical Heritage* (1978), and Dan S. Collins, *Andrew Marvell: a reference guide* (Boston, 1981). Nor do I attempt any survey of twentieth-century criticism, for which these and other lists provide much guidance.

Marvell's birth at Winestead in the East Riding of Yorkshire was soon followed by his family's move to Kingston-upon-Hull. One of the few major ports on the east coast of England, Hull had prospered as the silting of the Ouse made York less accessible to shipping. His father's ministry at the Charterhouse (on the outskirts of Hull) invited his role as a preacher also at the Holy Trinity Church, the major congregation in Hull. Favoured by the Hull mercantile community, the rev. Marvell in due course married his two elder daughters into prominent local families and was honoured with bequests. As a churchman he found himself a figure of moderation, challenged by the rise of Laudian religion at the archbishop's seat in York at the same time as more radical Protestantism flourished in Hull. In the listings below, I have included entries for the rev. Marvell's life even during the younger Marvell's absence from Hull, since the father's example informs the son's allegiances (and suspicion of the Athanasian creed), especially in later years when the son entered contests over the Restoration settlement of the English Church. His father's and his family connections also helped Marvell find promotion in the 1650s, with Fairfax and with Cromwell, until his eventual success as a Cromwellian placeman recommended him in turn to the Hull constituency that then elected him to parliament in 1659 and again in 1660 and in 1661. Likewise, Marvell's Restoration service to the Hull Trinity House, the shipmasters' guild, which as a corporation was second only to that of that town itself, thrived owing to his assiduity as a man of business but also to family association, conspicuously with his brother-in-law, the prominent dissenting merchant, Edmond Popple.

Most of what Marvell learnt from his father may have been learnt by the age of 12, however. That is when the young Marvell was sent to Trinity College, Cambridge, with which his association lasted the better part of eight years, as he went from the humble dependence of a subsizar to his election to a scholarship at the college. Here his notable gifts as a linguist could be developed in the wider university curriculum of the day; in later years, his admirable Latin became his stock in trade as a humanist secretary. Owing to the expense of travel and the long onslaught of the plague in Hull in 1635 and after, he may never have returned home during the mid- to late 1630s. His absence from Hull was marked by the wide waste of the plague, by his sisters' marriages, by the deaths of his mother and of a relation who served the Marvell household, and by his father's remarriage. The prolonged remove from his family may have made him especially susceptible to other influences: he seems when 18, for example, somehow to have been lured by Jesuits from Cambridge to London. Not much is known about the episode. It was enough to bring a visit south from his father, however, followed by Marvell's return to Cambridge. There he remained at least until his father's death a year later (by drowning, 23 January 1641), after which he seems to have made his way to London again. By the time Hull played its historic part in the outbreak of the first Civil War in April 1642, he may already have been on the continent. Except for his Yorkshire employment with Fairfax in 1650–52, Marvell seems only to have visited Hull three times in the rest of his life: in 1666, a three-month trip in the summer of 1674, and a fortnight or so in the summer of 1678.

About Marvell's life in his twenties we still know too little. After the spring of 1642 and before the autumn of 1647, he spent four years in Holland, France, Italy and Spain, and thus seems to have learnt Dutch, French, Italian and Spanish, as Milton reports in writing on his behalf in 1653. A decade later it might be reported of Marvell that he 'hath spent all his time in travelling abroad with Noblemens Sonnes and is skilled in several languages' (see October 1656 below); he has long if inconclusively been associated with the young Duke of Buckingham and his brother, the Lord Francis Villiers, on their travels. Marvell's ensuing careers as poet and tutor, and later as satirist and prose controversialist, drew much on his long education at home and abroad. Of his idiomatic French we have an example in his note to the Genoese diplomat Francesco Bernardi (20 November 1658), with more in the speeches he delivered in French during the Carlisle embassy's visits to Sweden and Denmark. He taught at least French and Italian to Mary Fairfax, and his wide reading in those languages appears from his writings. If his knowledge of Dutch and Spanish was comparable, he must have been a very remarkable linguist. Moreover, Marvell's handwriting was shaped in this period, since the unmistakable, fluent, regular italic script on which he now settled differs from his earlier hand. The change shows between his signatures on the Savile (1642) and Meldreth (1647) deeds, and further in his letter to Cromwell (28 July 1653). This mature script is a feature of his secretarial career, whether in his work in Whitehall in the Protectorate, his part in Carlisle's embassy in the early 1660s, or his Restoration service to his constituency and to the Hull Trinity House. Its regularity is not much deformed even by haste, even where he knew (as with documents under correction) that he was not writing final copy. Marvell's script became something like a signature, then as now. Even his unsigned letters were plainly recognizable to his correspondents, and around 1680 the Lord Wharton could note on another anonymous document in Marvell's hand that it was 'in the hand writing of a friend deceased' (Bodl. MS Carte 77, 598ᵛ).

There is a strong likelihood that most of Marvell's poems were written in the decade 1647–58. His education and travels plainly animated his sense that he might sophisticate English poetry as he found it, especially upon his return from the continent ca. 1647. Any close dating of Marvell's lyrics is difficult, and I hope not to have pressed the evidence too hard. But just as he had an intimate and often intricate relation with his patrons, aristocratic and institutional, so too his poetry shows a striking intimacy and intricacy in relation to its pretexts. If his poetry is at all datable by allusion, association, and occasion, the evidence from his lyrics indicates that Marvell wrote chiefly in response to English and continental poetry published in the 1640s and early 1650s and that his compositions flourished in London literary circles, also in the Fairfax household and in Protectoral court culture (and its later legacy, as with his friendship with Philip, Lord Wharton). Returning to London from the continent in 1647 he met with fresh volumes of poetry by Cowley, Crashaw, Waller and Milton, among others, which demanded his response as a lyric poet. His writing of poetry seems then to have been sustained by his stay as tutor to Mary Fairfax at Nun Appleton in his native Yorkshire (1650–52). His return to London in 1652 may have refreshed his poetic ambition; although this seems impossible of proof, a different sort of performance seems to have been prompted by the culture of the metropolis. Different again is the more public poetry that followed in the time of Marvell's service as William Dutton's tutor, first at Eton and then abroad (1653–57), when even more private work like 'Bermudas' departs from his previous estate poetry. Some laureate career coloured his advancement in the Protectoral court, as that government approached its dissolution. In the Restoration, his literary gifts seem in the main to have found other expression. Had he written lyric poetry more regularly in the preceding years and in the succeeding decades, my sense is that he would have written more of it and that more might have survived and in different sources.

Just when Marvell wrote which of his lyrics is usually a matter of no very sure inference from source and context. Although the student of Marvell can now benefit from many decades of modern scholarship, the most recent editor of his poems rightly comments that 'many of the lyrics remain undatable with any certainty' (Smith xiv). A poem's date of composition may be no simple matter in any case, even if understood simply as the writing and rewriting by a poet of a given work. That Marvell may have kept revising his poems seems possible, but not probable: the early and late versions of 'Dignissimo suo Amico Doctori Wittie', 'Angelo suo Marvellius', and 'The First Anniversary' show only small changes over more than 20 years. If he did revise, his having in view the publication of some collection of his poems seems the likeliest reason for reworking earlier materials. But my acquaintance with Marvell the MP, controversialist and man of business in the 1670s suggests him most unlikely to offer up quite such a hostage to fortune, or not at any late date. Of the lyrics, only 'The Garden' has been persuasively dated to the Restoration: here Allan Pritchard's case can be strengthened by further evidence of the late date from extra lines in the companion poem '*Hortus*', where Marvell supplies a witty description of the faithless Charles II, amusingly reunited with the royal oak ('*Jupiter annosam, neglecta conjuge, Quercum / Deperit*'). This seems the exception that proves the rule. Although we may imagine other possible Restoration scenarios – Marvell admiring mowers, perhaps, at a rural retreat in Highgate, or recollecting them in tranquillity (?) at his private lodgings in Covent Garden – these do remain possibilities rather than probabilities.

The 1681 *Miscellaneous Poems*, brought to the press two years after Marvell's death by his 'widow', provides a very uncertain witness to his authorial intentions and more uncertain still to the dating of most of its contents. Its order is important because it may reflect in whole or in part the organization of some compilation from his hand. But chronological inferences are not much to be drawn from it. At first glance, the 1681 volume shows three distinct categories in AM's poetry: the lyrics (pp. 1–52: 'A Dialogue between The Resolved Soul, and Created Pleasure' through to 'The Garden' and '*Hortus*'); the poems addressed to named persons (pp. 53–108: 'To ... *Maniban'* through to 'Upon Appleton House' and 'On the Victory obtained by Blake'); and the state poetry from Commonwealth and Protectorate (pp. 111–39: 'The Character of Holland', 'The Horatian Ode' and 'First Anniversary', through to 'Two Songs at the Marriage of the Lord Fauconberg and the Lady Mary Cromwell'). But with the lyric category a different sequence suggests itself. Since the epigram 'To ... *Maniban'* belongs to the mid- to late 1670s (see 26 June 1677 below) and 'The Garden' and *'Hortus'* to 1668 or later, they may together be seen as Restoration work supplementing a previous body of lyric poetry that had perhaps been readied for the press at an earlier date. Since that body of poetry apparently included 'Tom May's Death', the likely date for any possible publication may have been ca. 1661 after the exhumation of May's body from Westminster Abbey; and if some printing was then in prospect, the possible debt of another poem, 'The Nymph Complaining for the Death of her Fawn', to a 1662 publication may reflect some revision of Marvell's lyrics at that date, possibly coinciding with his stay in Holland that autumn and winter. Whether or not the lyrics were thus assembled and revised by the early 1660s, they too seldom leave evidence of their original dating. (The first poem in *Miscellaneous Poems* (1681), 'A Dialogue, Between the Resolved Soul, and Created Pleasure', is the only other of these lyrics suggested as dating from the Restoration (Smith 33), but here the perceived debt to *Paradise Lost*, first proposed by Leishman, seems no necessary one, with Cowley's 'The Soul', from *The Mistress* (1647), the nearer influence.)

The lyrics are quite distinct from the much more datable occasional poems that fill out the 1681 volume. In this gathering of *silva*, they are followed by Marvell's satire 'Flecknoe' and his commendatory poems and epigrams, including the epitaphs, and then by his Commonwealth and Protectoral poetry (whatever the status of the obtruded celebration of Admiral Blake and 'A Dialogue between Thyrsis and Dorinda'), with the 'Horatian Ode' displaced to a more 'Protectoral' place after the Fairfax estate poetry. Within these subgroupings, evidence of their occasions better dates the poems than their ordering does. Context has usually allowed some more specific date to be suggested for them below.

It took Marvell the better part of five years to win a place nearer the heart of the Protectorate. In September 1657, he joined Milton as a secretary for foreign tongues in working for John Thurloe at Whitehall. It is unclear how far his work as a tutor to the Cromwellian protégé William Dutton had already engaged him in Protectoral service, especially when he had taken that pupil to Saumur in 1655–56. That Marvell had no special status with Oliver Cromwell, as he insisted in self-defence later in the Restoration, appears from the episode late in 1656 when Dutton's uncle, seeking to contract Dutton in marriage to Frances Cromwell, only settled on Marvell to represent him to Cromwell after Sir William Killigrew had refused the same request. It was not long thereafter, however, that he made himself into a Protectoral state-servant and then placeman. By the time he did so, the desperate attempts to normalize constitutional arrangements had met with Cromwell's refusal of kingship; moreover, the growing fragility of the regime and of Cromwell himself had become apparent. After Cromwell's death, Marvell came nearer to the centre of power. His close identification with that government has long been understood from his revealing letter to George Downing (11 February 1659). We can now see more clearly how he was promoted for election in Hull in early 1659: he was given the good news of the government's funding of the magazine there so that he could deliver it to that constituency's representatives on the eve of the election. Since merchants in Hull hoped it might be made a free-port, there was further incentive to elect MPs who seemed near the centre of power (letter of Henry Robinson to Hull Corporation [3?]0 December 1658, Hull City Archives, BRL 633). With Richard Cromwell's loss of power in the spring of 1659, however, Marvell was suddenly at a disadvantage. We can now see his resulting lack of standing in the orders relating to him in the great Whitehall office shuffle of July 1659: rather than gaining lodgings there at this date, as has been supposed, Marvell at this point had to give up his lodgings, only to be found others, only to lose those in turn. The political changes in this year were such as might lead a Milton to rejoice in the opportunity for revolution; in the event, the revolution that did follow, the Restoration, may well have been viewed by Marvell as a welcome return to a more monarchical and courtly government in which to make his way. His constituency again handily voted him in over a republican candidate in the Convention Parliament (2 April 1660), and he once more polled well in winning his seat in the Cavalier Parliament (1 April 1661).

In the early years of the Restoration, Marvell's initial involvement as a parliamentarian yielded to state service in 1662–65. Whatever his circumstances, he was perhaps also discouraged by an unwelcome settlement of the Restoration Church and the emerging temper of the Cavalier Parliament. Only in the sessions of 1667–68 – buoyed by the changes that encouraged his also writing 'Last Instructions', with Buckingham's eminence in the Cabal administration perhaps another source of hope – does he again find a more significant role as a proponent of Comprehension in the national church, speaking also to other causes of the hour. The failures of moderate churchmanship, especially with the renewal of the Conventicle Act (1670), seem to have sharpened Marvell's misgivings about the Cavalier Parliament and about the High Church bishops against whom he wrote so bitterly in the 1670s. He continued to serve his constituency unstintingly, although significant runs of his constituency correspondence from the early 1670s have been lost. With the Declaration of Indulgence (1672) he found other means by which to promote his political and ecclesiastical objectives. In part this involved seeking allies elsewhere, in his association, for example, with some prominent figures in the House of Lords and even further afield with his communications with the Dutch during the Third Anglo-Dutch War in 1674. Seldom speaking in the House now – with the notable exception of his intervention and discomfiture in late March 1677 – he turned to the clandestine printing of his major works of controversy and perhaps to composing some of the many political satires circulated in manuscript and later attributed to him. The lengthening periods between sessions of parliament invited such work.

During sessions of parliament, Marvell's duties as MP occupied much of his time. His assiduity as an MP is no mere artefact of his secretarial discipline in reporting to his constituency but is corroborated by visitors' reports of the difficulty in meeting with him when he was so engaged in the House of Commons. That engagement followed from personal and political commitments, from his wish to be indispensable, and from his constituency's payment to him of 6s.8d. per day in session (and the potential, should the Cavalier Parliament ever be dissolved, of his failing of re-election). Much of an MP's work might leave little trace: comparatively little survives from this period except for the Commons Journal and private records of parliamentary debates. Marvell did not often speak in parliament, although then sometimes in fraught circumstances; these I have listed in full. His unease about his interventions seems to have been genuine; moreover, his incidents with Clifford (18 March 1662) and with Harcourt and Seymour (late March 1677) reveal some lasting difficulty with the demands of public life.

Marvell's committee-work is here only represented when he is named to a committee, whether by name or more generally as a Yorkshire MP or as an MP for one of the sea- or outports (I have not listed committees open to all MPs). Committee assignments where interested parties are listed collectively might become a significant part of an MP's business. Marvell's involvement, for example, as one of the MPs for seaports in the attempted bills concerning the repair of Dover pier (1667, 1671) allowed him to represent Hull's needs and won him lasting favour with the Deptford Trinity House, whose interest he had helped to maintain. The listings below cannot specify when those committees sat, in part for reasons of space in this volume but also because committee meetings and attendance from that time are no certain matter. Like many other MPs, Marvell was sometimes double-booked as a committee-man; he also attended some committees to which he was not named; and he failed to attend some committees to which he was named. Nor do I include names adjacent to Marvell's in these committee listings, although it is tempting to read more into those with whom Marvell is grouped – for instance, when he is named in a committee listing for a supply bill (26 January 1671) between Sir Richard Powle and Sir William Coventry (great country figures in the 1670s but the latter disparaged by Marvell in 'Last Instructions') or is named in two lists, 2 March 1671, next to Hugh Bethell, a Yorkshire MP and Fairfax and Wharton supporter, later thrice worthy in Shaftesbury's estimation. Even the court figures with whom he may thus be found, for example Sir John Birkenhead, can seem interesting companions for Marvell the satirist and controversialist. But the uncertain manner of recording nominations to committees makes such placements too unreliable an indicator of the company Marvell kept in the House of Commons. Nor have I cited his presence at particular communion services at St Margaret's Westminster, where MPs were certified as communicants in the Church of England and which he attended. Any persistent absence would have been noted.

As a parliamentarian Marvell was usually slow to volunteer for committees with any very political cast, preferring to appear a keeper of local business. He had an interest in not getting above himself and not squandering advantages that might be needed for other services to Hull. Moreover, he usually did not sit on committees where Hull was already represented by his very active fellow-MP, Col. Anthony Gylby, who had been elected on the Duke of York's interest and was associated with the military in Hull. Marvell had differences with Gylby that expressed themselves early in their service to Hull. Whatever their personal animus, their dispute also reflects differences between town and garrison or between a regional mercantile community and the court in London. But their sometimes close cooperation over the years, whether acting for Hull or for its Trinity House, shows a lasting professional relationship. They understood each other's usefulness in the demanding work of protecting their constituency's interests.

During sittings of parliament, Marvell's assiduity as a correspondent to his constituency appears from his often making all three posts a week. This required special effort: he sometimes wrote during a lull in parliamentary action, or at dinner-time, or late at night just in time to send the letter. A grey area is his possible inconsistency in citing Westminster or London as his place of writing (and my inferences in the listings below – marked in square brackets – where he has specified neither). The Westminster address seems straightforward since he could write from the House of Commons with postal privileges. But in one case he missed dinner to write a letter to his constituency with present parliamentary news (4 November 1667) yet addressed the letter as from London. Sometimes he gives no place with the letter plainly written and posted from Westminster. Moreover, his lodgings in James Shaw's house in Maiden Lane, Covent Garden, may complicate the matter. When he took these up is unclear: he only wrote to his constituency using this address after joining the Great Russell Street household with Edward Nelthorpe and Richard Thompson (June 1677), but he had been there at least since the beginning of 1677 and possibly long before. Did he rightly distinguish this as Westminster or more loosely style it London? Nor does his stock of paper change depending on whether he wrote from one or the other. Marvell almost always used a parliamentary supply of paper as appears from the paper-stocks in Gylby's letters of like dates; even in Holland in 1662–63, Marvell wrote on the same paper he had been using at the House of Commons.

The quantity of Marvell's constituency correspondence has here required its citation in brief, cross-referenced to its publication in the second volume of Margoliouth's *Poems and Letters* (3rd edn Oxford, 1971). My distinction in the listings below between news and business follows from the correspondence being in the main newsletters summarizing parliamentary and sometimes further national and international affairs, but also sometimes reporting Hull's business in parliament or elsewhere in London. The candour of Marvell's first such effort (11 November 1660) soon gave way to a less personal style of information. Especially late in this career, Marvell prided himself on his thoroughness in sending letters to Hull with the Tuesday, Thursday, and Saturday posts, almost regardless of the weight of business. The mail normally took three days to reach that destination.

The Hull Trinity House correspondence follows from Marvell's work in London on behalf of this corporation, in parliament, in the law courts, and at Court. Most of these letters concern the Spurn Light: owing to the fees the Hull Trinity House might win from ships passing by this navigational aid, there was a long contest with other interested parties over building it. Here I have sought to trace only Marvell's part in the very many papers surviving from this business. The case of Edmund Clipsham's attempted evasion of duties (1676–77) engaged Marvell more briefly. With his letters to the Hull Trinity House, I have not specified which warden is addressed, with some exception made for correspondence involving his brother-in-law, Edmond Popple. Concerning Marvell's involvement with the Deptford Trinity House, I have supplied much fuller listings than have hitherto been available. That London corporation was grateful to elect this MP to sit among its Elder Brethren in May 1674. His participation in its meetings at Water Lane, near the Tower of London, supplies fresh evidence of his consistent presence in London in the last years of his life.

Whatever his later Whig reputation as a model MP, Marvell was not above seeking other means of preferment in the Restoration. There is the abiding mystery of his service to Carlisle in Holland in 1662–63, on the eve of the Second Anglo-Dutch War, which did not require Carlisle to stay in Holland, as is evident from his continued attendance at Privy Council. The speculation that Marvell was sent to trepan republican conspirators against the English crown seems too doubtful, since his Protectoral career made him the wrong bait with which to catch such fish (compare Colonel Bampfield's attempts to come in from the cold, in his letters from Holland in 1663, PRO, SP84/167/113ff.). Having exposed himself to rebuke from his constituency, Marvell made certain when next on embassy with Carlisle that his excuses were made and his position as MP assured. I have given much space to the

Carlisle embassy, but this was the culmination of Marvell's court service, and the descriptions by Miège and in the letters by Carlisle/Marvell are full of interest, with fresh examples of the latter cited below.

Within parliament, Marvell might make himself something of a retainer to one or another of the Lords. Long before the party system emerged, there were shifting interest groups affiliated with prominent figures in and out of court. In addition to his service to the Earl of Carlisle and what may have been a long association with the Duke of Buckingham, Marvell in the Restoration had significant connections with the Earl of Anglesey, Philip Lord Wharton, and the Boyle family, among others. Such connections played a part in his work as a controversialist in the 1670s, if not before. Even in a work like *Remarks* (1678), where Marvell reacts against the orthodoxies of his youth and the certainty with which they had been expressed, he seems also to defend a publication by the dissenting minister John Howe because it was addressed to Robert Boyle. A visibly partisan work, like the *Account* (1677), might find support from Wharton in his publishing campaign of 1676–77, as did Marvell's antiprelatical prose, which may in one case (the *Short Historical Essay*) have been held over from some earlier composition for present publication in a new season of episcopal excess. In a strongly hierarchical culture – much as that hierarchy had been challenged by the events of mid-century – such affinities allowed an intimacy with power from which Marvell might benefit. The affective side to such intimacy is hard to judge but may well have made Marvell the readier to promise service to the great and the good. The friendship with Wharton, for example, seems of a piece with Marvell's warm relations with others nearer his own station, like Sir Edward Harley, James Harrington, John Rushworth, Jeremy Smith, John Pell, the wealthy Thompson brothers in Yorkshire, and Milton.

Marvell's most ardent affection, at least on record, was for his nephew William Popple, who was in London for much of the 1660s before going to Bordeaux in 1670, where he then received many of Marvell's most revealing letters. They saw each other again only in 1674, when Marvell in London awaited his nephew's arrival from France before journeying north to Hull together. Popple, who moved back to England in the late 1680s, also came to possess a most important copy of Marvell's *Miscellaneous Poems* (1681), which features manuscript corrections, the Cromwell poems, and further Restoration satires by Marvell or more loosely Marvellian (now Bodleian MS Eng. poet. d. 49). The vexed question of Marvell's possible marriage to his sometime landlord and housekeeper Mary Palmer remains (see 13 May 1667 below). He only belatedly came to share her address in Westminster in the 1670s, although if her story were true his desire for secrecy might explain any and every subterfuge and the resulting lack of better evidence for their marriage. But it is puzzling that Marvell, who immersed himself in controversy in 1672 and after, and was aware that High Churchmen were gathering calumnies against him, should at that date begin to use Mary Palmer's address, which could associate him with a shameful marriage. My doubts about Mary Palmer's claims (made after Marvell's death) are such that I have in great part referred to her by that name, which she was buried under, although when I come to the legal documents after Marvell's death I refer to her interchangeably also as Mary Marvell. Marvell's sexuality and psychology have recently been explored by Paul Hammond (1996) and by Derek Hirst and Steven Zwicker (1999) in ways that further inform Marvell's long bachelorhood and his representations of desire.

The entries below for the century after Marvell's death are differently organized, both for reasons of space and since more specific dates are often unavailable within a year. I have tried to be inclusive, with the following exceptions. I have not listed many of the later seventeenth- and eighteenth-century book-sale and library catalogues in which works by Marvell surface, with or without attribution, although I have included some of the collections left by persons known to be close to Marvell – Benjamin Worsley and the Earl of Anglesey, for example – as well as a few eye-catching entries, such as the attribution to Marvell of *The Character of Holland* in *Bibliotheca Digbeiana* (1680), before its publication as his in *Miscellaneous Poems* (1681). We still lack any more comprehensive indices of items in sale and library catalogues; moreover, the former can prove a deceptive guide to book-ownership, since booksellers might 'salt' these offerings with other wares. Another omission is of many book-advertisements naming Marvell, where especially newspaper notices of the successive editions of *Poems on Affairs of State* often and repeatedly cited Marvell among other contributors to those collections, which must have led to his wider identification as the author of such satires in the 1690s and after. Great uncertainties also attend the dating of later manuscript copies of poems and especially satires by Marvell and/or attributed to him, and the relationships between these manuscripts in great part remains to be charted, especially as these proliferate in the 1680s and later. I have elsewhere analysed the attributions ('Marvell's Ghost', 1999), but until these materials are more fully mapped, the best guides remain Peter Beal's Marvell entries in his *Index of English Literary Manuscripts* and Nigel Smith's list of variants in *The Poems of Andrew Marvell* (we await Harold Love's *English Scriptorial Satire, 1660–1714*). I have not much cited these manuscripts in the listings below. Nor have I cited every advice-to-a-painter poem or reference to such, since the specific connections of such poems to Marvell's example(s?) seem too tenuous.

This book ends too arbitrarily in 1780, a century after Marvell's death and just after the first publication of his complete works. The very last entry points back beyond the first entries to Marvell's Cambridgeshire ancestry. And even as this listing goes to press, fresh discoveries beckon. But here this work must end for the present, 'Having I hope thus far done you right in matter of Chronology'.

An Andrew Marvell Chronology

1584

March

1 (Sunday) AM's mother Anne Pease (daughter of George and Ann Pease) baptized in Flamborough, Yorks. (Yorks. East Riding RO, PE85/1, 7ᵛ)

ca. 1585

Birth of the poet's father Andrew Marvell at Meldreth, Cambridgeshire; his family seems long to have farmed there and a manor in the village was known as the Marvells as late as the nineteenth century. For evidence of early sixteenth-century Marvells (also Marwell, Merwell) in Meldreth and Shepreth, see extracts from Ely Cathedral Registers in William Cole's transcriptions (1780 below). Thomas Fuller is informed by the rev. AM's 'son-in-law' that this 'Andrew Marvail was born at Mildred in [Cambridgeshire], and bred a master of Arts in Trinity-colledge [*sic*] in Cambridge'. (Fuller 159)

1601

Andrew Marvell (senior) matriculates at the 'Puritan' Emmanuel College, Cambridge. (Venn, *Alumni Cantabrigienses*)

1605

Andrew Marvell (senior), elected a scholar in 1604, graduates BA, Emmanuel College, Cambridge. (Venn, *Alumni Cantabrigienses*)

1607

Andrew Marvell (senior) ordained as deacon at York. (Marchant 262)

1608

March
Andrew Marvell (senior) ordained as deacon at York. (Marchant 262; Kelliher 2004a)

November
Andrew Marvell (senior) 'licensed by the bishop of Ely to serve as curate and schoolmaster at Melbourne, adjacent to his birthplace' (Kelliher 2004a). Proceeds MA. (Venn, *Alumni Cantabrigienses*)

1609

January

8   (Sunday) The curate Andrew Marvell's first entry in the burials section of the Flamborough parish register, with more to follow, also under baptisms, until 1614. (Yorks. East Riding RO, PE85/1/late in the register, and 15^v–16^v)

May

30   (Trinity Sunday) Andrew Marvell (senior) ordained as priest at York. (Marchant 262; Kelliher 2004a)

1612

October

22   (Thursday) In Cherry Burton (near Beverley), 'Andrew Marvell and Anne Pease were maryed', as noted in the parish register. (Yorks. East Riding RO, PE69/1/24)

1614

April

23   (Saturday) The rev. Andrew Marvell moves from Flamborough when presented with living in Winestead-in-Holderness, ca. 14 miles east of Kingston-upon-Hull: 'Andrewe Marvell parson of Winestead was inducted into the corporall and peaceable possession of the sayd parsonage by Mr Marmaduke Brooke, deane, parson of Rosse upon Easter even, being Georges day' – entered in the parish register in the rev. Marvell's hand (Winestead Parish Register, 'Oenotopia', Yorks. East Riding RO, PE125/1/4^r, 1^r, 17^v, 30^r).

1615

March

14   In Winestead, 'Anne the daugher of Andrew Marvell borne March 14to being Tuesday in the night and was baptised upon the Annunc: Mart. 25°', as entered by her father in the parish registry. (Yorks. East Riding RO, PE125/1/4^r)

1616

October

20   (Sunday) In Winestead, 'Mary the daughter of Andrewe Marvell borne October 20 ~~and~~ was baptiz: upon Simon and Jude's day, Octobr, 28vo', as registered by her father. (Yorks. East Riding RO, PE125/1/4^v)

1618

September

28 (Monday) In Winestead, 'Elizabeth the daughter of Andrewe Marvell borne Sept. 28 and bap. Octb. 6to', as registered by her father. (Yorks. East Riding RO, PE125/1/4^v)

1620

The rev. Andrew Marvell licensed as a preacher. (Marchant 262)

November

12 (Sunday) In Winestead, AM's grandmother 'Ann Pease widow was buryed', as registered by her son-in-law, the rev. Andrew Marvell. (Yorks. East Riding RO, PE 125/1/17^v)

1621

March

31 (Saturday) In Winestead, 'Andrewe the sonne of Andrew Marvell borne Martii ultimo being Easter-even was baptized Apr: 5to', as registered by his father. (Yorks. East Riding RO, PE 125/1/4^v)

1623

September

7 (Sunday) In Winestead, 'John the sonne of Andrew Marvell borne 7^{bris} 7mo was baptized Sept: 9no', as registered by his father. (Yorks. East Riding RO, PE 125/1/4^v)

1624

September

20 (Monday) In Winestead, 'John the sonne of Andrew Marvell buried', as registered by his father. (Yorks. East Riding RO, PE 125/1/18^r)

30 The rev. Andrew Marvell elected Master of the Hull Charterhouse (has a dozen occupants) in Sculcoates, near Hull, and becomes preacher at Holy Trinity Church. Hence the family came to live 'at the separate house of the Master of the Charterhouse ... These almshouse buildings were outside the town, about a quarter of a mile north of the walls and some fifty yards from the River Hull. There were gardens belonging to the Charterhouse' surrounded by a brick wall. Only near neighbours the Alureds, minor gentry

occupying the Charterhouse itself. Presentation sealed 2 October 1624. (BRB 3:127; Margoliouth 351; Burdon 1982, 33)

The rev. Andrew Marvell 'became Minister in Hull, where for his life time he was well beloved. Most facetious in his discourse, yet grave in his carriage, a most excellent preacher, who like a good husband never broached what he had new brewed, but preached what he had pre-studied some competent time before. Insomuch that he was wont to say, that he would crosse the common proverb, which called *Saturday the working day, and Munday the holy day of preachers'* (Fuller, 159). 'He attracted a little over £60 in funeral bequests, the most conferred on any one cleric in either town [Hull or Leeds] throughout the whole period' (Cross, 23).

1625

April

6   (Wednesday) Public proclamation in Hull of the death of King James (d. 27 March 1625) and succession of King Charles; declaration published on scaffold set up for the purpose in the market, attended by the burgesses and the mayor and aldermen in scarlet gowns. (BRB 3:134)

August

Accounts for the Charterhouse audited, showing annual rents of £123 6s.11d. (Cook 141)

November

15   (Tuesday) The Hull Corporation settles the disagreement between Richard Perrott, minister at Holy Trinity Church, and the rev. Andrew Marvell over the latter's preaching at that church. (BRB 3:141)

1626

Late winter? Ships transporting 1350 soldiers set sail from Hull to support the king of Denmark, early in the Thirty Years War. (Tickell 297)

The rev. Andrew Marvell licensed as a lecturer, Holy Trinity Church. (Marchant 262)

At the Charterhouse, the rev. Andrew Marvell enlarges 'the hospitall for women' by six rooms; there is also much rebuilding and repair of the chapel, rooms and 'studie', costing £108 15s.5d. With the new rooms completed, he drafts an account of 'Things to be considered about the Hospitall called God's house, and the disposing of its revenues', which first outlines the finances and obligations of the institution. It then requests that the common hall 'be imployed as a perpetuall library for the maister of the hospitall and any other about the towne upon due caution'. In excusing his interest in this project, he notes that with 'infirmityes seasing upon me daily, I am not like long to enjoy it, but shall leave it to a successor'. Having 'a competent library' will attract better candidates for the mastership of the Charterhouse, will be of use to the ministers and scholars of the town and county, and will be a credit to Hull. (Hull Central Library, MS 'Sermons &c. of the Rev. Andrew Marvell'; Cook 141–2, 144–50)

1627

April

28   (Saturday) The rev. Andrew Marvell dedicates a copy of his sermon 'Israel and England parallel'd' to his patron Anne Sadleir, 'who hath beene a constant benefactresse to me and to my family' (London, Inner Temple, MS 531C). Whatever his unfriendliness to the Roman church in this sermon, another gift to Mrs Sadleir of unknown date is a nicely rubricated fifteenth-century MS exposition of the Ten Commandments, Pater Noster, Ave Maria, Directions for visiting the sick, and so forth, which she inscribed 'Mr. Andrew Marvell gave me this booke', possibly AM rather than the rev. Marvell. She in turn gave it to the minister William Parsons (13 November 1649), whose widow then gave it to the minister Meshach Smith, who bequeathed it to his brother-in-law John Worthington in 1707 (Cambridge University Library, MS Nn.4.12). A Bible belonging to the rev. Marvell is reported in a nineteenth-century sale catalogue (Beal 1993, 28).

October

13   (Saturday) Marvell's grandfather noted as having removed from Meldreth, Cambridgeshire, 'into Yorkshire': he seems to have moved to Hull with a grandson Andrew (son of Edward) in part to avoid the Forced Loan in Cambridgeshire. (PRO, SP16/52/82; Wall 1958b)

1628

April

2   (Wednesday) The rev. Andrew Marvell signs the will of Henry Alured, which specifies that AM's mother Mrs Marvell is (with the widow of the former Master of the Charterhouse) to determine what Alured's daughter should need by way of household goods

as the latter furnishes her house. (York, Borthwick Institute: Prob. Reg. 40, 247 ⁻ᵛ, will proved in May; Burdon 1982, 37)

13   'Andrew Marvell yeoman', the poet's grandfather, buried in Holy Trinity Church, Hull. (Wall 1958b)

June

4   (Wednesday) 'Andrew, son of Edw. Marvell', AM's cousin, buried in Holy Trinity Church, Hull; he had been baptized at Meldreth, Cambridgeshire, 16 November 1626. (Wall 1958b)

1629

Likely date of AM beginning attendance at Hull Grammar School where he seems to have been enrolled until going up to Cambridge in 1633, by then 'very well educated in Grammar learning'. This would have been owing to the instruction of James Burnett until 1632 and in 1632–33 his successor Mr Stevenson. AM is likely also to have been schooled at home, however, since his learned father had some role as a tutor (see 22 October 1637 below). (*MPW* 2:46; Wood, *Athenae*, 2:619; Margoliouth 351; Legouis 1928, 5–6).

September

30   (Wednesday) The rev. Andrew Marvell reaches an agreement with the Hull Corporation over the maintenance of Elizabeth Whincop, widow of the former master of the Charterhouse. (BRB 3:198)

1630

August

10   (Tuesday) The rev. Andrew Marvell among the witnesses of an earlier deed (1630) for delivery of bows and arrows from Castle at Hull to Tower of London, as well as other documents; this year there was further preparation of Hull's defences. (BRL 243, BRD 827A; Wildridge 11; Stanewell 125, 188, see also 155, 156, 157; Tickell 305–6)

October

15   (Friday) The rev. Marvell left 40s. in the will of George Pease, merchant, of Holy Trinity. (York, Borthwick Institute, Prob. Reg. 41, 334ʳ–335ʳ)

31   With the rev. Andrew Marvell's consent, the Hull Corporation gives the blind Leonard Storr a place in the Charterhouse; Marvell is also instructed to confer with the late William Gee's widow about Gee's legacy to the poor of Hull (£6 13s.4d.). (BRB 3:242)

1631

January

22   (Saturday) The rev. Marvell left £13 6s.8d. in will of Thomas
          Ferries, alderman, of Holy Trinity. (York, Borthwick Institute,
          Prob. Reg. 41, 334^r–335^r)

1632

April

17   (Tuesday) In the Easter season, the rev. Marvell and another
          minister, Richard Harrington, correspond in four letters energet-
          ically disputing Christ's descent into hell. Puritanically arguing
          against that tradition, the rev. Marvell's closeness of reasoning
          and suspicion of the Athanasian creed are soon matched by his
          animus in disputation, winning Harrington's reproach that
          'Your later letters are full stufft with swellinge (I may justly
          retorte) snarling bitinge belchinge termes... All which smell
          ranklie of a proud (to say noe worse) and hautie spiritt.' (BRL
          247, 247a, and BRL 247b, the last dated this day)

1633

The depredations of privateers (especially from Dunkirk) and even pirates
('from Sallee and Algiers'), as well as Dutch claiming 'a right to fish on the
coasts of England' leads to raising of ship money, especially in ports such as
Hull, and resulting discontents (Tickell 307–8). Later writing to his constituency, AM can recall ('though then a child') 'those blessed days when
the youth of your own town were trained for your militia, and did
methought become their arms much better then any soldiers that I have
seen there since' (*PL* 2:2) – this likely preceded his departure for Cambridge
at the end of this year.

Perhaps this year Samuel Cooper (?) paints the miniature of a boy who may
be AM, as claimed in the late nineteenth century (reproduced in Patterson
2000a, 12, from John L. Propert, *History of English Miniature Art*, 1887, 3:246).

December

14   (Saturday) AM matriculates as subsizar from Trinity College
          (Cambridge), funded by the college and obliged to menial
          service. His annual livery money is 6s.8d. and he receives 4d. a
          week for food. (Cambridge Univ. Archive: Matr. 6 (CUR 101.2),
          f. 1254; see Kelliher 1978a, 19–20)

29   AM's oldest sister Anne marries James Blaydes in the Charterhouse
          Chapel. (Sykes, 1896, 189; Legouis 1928, 15)

1635

'In the month of July, anno 1635, the plague, which, for some time past, had raged in several of the sea-port towns abroad, made its appearence in [Hull], notwithstanding all the wise precautions taken to prevent it, and spread with great rapidity. Many of the inhabitants left their houses, and fled into the country: strict watch was kept both night and day; and the gates were kept continually shut, except when provisions were bought in: all assemblies and meetings were forbidden; the schools were discontinued, and the churches entirely unfrequented. The whole town soon exhibited a scene of horror, silence, and distraction: the streets were unfrequented, and the country people fearing to attend the markets, made provisions excessively dear.' (Tickell 308)

December
31   (Thursday) The rev. Marvell left £5 in will of Alexander Swan of St Mary's. (York, Borthwick Institute, Orig. Wills, April 1636)

1636

August
18   (Thursday) AM's second sister Mary marries Edmond Popple (*'nauta'* – he is at this date a pilot between Hull and London) in the Charterhouse Chapel. (Sykes 1896, 190)

October
18   (Tuesday) St Luke's day: the rev. Marvell preaches 'A Sermon upon Swearing a new Mayor at Hull (A° 1636)', with the text Eccl. 8:2 (Hull Central Library, MS 'Sermons &c. of the Rev. Andrew Marvell,' 121–5).
            Cambridge too now begins to suffer from the plague.

1637

AM (again) receives a sizar's livery money of 6s.8d. at Trinity College, Cambridge. (Senior Bursar's Audit Book, 1637–59, 11ᵛ [the previous book has been long lost]; Kelliher 2004b)

March
The birth of Princess Anne (17 March 1637) occasions a congratulatory collection to which AM contributes two poems, a Horatian 'Ad Regem Carolum Parodia' in Latin sapphics, and the Greek *'Pròs Károlon tòn basiléa'*, in *SYNODÌA* [Gr.], *sive Musarum Cantabrigiensium Concentus Et Congratulatio*... (Cambridge, 1637), K4ʳ–L1ʳ . The former draws heavily on Horace's Actium Ode (*Odes* 1:2); the latter makes numerological play of this being Charles's fifth child (*PL* 1:238–9; Smith 5–10; Haan 19–56). In this year Richard Lovelace visits Cambridge, where his literary acquaintance may

have included AM, who in 1648–49 joins with the others in commending
Lucasta (Lovelace, ed. Wilkinson, xxi).

April

6 (Thursday) The rev. Andrew Marvell (Charterhouse, Hull) writes
to ? on Maundy Thursday, despite weight of business, to argue
with characteristic verve against the right to the sacrament of
all who present themselves, raising points of theology meant to
rescue his Calvinist position from the Arminian. Concludes:
'Pardon me I beseech you: I write I know not what: I am weary;
full of distractions. I preached to day; must preach to morrow
[Good Friday]. Much Company about me, many avocations. I
have not had two houres to forethink and make up this scrible.
Let none eyes but your own see this abortive. Read, Censure
freely, send back my paper that I may see what I have written.
Your man Calls me of; and must be gone...' (BL, MS Lansdowne
891, 118^{r-v}; reproduced in part in Kelliher 1978a, 20–2)

August

18 (Friday) Plague again visits Hull, and will build to a crisis in the
following months. (Sykes 1893, 468; Tickell 310–11)

September

28 (Thursday) The rev. Marvell left £5 in will of John Ramsden of
Holy Trinity, alderman and merchant. (York, Borthwick Institute,
Orig. Wills, February 1637/38)

October

22 (Sunday) Death of AM's godfather John Duncalfe of Patrington,
who had just on 11 October 1637 willed 'to Andrew Marvell my
Godson ten shillings'; moreover he gives 'unto Andrew Marvell
clerk twenty shillings in gold and my desire is that he shall have
the tuition of my two sons respectively according to the Law in
that case provided'. Duncalfe's will is proved at York, 7 February
1637/8. (Wall 1958a)

29 Jane Pease, servant to the Marvells, is buried in the Church of
Holy Trinity, Hull. (Sykes 1896, 202)

December

7 (Thursday) Death of John Ramsden, mayor, of the plague, at
whose funeral the next day 'Mr. Andrew Marvell ventured to
give his Corps a Christian Buriall and there was preach't a most
excellent funeral Sermon to the Mournfull Auditors which was
after printed' – this seems to have been an exceptional public
occasion during the privations of the plague. (Pryme, Hull CA,
DMX/132, 99; Kelliher 2004a notes that the sermon survives in
BL, MS Harl. 6356, 153–62)

1638

January

3 (Wednesday) In recognition of 'services and constant attention ... during the plague', the rev. Marvell with two other preachers voted 20s. each by the Hull TH. (Brooks, ed., *The First Order Book of the Hull Trinity House 1632–1665*, 26)
The rev. Marvell was in the course of year given £56 3d. for payments 'to the poore people in gen'all this yeare, they being sometimes more sometimes fewer, with dyvers extraordinary paym'ts and disbursem'ts for them in respect of the contagion of the pestilence amongst them, whereof dyv'rs of them dyed'. (Cook 143)

February

2 (Friday) At Trinity College, Cambridge, is performed Abraham Cowley's *Naufragium Ioculare, Comoedia* (1638): the sententious tutor Gnomicus may have been played by AM in view of the intermittent references to him as 'vir admirabilis' – among his many tags is the opening of Lucan's *Pharsalia* (B8^v). (Duncan-Jones 1975, 267; *Naufragium* C4^v and especially G4^r, and perhaps cognates on C4^v, C5^r, E3^{r-v}, F5^v, G1^r, G1^v, G3^r)

4 Birth in Hull of AM's nephew, William Popple. (BL, Add. MS 8888, 133^v)

April

13 (Friday) Autograph entry 'Andreas Marvell discipulus juratus et admissus' (Cambridge, Trinity College, Admissions and Admonitions, 1560–1759, 266). This marks AM's advancement to fellowship in the college as a scholarship student.

28 Anne Marvell, mother of the poet, buried in the Church of Holy Trinity, Hull. (Sykes 1896, 202)

June

Plague finally abates in Hull: 'The town had now been infected for upwards of three years, and all commerce was totally extinct.' The wide misery and heavy costs of the calamity met with some relief from other York ridings and from further afield, but of 'this terrible pestilence' it was calculated that some 'two thousand seven hundred and thirty persons died, exclusive of those who fled out of the town and died elsewhere, and even who died of other disorders, which according to one authority almost doubled the number'. (Tickell 310–11, drawing on Pryme, Hull CA, DMX/132, 100)

November

27 (Tuesday) AM's father remarries, to the 'generosa' Lucy Alured (b. 21 June 1592) at Norton, Derbyshire, widow of William Harries

(d. ca. October 1631) and earlier widow of Francis Darley (d. 1616); the Alureds were the rev. Marvell's neighbouring family in Sculcoates. (Legouis 1928, 17; Burdon 1982)

Ordered in the court of the Archbishop of York, the Laudian Richard Neile, that daily prayers be said in Hull Trinity Church and that the East Riding Archdeaconery official Edward Mottershed 'should intreate the helpe of Mr Marvill who is likewise admitted in partem Curae therein or some other fitt to be allowed to read prayers in the sayd Chapple' (in view of the expected intransigence of the minister Richard Perrott and especially his curate John Gouge) (BRM 166). Referring either to Neile or his successor, John Williams, AM later mocks 'proud Cawood Castle' and 'Th'Ambition of its Prelate great' ('Upon Appleton House,' 363–6).

1639

February

27   (Ash Wednesday) AM subscribes to three articles (upholding the King, Book of Common Prayer, and Thirty-Nine Articles) for his Bachelor's degree. Among his contemporaries at Trinity College are Richard Culverwell, Samuel Collins, Abraham Cowley, Martin Clifford, William Disney and Samuel Barrow, and among the fellows Herbert Thorndike; the Villiers brothers attend shortly after. (Cambridge Univ. Archive, Subscriptiones II, p. 9, and reproduced Kelliher 1978a, 23–5; Cambridge, Trinity College, Admissions and Admonitions, 1560–1759, 39ff. 266–9)

March

22   (Friday) The rev. Marvell witnesses will of William Robinson of Tripet, near Hull, in which he is left £5 (York, Borthwick Institute, Orig. Wills, July 1639)

April

4   (Thursday) Charles I spends the night in Hull on a visit to inspect the fortifications and magazine there. (Toynbee; Tickell 316–22)

August

AM the elder much repairs and rebuilds the Charterhouse over the next 'yeare and 1/2' (up to his death in January 1640/1), presumably owing to problems that had accumulated during the difficult plague years and the renewed income available in better times. (Cook 151, 173)

14   (Wednesday) Before the chancellor (the vicar-general from the Chancery Court, York), the rev. Andrew Marvell at Holy Trinity Church, Hull, is ordered 'to reade the later part of the prayers or divyne service mencioned and expressed in the book of Common prayer in the manner and forme as therein is

prescribed, in his hood and surplize upon Wednesdayes being lecture dayes and sundayes and at other tymes when he useth to preach at the said Chappell'. (Marchant 262)

October

12   (Saturday) The rev. Andrew Marvell appears in private before the chancellor; ordered 'to read the whole Second service in such manner and forme' as before. (Marchant 262)

December

14   (Saturday) The absent rev. Andrew Marvell submits certificate 'but the order was continued' that he read the second service from the Book of Common Prayer (Marchant 262). This absence may have followed from the father's intervention at the time of AM's flirtation (?) with Catholicism, later reported as his entanglement with Jesuits, which demanded the father's trip to London where he is reported to have found his son 'in a Bookseller's Shop' – presumably in employment, unless just browsing – and then to have sent him back to Cambridge. (See January 1640 below; Cooke 1:5; Kelliher 1978a, 25)

1640

January

Letter to AM's father from John Norton, another Yorkshire minister, concerning the recruitment by Roman Catholics at Peterhouse of that Norton's son, and seeking advice as to what the rev. Marvell had done in his similar case; Norton urges some exemplary punishment on the perpetrators. (BRL 247; Wildridge 166–7; Margoliouth)

31   (Friday) The episcopal order to follow the prayer-book is continued on the rev. Andrew Marvell. (Marchant 262)

May

29   (Friday) In a suit between Robert Legard and the mayor of Hull, the rev. Marvell among those now witnessing earlier letters (7, 31 August 1638) concerning the fortifications of Hull (BRL 272, 274; Wildridge 22).

October

'D[ominu]s Mervile' recorded among the Lady Bromley scholars receiving 3s.4d. quarterly over the previous year in accounts, Michaelmas 1640, at Trinity College, Cambridge (Senior Bursar's Audit Book, 1637–59, 23ᵛ [the previous book seems to have been long lost]). A late eighteenth-century copy of college records cites AM a 'dry' chorister 1640–42 (this did not require him to sing) – this is puzzling, in view of AM's prolonged absence from Trinity in the summer of 1641 and presence in London in February 1641/42 (unless there be some confusion with his younger contemporary, Andrew Meverell, B.A. 1642). (BL, Add. MS 5846, 133ᵛ, 134ʳ; Kelliher 1978a, 22–3; Kelliher 2004b)

December

21   (Monday) The rev. Marvell left £3 and made trustee for building the hospital provided for in the will of Sir John Lister of Holy Trinity. (York, Borthwick Institute, Orig. Wills, February 1640/41)

1641

Fourteen sermons of the rev. Andrew Marvell survive in an octavo volume at Hull Central Library (MS 'Sermons &c. of the Rev. Andrew Marvell'): a number of these are New Year's sermons and one with further materials appended addresses the city's suffering during a time of plague (all otherwise undated). These and adjacent materials invite further consideration of his activity as a minister and the moderation of his churchmanship: especially revealing of his difficulties in satisfying more radical elements in the Hull congregation as well as the Laudian Archbishop Neile at York is the rev. Marvell's undated 'Complaint against the perverse behaviour of some of the Inhabitants of Kingston upon Hull' (ff. 207–11), which laments 'some discourtesyes, & injuriious Carraiges, which I have experienced since my Coming to Hull; especially at their hands, from whome I promised my selfe most incouragement in the worke of my ministry.' His 'doctrine in the point of Christs merit' (207ʳ⁻ᵛ) has not met with open discussion from his opponents, who meet in private groups rather than in the church proper; moreover, these anabaptists disagree with his position on paedobaptism and traduce 'my doctrine Concerning the lawfull and profitable use of Godfathers in baptisme'. Worse, 'They have undertaken to inveigle others Closely, and among the rest one of mine owne family. A Sinister Course in persuading of any opinion to sett upon weaklings who it is likely may be Carryed about too easily. 2 Tim: 3, 6 Eph 4, 14'. Moreover, 'Some of them played the informers, relating my doctrine and maner of preaching to those who were more diligent to inquire and seeke narrowly into my ministry then charitable to advise me in any thing, or Christianly wise in their owne Courses to avoid scandall'. They condemn him for wearing surplice, although other ministers whom they like more are uncensured on this score. Finally, 'All these reproaches Cast upon my ministry have been Whisperings and back-bitings. to draw, as may be supposed, either my person or my doctrine into disgrace and obloquy, with the people set under my ministry. For they have beene uttered in my absence, unto others Covertly'. This despite his own candor and readiness to welcome them in discussion at all times 'if in the Compasse of my Calling, however [much] my occasions are oftentimes urgent'. The volume also includes a translation of the Racovian Catechism, perhaps to be associated with visits by Paul Best to his native East Riding (Driffield, Beverley). The rev. Marvell's otherwise moderate ecclesiology also appears from his 'notes on the necessity of observing church ritual' Kelliher 2004a, citing BL, MS Harl. 6356, 197ʳ⁻ᵛ).

January

23   (Saturday) The rev. Andrew Marvell drowns: 'crossing Humber in a
             Barrow-boat [i.e. from Barrow Haven, Lincs.], the same was sand-
             warpt, and he drowned therein, by the carelessness (not to say
             drunkenness) of the boat-men, to the great grief of all good men'
             (Fuller, 159, and in margin: 'With Mrs Skinner (daughter to Sir Ed.
             Coke) a very religious Gentlewoman.'). Later versions of the story
             embellish it increasingly, with *Biographia Britannica* claiming
             that the mother of the drowned woman supported AM thereafter
             (see below 1760): 'Mrs. Skinner' (that is, Cyriack Skinner's mother
             Bridget of Thornton College, Lincs.) died only in 1653 and her
             will leaves nothing to AM (Margoliouth 357–9), but such report
             may reflect the sponsorship by her sister Anne Sadleir of AM's
             father and family (see 28 April 1627 above; 1653 below).
             Already in the 1640s, Fuller adds of the rev. Andrew Marvell
             that 'His excellent comment upon Saint Peter, is daily desired
             and expected, if the envy and covetousness of private persons
             for their own use, deprive not the public of the benefit thereof'.
             AM is thought to have left Cambridge, presumably once more
             for London, 'shortly after his father's death' (Kelliher 1978a,
             26). If local Hull tradition be accepted, AM may have taken
             some clerkship in Hull at this date, perhaps with his brother-
             in-law Edmond Popple (leading to municipal memorabilia of
             that service in 80 High Street, a piece of patriot oak and the like,
             Margoliouth 355–6); if so, he must have abandoned any such
             work soon enough to be witnessing documents in London in
             February 1641/42.

March

15   (Monday) The rev. Andrew Marvell's successor, William Stiles,
             elected Master of the Charterhouse. In Stiles, the Hull Corporation
             gave preferment to a less moderate Puritan. (Cook 151–2)

May

8   (Saturday) AM's stepmother, Lucy Marvell, presents accounts
             for the Charterhouse and pays balance of £75 2s. to the new
             master, William Stiles. (Cook 151)

July

23   (Saturday) Exactly six months after the rev. Andrew Marvell's
             death, 'Jane Grey, the remarried widow of his brother Edward
             (d. 1631) [makes] over to young Andrew $47\frac{1}{2}$ acres of copyhold
             land that the Marvells had long farmed in Meldreth, Cambridge-
             shire ... These he at once mortgaged to his brothers-in-law
             Edmond Popple and James Blaydes for £260, repayable in two
             instalments by the eve of his majority; nine years later they

were still unredeemed. At the same time he paid a fine of £3 to retain the house and $2\frac{1}{2}$ acres which can be identified with the property traditionally known as the Marvells and nowadays as Meldreth Court.' (Kelliher 2004b, citing London Metropolitan Archives, H1/ST/E79/24, m.37)

September

24 (Friday) Trinity College 'Conclusion Book' entry cites AM among those who 'in regard that some of them are reported to be maryed and the other looke not after their dayes nor Acts, shall receave no more benefitts of the College, and shalbe out of their places unles thei shew just cause to the College for the contrary in 3 months'. (Trinity College, Cambridge, Conclusions and Admonitions 1607–73, 169; see Kelliher 1978a, 26)

1642

If any of AM's lyrics date from the period before his departure to the continent, they seem likely to include 'The Coronet' with its conspicuous indebtedness to Donne and Herbert (Smith 46–9). At this date, AM may be connected to Gray's Inn, which had Yorkshire associations and which lay nearby to the west of his Cowcross address (Burdon 1978, 46; Kelliher 1978a, 31).

February

8 (Tuesday) In London, AM witnesses deed by which Thomas Viscount Savile, Baron of Pontefract and Castlebar (1590?–1661?) acquires property from Sir William Savile of Thornhill (1612–44). (Burdon 1978)

10 In London, AM witnesses deed by which Thomas Viscount Savile, Baron of Pontefract and Castlebar (1590?–1661?) acquires property from Sir William Savile of Thornhill (1612–44). (Burdon 1978)

17 AM is living in London, where he signs the Protestation Returns in the Cowcross area, which includes St John Street and St John's Lane ('St Jones'). This is where Sir William Savile seems to have lived; it is also AM's and the Earl of Carlisle's address in May 1663 (Burdon 1978, 45–6, citing House of Lords' RO, Protestation Returns for Middlesex, Ossulton Division). AM does not appear in the list for the Irish contribution from St Sepulchre's, London, 11 March 1641/2, including the gathering at church door 23 February 1641/2 (PRO, SP29/193).

21 In London, AM witnesses mortgage by which Thomas Viscount Savile, Baron of Pontefract and Castlebar (1590?–1661?) acquires property from Sir William Savile of Thornhill (1612–44). (Burdon 1978; Kelliher 1978a, 31)

March

31   (Thursday) AM comes of legal age: 'Probably not more than a
            year after this date he disposed of some part of his patrimony to
            the purchaser mentioned in the Hull [Central Library, Andrew
            Marvell Meldreth] deeds, since the property there specified lay
            "betweene the lands late of the sayde Andrewe Marvell now John
            Stacey's on both sides". The sum raised by this earlier transaction
            may have been sufficient to enable him to finance at least part of
            the tour of the Continent from his own resources rather than
            from those of a wealthy, but so far determinedly anonymous,
            companion or pupil.' AM seems to have 'reserved the most valu-
            able portion [of this property], namely his grandfather's house, to
            the last'. (Kelliher 1978b, 125–6)

April

23   (Saturday) The parliamentary commander, Sir John Hotham,
            Governor of Hull, refuses to open that town's gates to King
            Charles and his royal troop.

August

22   (Monday) King Charles raises his standard in Nottingham.

October

16   (Sunday) Baptism of AM's niece Elizabeth, 'daughter of Robert
            More, gent. and Elizabeth Marvill', in Norton, Derbyshire.
            (Burdon 1982, 42)

1643

Whether already in 1642 or now, AM begins his 'foure yeares' travels on
the continent (Holland, France, Italy and Spain), which Milton cites in later
writing on his behalf (see 21 February 1653 below). This is the time of his
'travelling abroad with Noblemens Sones', which Hartlib later records (see
1645–46 and October–November 1655 below). Milton's report may well
respect AM's itinerary; that he had been to France before Italy seems wit-
nessed by the description of French youth in 'Flecknoe', lines 135–7. AM's
later editor Cooke (1726) is confident 'only that he was Secretary to the
Embassy at Constantinople' (1:6), of which other evidence has not surfaced
and which may confuse AM's career with Etherege's.

1645–46

In Rome, AM makes the acquaintance of Richard Flecknoe, priest, poet and
lutenist, whom he satirizes in 'Fleckno, an English Priest at Rome'. That
satire reports a visit to Flecknoe in Lent of 1645 (19 February / 1 March–6/
16 April) or more likely 1646 (11/21 February–29 March / 8 April) and

claims that AM had already suffered 'frequent visits' from him. Some un-
certainty remains whether AM was in Rome in the company of the Duke of
Buckingham and party to the dinners at the English College there in
December 1645, which included Buckingham and his entourage; nor has
any record surfaced of 'his Accession to the Poetical Academy in Italy:
Under the Presidency of the Lord Duke of Buckingham' (compare Burdon
1972; Chaney 347–50; Smith 166–74; Richard Flecknoe, *A Collection of the
Choicest Epigrams and Characters* (1673), 65; see also October–November
1655 below). Mathole suggests that possible echoes in AM's poem of later
publications by Flecknoe indicate a much later date of composition or revision for 'Fleckno'; if so, AM's animus may have been revived by Flecknoe's
quest for patronage from Richard Cromwell in 1658–59 or again by his
Restoration literary impostures (Mathole, chapter 3).

If Milton, in describing AM's sojourn on the continent, follows his itinerary, it is likely 1646 that AM has the Spanish fencing lessons to which he
later alludes (*PL* 2:324), as well as other Spanish experiences that find
mention in his poetry and prose.

1647

March

4   (Thursday) Abraham Cowley's *The Mistress* registered with the
           Stationers (*SR* 1:264), which collection strongly influences a
           number of poems from AM's hand either now or in the years
           to come, including 'A Dialogue, Between the Resolved Soul,
           and Created Pleasure', 'Mourning' (see July 1648 below), 'The
           Definition of Love' (see also 1652 below) and 'To his Coy
           Mistress' (see also 1652 below; *PL* 1:252–3), 'The Match' (Smith
           125–7, citing also Thomas Philipot, *Poems*, 1646, 31–4). Cowley
           was three years AM's senior at Trinity, Cambridge. AM may
           have exceeded him in making a mistress of his own desire; he
           seems also to have learnt from Cowley the use of eight-line
           stanzas formed of tetrameter couplets.

November

11–14   (Thursday-) King Charles escapes from Hampton Court to the
           Isle of Wight, where he is conducted to Carisbrook Castle and
           imprisoned anew, which alteration AM in 'An Horatian Ode'
           supposes a Cromwellian stratagem ('That Charles himself might
           chase / To Cares-brook's narrow case', 50–1).

12   AM is back in England by this date, when he sells the rest of his
           Meldreth property, it seems for £80, as evident from the 'coun-
           terpart deed recording the bargain and sale by "Andrew Marvell
           of Kingstone super Hull ... Gentleman" of land and other

property in Meldreth, Cambridgeshire, to "John Stacey of Orwell in the country of Cambridge gentleman" ', with AM journeying to Meldreth to effect the sale. (Kelliher 1978b, 125–9; Kelliher 2004b; Hull Central Library, Andrew Marvell Meldreth deed)

December

23   (Thursday) AM again present in Meldreth to complete the sale of that property, as noted on verso of the Hull Central Library, Andrew Marvell Meldreth deed.

1648

After his return from the continent, AM seems immersed in the counter-revolutionary ferment of London and a resurgent Cavalier literary culture. In the spring–summer of 1648, the onset of the Second Civil War begins to involve the British nations in fresh bloodshed; the insurgencies are met with the greater ferocity by the army.

A number of AM's lyrics are thought likely to date from this time on the basis of the poems they echo (see also 4 March 1647 above). These include 'On a Drop of Dew' and its Latin twin *'Ros'* (drawing on Crashaw's 'Eyes and Tears' in *Steps to the Temple*, 1646), as well as 'The Nymph Complaining' (drawing on Richard Fanshawe's translation of *Il Pastor Fido*; Smith 65–71). Still more difficult to date are AM's 'Young Love', 'Eyes and Tears', and 'The Fair Singer' (the latter may recall a line from *Areopagitica*, Smith 72–4, 96–7). If it is AM who rewrites Henry Ramsay's 'A Dialogue [between Thyrsis and Dorinda]', it may well be now that he revises the shorter original version, which had been set to music by William Lawes (d. 1645). In addition to the manuscript and print copies listed in Beal 1993 and Smith, there is an early separate of the long version of the poem in Longleat House, Whitelocke Papers, Parcel 5, 'Verses', with musical passages indicated after lines 12 and 18 (Beal 1993, 29–30; Bodl. MS Rawl. poet. 199, 52–3; BL, Add. MS 31432, 12^v–14; *PL* 1:248; compare Smith 242–3, 432–3).

February

4   (Friday) Richard Lovelace's *Lucasta* is licensed on this date, to which AM contributes a commendatory poem over his name (a7^{r-v}) and perhaps written months after this since he perhaps refers to a Kentish Petition of May 1648 and to the sequestration of Lovelace's estate, 28 November 1648. Although silent on the execution of Charles I, 'To his Noble Friend, Mr. Richard Lovelace, upon his Poems' may date as late as May 1649, since such materials might be incorporated late in the publication of such a volume, which is only then registered with the Stationers (14 May 1649), coming to Thomason's hands 21 June 1649. AM's poem is followed by John Hall's commendatory verses; in

some copies of the book, these poems are given pride of place after the dedication. Poems by Lovelace are echoed in a number of AM's poems. (Lovelace, ed. Wilkinson, lxxvi–lxxvii; Kelliher 1978b, 122–3; Smith 18–22)

May
The threat of counter-revolution reaches new heights: with the earlier Welsh insurgency contained, new petitions signal the imminent revolt of the counties; the danger from Scotland is compounded by the volatility of London itself.

21–   (Whit Sunday) Kentish Rising begins, prelude to Second Civil War.

July?
The anonymous *An Elegy upon the Death of my Lord Francis Villiers* is published (single sheet, quarto), of which the copy at Worcester College, Oxford, has an attribution by George Clarke (1660–1736) 'by Andrew Marvell', which is confirmed by internal evidence. Francis, son of George Villiers, first Duke of Buckingham, and younger brother of George, second Duke of Buckingham, 'was killed in a skirmish near Kingston-on-Thames', 7 July 1648; Marvell seems to have had some personal familiarity with him, perhaps stemming from acquaintance during their travels on the continent ca. 1646. (*PL* 1:435; Allison 114; Smith 11–17)

Not long after the Villiers elegy, it has been proposed, AM writes the poem 'Mourning,' which again features a Chlora, now weeping 'of late' (though its cynical note seems at a remove from the elegiac anger of the former poem: Donno ed., 228; Smith 98–101).

August
17–   (Thursday-) Cromwell's victory over the Scots at Preston effectively ends the Second Civil War.

October
14/24   (Saturday) Treaties of Westphalia signed, the foundation for French pre-eminence in continental affairs in the decades to come.

December
6   (Wednesday) In Pride's Purge, the Army prevents Presbyterian MPs from sitting in parliament, thus radicalizing that governing body and preparing for the trial and execution of King Charles.

1649

January
30   (Tuesday) Execution of Charles I at Whitehall, outside the Banqueting House. The crisis of the English Revolution and

an event that made a deep impression on Marvell, as the famous lines from 'An Horatian Ode' declare, also alluded to in his Restoration verse and prose. It has been seen by David Roberts (2002) as determining references to sacrifice, blood and sin in a number of Marvell's lyrics not otherwise easily datable: whether this need be with 'The Nymph Complaining for the Death of Her Faun' its most recent editor doubts, but if anywhere then in 'The Unfortunate Lover', likely written during these months. (Smith 67, 85–91)

May

23   (Wednesday) Burial of Andrew More, nephew and perhaps godson to AM, Holy Trinity, Hull. (Burdon 1982, 43)

June

24   (Sunday) Death of Henry Lord Hastings (smallpox), the day before his wedding to Elizabeth de Mayerne, daughter of Theodore de Mayerne, royal physician to the Stuarts and later to Cromwell. To the memorial volume *Lachrymae Musarum* published in the next months (1649), AM belatedly contributes an elegy, 'Upon the Death of Lord Hastings' (E8^v–F1^r, F1^v–F2^v), joining Robert Herrick, John Denham, John Hall, Marchamont Nedham and John Dryden among others. (Smith 23–9)

1650

January

30   (Wednesday) On the anniversary of the regicide may have been published the second edition of *Lachrymae Musarum* (thus dated by Thomason), the memorial volume for Henry Lord Hastings in which AM's elegy is inserted in some copies, now conspicuously promoted in the order and bound after Herrick's and Denham's and before John Hall's contributions (A3^v, 42a–d).

June

Late June or July: Marvell writes 'An Horatian Ode Upon Cromwell's Return from Ireland'. Very much in the ascendant, Cromwell returns from Ireland to London, 1 June; the Council of State adopts the resolution to invade Scotland 20 June. (Worden 1984; Smith 267–79)

25   (Tuesday) Reluctant to participate in any pre-emptive invasion of Scotland, the Lord General Fairfax resigns his commission. Whether AM already joins the Fairfax household now in its move north is unclear: although he is established in his role as tutor to Mary Fairfax by this autumn ('To his worthy Friend

Doctor Witty'), it has been thought that 'Tom May's Death' 'is
not the sort of poem Marvell would have written under Fairfax's
roof' (*PL* 1:277; see below 13 November 1650).

November
AM is likeliest now to have written the Latin and the English commendatory poems to the Hull doctor Robert Witty, whose translation
into English of James Primrose, *De Vulgi In Medicinâ Erroribus Libri
quatuor* (1638), was readied for the press this month (with the dedication
dated 30 November and the preface 2 December 1650, Primrose, *Popular
Errours* (1651), A4ʳ, A6ᵛ). The elaborate wit of AM's Latin poem, which
laments the excesses of printing in recent years and commends the *'Utile
... venenum'* of tobacco (A8ʳ), yields in the English poem to a commendation of translations that neither blot nor add beauties to the original,
and to a description of AM's student Celia (presumably Mary Fairfax)
being introduced to French and Italian, followed in deference to
Primrose's work with a more anti-feminist turn (A8ᵛ–B1ʳ). The poems are
both signed 'Andrew Marvell A.[ndreae] F.[ilius]', with the latter emphasis in keeping with the Hull company of the commendatory poets here
assembled (Wood, *Fasti*, ed. Bliss, 1:450). His friendship with Witty
lasted to the end of AM's life.

13   (Wednesday) Thomas May dies, after which AM writes the
satirical 'Tom May's Death.' Question has been raised whether
some lines in the poem (85–90) are informed by the later
exhumation of May (warrant of 9 September 1661), although
the stance of the poet seems quite capable of generating that
passage already in 1650. Owing to the poem's absence from
Bodl. MS Eng. poet. d. 49, doubts have been raised about its
attribution to AM, but the politics of the 'editor' of that compilation may better explain its omission of AM's scathing view
of republican impostures.

1651

Likely written this year, AM's Latin distichs 'Epigramma in Duos montes
Amosclivum Et Bilboreum. *Farfacio*' provide a study in contrasts, in which
all is governed by Fairfax, concluding with a teacherly compliment to AM's
pupil, Mary Fairfax. The companion piece, 'Upon the Hill and Grove at
Bill-borow. To the Lord Fairfax', in ten tetrameter stanzas, supplies a wittier
set of figures celebrating the general and his daughter, peace and retire-
ment (Hodge 349–50, supposes the latter to be Restoration work, without
considering that AM only once returned north before Fairfax's death; see
Smith 203 for a better reading of stanza VI). Composition in the Fairfax
period has also been proposed for AM's Spenserian 'Clorinda and Damon'
(Smith 59–60).

February
Late this month, AM writes 'In Legationem Domini Oliveri St. John ad Provincias Foederatas', which epigram turns on whether the Dutch wish to deal with an Oliver (as in Cromwell) or a St John. Parliament had chosen St John and the Yorkshireman Walter Strickland (brother-in-law to the Lady Frances Strickland to whom Robert Witty dedicated his translation of *Popular Errours*, now in press) to lead a grand embassy to negotiate a close alliance with Holland; the appointment came 14 February 1650/51. Writing as if the embassy is in prospect, AM in Yorkshire presumably composes the poem in time for the embassy's departure from London early in March (*PL* 1:308; Smith 257–8).

May

3   (Saturday) Date of publication of Dr Robert Witty's translation of James Primrose, *Popular Errours. Or the Errours of the People in Physick* (1651, Thomason), with AM's commendatory poems (see November 1650).

June
This is likely the mowing season, AM's first at Nun Appleton, that invited his writing the Mower poems ('The Mower against Gardens', 'Damon the Mower', 'The Mower to the Glow-worms', and 'The Mower's Song'), although a hot summer the next year has been thought to find mention in 'Damon the Mower' (lines 9–10; Smith 135), the second in this sequence of four as published in *1681*. Allied to these in subject is 'Ametas and Thestylis Making Hay-Ropes', which follows the Mower poems in *1681*. AM's fascination might well have first found expression now, although he did not lack for opportunity to write thus, early or late.

ca. July
Composes 'Upon Appleton House' (Hirst and Zwicker), which poem seems to register AM's joy at the wonders of summer on Fairfax's estate, as well as his reading of William Davenant's newly published *Gondibert* (Thomason corrects the 1651 imprint of his copy to 1650), William Cartwright's *Comedies, Tragi-Comedies, With other Poems* (23 June 1651, Thomason), and Cleveland's *Fuscara* (1651). The 97 eight-line tetrameter stanzas supply a history of Fairfax's estate, justifying what might seem the sacrilege of its having been taken from church-lands, and supplying a panorama of the house, its gardens, and the adjacent landscape, through which the wandering 'I' makes his way, honouring first the 'Master', Lord General Fairfax, and finally his daughter, the 'young Maria', who dignifies the evening scene with which the poem concludes.

Also inspired in some part by *Gondibert* are passages in 'Music's Empire', for which a date from the Nun Appleton time as well as from AM's later service to the Protectorate have been proposed (Smith 148–51; Griffin 90–1). The scale of its conception leads me to prefer the latter.

1652

The date of AM's return from service in the Fairfax household is not known, but he seems still to have been in the north this summer when he read Edward Benlowes, *Theophila* (1652), which informs 'The Picture of Little T.C. in a Prospect of Flowers', in some part portraying the young Theophila Cornewall at Thornton Curtis, Lincolnshire (whose grandmother is confusedly associated with AM's father in accounts of his drowning; Margoliouth 359–60; Smith 112). Later this year he seems again to be moving in fashionable circles in London, since he will testify to having now met 'Mr Georg Colt and Elizabeth his wife ... and ... Adryan Scroop and John Spencer'. (Deposition in *Dutton v. Colt*, PRO, C24/814/26, and Kavanagh 2003)

AM writes 'To his Coy Mistress' perhaps now: the poem is difficult to date more specifically in this period (Smith 75) but here AM is at the height of his power and synthesizing freely; moreover, a date in the early 1650s helps the wit of proposing to wait 'Till the Conversion of the Jews': if not already underway (as proposed by Edmund Hall, *Lingua Testium*, 1651, 13–14), 'the time of their conversion is not far off' (D.T., *Certain Queries*, 1651, 21) and in 1653, it could be thought 'very probable that the calling of the jewes will beginn in this enseuing year of our Lord 1654', *SR* 1:435). Now too seems the likeliest date for 'The Gallery', whether written in Yorkshire or London, which seems to refer to the sale of the royal paintings in 1650 and draws on materials published in 1651 by William Cartwright (*Comedies*, 23 June 1651, Thomason) and William Davenant, and having those and other features in common with 'Upon Appleton House', more certainly dated to the previous summer (Smith 92–5). 'Daphnis and Chloe' may well also date from this return to London, with its cynicism and capacity to incorporate in libertine lyric a reference to the 'headsman' and his 'parting stroke' (this poem has also been seen as near to 'To his Coy Mistress', Smith 102–6); so too 'The Definition of Love', which to my ear shares this 'mature' voice, and which may draw on a 1650 publication as well as Cowley's *Mistress* (Smith 107–11).

January

3   (Saturday) James Howell, *The Vision: or a Dialogue between the Soul and the Bodie* is registered with the Stationers (*SR* 1:387; Thomason dates his copy 14 January 1651/2), which work seems echoed in the title and contents of AM's 'A Dialogue between the Soul and Body'. (*PL* 1:249–50; Smith 61–4)

1653

In an exchange of letters between Roger Williams and Anne Sadleir, in which the former advises the latter to read Milton's *Eikonoklastes*, the scandalized Sadleir observes 'you should have taken notice of God's judgment upon him, who struck him with blindness; and, as I have heard, he was fain to have the help of one Andrew Marvell, or else he could not have finished that most accursed libel' (Trinity College, Cambridge, MS R.5.5, undated; see also Arnold Hunt). Although Sadleir was an informed patron of letters who had long known AM's father (see 28 April 1627 above), the cooperation she reports between Milton and AM seems likeliest to have been on the *Defensio secunda* (published May 1654), a passage of which seems recalled in 'Angelo suo Marvellius' (see 23 February 1654 below). *Eikonoklastes* was published well before Milton's final blindness.

February

21   (Monday) 'Letter of Mr. Milton Concerninge Mr. Marvaile':
            Milton writes to the Lord Bradshaw, President of the Council of
            State, recommending AM for employment, especially as
            Milton's assistant in place of the late Georg Weckherlin (d. 13
            February 1653): 'there will be with you to morrow upon some
            occasion of busines a Gentleman whose name is Mr Marvile; a
            man whom both by report, and the converse I have had with
            him, of singular desert for the state to make use of; who alsoe
            offers himselfe if there be any imployment for him. His father
            was the Minister of Hull and he hath spent foure yeares abroad
            in Holland, France, Italy, and Spaine, to very good purpose, as I
            beleeve, and the gaineing of those 4 languages; Besides he is a
            scholler and well read in the latin and Greeke authors, and noe
            doubt of an approved conversation, for he com's now lately out
            of the house of the Lord Fairefax who was Generall, where he
            was intrusted to give some instructions in the Languages to the
            Lady his Daughter ...' Milton adds that he believes AM will 'in a
            short time' make as good a public servant as the late Anthony
            Ascham, the English republic's Resident in Madrid who had
            been assassinated in 1650 (PRO, SP 18/33/152). In the event,
            that position went to Philip Meadows, with AM being remem-
            bered for later employment.
Around this date, AM wrote the original version of 'The Character of
Holland', which satire seems to follow from the English victory over the
Dutch fleet 18–20 February 1653 (lines 137–40). The Miltonic allusions in
the poem coincide conspicuously with AM's approach to Milton for
employment. Its publication only in altered form for a successful season in
a later Anglo-Dutch War (1665) suggests that its audience was as yet
restricted to his potential employers.

April

20 (Wednesday) Oliver Cromwell discharges the Rump Parliament, forestalling its self-dissolution and a fresh general election. (Worden 1974, 345–84)

July

28 (Thursday) AM, having moved to Eton to be tutor to Oliver Cromwell's *protégé* William Dutton (and possible son-in-law in prospect), writes Cromwell about the boy, whom he has interviewed in the presence of John Oxenbridge (a Fellow at Eton College, and brother-in-law of Oliver St John). Perhaps hedging his bets, he finds in the 11-year-old Dutton a promising mix of modesty and emulation. Thanks Cromwell for 'having placed us in so godly a family' as the Oxenbridges (newly installed at Eton, October 1652). A fascimile of the letter is supplied in *PL* 2:304a^{r-v} (London, Society of Antiquaries, MS 138, ff. 152–3; *PL* 2:304–5). AM will be Dutton's tutor for three and a half years. He now also meets John Dutton of Sherborne, William's wealthy uncle, who raises his nephew 'at A great rate and charge'. (AM and Poulton depositions, PRO, C24/814/26)

AM's present connection to John Oxenbridge has been understood to have occasioned 'Bermudas', which poem conspicuously responds to Edmund Waller's 'The Battle of the Summer Islands' (published 1645). Oxenbridge had visited the island and 'had recently been made (on 27 June) one of the Commissioners for the government of the Bermudas'; the date may be later in 1654 if indeed the poem anticipates 'Cromwell's intended expedition to the West Indies, which sailed in December 1654'. Oxenbridge had served as chaplain to Col. Robert Overton in Hull, where in municipal government they worked with Alderman William Popple (sr) (*PL* 1:246; Smith 54–5; see 2 June 1654 below; Bodl. MS Tanner 57, 167–9). Near Eton at the 'Anglican stronghold' of Richings, AM meets John Hales (1584–1656 [May]) and so 'convers'd a while with the living remains of one of the clearest heads and best prepared brests in Christendom'; later in *RT*, AM was glad to quote at length from the Arminiam Hales's *Tract Concerning Schism* (1642) which 'I had read many years ago' (*MPW* 1:130–4, 395–6; Legouis 1968, 97–8).

December

12 (Monday) Dissolution of the Barebones' Parliament.

16 Cromwell installed as Protector by the terms of the Instrument of Government.

1654

Ca. 1654? AM the elder's name memorialized among the recent masters of the Charterhouse in an epigram by the present incumbent, John Shaw, inscribed inside that building: 'Masters, of old, next, since, late, now, I saw, / Here Briscen, Wincop, Marvel, Stiles, and Shawe.' (Shaw, 148)

February

23   (Thursday) AM (Eton) sends the Latin verse-letter 'Angelo suo Marvellius' to Nathaniel Ingelo, chaplain to Bulstrode Whitelocke's embassy to Sweden, signed 'Tuus Marvellius' (copy in Longleat House, Whitelocke Papers, vol. 124a, 178ᵛ–180ʳ [Journal 1653–4]; Holberton). These elegiac distichs are only locally revised when published as 'A Letter to Doctor Ingelo, then with my Lord Whitlock, Ambassador from the Protector to the Queen of Sweden' in *1681* (130–4; Kelliher 1969, 54–7; Holberton). Ingelo is a Fellow of Eton whose acquaintance with AM seems to have been made between AM's arrival there in July 1653 and the embassy's embarkation in November 1653. AM praises Queen Christina with reference to her portrait, received by Cromwell already the previous May; he celebrates the Anglo-Swedish alliance against Holland and proposes a crusade against Rome, the Palatine, Spain and Austria (*PL* 1:315).

March

30   (Thursday) After some sticky negotiation over articles in the Anglo-Swedish treaty, the English ambassador to Sweden, Bulstrode Whitelocke, shows Queen Christina (who had fallen 'into discourse of poetry', or of England according to Whitelocke's original) 'a Copy of verses he had then about him, made by an English gent[leman] and sent hither to Wh[itelocke]. the Q[ueen] was much delighted with them, and read them over severall times, and highly commended them, as she did those that Dr Whistler made, and she desired copyes of them, which were sent to her.' The poems had arrived a week before. The entry in Whitelocke's journal on which this is based makes plain that it is AM's poem to Ingelo that is first meant; and that thereafter she bids him 'lui laisser les Articles jusques au lendemain et alors retourner vers elle' (leave the articles with her and come back tomorrow: Longleat, Whitelocke Papers, vol. 124a, 186ʳ; Whitelocke 346; Holberton). That the contemporary transcription of AM's poem by Jean Scheffer is taken from an incomplete example of such a copy shows from its breaking off after line 72, where the Whitelocke manuscript also starts a fresh page (see 1751 below; Kelliher 1969).

April

8   (Saturday) The song 'A Dialogue between Thyrsis and Dorinda' influences Thomas Washbourne's 'A Pastoral Dialogue Concerning the Joyes of Heaven, And the Paines of Hell', in his *Divine*

Poems (1654), 84–6, registered with the Stationers this day, in print by 28 June (*SR* 1:445; Thomason). Washbourne's 'Rounde-layes' recalls Henry Ramsay's 'A Dialogue [between Thyrsis and Dorinda]'; his 'musick of the spheares / ... ears' the longer version associated with AM since its publication in *1681* (*PL* 1:248; compare Smith 244).

May

AM supplies two epigrams in praise of Oliver Cromwell perhaps now to accompany a portrait of the Protector sent to Queen Christina of Sweden in celebration of the treaty signed at Uppsala, 28 April 1654. '*In Effigiem Oliveri Cromwell*' and '*In eandem Reginae Sueciae transmissam*' enjoyed some manu-script circulation with attribution to AM, but it seems only after their appearance in *1681* (Beal 1993, 31–2); also in translation, 'With Cromwells Picture to Christina Queen of Sweeden by Andrew Marvell in Latin': 'Queen of the North Virgin renown'd in Warr, / Of all the Artick Pole the Brightest Starr: / These Wrinkles See, the effect of Steel & years / Thus Old, but prompt in Arms my Face appears / While through the untroden paths of fate the hand / Makes way & does the Peoples strong command / But this my humbler Form submits to Thee / Nor to Crown'd heads, will alwaies dreadfull bee' (in Hertfordshire RO, MSS D/EP F.83). One of the Robert Walker portraits of Cromwell includes the latter verses, 'Bellipotens virgo ...', as if for presentation (in the collection of the Duke of Grafton: Edward Holberton, private communication, citing Noble 1:307–8, with the portrait reproduced in Ashley 161).

[31? (Wednesday) AM (Eton) writes to Milton about having just presented to John Bradshaw the newly printed *Defensio secunda* (Thomason's copy dated 30 May). (Letter lost, but can be inferred from AM's next letter to Milton, 2 June)]

June

2 (Friday) Letter from AM (Eton) 'For my most honoured Freind John Milton Esquire, Secretarye for the forraine affairs' ('at his house in Petty France Westminster'). Reports on his presentation to 'my lord' [John Bradshaw] of Milton's newly published *Pro populo Anglicano defensio secunda* and reassures Milton that he delivered the letter for Bradshaw that Milton had supplied, and that Bradshaw has expressed esteem for Milton's person and work; also cites Milton previously having written to Bradshaw on AM's behalf. Thanks him for the copies of *Defensio secunda* that Milton has given to him and to John Oxenbridge. He will 'now studie it even to the getting of it by Heart', so much does he admire its reaching the 'to the Height of the Roman eloquence'. Refers to their friends Col. Robert Overton and Cyriack Skinner. (Copy in BL, Add. MS 4292, 264; *PL* 2:305–6)

August

3   (Thursday) AM witnesses leases of college houses at Eton to
             John Oxenbridge and William Barnsley (brewer). (Blakiston)

1655

January

AM and Milton's friend, Colonel Robert Overton (see 2 June 1654 above),
arrested at Cromwell's instigation in January and kept in Tower until 16
March 1658/9.

17   (Wednesday) Anonymous publication of AM's *The First Anni-*
             versary of the Government Under His Highness The Lord Protector
             ('Printed by Thomas Newcomb, and are to be sold by Samuel
             Gellibrand at the golden Ball in Pauls Church-yard, near
             the West-end, Anno Dom: 1655'; dated thus by Thomason, E.
             480:1). An impressive panegyric of 402 lines celebrating the
             anniversary on 16 December 1654, published in a plain and
             handsome printing of three sheets quarto, 20 leaded lines per
             page. In service to the Protectorate, AM's apocalyptic praises of
             Cromwell's person and statecraft combine with censure of more
             radical religion; he is also concerned to explain away
             Cromwell's coaching accident (29 September 1654). Evoking
             the wonder of foreign princes at Protectoral triumphs, AM con-
             cludes the poem with a second-person address to Cromwell as
             'great Prince'. The publication is advertised in *Mercurius*
             Politicus, no. 240 (11–18 January 1654/5). The poem is later
             republished in *1681*, only to be removed in printing from that
             book. (*PL* 1:319–28; Smith 281–98; Hirst; Raymond 2001)

May

29   (Tuesday) To 'Master Newcombe' is registered 'a booke called
             An Anniversary on the Lord Protector by Andrew Marvell', with a
             sixpence fee for the registration of copy. (*SR* 1:484)
             In part a corrective to AM's *First Anniversary*, Edmund Waller's
             A Panegyric to my Lord Protector is also registered with the Sta-
             tioners by Thomas Newcombe, who publishes it in small folio;
             it is reprinted in quarto for Richard Lowndes, which Thomason
             has by 31 May. (Raylor 22, 31; Waller, *Poems*, ed. Thorn-Drury,
             322–4; *SR* 1:484)

October–November

John Dutton sends his nephew William Dutton with AM his tutor and
other of Dutton's servants 'for his better accomplishment to travell beyond
sea' (Poulton deposition, PRO, C24/814/26). Soon after 3 October, Samuel
Hartlib's 'Ephemerides' reports from Dr John Worthington: 'There is one

Marvel of 40. y. of age who hath spent all his time in travelling abroad with Noblemens Sones and is skilled in several languages, who is now again to goe with one's Sone of 8. thousand a y[ear] who is fitter to bee a Secretary of State etc. Hee is advised to make the like contract as Page hath done being thus far in y[ears]' (Sheffield University, Hartlib Papers, 29/5/50A, yielding a departure date a little later than implied by Henry Poulton; Page was a 'fellow of Kings Colledge in Cambridge and once Orator there [who] hath from beginning of these troubles travelled into forraigne Parts and learned' and who had been newly employed 'by the Earl of Devonshire as Governour to his Son and hath an Annuity of an hundred lb. settled upon him' (Hartlib Papers, 29/5/8A–B, 29/5/43A).

1656

Apparently during his visit to France with William Dutton this year, or upon his return and preparation for employment at Whitehall in 1657, AM writes the Latin triplet translating four lines from Georges de Brébeuf's translation of Lucan, *La Pharsale* (Paris, 1654), Bk 3, ll. 395–8; this in turn is translated into English by Sir Philip Meadows, who was preferred over AM as secretary for foreign tongues in 1653, and who will open the position for AM when Meadows becomes ambassador to Denmark in 1657. (Bodl. MS Eng. poet. d. 49, 63–4; *PL* 2:274–5; Smith 189)

January
16/26 (Wednesday) Alex. Calander (Paris) writes to Joseph Williamson (Saumur) with postscript 'Si vous visités [sic] Mr Ditton et Monsieur Merville son Gouverneur je vous supplie de leurs faire' his humble regards. (PRO, SP18/123/98ᵛ)

19/29 René Augier (Paris) writes to John Thurloe [Whitehall] reporting that 'I have according unto your Honour's Direction sent the Inclosed unto Mr. Marvin [sic] att Saumur, and have also written unto him the place of my Abode here, that he maye make use of me for his Letters and Otherwise. / Yesterdaye the King daunced his New Balet repeating it unceassantly, and thinking upon nothing else ...' (Bodl. MS Rawl. A34, 599; *Thurloe*, 4:437)

February
13/23 (Thursday) René Augier (Paris) writes to John Thurloe [Whitehall] enclosing 'a Pacquett directed unto me by Mr. Marvill'. (Bodl. MS Rawl. A35, 132; *Thurloe*, 4:533)

March
7/17 (Wednesday) AM's pupil William Dutton still in Saumur with his tutor, since G. George (Paris) forwards to Joseph Williamson

(Saumur) mail for Dutton that he has found at the post-office and which otherwise would have been lost. (PRO, SP18/125/50[r])

June
Late this month, the ailing John Dutton speaks with Oliver Cromwell about permitting William Dutton to 'come home from beyond sea with what Speede conveniently mighte be and Commanded this Deponent to certifie the same by way of letter to Mr Marvell then tutor to the said Complainant William Dutton'. (Benjamin Billingsley deposition, PRO, C24/814/26)

This summer, AM (Saumur) seems to have sent to Milton a letter informing him of the demand for one of his books (the *Defensio* or *Defensio secunda*, or *Defensio pro se*?). When Milton then sends the book, AM writes again to report its good reception there (see 1 August 1657 below).

August
John Dutton, very ill of a dropsy, writes to Cromwell asking permission for William Dutton's return from the continent, wishing to see that nephew and to instruct him in the ways of Dutton's estate. (Benjamin Billingsley deposition, PRO, C24/814/26)

15   (Friday) Letter from James Scudamore (Saumur) to Sir Richard Browne (Paris): Dutton's 'Governour is one Mervill a notable English Italo-Machavillian'. Dutton will later marry this Scudamore's sister, Mary. (BL, Add. MS 15858, 135; Duncan-Jones 1949; *PL* 2:377–8)

September
Permission having been secured from Cromwell by John Dutton, William Dutton is recalled with his tutor AM to the ailing uncle's estate at Sherborne so 'that he might impart to him all the busines of his estate and have his Assistance', since he claims just to be his 'Nephewes Steward'; William Dutton later reported to have arrived back 'about Michaelmas'. (AM and Dring depositions, PRO, C24/814/26)

ca. 29   (Monday) AM is sent by John Dutton from Sherborne to London to transact business relating to the settlement of that estate, 'about Michaelmas'. (AM deposition, PRO, C24/814/26)

October
ca. 11   (Saturday) The lawyer Henry Poulton (husband of William Dutton's older sister Elizabeth) later deposes that around this date AM was sent to get him from London by John Dutton, which Poulton hastened to do owing to John Dutton's illness, and so 'two or three dayes after ... did accompaney the said Mr Marvell to Shierborne' arriving late. The next morning John Dutton welcomes his 'Nephew Poulton' and explains the

intended legacy to William Dutton; he recruits Poulton as a trustee, who stays on three or four days. (Poulton deposition, PRO, C24/814/26)

John Dutton asks of AM that should Dutton die while his nephew William is in London, AM 'should bring downe some good Companey of Friends' to protect William's interest in the estate. With his pupil William Dutton, AM is instructed in the management of the Sherborne properties and daily guided around those, until winter weather fatally worsens John Dutton's condition. (PRO, C24/814/26)

21 The will proved of William Popple, Edmond Popple's father and William Popple's grandfather, with most of his considerable property willed to Edmond and his heirs. (Copy in Hull Central Library, Wills 650 00 Popple, William 65)

1657

According to AM's later self-defence (*RT2*, 1673): 'I never had any, not the remotest relation to publick matters, nor correspondence with the persons then predominant, until the year 1657. when indeed I enter'd into an imployment, for which I was not altogether improper, and which I consider'd to be the most innocent and inoffensive towards his Majesties affairs of any in that usurped and irregular Government, to which all men were then exposed.' (*MPW* 1:288)

January

ca.11 (Sunday) AM is finally sent to London by the dying John Dutton in lieu of Sir William Killigrew (the dramatist, who has been staying in the house at Sherborne) to urge on Oliver Cromwell the match between William Dutton and Cromwell's daughter Frances. Dutton desires AM 'to make haste back with all possible speede' and is told by him now and in the preceding days of £4000 per annum and almost £2000 in reversion that John is leaving William. (AM and Killigrew depositions, PRO, C24/814/26; Morgan 123)

13–14 John Dutton is 'suddenly over nighte taken very ill and early the next morning dyed'; 'He was not buried until 18 February, but Cromwell's letter of condolence to his widow is dated 23 January'. (Poulton and Killigrew depositions, PRO, C24/814/26; Kavanagh 2003; Morgan 124)

May

29 (Friday) First news of Blake's victory, 'brought in to us this morning by Mr Secretary [Thurloe] ... a totall rout given to the Spanish Fleete at Santa Croue by Generall Blake'. (William Lister [Inner Temple] newsletter, BRL 632)

June

Likely date of the original version of the poem 'On the Victory obtained by Blake over the Spaniards, in the Bay of Santacruze, in the Island of Teneriff. 1657', published in AM's *1681* although excised from Bodl. MS Eng. poet. d. 49 and attributed to 'R.F.' in the revised and shorter version dated 9 July 1657 in Roger Boyle, Lord Broghill's papers (Petworth House Archives, Orrery Papers 13187), also extant as 'To his HIGHNESSE. In his late Victory in the Bay of Santa Cruz, in the Island of Tenariff' in the Hartlib Papers. Owing to its failings, this poem has long been doubted as AM's work, and the Boyle copy with its reattribution to 'R.F.' suggests the circulation that may have led to its later publication in shortened form in John Bulteel's *A New Collection of Poems and Songs. Written by several Persons* (1674), 109–16. (Sheffield University, Hartlib Papers, 55/15/1A–2B; Stocker and Raylor; Duncan-Jones 1995; Smith 423–7)

22   (Monday) 'Andrew Marvell of Kingston upon Hull Esqʳ aged 37 yeares or thereabouts being produced a witnes &c deposeth' in response to interrogatories in the case of *Dutton vs Colt*. Testifies to John Dutton's arrangements near the end of his life for William Dutton's inheritance of the Sherborne estate, with emphasis on the tender affection of the uncle for the nephew. Signs both pages of the document. Listed with other deponents as 'paid'. (PRO, C24/814/26)

25   Sir William Killigrew (the playwright, 'aged 51 yeares or thereabouts') deposes in *Dutton vs Colt* that 'Mr Marvin' had at his suggestion performed John Dutton's dying wish (refused by Killigrew) to visit Oliver Cromwell to treat in the proposed marriage of William Dutton to Frances Cromwell; also that Killigrew had shared with AM some of Dutton's plans for improving the Sherborne estate. (PRO, C24/814/26)

July

'James Fraser, a visitor to London in July 1657, left an account of his experience [of Cromwell] that may have been informed by a Royalist reading of *The First Anniversary* ...' (Raymond 2001, 349–50, citing Aberdeen University Library, MS 2538, 1:30, 33)

4   (Saturday) Henry Poulton of Lincoln's Inn deposes in the case of *Dutton vs Colt*, affirming John Dutton's high regard for his nephew William Dutton and describing the provisions he made for him. (PRO, C24/814/26)

August

1   (Saturday) In a letter from Milton to Henry Oldenburg, reference to '*vir doctus quidam, familiaris meus*' who spent previous summer at Saumur and wrote that Milton's work in demand there, with the copy then sent along much admired. (Milton, *Works*, 12:96–9; Milton, *CPW*, 7:502–3; Duncan-Jones 1953)

September

2   (Wednesday) AM begins official employment as a secretary for
           the foreign tongues on an annual salary of £200; his first quar-
           terly pay is later noted as due 2 December 1657. (Bodl. MS Rawl.
           A62/1, 49; *Thurloe*, 7:487)
           Soon? after this, in response to a petition by the Scottish
           Guinea Company, seeking to recover the St Andrew of
           Edinburgh (taken in 1636 or 1637 but with redress only now
           seeming possible, despite the outrage also of the murder of its
           men by the Portuguese governor of San Tome), John Thurloe
           notes: 'Mr Marvill. I desire you to write a Letter upon this peti-
           tion to the K. of Portugall.' (PRO, CO1/13/84; *PL* 2:380)
           Perhaps dating from this period of state service is the oval
           'Nettleton' portrait of AM, which the poet's great-nephew Robert
           Nettleton gave to the British Museum in 1764, now at the National
           Portrait Gallery (discussed and reproduced in Kelliher 1978a, cover
           and frontispiece, 80); it may in AM's lifetime have remained in
           his possession, since the engraved frontispiece to *1681* seems to
           derive from it. The face resembles that in the 'Hollis' portrait (see
           31 March 1662 below), with rolling shoulder-length brown hair
           (with skull cap), strong eye-brows and nose, and thin moustache (a
           square copy is in the Hull Guildhall, Lord Mayor's Dining Room).
           A possible Lely portrait of AM, now unknown, is later recorded by
           George Vertue in the hands of AM's great-niece Katherine Popple's
           husband, a younger brother of the third Earl of Shaftesbury (*PL*
           1:286; Duncan-Jones 1968), although this may be by Gaspar Smith
           or Smitz (Collins-Baker 2:217). In the Court Room at the Hull TH is
           a later portrait said to be AM, which seems not to be him or by Lely.

ca. 4   AM translates a Latin despatch about Baltic affairs from
           Hamburg to Thurloe (1 September). (Bodl. MS Rawl. A53, 242–3;
           Kelliher 1978b, 130)

ca. 11   AM translates another Latin despatch about Baltic affairs from
           Hamburg to Thurloe (8 September). (Bodl. MS Rawl. A53, 302;
           Kelliher 1978b, 130)

24   'The L[ord] Fairfax his daughter & heir [Mary Fairfax] was
           marryed to the D[uke] of Bucks' (Whitelocke, 476).

October

ca. 31?   (Saturday) AM translates letter of 6 November 1657 (n.s.) in
           which Marshall Turenne writes Bordeaux, the French
           Ambassador, from the camp at Rumingen; at issue is the preser-
           vation of Mardike after it has been taken and the degree of
           English involvement in France's conflict with Spain. (Bodl. MS
           Rawl. A55, 221–2; *Thurloe*, 6:578–9; Kelliher 1978b, 130)

November

ca. 2   (Monday) AM translates letter from D'Ormesson (Calais) [to Thurloe], dated 10 November (n.s.), about the success at Mardike, French mobilization, defences. (Bodl. MS. Rawl. A55, 255; *Thurloe*, 6:584–5; Kelliher 1978b, 130)

9   In AM's hand with Thurloe's corrections, endorsement, and added punctuation is 'The Answer of the High Commissioners to the Lord Nieupoort 9 Nov: 1657' about the marine treaty with Holland, which Thurloe notes 'Read & agreed 9 Novem. 1657'. (Bodl. MS Rawl. A55, 249–50ᵛ; *Thurloe*, 6:601–2; Kelliher 1978b, 130)

19   AM's 'Two Songs at the Marriage of the Lord Fauconberg and the Lady Mary Cromwell' celebrate the wedding at Hampton Court of the Yorkshireman Thomas Belasyse (1627–1700), second viscount Fauconberg (and a distant cousin of the Lord Fairfax), to Cromwell's third daughter, Mary (1637–1712). 'Younger sister' to this 'Cynthia' is Frances Cromwell, who had on 11 November married Robert Rich, grandson of the Earl of Warwick.

27   Letter from the Dutch ambassador Nieupoort notes that 'Mr Marvell came to me'. (*Thurloe* 7:513)

December

ca. 14   (Monday) AM translates from Latin 'a proposal made by the Swedish to the English Commissioners' arising from negotiation of the previous week; he also translates from Latin 'A Memoriall from the Swedish Commissioners' to similar effect. (Bodl. MS Rawl. A56, ff. 65–6, 153, and *Thurloe*, 6:677–9; Kelliher 1978b, 130)

ca. 16   AM translates from Latin 'the answer of the English to the Swedish Commissioners'. (Bodl. MS Rawl. A56, 178–9 [with Latin 174–6], and *Thurloe*, 6:684–6; Kelliher 1978b, 130)

ca. 19   AM translates from Latin 'The Answer of the Swedish Commissioners given in to those of England 19 Dec: Anno 1657'. (Bodl. MS Rawl. A56, 246 [with Latin 244–5], and *Thurloe*, 6:696–7; Kelliher 1978b, 130)

1658

Kelliher (1979, 149) draws attention to an unspecified letter of 1658 ('belonged in the 1840s to Dawson Turner and was sold at Puttick & Simpson's, 6 June 1859, Lot 677'; Beal 1993, 20).

January

7   (Thursday) AM translates letter from George Fleetwood and Johann Friderich von Friesendorff to Council of State: at issue is

Anglo-Swedish reconciliation, especially restitution for shipping losses owing to English depredations (with the English commissioners seen as not having lived up to treaty commitments), and recalled is the services in yesteryear of the Swedes against the Dutch. (Bodl. MS Rawl. A63, 27–9 [Latin is MS Rawl. A57, 82–4]; and *Thurloe*, 6:735–8 [also 7:813–6]; Kelliher 1978b, 131)

11/21   AM writes to Sir William Lockhart, ambassador to Paris, concerning message from Thurloe that was instead to be prepared by Lord Fauconberg, and is now again delayed by Thurloe's indisposition (this note is intercepted in France, copied, and sent on). (PRO, SP78/114/17, printed from original in *Thurloe*, 6:743; manuscript copy is Bodl. MS Clarendon 57, 42; *PL* 2:306)

15   During Thurloe's indisposition, AM writes on this day to Col. William Jephson in Wismar, as noted in Jephson's letter to Thurloe of 31 January / 10 February 1657/8. (Bodl. MS Rawl. A46, 299, and *Thurloe*, 6:770)

16/26   Letter from Sir William Lockhart (Paris) to Thurloe [Whitehall], saying he has received two letters from AM and is glad to learn from AM's note of 11/21 January that Thurloe is on the mend. (Bodl. MS Rawl. A57, 70, and *Thurloe*, 6:747)

28   As Thurloe (Whitehall) recovers from illness, he uses AM as amanuensis for political letter to George Downing (English Resident at The Hague). (BL, Add. MS 22919, 11–12; Kelliher 1978b, 130)

30 / 9 Feb.   Letter from Sir William Lockhart (Paris) to Thurloe [Whitehall]: 'I have detaind Mr Compton a whole weeke in expectation of sending by him a returne to those commands Mr Marvale putt me in hope I should have received from your lordship ere this .... My lord I ame exceedingly sorry to heare that your lordship hath not yett recovered your strenth.' (Bodl. MS Rawl. A57, 234, and *Thurloe*, 6:769)

February

– 4   (Thursday) In the preceding couple of weeks, AM translates 'The Justice of the Swedish Cause and the danger of the Protestant Cause involved therein' producing 'forty neatly-copied pages of translation from a political tract composed apparently by the Swedish envoy to England, Johann Friderich von Friesendorff .... the tract was aimed at persuading the Protector to lead his navy and that of Sweden against Holland and Spain'. (BL, Add. MS 4459, 175–96ᵛ; Kelliher 1978b, 130, 131, 133; *MPW* 1:441–9)

10   Letter from Col. William Jephson to Thurloe cites 'Mr. Marvell's letter'. (*Thurloe*, 6:770)

18   Letter in AM's hand from Cromwell (signed 'O.P.') to the Marquess of Brandenburg, requesting the punishment of one of Brandenburg's naval commanders for his treatment of an English ship's captain. (English copy for Latin translation, Bodl. MS Rawl. A57, 358, reproduced in Kelliher 1978a, 70–1; *Thurloe*, 6:812)

March

18   (Thursday) AM successfully supports petition to the Protector and Council of Giovanni Bernardo Isola, employed in Holland by the State of Genoa, for a pass to France. (PRO SP25/78/507, and *CSPD 1657/8*, 333)

29   In Council of State, 'on desire of Mr. Merville', a pass beyond sea is granted to John Duke, son of Sir Edward Duke of Suffolk. (PRO, SP25/78/527)

April

ca. 9   AM pens 'Papers, including the draft (fols. 380–2) of a letter for, and "Instructions to Philip Meadowe envoye extraordinary to his Majesty of Sweden" (fols. 385–7), with revisions in another hand'. (Bodl. MS Rawl. A58, 380–7, and *Thurloe*, 7:63–4; Kelliher 1978b, 130)

11/21   Letter from Sir William Lockhart (Paris) to Thurloe: 'The last post broght me two from your Lordshipp and one from Mr Marvell, with a letter inclosed to his eminency which I delivered upon fryday last ...' – the English ambassador supplies news of international relations, centring in Anglo-French concerns. (Bodl. MS Rawl. A58, 325, and *Thurloe*, 7:69)

20   AM pens 'His Highness Letter to the Duke of Venice on the behalfe of Col. Holdip': 'Serenissime Princeps, Illustrissime Senatus, Richardus Holdipp, nuper in exercitu Nostro Tribunus militum ...'. (Bodl. MS Rawl. A58, 388, and *Thurloe*, 7:83; Kelliher 1978b, 130)

23   Death of Jane Oxenbridge (aged 37), first wife of John Oxenbridge, in whose residence at Eton AM had lodged. AM's Latin 'Janae Oxenbrigiae Epitaphium' was used for her monument in Eton College Chapel: it praises her loyalty to her husband on his travels 'Religionis causa' to Bermuda as well as her support for his evangelical work in England; it also refers in some detail to her long-failing health, which seems to have had its inception near the time of AM's arrival in the household. AM's note indicates the epitaph had been written before the Restoration; the monument was painted over at the Restoration and removed in 1699. (Included in *1681* and copied independently into a number of antiquarian compilations: see Kelliher 1978b, 134–9; Beal 1993, 32–3; Smith 192–4)

27   Samuel Hartlib refers to AM in writing to Robert Boyle about collection for Polish Protestants: 'But Mr. Marvel did send again another express unto him [Roger Boyle, Lord Broghill], that his business was laid seriously to heart. Mr. Dury doth bestir himself daily for him [Broghill]. Yesterday he went to Hackney to speak with Sir Thomas Winor [Viner], about the contents of his highness's letter for advancing of four or five hundred pounds, for the relief of the twenty families. But the poor man excused himself, that he had no money, and because the other treasurer was absent, that should concur with him. The collection is begun to be made in several churches in London; but what farther expedient they will find out for the advance-monies, I cannot tell.' (Boyle, *Works* 5:274)

May

12   (Wednesday) Order in Council of State delivered to AM 'That the Treasurers for the monies ariseing by the Collecion for the Poore Protestants Exiled out of Poland doe advance five hundred pounds for the releife of the xx^{tie} Bohemian familyes; upon the Creditt of that Collection to be paid to such person and distributed in such manner as the Committee for that affaire shall direct.' (PRO, SP25/78/615)

         AM also ordered by Council of State to attend to the business of 'the Committee on the Piedmontese Protestants to consider who shall receive the 500*l*. and how it shall be disposed of'. (PRO, SP25/78/615, and compare *CSPD 1658–59*, 21)

June

8   (Tuesday) AM ordered to refer to a committee of army officers and Hull worthies the questions of the need for the magazine in the manor house in Hull and its expected cost to the govern-ment, following Strickland's report to Council of State on the Hull petition that it be kept in good repair. (PRO, SP25/78/668, and *CSPD 1658–59*, 52)

13/15   Dunkirk taken in the campaign in the Spanish Netherlands by French and English forces and delivered to the English according to the terms of Cromwell's treaty with Louis XIV.

29   'On desire of Mr Marvell', Council of State grants pass for William de Gerbert, merchant to go to France. (PRO, SP25/78/724)

July

9   (Friday) AM (Whitehall) serves as amanuensis for 'Mr Secret-aryes Letter to Resident Downing [The Hague] concerning the Mediation betwixt Portugal & the States-Generall'. (Bodl. MS Rawl. A60, 88–9, and *Thurloe*, 7:253; Kelliher 1978b, 131)

24 AM plays a part in reception of the Dutch ambassador Willem Nieupoort. Thurloe arranges for 'a Barge of his Highness [Cromwell] to be made ready to be sent to [the ambassador] with a gentleman cald Marvell, who is employed in the dispatches for the latine tongue'. The same day Thurloe writes to Nieupoort that AM, as Nieupoort has it, 'was expresly sent unto me to salute mee and to speake with mee concerning my reception and that he would say nothinge more concerning the same, that it would be most acceptable to his Highness as it could best express and declare the great esteeme which he hath of your H[igh] and M[ighty] L[ordships], the States-General of Holland]'. (Bodl. MS Rawl. A60, 262, and *Thurloe*, 7:298)

25 AM arrives at the Dutch ambassador's (Gravesend) 'before the sermon in the morning, to bid [Nieupoort] wellcome in the name of his Highness the lord Protector and to present [him] a publick reception with Barges and Coaches, as also an Entertainement such as is usually given to the chiefest Ambassadors'. But out of consideration for the Protector and the protectoral court, in mourning for the death of Elizabeth Cromwell, Nieupoort begs off these honours, and accompanies AM that night to London, in anticipation of Cromwell's coming the next day from Hampton Court to Whitehall. But the grief-stricken Protector does not leave Hampton Court after all and so Nieupoort visits there with Thurloe then managing the meeting. (Bodl. MS Rawl. A60, 263–5, and *Thurloe*, 7:298)

29 AM writes the endorsement specifying 'The Case betwixt the Creditors of the late Dukes of Hamilton and the Earle of Abercorne' on that document. (PRO, SP18/182/79)
Council of State orders AM to recover money from the commissioners for prize goods in the matter of Portuguese ship, the Lady Mary ('nostra seniora de Rosario, otherwise called'), following a claim by the Portuguese ambassador. (PRO, SP25/78/757)

30 Willem Nieupoort, Dutch ambassador, writes to States General of Holland, describing his reception in England and citing AM's role (9 Aug. n.s.). (Bodl. MS Rawl. A60, 262–6, and *Thurloe*, 7:298–9; *PL* 2:380–1)

August
18 (Wednesday) AM writes and signs receipt for £15 he receives from the under-clerk of the Council Matthew Firbank 'by Mr Secretaryes order for J:J: and H:M: for the publick Service'. (PRO, SP18/200/184ʳ)

September

1   (Wednesday) AM receives from Thurloe £6 6s. reimbursement for expenses the previous year (30 September 1657–12 August 1658) which AM has listed: 'For a coach twenty times to my Lord Fleetwood and Mr Friesendorffs', 'For a coach to Mr Petcombes [the Danish resident] foure times', 'For a Coach to my Lord Whitlocks and to Mr Barkman [secretary of the Swedish envoy] severall times', 'For a coach to the French Embassadours thirteen times', 'For going by water to Dr Walker [Walter Walker, judge advocate of the Admiralty Court] severall times', 'For a Coach to the Portugal Embassadours seaven times', 'For a coach to Hampton Court and returning about publick business', and 'Charges of three days fetching the Dutch Embassador from Gravesend'. Holograph and receipt signed 'Andr: Marvell'. (PRO, SP18/200/188)

3   AM paid £50 quarterly salary 'for attending the publique service, and was due 2° X^{bris} 1657'. (Bodl. MS Rawl. A62/1, p. 49; *PL* 2:380)

Death of Cromwell at three in the afternoon. Richard Cromwell declared Protector. AM soon laments the loss in 'A Poem upon the Death of His late Highnesse the Lord Protector', which in 324 lines celebrates Cromwell as 'Heavens Favorite', praises his military and political career and proposes Cromwell's grief at his daughter Elizabeth's death as having led to his death. 'I saw him dead', AM reports, contrasting the living Cromwell's vigour with the 'wither'd' corpse. The elegy finally endorses the succession of Richard ('A Cromwell in an houre a prince will grow'). Although registered for publication in a memorial volume (see 20 January 1658/9 below), the poem is then omitted from that work; it was then printed at least in part in *1681* only to be withdrawn from that publication (see 1681 below).

5   J.F. Schlezer (agent of the Elector of Brandenburg) to Thurloe (Whitehall): has shown his master letters concerning the Baltic conflict delivered by AM. (Bodl. MS Rawl. A61, 33, and *Thurloe*, 7:373; Legouis 1928, 201)

7   'Mr Merville' listed with John Milton and John Dryden among the 'Lattin Secretaryes' allotted mourning cloth for Cromwell's funeral. (PRO, SP18/182/159)

16   AM notes on the petition of Mahamet, Mustaoth, Hamat and Abdullah, Turks escaped from Spanish imprisonment, that: 'The same is also petitiond for Abducadir, Achmet Sillau, and Hamet, of Sally.' (PRO, SP18/182/194)

October

1	(Friday) Letter from Thurloe (Whitehall) to Downing (The Hague) in AM's hand, signed by Thurloe; also in AM's hand is another such note of uncertain date, but after Oliver Cromwell's death and before the end of Richard Cromwell's regime (ca. 3 September 1658–25 March 1659). (BL, Add. MS 22919, 51, 52–3; Kelliher 1978b, 131)
8/18	Letter from the Dutch ambassador Nieupoort (Westminster) to the States General (The Hague): 'And although the Secretary of State were not yet recovered enough to look after publique affaires yet I wrot him a letter praying him that the Protector might be informed of the promises made unto him heretofore in this matter and that he would not treate apart with Swede who had so unexpectedly violated the Treaty of Denmark made by the mediation of a Minister of England and he send me answer by the sieur Marfelt [orig. 'Mr Marvelt'] that he had read my letter and although he was yet so indisposed in health that he could not goe to counsell that he would endeavour that nothing should be done in hast but that conferance should first be had with me and nothing be done by surprise.' (Bodl. MS Rawl. A61/2, 275 (Dutch original 279–80), and *Thurloe*, 7:434)

November

17/27	(Wednesday) Letter from the Dutch ambassador Nieupoort to States General: Nieupoort presents Thurloe with another memorandum concerning Dutch shipping losses and 'Afterward Mr. Marvell came to me with a letter from the secretary Thurloe, and a great writing signed by the commissioners Fiennes and Wolsely, Jones, Strickland, and Thurloe' in response to Nieupoort's memorandum of 6 November (Bodl. MS Rawl. A62, 276, and *Thurloe* 7:513)
20	AM writes in idiomatic French from Whitehall to Francesco Bernardi (London): on behalf of Richard Cromwell ('Son Altesse Serenissime') [and in lieu of the ailing Oliver Fleming] invites the Genoese diplomatic representative to attend the funeral of Oliver Cromwell the following Tuesday (signed André Marvell). (Archivio di Stato di Genova / Archivio Segreto, inserto 1, for which my thanks to Stefano Villani)
23	As one of the 'Secretaryes of the French and Latin Toungs', AM in Oliver Cromwell's funeral procession, listed with Dryden, Peter Sterry, Milton, Hartlib sr (Pell and Bradshaw crossed out). (BL, MS Lansdowne 95, 41^v)
26	Noted by the Dutch ambassador Nieupoort (in his letter to the States General the next day) that late this day 'Mr Marvell came to me with a letter from the secretary Thurlo and a great writing

signed by the Commissioners Fiennes and Wo[l]sely Jones Strickland and Thurlo being an answer of my Memoriall of the 6th'. (Bodl. MS Rawl. A62/1, 276, and *Thurloe*, 7:513)

December

4   (Saturday) 'Richard [Cromwell] by advice of his Councell resolved to call a Parlement to meet on the 27 day of January next.' (Whitelocke 501)

16   Council of State orders that the Court of Admiralty review the complaint of Patrick Hayes against the city of Hamburg: minutes note this as 'd[elivere]d Mr. Marvel'. (PRO, SP31/17/33, p. 307; original (unseen) at Longleat [p. 228])

21   Council of State orders that Hull be paid £60 per annum to rent manor house for a magazine, 'the State keeping it in repaire': noted as 'd[elivere]d Mr. Marvil'. (PRO, SP31/17/33, pp. 326–7; original (unseen) at Longleat [pp. 242–3])

     Council of State orders that a petition against the Governor of Jersey for seizure of 'a parcell of Wool' be referred to 'Dr. Walker his Highness Advocate' of the Court of Admiralty: noted as 'd[elivere]d Mr. Marvill'. (PRO, SP31/17/33, p. 343; original (unseen) at Longleat [p. 251])

     Council of State orders that a petition for a ship seized by the Dutch find representation to the ambassador Nieupoort: noted as 'paper sent Lord Ambassador Nieupoort by Mr. Marvill 23°'. (PRO, SP31/17/33, 349–50; original (unseen) at Longleat [p. 254])

23   AM sends paper regarding Stevenson's petition (see 21 December above) to Dutch ambassador Nieupoort.

     Council of State grants a license to the Duke of Holstein's envoy for transport there of 100 barrels of gunpowder: noted as 'd[elivere]d Mr. Marveil'. (PRO, SP31/17/33, 357–8; original (unseen) at Longleat [p. 260])

28   Edmond Popple, sheriff of Hull, seeks authorization for 'his brother in law Mr Andrew Marvell' to be made 'a free Burgesse of this Corporation' *in absentia*, which is granted 'accompting the good service he hath allready done for this Towne'. (BRB 4:274; *PL* 2:372)

1659

The longer revision of 'A Dialogue between Thyrsis and Dorinda', which has been proposed as AM's improvement on a much circulated song originally from the 1630s (see headnote to 1648 above), now finds print publication with musical setting in John Gamble, *Ayres and Dialogues ... The Second Book* (1659), 66–9; it will be republished in a succession of Restoration song-books. (*PL* 1:247–9; Smith 242–5)

January

9   (Sunday) Letter from Robert [ ] [East Yorks.] to Capt. Adam
           Baynes: in a critical account of the elections in the area, espe-
           cially the lack of due notice in York, includes comment, 'who at
           Hull I am not able to thinke, the town is soe much divided; but
           beleive that one Mr Marveile who is the Lattin Secretary at
           White-Hall, and one Mr Ramsden a merchant may carry it,
           except Sir Henry Vane who has a considerable party, carry it by
           the divisions of the rest .... Hull chuses on Monday next'.
           Explains that delay of writs for Beverley and Hedon seems
           designed to influence that election based on the result in Hull,
           so that should Strickland fail in Beverley 'he may make his
           interest stronger at the other places'; postscript reports
           Strickland's success. (BL, Add. MS 21427, 262^v)

10   AM first elected (with Matthew Alured) to sit for Hull in Richard
           Cromwell's brief-lived parliament. With help from the
           Cromwellian court, he overcame the rival bid of the republican
           Sir Henry Vane – 'it was said he had the majority' – who had
           been member for Hull in the Long Parliament. (BRB 4:277;
           Ludlow 2:51).

15   Fragment of a letter from AM (Whitehall) perhaps to Edmond
           Popple (signed 'Your most obligd affectionate cosin Andr: Mar-
           vell'), presumably about his recent election: 'Pray what say our
           86 men of the businesse & of me?' (facsimile in Thane 1788,
           vol. 2, sixth plate from end; Legouis 1923, 418)

20   Entry in Stationers' Company, Liber E (Entries of Copies), 114:
           '20 January 1658[–59] Mr Henry Herringman Entred for his
           Copie under the hand of Mr Pulleyn Warden) a booke called
           Three Poems to the happy memory of the most renowned
           Oliver late Lord Protector of this Commonwealth by Mr
           Marvell. Mr Driden Mr Sprat' (*SR* 2:211). In the event,
           Herringman seems to have ceded this publication to the printer
           William Wilson and AM's poem was replaced by Edmund
           Waller's 'Upon the Storme and Death of his Highnesse Ensuing
           the same' in *Three Poems Upon the Death of his late Highnesse
           Oliver Lord Protector* (1659), F1^r–F2^r – this likely follows from the
           changing political circumstances that spring, which soon made
           AM's praises of Richard Cromwell inopportune (Macdonald
           3–5).

27   Parliament meets, the session lasting until its dissolution
           22 April 1659.

February

5   (Saturday) AM named to parliamentary committees to examine
           the petition of Elizabeth Lilburne, widow of John Lilburne, and

further to examine how the northern countries 'may be supplied with a learned, pious, sufficient, and able Ministry'. (*CJ* 7:600)

11   AM (Whitehall) writes to George Downing (The Hague): newsletter regarding parliamentary debates, distinguishes republican position from that 'on our side', namely the two thirds of the house supporting Richard Cromwell as Protector. (BL, Add. MS 22919, 78; *PL* 2:307–8; facsimiles in Kelliher 1978a, 75 and back cover)

18   Letter from Thurloe (Whitehall) to George Downing (The Hague) in AM's hand, signed by Thurloe, with petitions for redress for damages to English shipping. (BL, Add. MS, 22919, 81–2; Kelliher 1978b, 131)

March

3   (Thursday) Hull Corporation to meet 7 March 'to consider of instruccions to be sent to Mr Ramsden and Mr Marvell to present to the Parliament'. (BRB 4:280)

25   Letter from AM [Whitehall] to George Downing (The Hague), promising a further fuller communication from Thurloe, and supplying parliamentary news in brief from the standpoint of an ardent Cromwellian. (BL, Add. MS 22919, 14–15; *PL* 2:308)

31   AM named to committee to examine if the county palatine of Durham should have parliamentary representation. (*CJ* 7:622)

April

13   (Wednesday) AM named to committee to examine the petition of the supernumerary disbanded forces in Lancashire. (*CJ* 7:638)

14   In parliament, resolved 'That it be referred to Mr. Attorney-general, Serjeant Maynard, Mr. Marvell, Mr. Dixwell, Mr. Scot, Mr. Annesley, Lord Marquis of Argyle, etc. to consider how to remove, and where to place, the conveyances, records, and other writings, now remaining at Worcester House, so as they may be disposed of, for their safety, and the service of the Commonwealth.' (Burton, 4:425–6; *CJ* 7:639)

21–22   Army causes dissolution of Richard Cromwell's parliament.

May

5   (Thursday) AM paid £28 13s.4d. knight's pence, parliamentary salary for 86 days (styled 'sixty eight dayes' in BRB) vs. John Ramsden's 106 days. (BRB 4:284; BRF3/22/16ᵛ)

9   The restored Rump Parliament meets, for first time since 20 April 1653; will sit until the Army forces an interval from 13 October to 26 December 1659.

10   Sir Henry Vane sitting in the restored Rump Parliament writes to his Hull constituency rejoicing in the turn of events that has overcome 'the practices of some and the Influence of [the] Court party'. (BRL 635)

27 AM translates into English a letter in French from the Lübeck agent Martin Bökell (27 May, London) to the Council of State. (PRO, SP82/9/219ʳ (217ʳ original); Kelliher 1978b, 132)

June

16 (Thursday) The mayor and burgesses of Hull give 'our well beloved friend Andrew Marvell of the Citty of Westminster Esquire' power of attorney 'to receive rent for the Hull Manor house' used as a magazine. (BRD 867; see 21 December 1658 above)

ca. 30 'Forme of the Ratification of the Treaty at the Hague as it is passed under the greate Seale': drafted in AM's hand in English and Latin, relating to treaty agreed between England and the United Provinces on 11/21 May, after the dissolution of parliament. (Bodl. MS Rawl. A66, 15; Kelliher 1978b, 132)

July

12 (Tuesday) AM translates into English a letter in Latin from the Lübeck agent Martin Bökell (11 July, London) to the Council of State. (PRO SP 82/9/243 (245 original); Kelliher 1978b, 132)

14 Council of State orders 'That Mr Marvell latine Secretary imployed by the Councell doe continue in his former lodgings in Whitehall'. (Bodl. MS Rawl. C179, 178; compare *PL* 2:382)

16 Council of State orders 'That Mr Goodwyn have the Roomes in Whitehall formerly Capt. Bishops, and now Mr Marvells, and that some other lodgings be lookt out for Mr. Marvell'. (Bodl. MS Rawl. C179, 187)

18 Council of State orders 'That the lodgings which were Mr Wings be assigned to Mr Marvell, those formerly allotted him being afterwards given to Mr Robert Goodwin' but a week later AM's new rooms were given to Brampton Gurdon. (Bodl. MS Rawl. C179, 196, 217)

August

ca. 6 (Saturday) AM translates from Latin 'the further agreement upon the Treaty at the Hague' (4 August), read and approved in Parliament, 9 August 1659. (Bodl. MS Rawl. A65, 403–6, and *Thurloe*, 7:705; *CJ*, 7:754; Kelliher 1978b, 132)

ca. 22 AM translates from Latin 'a Letter from the States Generall of 20ᵗʰ August concerning a Ship of theirs assaulted, by the Portland', also thus endorsed by him. (PRO, SP84/162/322ʳ–323ᵛ [original 324]; Kelliher 1978b, 132)

October

Council of State appoints a committee of seven, with AM as secretary, to treat with the Portuguese ambassador, Francisco de Mello e Torres (Kelliher 1979, 148).

13 (Thursday) In Lambert's *coup d'état*, the army expels the Rump.

25   At its final meeting, the Council of State orders AM's salary (and
            that of Milton) to be paid, 'at 200 li: per ann each' yielding each
            £86 12s (PRO, SP25/107/143). The next day the Committee of
            Safety is formed.

1660

AM keeps his place in Whitehall as late as April, and perhaps longer.
Later listed in Wharton papers among 'Names of the members of
the Commons house. 1660', and further noted (in another hand –
perhaps Wharton's) as if in the Yorkshire interest of the MP Hon. James
Darcy (Bodl. MS Carte 81, 77ʳ). AM may have made a speech at the
Rota Club this winter 1659/60, where his friend Cyriack Skinner presided
(this according to the hostile report of Samuel Butler, *The Transproser
Rehears'd*, 146); although conspicuously not among republicans under
the Protectorate, and unremembered by Aubrey among the participants,
AM was in Westminster and could have attended from November 1659
'till Feb. 20 or 21' when 'upon the unexpected turne upon generall
Monke's comeing-in, all these aierie modells vanished' (*Brief Lives*,
1:289–91).

February
21   (Tuesday) General Monck forces readmission to parliament of
            the Presbyterians ejected in Pride's Purge.
22   Writs issued for a new parliament to meet 25 April 1660.

April
2   (Monday) AM elected member for Hull in the 'Convention' par-
            liament, polling second with his 141 votes after John Ramsden's
            227 (AM's republican relation Col. Matthew Alured a distant
            fifth at 55). (BRB 4:303)
4   Letter in Latin from AM (Whitehall) to Francisco de Mello e
            Torres, Portuguese ambassador to England, concerning a treaty
            now under discussion, and the advantage to the ambassador at
            home and in England should he sign it; in signing off AM seems
            to distance himself from the diplomatic pressure being exerted
            on the Portuguese (Mello signs the treaty with the Council of
            State on 18 April). (Sotheby's, 24 July 1978, lot 108; BL, RP 3791
            (photocopy); Kelliher 1979, 148–9)
            Declaration of Breda dated this day, in which Charles Stuart
            promises peace, pardon, and 'a liberty to tender consciences'.
25   Parliament meets, in a session that, with an adjournment on
            13 September until 6 November 1660, lasts until its dissolution
            29 December 1660.

May

29   (Tuesday) Restoration of Charles II.
          Letter from AM (Westminster), cosigned by Ramsden, to 'the
          Commissioners of the Militia for the town & County of King-
          ston upon Hull', responding to theirs of 25 May and urging
          restraint in their prosecution of present business, owing to the
          Council of State having been disbanded. (Pierpont Morgan
          Library, LHMS, Misc. English; facs. in Verlyn Klinkenborg,
          British Literary Manuscripts, no. 50; *PL* 2:309; Bühler)

June

25   (Monday) AM named to committee to examine the University
          of Oxford petition. (*CJ* 8:74)

30   AM named to committee to examine questionable publications
          in the King's and bishops' names. (*CJ* 8:78)

July

16   (Monday) In a committee of the whole House of Commons,
          debating the settlement of religion, AM seeks to make sure that
          the question put to the vote is that of both 'the Protestant Faith
          according to the Scriptures and the Governement of the Church
          accordinge to Lawe', thus aiming 'to mix both [Doctrine and
          Discipline] together' to preempt further consultation and votes
          on the latter issue, 'the Discipline of the Church' – in sum,
          trying with others to forestall the eventual Restoration settle-
          ment by instead achieving an episcopal church without deans
          and chapters. The decision is reached to readdress the issue in
          October. (Bodl. MS Dep.f.9, 79^v, 77^r–79^v; see also 15 October
          and November entries below)

23   House of Commons nominates AM 'together with the Members
          that serve for the Universities' to prepare an answer to a letter of
          congratulation from the Elector Palatine, should Charles II
          think it fit. (*CJ* 8:98)

August

29   (Wednesday) AM named to committee to consider reparation
          to the Earl of Bristol out of the properties of Carew Raleigh.
          (*CJ* 8:140)

September

3   (Monday) AM added to committee to examine moneys spent to
          redeem captives at Algiers and Tunis. (*CJ* 8:148)

4   AM named to committee on 'draining of the great Level of the
          Fens'. (*CJ* 8:149–50)

6   Hull Corporation accords AM his knight's pence of 6s.8d.
          per diem, for 137 days, or £45 13s.4d. (BRB, 4:315)

13   Parliament adjourned until 6 November 1660.

October

15   (Monday) Worcester House Declaration announces Charles II's
            intention to call conference to implement the Declaration of
            Breda granting 'liberty to tender consciences'.

November

6   (Tuesday) Parliamentary session continues after the adjourn-
            ment. AM named to committee 'for settling the Militia'.
            (*CJ* 8:175)

7   AM named to committee for bill for endowing vicarages.
            (*CJ* 8:177)
            Hull Corporation accords a barrel of ale each to the MPs John
            Ramsden and AM. (BRB 4:331)

9   AM named to committee 'to examine the petition of Michael
            Crake', the House of Commons' sergeant at arms. (*CJ* 8:180)

14   AM named to committee to examine a bill 'for preventing the
            voluntary Separation, and living apart, of married Persons'.
            (*CJ* 8:183)

15   AM named to committee for Bill settling 'a Chapel of Ease in
            the Forest of Waltham'. (*CJ* 8:183)
            AM reports from committee to the whole House on amend-
            ments 'to the Bill for erecting and endowing Vicarages out of
            impropriate Rectories.' (*CJ* 8:184; see also *MPW* 1:298)

17   LHC: AM (W) sends the first of his constituency letters extant.
            Its liveliness of style and the frequent interjection of opinion
            distinguish it from most of his constituency letters to follow.
            The bill for supply is discussed at length – 'it will be each mans
            ingenuity not to grudge an after-payment for that settlement
            and freedome from Armyes and Navyes which before he would
            been glad to purchase with his whole fortune' – though AM
            does 'not love to write so much of this mony news'. (*PL* 2:1–3)

20   LHC: AM (W) reports on business; sends parliamentary and
            other news. (*PL* 2:3–4)

22   LHC: AM (W) reports business, parliamentary news. (*PL* 2:4–5)

24   AM a teller with [Hugh] Boscawen for the unsuccessful Yeas
            (117, vs 131 Noes) in a vote on bringing in legislation based on
            Charles II's Worcester House Declaration for a first reading the
            following Tuesday. (*CJ* 8:191)

26   Named to the committee for a bill settling the debts of the Earl
            of Cleveland. (*CJ* 8:192)

27   AM further reports from committee for endowing vicarages on
            amendments, which bill is passed with the amendments; and
            reports from the same committee bidding the king to write to

the colleges of the universities to put this legislation into effect. (*CJ* 8:193)

LHC: AM (W) sends parliamentary news, including 'I made my second Report [from committee] of that very good Bill for erecting and augmenting Vicarages out of all impropriations belonging to Arch Bishops Bishops Deans and Chapters'. Asks whether his fellow MP Ramsden is to be expected at Westminster. (*PL* 2:5–6)

28   In the Commons, the Yeas are unsuccessful (157 to 183) in the division on the 'Bill for making the King's Majesty's Declaration touching Ecclesiastical Affairs, effectual' (the bill providing 'ease for tender consciences'). (*CJ* 8:194)

29   Hull Corporation orders a barrel of ale to each of the town's MPs. (BRB 4:335)

LHC: AM (W) sends parliamentary and other news. 'Tis much refreshment to me after our long sittings daily to give you account what we do ...' (*PL* 2:6)

December

4   (Tuesday) LHC: AM (W) sends parliamentary and political news. Consecration of bishops – 'Tis thought that since our throwing out the bill of the kings declaration [see 28 November above] Mr Calamy and other moderate men will be resolute in refusing of Bishopricks.' Bill of Attainder has been before the house and question of 'Cromwell Bradshaw Ireton and Pride ... tis orderd that the Carkasses and coffins of the foure last named shall be drawn, with what expedition possible, upon an hurdle to Tyburn, there be hangd up for awhile and then buryed under the gallows'; Militia Act set aside since 'Tis better to trust his Majestyes moderation'. (*PL* 2:7–8)

8   LHC: AM (W), cosigned by fellow MP John Ramsden, reporting parliamentary business and news; postscript with further business. No amount of money will belatedly get a private bill [for division of Hessle parish] through the small remainder of this crowded session. (*PL* 2:8–9)

11   LHC: John Ramsden (W), cosigned by AM, reporting business in the main with brief parliamentary news. (*PL* 2:10–11)

15   House of Commons orders 'That Mr. Milton, now in Custody of the Sergeant at Arms attending this House, be forthwith released, paying his Fees.' (*CJ* 8:208)

17   'The celebrated Mr. John Milton having now laid long in custody of the serjeant at arms, was released by order of the house. Soon after, Mr. Andrew Marvel complained that the serjeant had exacted 150 l. fees of Mr. Milton; which was seconded

by col. King and col. Shapcot. On the contrary, sir Heneage Finch observed, That Milton was Latin Secretary to Cromwell, and deserved hanging. However, this matter was referred to the committee of privileges to examine and decide the difference' (Cobbett 4:162; see also Edward Phillips, in Darbishire 74). 'A Complaint being made, that the Sergeant at Arms had demanded excessive Fees for the Imprisonment of Mr. Milton; / Ordered, That it be referred to the Committee for Privileges, to examine this Business; and to call Mr. Milton and the Serjeant before them; and to determine what is fit to be given the Serjeant for his Fees in this Case' (*CJ* 8:209).

18 LHC: AM (W), cosigned by John Ramsden, reports on business with parliamentary and other news. (*PL* 2:12)

25 LHC: AM (W), cosigned by John Ramsden, sending mostly parliamentary with brief other news; brief business postscript. (*PL* 2:13)

29 Dissolution of Convention Parliament.
LHC: AM (W), cosigned by John Ramsden, reporting dissolution of parliament, summary of legislation passed during the session, and other news. (*PL* 2:14)

1661

AM's ongoing familiarity with Milton is suggested by his later reference to Samuel Parker's presence at this time in Milton's Jewin Street household, which may have come from Milton, but seems as likely first-hand (*RT2*, in *MPW* 1:418). AM listed by Wharton in 'Names of freinds 1661', and this on primary list 'for 'Myselfe', in rough copy and fair (Bodl. MS Carte 81, ff. 80r, 82r). AM also named in the printed list of all the MPs in the new parliament this year.

January
3 (Thursday) LHC: AM (W) writes singly, promising service between parliamentary sessions while he is still in London; reports business and other news. (*PL* 2:14–16)

12 LHC: AM (W) acknowledges receipt of letter of 8 January 1661; reports business concerning the farming of excise; promises newsletters in place of Gilbert Mabbott who is 'shortly to goe for Ireland'; early and late professions of grateful service; news. (*PL* 2:16–17)

13 Hull Corporation pay £37 13s.4d. to MPs Ramsden and AM, of which Ramsden gets £20 because of extraordinary charges, and AM £17 13s.4d. (BRB 4:342)

17 LHC: AM (W) sends news-book with brief cover-note with further news. (*PL* 2:18)

February

7   (Thursday) LHC: AM (W) reports parliamentary business of Hull's Commission of Lieutenancy, which goes to Hull's status as a town, and news from home and abroad. (*PL* 2:18–19)

17   LHC: AM (W) reports parliamentary business. (*PL* 2:19–20)

March

7   (Thursday) LHC: AM (W) sends note regarding Hull Commission of Lieutenancy to be sent on after sealing 'to morrow'. (*PL* 2:20)

9   LHC: AM (W) reports that he has received Hull Commission of Lieutenancy. (*PL* 2:20–1)

13   AM paid an extra £10 for 'charges about Ld Bellasyse Commission for Ld Leiutenancy' [*sic*] to 'be payd to Mr Edmond Popple for the use of Mr Andrew Marvell towards the paying the charges and Fees for the procureing the Lord Bellasies Patent for Lords Lieutenant ...' with some allowance to 'Mr Marvell for charge of postage of letters since he held intelligence with this board'. (BRB 4:352)

[19   LHC: this letter fails of delivery because 'all were stoppd'. Substance reported in letter of 26 March 1661.]

[21   LHC: this letter too seems to have failed of delivery because of the stop on mails.]

26   LHC: AM (W) promises cooperation with Colonel Gylby if they are both elected, refusing to see any 'inconsistence ... betwixt Colonell Gilbyes intrest & mine'. Parliamentary business. Mail for AM just to be addressed 'to be left with William Popple Merchant London' without further address so that AM can collect it directly. (*PL* 2:21–2)

28   In connection with the Belasyse patent (Commission of Lieutenancy, 7–13 March above), £7 10s. paid back to Hull Corporation by Popple from AM. (BRB 4:354)

April

1   (Monday) AM re-elected to parliament with Col. Anthony Gylby: initial voice vote does not settle who comes first; then Gylby polls at 294, AM 240, Ramsden 122, Edward Barnard 195. (BRB 4:355)

6   LHC: AM (W) reports that the raising of trained bands likely to be changed, but Hull can proceed with its two companies if it wishes. Knights of Garter and Bath made in preparation for coronation; French report that Northwest Passage has been discovered; gratitude for having been selected anew to represent Hull in parliament (as per letter received from mayor of Hull). (*PL* 2:22–3)

11	'A letter to be written to Mr Marvell, to repayre to the Wine Licence office at London and to make clame there that this Towne by Vertue of the [ ] Statute of King Edward the Sixt doe clame fower licenses to be due to them.' (BRB 4:356)
16	LHC: AM (W) sends brief note with enclosure. (*PL* 2:23)

May

8	(Wednesday) Parliament meets in a session that, with an adjournment from 30 July to 20 November 1661 (and a Christmas recess), continues until its prorogation, 19 May 1662. Sir Edward Turnor chosen Speaker.
9	Letter from MP Anthony Gylby ('att Mr Binns his house, in St Peeters streete, nere the Olive tree, in Westminster') to the mayor of Hull about the beginning of the parliamentary session. Accidentally has found himself 'within four or five dores of Mr Mervells' lodgings: 'I very well like of Mr Mervels conversation, and I doubt not but wee shall both of us indevour to be serviceable to those that sent us hither, and alsoe very freindly to one the other, noe place beinge able to afford (for any thinge I can perceive) any two Members more of a Judgement then we shall bee, we expect your Commands, which wee beleeve (by this time) you have prepared.' (BRL 651)
11	AM appointed to committee of elections and privileges, to meet that afternoon and every Tuesday, Thursday and Saturday. (*CJ* 8:246)
14	AM named to committee for a bill confirming the Acts of Pardon, Indemnity, and Oblivion, and others, to meet the next day. (*CJ* 8:249)
16	LHC: AM (W) reports parliamentary news and business. AM explains that his and Gylby's writing separately should not be taken as any sign of difficulties between them, 'For there is all civility betwixt us'. (*PL* 2:23–4; compare 1 June 1661 below)
18	AM (W) writes with his fellow MP Col. Anthony Gylby to Hull Trinity House [TH], in response to a letter from that society and apparently for the first time, and promise their service. (NTH52/1; *PL* 2:247–8)
20	LHC: AM (W), but signed only by Gylby, reports parliamentary business (in AM's hand and addressed by him). (*PL* 2:25–6)
30	LHC: AM (W) sends parliamentary news; 'I am somthing bound up that I can not write about your publick affairs but I assure you they break my sleepe.' (*PL* 2:26)

June

1	(Saturday) LHC: AM [W] reports that 'The bonds of civility betwixt Colonell Gilby and my selfe being unhappily snappd in

pieces, and in such manner that I can not see how it is possible ever to knit them again, the onely trouble that I have, is least by our misintelligence your businesse should receive any disadvantage.' Cites the election as the origin of their dispute, but subsequent differences seem also to have emerged. Parliamentary business. (*PL* 2:27–8)

15   LHC: AM (W) reports parliamentary business, in which AM touts his own role in committee of grievances on Hull's behalf; supplies the text and advises on the act separating Hull Trinity Church from its mother-church of Hessle; parliamentary news. (*PL* 2:28–31)

17   LHC: AM [W] reports parliamentary business and news. (*PL* 2:31–2)

20   LHC: AM (W) reports parliamentary business involving also Hull TH; 'I must beseech you also to listen to no litle storyes concerning my selfe. For I believe you know by this time that you have lately heard some very false concerning me.' (*PL* 2:32–3)

27   AM named to committee for the better ordering of the fens in Lincolnshire and for the trustees of Henry Neville to sell land to pay his and his son's debts. (*CJ* 8:281)
     LHC: AM (W) reports parliamentary news and business, including Conformity Act expected. (*PL* 2:33–4)

28   Yorkshire members named to committee to restore Thomas Radcliffe's estate to him. (*CJ* 8:284)

29   AM named first to committee for bill dividing Hull Trinity Church from Hessle, to meet the following Monday. (*CJ* 8:284)

July

4   (Thursday) Hull Corporation orders 'that a letter be writt to the two members of Parliament for this Towne to acquaint them that the bench conceives it very necessary that the Towne should fall upon the Eleccion of Aldermen, in the place of those sent who were displaced by his Majesties order and to desire their advice and speedy result thereupon'. (BRB 4:372)
     AM named first to committee for distinguishing the parish of Stanstead from that of Wrotham, to meet that afternoon. (*CJ* 8:289)

22   Amidst much business, the House of Commons passes the bill for dividing Hull Trinity Church from Hessle; 'Col. Gilby is to carry up the same to the Lords.' (*CJ* 8:307)

25   AM named to committee for the bill for 'Paving, Repairing, and Cleansing the Streets and Highways of Westminster', to meet that afternoon. (*CJ* 8:311)

30   Parliament adjourns until 20 November 1661.

August

9   (Friday) Hull Corporation agrees that AM is to take up the business of the renewal of the town's charter under way in London, with its lawyer Charles Vaux to go and attend for the duration. (BRB 4:373)

29   AM allotted £28 from Hull Corporation, being 6s. 8d per diem, for 84 days of preceding session of parliament (Col. Gylby will return his like payment, 17 October 1661). (BRB 4:382, 389)

September

9   (Monday) Warrant for exhumation of Thomas May from Westminster Abbey: this has been thought a possible occasion for some of the harshest lines in AM's 'Tom May's Death', possibly revised now or hereafter. (*PL* 1:303; Rees 484–5)

November

7   (Thursday) 'This day Milton's booke against the portrature of his sacred Majestie beeing by order of his Majestie amongst other bookes to be burnt the sayed booke was this day burnt in the Common Hall of this Towne [of Hull].' (BRB 4:399)

8   Hull Corporation orders barrels of ale for its friends in London, including AM. (BRB 4:402)

20   Parliament sits again.

December

3   (Monday) Hull TH drafts letter to Gylby asking his and AM's assistance with securing the grant of the Spurnhead lighthouse. (NTH52/1)

11   Yorkshire members among those named to committee for better regulating the Yorkshire cloth trade. (*CJ* 8:329–30)

18   House of Commons agrees to the amendments from House of Lords 'to the Bill for dividing Trinity Church in Kingston upon Hull from Hasle'. (*CJ* 8:335–6)

20   Christmas recess of parliament, until 7 January 1662. Corporations Act comes into force, requiring all persons governing cities and corporations to be of the Church of England.

25   For taxes first due this day, AM is named among the commissioners for assessment in Hull (among 20 local dignitaries), to which local office he is renamed (or renewed) to the end of his life, with the exception of 1663. (*Statutes of the Realm*, 5:342, 544, 572, 582, 591, 619, 773, 809; compare 5:458)

1662

Thomas Fuller's warm tribute to the rev. Andrew Marvell is published in *The History of the Worthies of England* (1662), 159 (see 30 September 1624 above). Fuller died in 1661 and this entry was likely composed in the 1640s; the present publication in aid of the Restoration church settlement describes a church that Marvell will redescribe with reference in *RT2* to his father's example. (*MPW* 1:241, 288–9)

Although the resemblance may be only that, AM's 'Nymph Complaining' (lines 71–92) has been associated with Rowland Watkyns's 'The Holy Maid', in *Flamma Sine Fumo: or, Poems without Fictions* (1662) 104–6. (Smith, 66–7)

January

1   (Wednesday) John Dryden, *To My Lord Chancellor, Presented on New-years-day* (1662): seems to recall AM's 'An Horatian Ode' (lines 19–20, 41–2, 9–10), in describing the King's and the Chancellor's virtues:

> ... both are for each other's use dispos'd,
> His to inclose, and yours to be inclos'd;
> Nor could another in your room have been
> Except an Emptinesse had come between. (lines 39–42)

'An Horatian Ode' seems also to inform the description of Clarendon's policy: 'How strangely active are the arts of peace, / Where restless motions less than war's do cease' (lines 105–6). Republished in *Annus Mirabilis* (1688) and thereafter. (Dryden, *Poems*, ed. Hammond and Hopkins, 1:64, 67; Macdonald 10–11, 15)

7   Parliament reconvenes after Christmas recess.

11   AM named to committee for settlement of an estate to Lady Wandesford (wife of a fellow Yorkshire MP). (*CJ* 8:343)

29   AM named to committee for bill to prevent frauds in customs. (*CJ* 8:353–4)

February

11   (Tuesday) Hull TH drafts letter to AM and Gylby that outlines its interest in a Spurnhead light and the related collection of shipping duties. (NTH52/1)

17   AM a teller with [William] Sandys for the unsuccessful Yeas (63, vs 77 Noes) in a vote on a proviso touching soldiers and their families in garrison towns, which was to have been added to the bill for poor relief. (*CJ* 8:366)

19   Yorkshire members among those enlisted for committee to reverse the Earl of Strafford's attainder. (*CJ* 8:368)

25   AM and Gylby write to the wardens of Hull TH (one of them is now AM's brother-in-law Edmond Popple), with text of a petition, to be corrected and sent back in duplicate (concerning the proposed Spurnhead lighthouse). Enclosed seems to have been AM's copy of a parliamentary bill to this purpose that had been read in the Lords, 8 July 1661. (NTH52/1; *PL* 2:247–8, 372)

March

1   (Saturday) Hull TH drafts note concerning Spurnhead light; AM to speak to Lord Belasyse on its behalf. (NTH52/1)

3   Yorkshire MPs among those enlisted for committee for a bill regulating abuses in the packing and weighing of butter. (*CJ* 8:376)

5   AM named (with Gylby) to committee for 'a Bill for Increase of the Maintenance of Ministers in Corporate and Market Towns'. (*CJ* 8:379)

6   Gylby (London) to Edmond Popple (Hull TH): '... you have formerly heard by Mr Marvell, what we suppose fit to be done in your busines, if we shall now proceede acordinge to our intentions, it will be requisit that you place some mony in such hands as may be both responsable to you for it, and alsoe be fit to helpe to solicit your busines.' (NTH52/1)

7   Hull TH drafts letter asking Lord Belasyse's assistance with Spurnhead light, citing AM's and Gylby's involvement as MPs. (NTH52/1)

12   Yorkshire MPs among those enlisted for committee to settle Francis Tyndall's estate. (*CJ* 8:384)

14   Yorkshire MPs among those enlisted for committee to settle Henry Hilton's charities. (*CJ* 8:386)

15   Hull Trinity House records payment to Mr Hoare of £20 to be sent to Gylby and AM, with 4s. extra for the bill of exchange. (FTH1/5)

18   Ordered in the House of Commons that the Speaker, Sir Edward Turnor, examine 'the Difference between Mr. Marvell and Mr. [Thomas] Clifford, Two Members of this House ... [and] to hear Mr. [John] Scott, another Member of this House, who was present when this Difference did happen; and to mediate and reconcile the same between them if he can; or else to report it to the House, with his Opinion therein' (*CJ* 8:389). Scott was a Cavalier member from York; Clifford becomes 'a tall Lowse' in AM's 'Last Instructions', line 18.

19   Yorkshire MPs among those additionally enlisted for committee for the bill concerning the fishing trade. (*CJ* 8:390)

20   Speaker Turnor 'reports, That he had examined the Matter of Difference between Mr. Marvell and Mr. Clifford; and found, that Mr. Marvell had given the first Provocation, that begot the Difference: And that his Opinion was that Mr. Marvell should declare his Sorrow for being the First Occasion of this Difference; and then Mr. Clifford to declare that he was sorry for the Consequence of it: and that Mr. Clifford was willing to yield to this Determination, but that Mr. Marvell refused'; the two are directed to withdraw during the debate of the matter;

the resolution is that they be gravely reprehended; which leads to their apologies, with AM now acknowledging that he had given 'the first Provocation', which leads to the remission of this breach of privilege. (*CJ* 8:391)

22   AM (W) writes without Gylby's signature to Hull TH, noting his delay in correspondence owing to 'avocations lately in mine own particular' (likely the problem with Clifford), promising that their business has not suffered in the interim, and urging their attention to this 'thing of great consequence'. Verso has draft of response from Hull TH about the Spurn lighthouse location and the duties payable by passing shipping. (NTH52/1; *PL* 2:248)

23   Hull TH records previous payment of £100 to Gylby and AM 'about the lights', with £1 0s.2d. extra for the interim lender. (FTH1/5)

29   Hull TH draft another note to AM and Gylby and another draft follows of the Spurn Light petition to the King. (NTH52/1)

31   AM's 41st birthday: the 'Hollis' portrait of AM (City Art Gallery, Hull) portrays him in his 42nd year and was likely painted now before his departure for Holland in May 1662. This is the portrait the eighteenth-century republican Thomas Hollis has engraved by Giovanni Battista Cipriani (see 1760 below); it is engraved again by John Basire in 1776. (Discussed with reproduction in Kelliher 1978a, 80–2)

April

1   (Tuesday) AM (W) writes without Gylby's signature to Hull TH explaining in response to its letter dated 25 March that it should be understood that he always writes for both himself and Gylby, sending a petition to Lord Albemarle (General Monck) in AM's handwriting for their subscription, asking for £100 credit 'to reward such as will not otherwise befriend your businesse', and urging secrecy. It is likely that prorogation would soon make any legislation for the lighthouse moot. That petition begins 'May it please your Grace, We should at all times be very unwilling to give you trouble, but much more when your indisposition might rather require our prayers for your recovery then admit the importunity of businesse ...'. On 5 April, Hull TH adds a note: 'In answere to this was sent a bill of 100 li Credit a certificate with most of the hands in Hull and a letter to the Duke of Albermarle according to the Coppy annexed.' (NTH52/1; *PL* 2:249)

3   AM named to committee for the settling of Cuthbert Morley's (Yorkshire) estate. (*CJ* 8:394)

4	Yorkshire MPs among those enlisted for committee for bill preventing theft and rapine upon the northern borders of England. (*CJ* 8:396)
11	AM named second to committee for an ingrossed bill from the Lords, 'An Act Declaratory concerning Bankrupts'. (*CJ* 8:403)
28	AM among the MPs added to the committee for the bill for sowing flax and hemp. (*CJ* 8:415)

May

8	(Thursday) AM (W) writes to Hull TH with concern about discussing too much business via the mails, and notes that Gylby will eventually report in person. He apologizes that he must now go to Holland with the Earl of Carlisle, thus securing that Privy Council member to their interest, which service he is obliged to undertake owing to 'the interest of some persons too potent for me to refuse and who have a great direction and influence upon my counsells and fortune'. He promises to write weekly from Holland and has employed the lawyer John Cressett for their business, in which there has been much 'cunning and intricacy' on the part of rivals. (NTH52/1; *PL* 2:250–1)
12	Privy Council determines that neither Hull TH nor Col. Frowd have any valid claim to erect a lighthouse at Spurnhead, which lies in the King's disposal. (PRO, PC2/55/322ʳ)
	Presumably in the weeks before this date, AM and Gylby have in London been paid £100 'concerning the lighthouses', for which the Hull TH order book now records a reimbursement. (Brooks, ed. *The First Order Book of the Hull Trinity House 1632–1665*, 156)
13	AM cited as having delegated business of Spurn lighthouse to the solicitor John Cressett, in letter from Cressett (London) to Hull TH. (NTH52/1; *PL* 2:372)
19	Act of Uniformity receives royal approval. Parliament prorogued until 18 February 1663.
21	Caveat ordered in Privy Council that no grant for Spurnhead lighthouse be granted without a hearing of the Hull TH. (PRO, PC2/55/325ʳ)
24	In a postscript to Hull TH, John Cressett (London) adds he has 'now heard from your Brother Marvill who is safe at the Hague att Sir George Downeings house' (NTH52/1; *PL* 2:373). Whatever AM's errand in Holland, it did not much engage the Earl of Carlisle there in person, since the latter's presence in Privy Council meetings is little interrupted this year or the next, until his departure for Moscow (PRO, PC2/55–6). Carlisle's brother-in-law George Downing, a colleague of AM's in the

Protectorate and still English Resident at The Hague, later attests that Carlisle depends heavily on his secretary AM for languages and has to trust him completely (see 1/11 April 1664 below), which may be based on some present experience of AM as his visitor.

August

24   (Sunday, St Bartholomew's Day) Act of Uniformity in force, requiring widespread resignation of ministries by Presbyterian incumbents ('Black Bartholomew').

1663

The longer version of 'A Dialogue between Thyrsis and Dorinda' is included in the second edition of Samuel Rowlands, *A Crew of Kind London Gossips* (1663), 92–4. (*PL* 1:247; Beal 1993, 30)

January

9/19   (Friday) AM (Vianen [near Utrecht]) to Hull TH reassuring them of his eagerness to serve them, again promising 'frequente letters', and presenting an account of their monies spent (chiefly legal expenses). (NTH52/1; *PL* 2:251–3)

February

[3   (Tuesday) Hull Corporation writes to AM asking him to return to his seat in parliament (see 27 February, and 5 and 12 March below).]

10   Hull TH drafts letter to AM about Spurn business. (NTH52/1)

18   Parliament meets in a session that continues until its prorogation, 27 July 1663.

27   Hull Corporation: 'Sir Robert Hildyard acquainted the Board with a letter he received from the Lord Bellasyse about Mr Marvells absence from Parliament &c' Answered: 'It hath been comunicated unto us by Sir Robert Hildyard the absence of our Burgess Mr Marvell, In his present attendance in the service of the Parliament, and your Lordshipps care in makeing [way?] of an opportunity of a supply of which wee have very high esteeme and shall endeavor accordingly to improve. wee have had two letters from Mr Marvell the one wrote at his departure that he was to goe into Holland, not farr off, and would be ready at our call, and in a late letter dated at Vianen in Holland, to remember us that he did not forgett our service the copie of which sayd Letter, wee send here inclosed, To which wee wrote him our answer, That wee conceived It was his duty incumbent to attend the Kingdomes service, in Parliament and according to the trust reposed in him, wee expected that he would performe, If he doe not very shortly wee

hope not to loose your Loordshipps favor to procure for us that expedient, As wee may supply his absence by a new elecion of a Burgess which shall not want the testimony of our endeavors to place it ...'. (BRB 4:503)

March

5 (Thursday) John, Lord Belasyse to the mayor and aldermen of Hull: '[ ] be occation off choyse, off another [ ] serve in parliament: for your towne [and corpo]ration; assuring you that nott onely [ ] such person, who I may hearafter recom[mend] to you, but my self allso, shall be [ ] assiduous, and reddy uppon all occations [ ] you all the favor and service, in owr pow[er] allso I approve off your prudence and just[ ] in advertising Mr Mervell to returne, [ ] you proceed against him; and that in [ ] he neclect your service, then you have c[ause] to indeavor a new choyse, wherin you [ ] have my assistance ...'. (BRL 669)

12 LHC: AM (Vianen, near Utrecht) promises his swift return to parliament in response to 'your prudent and courteous letter of the 3^d of Febr:' such as 'would have brought me over though I had been at a greater distance'. (PL 2:34)

April

2 (Thursday) AM returns to the House of Commons, there to encounter an emollient royal answer to the Commons' anti-popery address.
LHC: AM (W) sends notice that he has returned and been in parliament that day; has ignored his 'own private concernments' to fulfil his obligation to them. (PL 2:34–5)

14 AM [W] to Hull TH regarding state of the lighthouse business, which should rest as it is for the time being; 'My memory of this businesse of yours was no small inducement together with my more publick obligations to hast me over to Parliament' (dated from postmark). Hull TH drafts letter in response thanking the MPs for their good work and trusting their discretion. (NTH52/1; PL 2:253)
Yorkshire MPs enlisted for committee to enable John Robinson to sell and dispose lands. (CJ 8:472)
LHC: AM [W] suggests Gylby's 'vigilance and sufficiency might well have excused my absence'; sends parliamentary news. (PL 2:35–6)

May

AM's nephew William Popple marries Mary, eldest daughter of Matthew Alured. (Burdon 1984, 384)

19 (Tuesday) LHC: AM (St John's St, Clerkenwell [where resides the Earl of Carlisle]) responds 'to yours of 5th of May' with brief

parliamentary news; reports that the Earl of Carlisle is to embark on an embassy to Moscow, Sweden and Denmark. (*PL* 2:36, 360)

June
6   (Saturday) LHC: AM (London) sends parliamentary news; 'I am forced by some private occasions but relating to the publick to be something lesse assiduous at the House then heretofore but my worthy Partner never failes.' (*PL* 2:37)

20   LHC: AM [London] reports his appointment as secretary to the Earl of Carlisle's embassy; aims to be excused by the Commons so that Hull must not think of replacing him as MP; the adjournment of parliament may last almost as long as the embassy; and Hull's interests will continue to be well-represented by Gylby. (*PL* 2:37–8)

23   LHC: AM (W) sends brief note with parliamentary news. (*PL* 2:38)

26   MPs from any of the seaports enlisted for the committee for a bill settling the possession of marshes reclaimed from the sea. (*CJ* 8:511)

July
9   (Thursday) Gylby (London) writes Hull TH with enclosures delivered to him and AM by Scarborough MPs protesting the new grant to Hull; 'Mr Mervell tells me he will by this Post give you alsoe this Accompt.' (NTH52/1)

20   About to depart for Archangel, AM (London) writes to Trinity House (Hull), excusing himself as he sets off – 'which I do with his Majestyes good liking, by leave from the House and with the assent of our Bench' – and professing his lasting regard for their business, which now stands in a good posture; he recommends, should the need arise, that they write to secretary of state William Morice using AM's name and engage their previous solicitor John Cressett, failing whom John Rushworth. Session of parliament will last a week longer (27 July). (NTH52/1; *PL* 2:254)

LHC: AM (London), as he embarks for Archangel and Moscow, cites Charles II's approval of his undertaking, as well as the 'leave given me from the house [of Commons] and enterd in the journall' (not found there), as well as the Hull Corporation's approbation; also Gylby's value for the management of affairs relating to Hull's garrison. (*PL* 2:39)

Before his departure, AM has William Popple repay 'the remaynder of the moneys expended about the light house' (£40 3s.4d) to Hull TH, with the payment made perhaps in August. (FTH1/5; *PL* 2:254)

22   AM sets sail from Gravesend in the frigate *Kent* with the Earl of Carlisle (PRO, SP29/81/223ʳ). Parliament prorogued, 27 July.

30   AM's brother-in-law Edmond Popple refuses to 'subscribe the declaration for renouncing the Covenant' in taking the oath of alderman. Two weeks later he refuses a second time and 26–27 November 1663 he accepts being fined £150; granted a year to pay the fine, he pays the whole amount 14 December 1663 (and will later be repaid £13 6s. for this early payment). (BRB 4:527, 529, 551–2, 553, 556, 597)

August

The Carlisle embassy to Muscovy, Sweden and Denmark is richly described in Miège and in Carlisle's letters, the latter written in AM's hand. In Moscow, the main aim was to retrieve for the English the White Sea trading route, a privilege lost owing to the tsar's revulsion at the regicide and the diminishing benefit of thus restricting commerce (Konovalov, Phipps, and especially Unkovskaya). Carlisle himself 'had a peculiar grace and vivacity in his discourse' (Miège 4) but no languages. In Russia his diplomacy proceeds in great part in English with Russian interpreters. AM's role as a humanist secretary was problematic in Moscow with the Russians liking to mistake his Latin when they sought grounds for disagreement; in Sweden and Denmark, by contrast, AM performs productively in Latin and in French.

19   (Wednesday) The frigate with AM and Carlisle reaches the bar of the Dvina, 'thirty miles' before Archangel. (Bodl. MS Clarendon 80, 165–6; PRO, SP29/81/223ʳ)

20   AM sent ahead to give notice of the embassy's arrival, is conducted from his lodging by six gentlemen to the castle, 'through a guard of six hundred soldiers'; delivers his message; and 'after much civility was brought back again in the same manner'. (*Ibid.*)

21–22   AM returns with the 16 boats sent by the Governor of Archangel to bring ashore the Earl of Carlisle's entourage. (*Ibid.*)

23   AM joins in disembarking as the Earl makes his entry into Archangel, saluted by ships in the roads and the garrison 'drawn up all along the shore'. Beginning of disputes about protocol. (*Ibid.*; Miège 24–5; PRO, SP29/81/223ʳ)

27   Letter in AM's hand from Earl of Carlisle (Archangel) to the Earl of Clarendon (London), reporting on the embassy's reception in Archangel. (Bodl. MS Clarendon 80, 165–6)

        Hull: 'This day the Accompt for Knights pence due to Coll. Anthony Gilbie and Mr Andrew Marvell for this last Session of Parliament was had ... And Mr Andrew Marvell served from the second of Aprill 1663 untill the 20th of July 1663 beeing a hundred and ten dayes at viˢ–viiiᵈ per day which in all is thirty six pounds Thirteene shillings and Fower pence.' (BRB 4:531)

September

3   (Thursday) Hull moneys taken out of the Corporation's iron
         chest to be paid 'to whom [AM] hath or shall order to receive
         it'. (BRB 4:533)

5–6   Belated arrival in Archangel of the merchant vessel shipping the
         rest of Carlisle's entourage and goods. (Miège 22)

12   Embassy departs Archangel, upriver by barge 'drawn up all
         along in boats by force of men for neare a thousand miles,
         against the streame of two rivers, first the Dwina and then the
         Sucana which froze not upon us till we came within thirty miles
         of Vologda'. (Bodl. MS Clarendon 80, 276; see also Miège 85–7)

October

This month Patrick Gordon (Moscow) receives from Carlisle (Archangel?) a
written request to purchase two silver trumpets with banners and twelve
halberds with fringes in Carlisle's livery. (Gordon *Diary*, 55–6)

17   (Saturday) Embassy reaches Vologda, where it stays awaiting
         winter, which will permit its overland journey to Moscow, but
         encounters further delays owing to unseasonal thaw. (Bodl. MS
         Clarendon 80, 276; Miège 95–96)

November

5   (Thursday) The embassy celebrates Guy Fawkes Day in Vologda
         with fireworks, a feast and a ball. (Miège 100)

21   Letter in AM's hand from Earl of Carlisle (Vologda) to the Earl
         of Clarendon (London), reporting on the journey of the
         embassy, matters of protocol, and on Muscovite affairs, espe-
         cially mobilization against Polish invasion; also recommending
         an embassy to Poland and seeking direction about any such
         mission on this embassy's return from Moscow; and noting
         expense of the present embassy. A few days before John Hebdon
         had noted the Earl of Carlisle's good reception in Vologda ('as
         honorably as possible these Parts cann aford') and hopes of
         good success as 'hee himselfe haith written to the King and
         Councell'. (Bodl. MS Clarendon 80, 276–9; PRO, SP29/84/
         12ᵛ–13ʳ)

December

Embassy remains in Vologda, but the arrival there of the Tsar's chief agents
leads to marked deterioration in the standards of diet and accommodation;
chief diversions are hunting, music and dancing (some traffic in tobacco).
(Miège 96–101)

3   (Thursday) 'This day Thirty Six pound thirteene shillings and
         fower pence is taken out of the [Hull Corporation's] Iron Chest
         and payd unto Mr Edmond Popple for the use of his brother
         Andrew Marvell Esqr [corrected from 'Mr'] given him by this

board for his service in the last Session of Parliament.' (BRB 4:555)

ca. 28   Carlisle having unsuccessfully sought good sledges from Nestrof, the Tsar's agent, AM is then dispatched to renew the request, and tells Nestrof 'freely' that this poor treatment 'was most undecent'. The disobliging Muscovite claims it sufficient honour to the English that he has been sent this far to meet them, to which AM replies that, Nestrof's quality notwithstanding, the agent may rate himself too high. (Miège 105–6)

1664

January

7   (Thursday) Carlisle's baggage is sent ahead on 60 sledges, with horses. (Miège 107)

15   The well-wrapped embassy departs Vologda, travels cross-country in sledges of its own hire. Hardships aside, 'the greatest part of us did nothing but sleep all the Voiage'. (Miège 106–7, 111)

February

3   (Wednesday) Reaches Yauza ('The Yawes') near Moscow, where embassy prepares for the formal entry into the capital. (Miège 107–8, 113)

5   Embassy readies itself for formal entry into Moscow that day, and after further delay arrives within sight of the city, only to be turned back so that the ceremonies can be performed the next day; the Tsar and his family too kept waiting for five hours in expectation. Uncomfortable night in the nearby village of Prutki. (Miège 107–8, 115–17; Bodl. MS Clarendon 81, 122ʳ; Gordon *Diary*, 56)

6   At Carlisle's command and in his name, AM writes a letter to the Tsar Alexei Mikhailovich, 'Illustrissime atque Excellentissime Imperator. Novum hoc & inusitatem ...', complaining of their treatment, unworthy of a delegation of 'Serenissimi Regis' Charles II, for which the apologies that have been tendered are inadequate. Observes that 'Rem hanc fabulae & ludibrio toti mundo futuram' ('this proceeding would give cause of talk and laughter to the whole World') and demands due correction of its perpetrators. (Miège 117–26)

Sumptuously dressed, and heralded by trumpeters on horseback, the ambassadorial train with Muscovite attendants approaches Moscow, and around two-o-clock in the afternoon begins to proceed the final two miles into Moscow through large numbers of troops and loud music. The numbers of troops are made to seem larger still by their peeling away once passed by the ambassador and galloping around 'to fill up a new station forward'. Some three hours later – after gifts, a further dispute about precedence, a formal Muscovite greeting and the English response – night has fallen as the embassy enters Moscow itself, and so it is with bonfires and great numbers of torches illuminating the glittering parade, all under the eye of the Tsar for whom it stops 'accidentally', that the embassy makes its way to the ambassador's residence, a large stone house in a good street near the Kremlin. (Miège 127–35, 139, 439; Bodl. MS Clarendon 81, 122ᵛ; Gordon *Tagebuch*, 1:341)

11   After four days of being 'shut up close in our House', during which efforts are made to master Muscovite protocol, and after the initial promise on February 7 of an audience on February 9, Carlisle finally has his audience with Tsar Alexei Mikhailovich. The English send ahead gifts of luxuries, fabrics, cannon, Cornish tin and a hundred pigs of lead; whereupon sledges are provided for Carlisle and his son, with AM 'standing and uncovered' in Carlisle's sledge, 'carrying in his hands upon a yard of red Damaske his Letters of Credence written in parchment, whose Superscription contained all the titles of the Tzar in letters of Gold'. (Miège 140, 144–6; PRO, SP91/3/103ᵛ–104ʳ, printed in Robbins 1957, 10–11; Bodl. MS Clarendon 81, 122ᵛ)

At the Kremlin the embassy proceeds through ranks of troops, past the splendid guards, to the vast hall of audience, where it meets the richly clad Tsar, with his lustrous throne and attendant lords, and some two hundred boyars in dazzling dress. Carlisle's greeting on behalf of Charles II, and the Tsar's Russian response, are followed by Carlisle's speech in English, translated sentence by sentence by his Russian interpreter, with a Latin copy by AM for submission. (Miège 146–53)

Carlisle's speech gives thanks for the Muscovite embassy to England (that of Prosorovskiy, 1662–63) and elaborates the praises of Charles II, celebrating his present power and dominion, and then cites the advantage of his friendship, recalls the English discovery of the Archangel shipping route in the reign of Edward VI, and expects that the English trading privileges (denied after the execution of Charles I) will now be graciously renewed. (AM's Latin document and the English version are printed in Miège 153–79)

After the speech, which was 'well approved of', Carlisle and his gentlemen, among whom AM, are given leave to kiss the Tsar's (right) hand, which is upheld by a boyar lest the Tsar be tired; the English gifts are formally presented, beginning with a cannon given as a relic of Charles I and a pair of pistols that Charles II had worn on his entry into London at the Restoration. Huge feast follows with many healths drunk. (Miège 180–4)

13 Again with due ceremony, another brief audience with the Tsar, and the first conference with his commissioners, including presentation of English claims for redress of the slight to the embassy at its approach to Moscow, and for the renewal of the trading privileges of the Muscovy Company, in terms 'given' by Carlisle to his secretary. (Miège 183–91)

17 A second conference at the Kremlin, where English claims answered but in a way 'quite contrary' to Carlisle's expectations, and so 'he thought fit thereupon to speak somewhat hard to them'; a casement window then crashes down and the commissioners wish Carlisle 'had spoken more gently'. (Miège 191)

19 Carlisle dines with the Tsar, in a meal lasting from two in the afternoon to eleven at night, with 'near five hundred dishes' served continuously and on very tarnished silver. He attempts more personal diplomacy, still hoping for the successful renewal of English trading privileges (PRO, SP91/3/104^r, printed in Robbins 1957, 11; Miège 290–5). AM, among others, is favoured with a whole head of a sturgeon. (*Dvortsovye Razriady* 3:571)

26 The written copy of the Muscovite response of 13 February is finally brought to Carlisle, explaining away the confusions suffered by the embassy on 5 February, and refusing privileges to the Muscovy Company, owing to its allegiances during 'the late Rebellion of England', and owing to the rapacity and bad faith of English merchants, including the sale of such 'prohibited commodities as Tobacco'. (Miège 192–4)

Now too ('as if ... to be revenged of the former Reparation required by his Excellencie') the commissioners complain that (AM's) Latin copy of the speech had given the Tsar the title only of *Illustrissimus*, reserving *Serenissimus* for Charles II, an egregious affront; and so 'a writing that was only given to satisfie a mans curiositie, who desired to see it, is now become a very great matter of State, every word of it is examined strictly'. (Miège 194–5)

29 Another conference, where Carlisle writes back at length, presumably in AM's hand and especially on the third point more entirely of his composition. First, concerning the slight to his embassy, 'Carlisle' observes that such is the Tsar's command that it is incredible that his posts, which 'would not miss a foot at midnight thorough the very desarts of Tartary, yet should

lose their way in broad day-light, within three or four miles of Mosco', and 'it appears the nearer one comes to Mosco men are more ignorant of the Roads'; and that the present excuses are not satisfactory. Second, concerning the trading privileges, he asserts that 'the late Rebellion' has been extinguished and pardoned, and hence can be no reason for present prejudice; that whatever the wealth of the English merchants, the Russian people have benefited more; and that the Tsar's letter to Charles II of 28 July 1661, had amounted to an invitation to the Muscovy Company to resume its privileges. Third, concerning the 'new matter' of how the Tsar had been addressed in the Latin version of Carlisle's speech, he styles it no true 'paper of State, nor written in the English Language wherein I treat, [nor formally presented] ... but only as a piece of curiosity, which is now restored to me and I am possessed of it'. But on 'the value of the words *Illustrissimus* and *Serenissimus* compared together, seeing we must here from affaires of State, fall into Grammatical contests concerning the Latin tongue', favours the commissioners and perhaps the Tsar with a disquisition on those words, with references to chapter and verse in Cicero, Lucretius, Ovid and Pliny, and noting that, since these titles are no proper classical usages, other modern instances must serve for guidance, and none of them is derogatory to the Tsar. In sum, 'I would have used *Serenissimus* an hundred times concerning his *Tzarskoy* Majesty, had I thought it would have pleased him better.' (Miège 196–220)

March

Very closely attended by the Tsar's troops, members of the embassy seek to explore Moscow. The main diversions for this 'Family' are their saunas and acting 'a handsome Comedie in Prose' of the music-master's composition. After the thaw they enjoy horse-racing, football, running at the ring and picnics.

10	(Thursday) Carlisle is held 'above four hours' by delegates of the Tsar, 'using all the arguments, turnes and scrues of the Russian suttlety' to promise privileges only after the wars with Poland and Crimea are over, 'but I held firme'. (Bodl. MS Clarendon 81, 124^v)
12	Letter in AM's hand from Earl of Carlisle (Moscow) to Charles II, describing progress of embassy; lamenting 'the slownesse of the winter and the greater slownesse of those Sonns of Winter, the Muscovites'; explaining that the difficulty over the form of address for the Tsar has been overcome. (PRO, SP91/3/ 103^r–104^v, printed in Konovalov 86–7, and Robbins 1957, 10–12)

Letter in AM's hand from Earl of Carlisle (Moscow) to Earl of Clarendon (London), describing the progress of the embassy much more fully, and explaining the unsuccess of his conferences to date, and the emphasis the Muscovites place on the war with Poland. (Bodl. MS Clarendon 81, 122–4; printed in Konovalov 87–8)

16   Westminster: parliamentary session of 1664 begins; continues until 17 May. AM named to committee of elections and privileges. (*CJ* 8:534)

17   Great dinner sent to embassy from the Tsar in honour of his birthday. (Miège 295)

19   Response from the commissioners, nettled by the tone of Carlisle's comments about the Russian posts and about the titles (see 29 February above): lamenting the lack of English support to Muscovy in wars against Poland and the Crimean Tartar, they offer the trading privileges only once those wars are over. (Miège 220–1)

22   Carlisle's response given in papers at conference, which in passing mocks the delay in the commissioners' answer, insists that he only has the power to treat for the entire and present renewal of the trading privileges, and cites English support for the Tsar in times past. Carlisle seeks private audience with the Tsar. (Miège 222–6).

April
1/11   (Friday) Carlisle's dependence on AM cited, in letter from George Downing (The Hague) to the Earl of Clarendon (London): Carlisle 'hath no language and so must wholy trust his Secretary and act by him', whereas Downing is entirely discreet and does his own coding in correspondence. (Bodl. MS Clarendon 107, 153ᵛ)

3   The great Palm-Sunday procession in Moscow observed by the embassy. (Miège 295–9)

11   Easter celebrations begin, including for 15 days the giving of coloured eggs. (Miège 299)

22   Carlisle (with his secretary and interpreter) has his private audience with the Tsar 'from ten a clock at night till one of the next morning', presenting the English claims in full in a long speech where, after his own preface, he speaks for Charles II at length in the first person as if to address the Tsar directly from the English crown. The speech rehearses more fully the points noted previously, and now offers mediation with Sweden and with Poland; copies of it in English and in Latin ('translated as near as possible, but not subscribed but by his Secretary' AM) are given to the commissioners. For some days after, one of the commissioners tries to get Carlisle to sign the Latin version,

which he eventually does but with the reservation 'Except any difference with the English.' (Miège, pp. 227–77, 451; *Dvortsovye Razriady* 3:581–2)

Carlisle also supplies memorials against the embassy's *pristaf* Pronchishchev (also a commissioner), and still seeks the reparation promised for the confusions of 5 February (Miège 278–80)

May

24   (Tuesday) Commissioners respond to Carlisle's papers given in conference 22 March, again nettled by the tone of his communication and effectively refuse all his demands. (Miège 280–1)

27   Commissioners respond to Carlisle's speech in private audience with Tsar of 22 April: they cavil at his claims and tone, misinterpret the Latin to Carlisle's disadvantage, insist on hearing the specifics of what Charles II might perform for Muscovy, and excuse Pronchishchev. (Miège 281–4, 451–2)

29   Celebration by the embassy of Charles II's birthday and Restoration. (Miège 299–300)

June

1   (Wednesday) Charles II having empowered Carlisle with the offer of that king's mediation in affairs between Muscovy and Poland, Carlisle has conference with new set of commissioners, and submits letter proposing that mediation. (Miège 284–7)

14   Letter in AM's hand from Earl of Carlisle (Moscow) to Charles II, describing the unsuccessful conclusion of the embassy, and explaining that the renewal of trading privileges has been postponed by the Russians until after their war with Poland, which is 'but a meere evasion' since then they will have no reason to grant them. (PRO, SP91/3/105^r–106^v; printed in Konovalov 91–2, Robbins 1957, 12–13)

Same day, another letter in AM's hand from Earl of Carlisle (Moscow) to Earl of Clarendon (London), declaring that 'all this Muscovia businesse proves a meer cheat on their part from the very beginning ... no [trading] privileges are to be had'. (Bodl. MS Clarendon 81, 282–3)

Same day, another letter in AM's hand from Earl of Carlisle (Moscow) to Secretary Henry Bennet (London), regretting failure of the embassy, and exclaiming 'What else was to be expected in a country where all other beasts change their colors twice a yeare but the rationall beasts change their soules thrice a day.' (PRO, SP91/3/107^r–108^v; printed in Konovalov 92, Robbins 1957, 13–14)

16   Carlisle refuses the Tsar's lavish leave-taking present to the English ambassador and embassy of thousands of sables. (Miège 302–6)

Hull Corporation pays Col. Gylby his knight's pence with no mention of the absent AM; on 3 December 1664, AM is likewise not listed among the London representatives of Hull to whom ale is being sent. (BRB 4:588, 5:9)

24   A leave-taking audience with the Tsar as Carlisle declares the end of this embassy to Moscow. Departure via Riga for Sweden: ambassador and his gentlemen in coaches, with the rest of the embassy on horseback. The rigours of the journey (especially flies) relieved by the fine weather, sheltering forests and grand rivers, and an 'incredible quantity of excellent Strawberries'. (Miège 288–9, 306–7)

30   Near the town of Tver', from which they have been shut out, 'Andreas Marvell Secretarius' writes a Latin letter 'Ex Mandato Excellentiae suae', signed by Carlisle, to Larion Lopuhkin 'Diack or Chancellor of the Embassy-Office' (Moscow) about Caspar Calthov, an English subject whose time of service to the Tsar having ended sought to escape from Moscow with the embassy, only to be arrested and gaoled. Asking for Calthov's release, Carlisle wonders 'ut Exitus Introitum nostrum referret, & postrema primis per omnia responderent' ('that my exit should bear resemblance with my Entry, and my last usage be as disobliging as my first'). (Moscow, Rossiiskii Arkiv Drevnikh Aktov, Angliiskie dela, 35/1/208, f. 166, of which a copy is printed with translation and comment in Miège 314–19, 459)

July

11   (Monday) Entry into Novgorod, where embassy well received. (Miège 321)

14   Entry into Pskov ('Plesco') where embassy well received, and supplied with a footguard lest they be waylaid as they travel by a band of Polish thieves. (Miège 322–3)

19   AM (Pskov) writes another Latin letter 'Ex Mandato Excellentiae suae', signed by Carlisle, to Lopuhkin, chancellor of the embassy-office in Moscow, requesting the liberty of Calthov as an English subject, and regretting that the tents lent to the embassy must be returned at the frontier rather than from Riga as expected (Moscow, Rossiiskii Arkiv Drevnikh Aktov, Angliiskie dela, 35/1/208, f. 164, of which a copy is printed with translation and comment in Miège 324–30, 459). Again AM's fine Latin finds misinterpretation, deliberately so in Miège's view, and issues in the Tsar's outrage at Carlisle's insolence and at his eagerness to find fault. The Tsar sends the ambassador Vasilii Jacovlevitsch Dashkov to England with a lengthy Russian complaint against Carlisle, including specific mention of these last letters from Tver' and

Pskov 'in the ambassador and his secretary's hands'. (Bodl. MS Barlow 52, printed in Konovalov 95–104, for translating which I am grateful to Maria Unkovskaya)

22   Arrival at frontier of Russia and Livonia, where the embassy is saluted by deputies of the governor of Livonia and greeted from the Swedish king and his mother, who have also commanded lavish provisions for its journey through that 'desolate' country. The Russian tents and coaches are returned and the gentlemen now travel by horseback, and the horses are poor. In Swedish realms the artillery salutes repeatedly surprise the embassy owing to their volume and frequency. (Miège 308, 332–3)

August

3   (Wednesday) Embassy reaches Riga, where it is well received. (Miège 308, 338)

4   Visit from Count Oxenstierna to Carlisle, and the next day from Carlisle to Count Oxenstierna in the Castle; the warm Swedish welcome includes three days entertainment at the town's charges. Fifteen days spent in the city, where the novelties include the use of featherbeds, disliked by some, 'in so much as one somewhat a Critick [AM?], took occasion to call them Beds of Ignorance, according to that expression of the Poet. *Non jacet in molli veneranda scientia Lecto.* Learning's not found in Beds of Down.' Despite stormy weather, profound relief 'in being out of all commerce with the Moscovits, [and] to find our selves amongst Christians of very good conversation'. (Miège 339–41)

10   Huge ceremonial entertainment of the embassy with 'much splendor and Pomp'. (Miège 341–2)

11   Ambassador Dashkov departs Moscow for England, with Tsar's complaint against Carlisle's insolence; will meet with a cold reception there. (Konovalov 76; Bodl. MS Barlow 52; Oxford, Queen's College, MS 284, 39ʳ–40ᵛ)

17   Carlisle's steward, Mr Taylor, cites AM's communications from the embassy to the English Secretaries of State in a letter from Riga to Joseph Williamson at Secretary Bennet's: 'the most passages and transaction of moment, in this Embassye are understood by you out of the papers that have binne transmitted by Mr Marvel.' (PRO, SP91/3/110ʳ–111ᵛ, quoted in Robbins 1957, 14)

18   Embassy departs Riga on a frigate for Stockholm, although bad weather delays its setting sail until the 22nd, and only on the 24th does it cross the bar of the river; these delays lead to lack of provisions, with the problem compounded by further storm and contrary winds. (Miège 342–7)

20	English parliament meets for further prorogation until 24 November 1664.
31	The frigate anchors at the Shares outside Stockholm, awaiting a favourable wind. AM is sent ahead to notify the Swedes of the embassy's arrival and to learn the time for formal entry into Stockholm. (Miège 347)

September

8	(Thursday) Formal entry into Stockholm, and warm welcome; embassy in new liveries 'in all points very rich and handsom'. (Miège 349–50; PRO, SP 95/5A/149ʳ, printed in Robbins 1957, 14)
11	Carlisle has audience with the nine-year-old King Charles XI, which 'little Hercules' he addresses in English with AM then delivering the same address in Latin. In Stockholm, the English delight in the courteous and civil natives, who combine a French gallantry with Lutheran religion; their entertainments include rich dinners, deer-hunting, a great ball and visiting the Swedish fleet. (PRO SP 95/5A/149ᵛ, printed in Robbins 1957, 14; Miège 352–8, 362–5)
12	Carlisle has audience with the Queen Mother (Hedvig Eleonora), whom he addresses in English with AM then delivering the same address in French. English diplomacy aims at alliance with Sweden and Denmark so that all three might control the Baltic trade, ending the present predominance there of the Dutch. (Miège 359–61; PRO SP 95/5A/149ᵛ–150ʳ, printed in Robbins 1957, 14)
13	Letter in AM's hand from Carlisle (Stockholm) to Charles II, describing the reception of the embassy in Stockholm; reporting that they have calmed Swedish fears that the English are allying against them; and proposing advantages of cooperation with Sweden against the Dutch, which would also discountenance Muscovy. (Miège 361–2; PRO, SP 95/5A/149ʳ–150ᵛ, printed in Robbins 1957, 14–16)

October

11	(Tuesday) Ceremonial leave-taking with Carlisle's compliments to the King in English again delivered in Latin by AM, and Carlisle's compliments to the Queen Mother in English again delivered in French by AM (here each pauses at the same point in the speech as if eloquence could go no further). (Miège 368–74)
13	After the royal audience, the embassy departs Stockholm for Denmark, continuing by water overnight in order to reach the frigate, but then embarkation further postponed owing to delay

in shipping its goods, and the weather turns for the worse. Under way, the chief shipboard recreation is a pair of tame bears brought from Russia, one playful as a spaniel, and the other eager 'to suck peoples fingers' and who pats 'with his foot if one passed by upon the Deck without treating him in that manner'. (Stockholm, Kungl. biblioteket, D 757, f. 209; Miège 376–9)

21   Burial at St Mary's Church, Beverley, of Lucy (Alured) Marvell, AM's stepmother. (Burdon 1982, 44)

25   Embassy arrives at Copenhagen and AM sent ahead to give notice of its arrival and to carry his credentials to the Chancellor; a warm reception, but the formal entry attempted the next day is delayed by the grounding of the ship and the need to prepare the ambassadors' residence in the city. (Miège 380–1)

27   Formal entry into Copenhagen, through a thronged harbour, and by the King's coach to the ambassadors' residence. Entertainments for the first three days ('Bacchanalian') and subsequent feasts, including cordial relations with French ambassador. (Miège 382–3, 406–7)

30   Audience with Frederik III, King of Denmark, where Carlisle presents compliments to the King in English, which are again delivered in Latin by AM; also compliments to the queen in English, which are again delivered in French by AM; also compliments to the crown prince Christian in English, which are presumably delivered in Latin or French by AM (printed in Miège 385–99). In the next six weeks negotiations continue toward allying Denmark with Sweden and England.

November

1   (Tuesday) Letter in AM's hand from Carlisle (Copenhagen) to Secretary Bennet, pleading debts incurred in the embassy; noting Carlisle's wife's present labour and then the birth of their son, and so asking a fortnight's delay in his return; and describing Swedes 'as those who desire to be the best friends of his Majesty, the Danes as those who are, but the Muscovites as those who care not to be'. (PRO, SP75/17/213^{r-v}; printed in Robbins 1957, 16)

16   Letter in AM's hand from Carlisle (Copenhagen) to Secretary Bennet: he recommends for employment a Mr Brooke who has been on the embassy. (PRO, SP75/17/223^{r-v}; printed in Robbins 1957, 17)

17   Feast to celebrate christening of Carlisle's son, Frederick Christian; the entertainments these weeks include dancing, hunting for hares, visiting the arsenal, inspecting the curiosities at the royal palace, a visit to Fredericksburg, and a waterfight between two fire-pump crews. (Miège 408–12)

24 Westminster: parliamentary session of winter 1664–65 begins; continues until 2 March 1665. AM named in his absence to committee of elections and privileges. (*CJ* 8:567)

December

3 (Saturday) Letter in AM's hand from Carlisle (Copenhagen) to the Navy Commissioners: he seeks reimbursement for £203 12s.11d. 'for provision for the Centurion for five weeks', with another smaller bill enclosed to be paid the bearer. 'Whereof no way doubting, I therefore advance my thanks to you as for a businesse already effected ...'. (Not addressed by AM.) (PRO, SP29/106/13)

10 Letter in AM's hand from Carlisle (Copenhagen) to the Navy Commissioners: 'Since mine to you of 3ᵈ Dec: the frose seems to be so set in, that upon a Consult of the Admiralty of Denmarke ... they conclude it impossible for me to stirre by Sea. So unless a day or two alter the weather I must resolve to take my journy by land.' Will make best provision possible for ice-bound ship; asks again for reimbursement; 'There is no arms against accidents.' (Also addressed by AM.) (PRO, SP29/106/81)

11 Ceremonial leave-taking with Carlisle's compliments to the King in English again delivered in Latin by AM; Carlisle's compliments to the Queen in English presumably delivered again in French by AM; Carlisle's compliments to the Crown Prince in English, presumably delivered again in Latin or French by AM; and Carlisle's compliments to Prince George in English, presumably delivered again in Latin or French by AM. (Printed in Miège 413–23)

15 Departs Copenhagen by ship, but then at anchor six days off Elsinore, awaiting better winds, and then a false start when bad weather closes in again. The beginnings of hostilities with Holland encourage a prompt return to England. (Miège 424–7)

29 The bad weather leads to change of plan in which the embassy will travel overland, without ceremony, via Hamburg, Bremen, Münster, Cologne, Brussels and Calais.

1665

January

5 (Thursday) In Buxtehude (west of Hamburg), AM attempts to force wagoner to do his bidding, 'clapping a pistol to his head', but the pistol is 'wrested from him' and he needs rescuing 'out of the hands of a barbarous rout of peasants and Mechanicks'.

As AM goes off to complain to the Governor, a riot ensues in which the entourage of the embassy fights off the mob. The embassy arrives in Bremen around 6 January and departs probably 8 January, reaching Münster on 11 January and departing again the same day. (Miège 427–33)

30 Embassy returns to London and is greeted with satisfaction by Charles II, who owing to Russian complaints asks that the ambassador 'give in writing a Narrative of all that had passed relating to himself' in the embassy to Muscovy. This document, 'The Lord Ambassadors Apology', is produced in the following days and is likely of AM's writing; it is printed in Miège (435–60). It defends the Earl against the charges brought from the Tsar by his ambassador Dashkov, and emphasizes the slights to the embassy throughout its progress in Russia, as well as contests over protocol ranging from huge delays of the embassy to the ambassador's having 'no napkin allowed him at dinner', with emphasis on the denial of the trading privileges and the mistreatment of English subjects. This apology is well received by the King; the Russian ambassador, having also met now with Carlisle, departs for home 'not over well satisfied with his Voiage'.

February
4 (Saturday) In London, AM witnesses Robert Bloome's signature, with Anthony Gylby, John Ramsden and John Cressett (ATH47/1; *PL* 2:373n). Whatever AM's assurances in his letter to the Hull TH before his departure for Russia (20 July 1663), the contest between the TH and merchants in Hull (who had at the Restoration promoted themselves as the Merchants Company) had built to a crisis by the end of 1664. The matter was brought before the Attorney General (Sir Geoffrey Palmer) and Solicitor General (Sir Heneage Finch) in a hearing of 20 December 1664, with Cressett (whom AM had recommended) acting for the Hull TH, one of whose delegates in London had been Edmond Popple. While awaiting the decision of the Attorney and Solicitor General, there was further dispute as the Merchants Company sought action at the municipal level, but with AM's and Gylby's mediation the parties agreed to attend the Attorney and Solicitor General on 6 February; on 17 February those arbitrators had decided against the merchants but urged reconciliation. (Brooks, ed. *The First Order Book of the Hull Trinity House 1632–1665*, 172–3)

8 Yorkshire MPs enlisted for committee for bill for the repair of Bridlington pier. (*CJ* 8:597)

22	Declaration of Second Anglo-Dutch War, after military preparations at least since the previous autumn and an onslaught against Dutch colonies in December 1664.
25	Yorkshire MPs among those enlisted for committee for the draining of Deeping Fen, Lincolnshire. (*CJ* 8:609)

March

2	(Thursday) Parliament prorogued to 21 June.
16	AM paid £10 6s.8d. by the Hull Corporation for the 31 days he has sat at end of this session (BRB 5:19). The lack of present constituency correspondence from him may reflect his belated return to parliamentary service, but may also follow if these letters remained in possession of the mayor of this date, William Skinner, whose namesake (a son?) is later noted as having given AM's letters 'to the pastry-maid, to put under pie-bottoms' (1708 below).

June

3	(Saturday) Battle of Lowestoft, in which the English fleet fails to press its triumph over the Dutch; this is soon the subject of Waller's celebratory 'Instructions to a Painter', which invited the rejoinders of successive 'Advices to a Painter' as well as AM's 'Last Instructions to a Painter'.
13	*The Character of Holland* entered under the hands of Roger L'Estrange and warden Octavian Pulleyn into the Stationers' Register (*SR* 2:357). Anonymous two-sheet folio with colophon imprint: 'London, Printed by T. Mabb for Robert Horn at the Angel in Popes-head-alley, 1665.' M867. AM's responsibility for this publication, with its abbreviated text and new eight-line conclusion applying it to 1665 and praising the Duke of York, has been doubted (*PL* 1:309), but, not least after the extra demands of skirting the hostile Dutch as the Carlisle embassy returned to England, he may have been ready to resurrect his promotion piece of yesteryear. (See also 5 August below; Barnard)
21	Parliament meets for further prorogation to 1 August.

August

1	(Tuesday) Parliament meets to be further prorogued to 9 October.
5	James, Duke of York, arrives in York as a precaution against any possible northern uprising; stays until 23 September. Likely occasion for the York edition of *The Character of Holland*, a folio broadsheet in two columns, printed by Stephen Bulkley, which seems taken from a corrected copy of the Robert Horn edition (see 13 June above). (Barnard; Leeds, Yorks. Archaeological Society, MS 13.44)

September
As the Great Plague reaches its height in London, 'This year in the month of Septemb. Andr. Marvel a burgess for Kingston upon Hull to serve in that parl. which began at Westm. 8 May 1661, became a sojourner in Oxford for the sake of the public library, and continued there, I presume, some months' for the meeting of parliament. (Wood, *Fasti*, ed. Bliss, 2:288)

30   (Saturday) In Oxford, AM signs the Bodleian Library 'Liber Admissorum' among 'Extranei Nobiles et generosi'. Of visiting MPs he is almost alone among such readers, the other being Winston Churchill, the historian, MP, and (Court) political writer (4 October 1665). (Bodl. Library Records, e. 533, 179ᵛ)

October
9   (Monday) Parliament meets in Oxford; session continues to 31 October.

11   AM named to committee of elections and privileges. (*CJ* 8:614)

12   In a postscript to a letter to the Hull Corporation, Robert Stockdale (Oxford) sends the regards of AM, who 'had writt to you this post but has not time'. (BRL 1194/17)

[13   Letter from Hull TH to AM, cited in AM's reply of 22 October]

15   LHC: AM (Oxford) has not yet had a response from the Hull Corporation concerning his letter before this session of parliament; sends parliamentary news. (*PL* 2:40)

22   LHC: AM (Oxford) sends parliamentary and other news. (Haverford College Library, Special Collections, MS 115; *PL* 2:40–1)

26   AM among those added to committee for bill against embezzling prize goods. (*CJ* 8:621)

31   Parliament prorogued until 20 February 1666. Legislation this session includes the Five-Mile Act which, with the Conventicles Act of 1664, reinforces earlier laws against nonconformist ministers.

November
2   (Thursday) LHC: AM (Oxford) sends parliamentary news including notice of adjournment and legislation passed. (*PL* 2:41)

December
9   (Saturday) AM [London] writes Hull TH about Spurn Light, dispute with Sir Philip Frowd over how much revenue it will raise and whether Frowd's income from it might be secured, and underlying question of whether to propose this act of parliament in his name or their own, since if the former the Commons especially may baulk, preferring some 'reall and maritime interest', and if the latter they would need to recuse

themselves from 'testimony' in their own cause. (NTH52/1; *PL* 2:255).

13   Hull: 'It is ordered that Mr Major doe make his command for the payment of seaven pound six shillings and eight pence unto Mr Andrew Marvell for his Knights-penny in attending at the Parliament at Oxford being two and twenty dayes which moneys shall be paid unto Mr Edmond Popple for the said Mr Marvell' (not Gylby it would seem, who has been managing the garrison at Hull during the plague season). (BRB 5:50)

1666

February
20   (Tuesday) Parliament further prorogued to 23 April.

April
'The Second Advice to a Painter' satirizes Edmund Waller's *Instructions to a Painter*, which was registered with the Stationers 1 March 1666/7 (*SR* 2:362). The poem finds print publication the next year as 'the last work of Sir John Denham' – plainly another witty thrust after that courtier's death – and is only belatedly and ambiguously associated with AM (Samuel Butler, *Transproser Rehears'd*, Oxford, 1673, 131–2, 134; Roger L'Estrange, *An Account of the Growth of Knavery*, 1678, 6; Yonge 23; Bodl. MS Aubrey 6, 104^r; Bodl. MS Eng. poet. d. 49, 157–86) with specific attribution to him in collections of state poetry in 1689 and after, in derivative MSS, and then in Thompson (von Maltzahn 1999); an attribution revived by Lord (1958; 1959; Lord, ed., *POAS*, vol. 1; Marvell, *Complete Poems*, ed. Lord, 117–44) and Patterson (1977; 2000a, 76–9, 85–97, 159–78; 2000c) chiefly on internal evidence, and Smith (321–41), but resisted especially by Margoliouth / Legouis (*PL* 1:348–50), Fogel and Chernaik (206–14). The internal evidence may be explained away if the Duke of Buckingham was indeed the author (as is soon implied in Christopher Wase's 'Divination', lines 91–110), or others in Buckingham's circle, since Buckingham seems to have had unusual access to AM's poetry; but in view of Buckingham's collaborative work elsewhere (*The Rehearsal*), AM may yet have been involved more directly with the present composition. Despite their merits, the Second and Third Advices are widely agreed to be 'aesthetically and intellectually inferior both to *The Last Instructions* and to *The Loyal Scot*' (Smith 322), which latter works are attributed with great confidence to AM in whole or in part. Correcting Waller's panegyric, 'The Second Advice to a Painter' redescribes with bitter wit some early episodes of the Anglo-Dutch War, in particular the Battle of Lowestoft (3 June 1665) and its aftermath; it is harsh to the English participants, except for Prince Rupert and Capt. Jeremy Smith (both associated with AM in later years). Its final address to the king again warns against Clarendon's ministry. The poem is dated April 1666 in Bodl.

MS Eng. poet. d. 49, 157, and may have been designed to greet the brief meeting of parliament this month. That it was then withheld from circulation until the September meeting of parliament is suggested by the belated reaction to it of Wase's 'Divination' (see September below).

9   (Monday) AM, in company of his nephews William Popple and Thomas Alured, as well as James Faireclough and Thomas Pooley, witnesses certificates of the Cambridge bookseller Anthony Nicholson and Dorothy Pocock to their cures (from the King's Evil and a breast tumour respectively) by Valentine Greatrakes, 'the Stroker', who is being promoted by the Boyles at this date. (Henry Stubbe, *The Miraculous Conformist*, Oxford, 1666, 83–5; Bailey)

23   Parliament further prorogued to 18 September.

May

17   (Thursday) AM has made one of his rare visits to his constituents in Hull. Date of payment of £1 14s. by Hull TH 'to Andrew Raikes for wines and meate when Coll. Gilby and Mr Marvell was ther'. (FTH1/5)

September

2–6   (Sunday–) Fire of London.

18   Parliament meets in session that continues to 8 February 1667.

21   AM named to committee of elections and privileges. (*CJ* 8:625)

Christopher Wase's 'Divination' supplies a heated response to 'The Second Advice to a Painter', controverting its attribution to his friend Sir John Denham, defending Waller, and associating it with the Duke of Buckingham (Bodl. MS Eng. poet. e. 4, 222–9; Lord, ed., *POAS*, 1:54–66). 'Divination' seems an immediate reaction to the wider manuscript circulation of 'The Second Advice', perhaps near this month's meeting of parliament, and it refers to the Fire of London; it was probably written before 1 October, since that is the date given for 'The Third Advice to a Painter' (see below), which responds to Wase's complaint that 'the kind Duchess [of York] is forbid to mourn / When her Lord parts, or joy at his return' (35–6) by then giving extraordinary voice to another duchess, Albemarle's wife.

October

1   (Monday) 'The Third Advice to a Painter' is composed around this date (given in Bodl. MS Eng. poet. d. 49, 172; Oxford, All Souls MS 174, 35^r); Pepys encounters it in manuscript only on 20 January 1666/67 (Pepys 8:21) and it is first printed with 'The Second Advice' ca. 1 July 1667 (see below). Whether AM contributed to this satire remains uncertain as does his possible hand in 'The Second Advice' (see April above; compare Patterson 2000c; Smith 321–6, 342–54). Centring in the debacle of the Four Days Battle with the Dutch (1–4 June 1666), the poem catalogues English

naval failures, even as its regard for the Dutch admiral De Ruyter anticipates the admiration voiced in 'Last Instructions'; the poem gives the Duchess of Albemarle a long and compelling role, in which the 'painter' motif is subsumed by the raging speech of this 'Presbyterian sibyl', not unsympathetically evoked (lines 171–434, answering Wase's 'Divination', 35–6). Its final apostrophe 'To the King' demands better morals and government from the crown (this much more decorously than in 'The Second Advice').

2	AM among those added to the committee to enquire into the causes of the Fire of London. (*CJ* 8:629)
23	LHC: AM (W) reports he is very busy; sends parliamentary news in brief. (*PL* 2:42)
27	AM named to committee for settling the estate of Thomas Mildmay. (*CJ* 8:642)
	LHC: AM (W) sends parliamentary news, including 'Many informations are daily brought in to the two Committees about the Fire of London and the insolence of Papists.' (*PL* 2:42–3)
31	AM alloted a barrel of ale by the Hull Corporation as one of 'the Townes Freinds'. (BRB 5:76)

November

6	(Tuesday) LHC: AM (W) sends parliamentary news. (*PL* 2:43–4)
13	'A Letter prepared to be sent to Coll. Gilby and Mr Marvell about the soliciting his Majesty and Councell and others concerned for the exchangeing of such persons Seamen belonging to this Towne as now are Prisoners in Holland.' (BRB 5:77)
	LHC: AM (W) sends parliamentary news, disclosing that 'The Reports from the Committees of the fire of London and insolence of Papists are almost ready for the house things of extraordinary weight and which if they were not true might have bin thought incredible.' (*PL* 2:44–5)
16	AM named to committee for bill voiding a lease made by Thomas Pride of lands in Redriff parish. (*CJ* 8:650)
20	LHC: AM (W) sends parliamentary news. (*PL* 2:45–6)
22	LHC: AM (W) reports his efforts following their request on behalf of Hull prisoners in Holland. (*PL* 2:46)
	In a simile comparing the Fire of London to the rise of a usurper from unsuspected origins, John Dryden, *Annus Mirabilis*, lines 849–60, seems to recall AM's 'An Horatian Ode', lines 13–34. Licensed 22 November and in print by the end of the year, *Annus Mirabilis* is republished in 1668, 1688 and thereafter. (Dryden, *Poems*, ed., Hammond, 1:107, 181–2; Macdonald 14–16)
28	Committee to inquire into the causes of the Fire of London revived with AM again among those added to it. (*CJ* 8:654)

December

1	(Saturday) LHC: AM [W] sends brief parliamentary and other news. (*PL* 2:46–7)
3	LHC: AM (W) sends parliamentary news in brief. (*PL* 2:47)
14	At his house at day's end, Samuel Pepys 'meets with, sealed up, from Sir H[ugh]. Cholmly, the Lampoone or the Mocke-advice to a Paynter ['Second Advice'], abusing the Duke of York and my lord Sandwich, Pen, and everybody, and the King himself, in all the matters of the Navy and Warr'. (Pepys 7:407)
15	LHC: AM (W) sends parliamentary news in brief. (*PL* 2:48)
20	For parliamentary committee, AM examines with John Jolliffe (Jolley; or perhaps John Holland) one Rebecca Eves, possible witness to Roman Catholic conspiracy behind the Fire of London, which testimony is soon published among others in *Londons Flames Discovered by Informations Taken before the Committee ...* (1667), 7, of which there are now three editions, at least one of which is by the printer Elizabeth Calvert, whose clandestine work will include *Directions to a Painter* (1667) (Smith and Bell); see also the fuller information in *A True and Faithful Account of the Several Informations Exhibited To the Honourable Committee appointed by the Parliament To Inquire into the late Dreadful Burning Of the City of London* (1667), 4, 15–16, which work is later republished in William Bedloe, *A Narrative and Impartial Discovery of the Horrid Popish Plot* (1679), 4, 8, and in *State Tracts: a Farther Collection* (1692), 27–8, 34.
22	House of Commons in a week's recess until 29 December.
	LHC: AM (W) sends parliamentary news in brief and thanks for 'our Hull liquor'. (*PL* 2:48–9)
29	LHC: AM (W) sends brief parliamentary and other news. (*PL* 2:49)

1667

Early this year AM is among those made commissioners of sewers for Hull (with Edmond Popple), which in view of his absence from the town must have been a matter of prestige more than service. (PRO, C181/7/420, late in entries for '1666')

January

5	(Saturday) AM named to committee for a bill setting the prices upon wine. (*CJ* 8:671)
	LHC: AM (W) sends parliamentary news. (*PL* 2:50)
7	AM named to committee for assuring a share of the manor of Iron Acton to Sir John Poynz. (*CJ* 8:672)
11	Yorkshire MPs enlisted for committee settling the late Henry Hilton's charities. (*CJ* 8:674)

12	LHC: AM (W) sends parliamentary news. (*PL* 2:51)
15	LHC: AM [W] sends parliamentary news. (*PL* 2:51–2)
18	AM named to committee reviewing defaulting MPs. (*CJ* 8:679)
19	LHC: AM [W] sends parliamentary news. (*PL* 2:52–3)
20	At Whitehall, Pepys's admiralty colleague John Brisbane lends him 'The Third Advice to a Painter' – 'a bitter Satyr upon the service of the Duke of Albemarle the last year' – which he takes home to copy. (Pepys 8:21)
22	LHC: AM [W] sends parliamentary news, including that 'the report of the Fire of London [is] full of manifest testimonys that it was by a wicked designe' (*PL* 2:53). With prorogation to follow, the lack of parliamentary response to the report seems soon to have led to its print publication (see 20 December 1666 above).
26	LHC: AM (W) sends parliamentary news. (*PL* 2:53–4)

February

2	(Saturday) LHC: AM (W) sends parliamentary and other news in brief. (*PL* 2:54)
4	AM among those added to committee for the Lord Abergaveny's estate. (*CJ* 8:688)
8	Parliament prorogued until 25 July.
9	LHC: AM (W) sends parliamentary news, including prorogation and list of bills passed; other news in brief especially regarding proliferation of fires, raising pious concerns. (*PL* 2:55)

April

2	(Tuesday) AM (London) writes to Philip, fourth Baron Wharton [Wooburn, Bucks (or perhaps Winchendon)], citing previous communication and professing loyal service to Wharton, and some business in hand which he trusts to have completed 'by the Terme' (Easter Term begins 24 April). Sends a couple of recent publications and reports London news, preparations against the Dutch, and political developments. (Bodl. MS Carte 103, 258–9; *PL* 2:309–10)
4	Hull: 'It is Ordered: That the Ninety six pounds due to Coll Gilby and Mr Andrew Marvell Burgesses of Parliament for this Towne shall forthwith be paid them by the Chamberlains being Forty eight pounds a peece for their Attendance at the last Parliament from the Eighteenth day of September last untll the Eighth day of February last past ...'. (BRB 5:87)

May

ca. 13	(Monday) AM perhaps marries his (later) landlady the widow Mary Palmer in the church of the Holy Trinity Minories, 'As by the Register book of the said church may appeare' according to

her claim after his death. She had previously been married to 'a Tennis Court Keeper in or near the Citty of Westminster'. AM lives at her address in the Little Armory (or Amboy) in Westminster in the 1670s (see 13 April 1672 and 1 December 1674 below) – I am grateful to Nigel Smith for discovering this the address of 'The Widow Palmer' in the 1670s (tax assessments at the Westminster RO). AM has Mary Palmer take up the lease and serve as housekeeper when he sought anonymity with the Nelthorpes and Thompsons in June 1677. The fullest discussion of the matter (Tupper) decides against Mary Palmer's claim but leaves the matter in doubt. No one seems to have known anything of the union during AM's lifetime and in the belated legal crossfire after AM's death her claim met with deep suspicion from interested parties in London. Holy Trinity Minories was one of the 'peculiar' churches with a right to solemnize marriages without banns or licence; very many clandestine marriages took place there. On one hand, this is consistent with the absolute secrecy Mary 'Marvell' says AM imposed on her; on the other, the relevant register of marriages at that church has long been lost and may have been (known to be) unavailable even in 1682 and likely very incomplete (its terminal date 26 March 1676 coincides with the death of the incumbent and the arrival of his successor, 14 April 1676). The balance of probabilities falls against Mary Palmer's claim, the more so since in 1670 AM does not seem yet to be sharing her address in Westminster (when 20 May he is instead to be reached at Richard Hill's in the Rhenish Wine Yard [off King Street], Westminster). (John Farrington bill of complaint; Mary Marvell answer, PRO, C6/242/13; Tupper; Tomlinson 204–5, 389; NTH52/1)

June

10–13   (Monday–) Dutch fleet under Admiral de Ruyter attacks English fleet laid up at Chatham, which culminates in the firing of ships and prize-taking described in AM's 'Last Instructions', lines 523–760.

27   LHC: AM (London) gives notice of royal proclamation for next session of parliament; postscript that 'The Dutch begin to appear again neare Graves-end.' (*PL* 2:55–6)

July

AM may write or contribute to the satire 'Clarindon's House-Warming' and compose the epigrams 'Upon his House' and 'Upon his Grand-Children'. Of the many satires ascribed to AM in the 1690s and after, 'Clarindon's House-Warming' seems a most compelling attribution owing to the virtuosity of its wit. As Clarendon's ministry became ever more unpopular, his recent construction of the grand Clarendon House invited the darkest reflections on the sources of his wealth. The poem's last line dates it after 25 June 1667 when a meeting of parliament was proclaimed for St James's Day (25 July; *PL* 1:340), which session the poem was likely meant to greet.

1   (Monday) Samuel Pepys and his friends read 'the several *Advices to a Painter*, which made us good sport', which publication near this date also appears from contemporary notice of the stationer Richard Royston being 'advised upon Wednesday last to endeavor the hindring of the Second and Third Advice to a Painter to be Printed. And was told that Francis Smith had offer'd the same to one Burden to be Printed.' (PRO SP29/187.2/83–84, note also 'They found *London's Flames* upon the Press at Leech's')

25   Parliament meets only to be prorogued after 29 July. LHC: AM (London) sends news in brief concerning meeting and adjournment of parliament; 'The Dutch have been fighting with us in the mouth of the river but I think with more damage to themselves then us'; peace expected daily. (*PL* 2:56)

29   Parliament prorogued until 10 October.

30   LHC: AM (London) communicates the announcement of peace with Dutch and the prorogation of parliament. (*PL* 2:56–5)

August

11   (Sunday) Soon after this date, AM writes to his fellow MP Sir John Trott, with condolences on the loss of his sons John and now Edmund (smallpox), and recommending 'The word of God: The society of good men: and the books of the Ancients' for consolation, as well as 'diversion, business, and activity'. He makes veiled reference too to the difficulties of the Lord Chancellor Clarendon, whose fall is imminent. Encloses the 'Edmundi Trotii Epitaphium' for the monument in the church in Laverstoke in Hampshire. AM presumably took this occasion also to write the similar 'Johannis Trottii Epitaphium' since he had been en route from Moscow to Tver' when that youth died, 28 June 1664. (*1681*, 66–70; copy in Yale, Beinecke Library, Osborn Collection, MS b. 136, 57–9; *PL* 2:311–13, 383; compare Smith 195)

       If the epitaphs in *1681* are in chronological order, the prose 'An Epitaph upon ——' (pp. 70–1) is from the next few years (before Frances Jones's memorial, 1672). It honours a man (unknown), of good descent and married but apparently childless, who is here cited as a paragon of moderation and virtue, and who is also 'Religious without Affectation'. (*PL* 1:142)

20   *Paradise lost* registered with the Stationers' Company for publication. (*SR* 2:381)

September

4   (Wednesday) AM ends (?) 'Last Instructions', which has been ani-
           mated by exasperation at the prorogation of parliament 29 July
           and which concludes with references to the beginning of the fall
           of Clarendon (26 August) and perhaps 'Coventry's resignation of
           the post of secretary to the Duke of York ... 2 September 1667'
           (lines 926, 935; *PL* 1:373). Two manuscripts of the poem are thus
           dated to the day (Bodl. MS Eng. poet. d. 49, p. 193; BL, Add. MS
           73540, f. 1; also the print *Last Instructions to a Painter, 1667* [see
           1689 below]) and another to this month (Yale, Osborn Collection
           'PB VII/15'). The publication history of 'Last Instructions' in manu-
           script and print is distinct from that of the Second and Third
           Advices, which difference may witness the separate origin as well
           as much greater length of AM's present work. Describing political
           and naval affairs over the last year, the satire richly merits Lord's
           claim that 'No other Restoration poem is more comprehensive or
           specific in its treatment of public affairs' (Lord, ed., *POAS* 1:97); it
           marks a different order of political engagement from the previous
           Advices, to which it refers, and is longer than both of those put
           together. Whereas 'The Third Advice' tires of the painter conven-
           tion, AM now adopts it afresh and gives it a sustained variety.
           Distinctive too is his emphasis on parliament and his brilliant por-
           trait of its contests and contestants in the session of the autumn
           and winter of 1666–67 and again in the abbreviated session of
           25–29 July 1667, turning to more recent recriminations after the
           Dutch triumph in attacking the English navy in the Medway.
           That Dutch raid, the final crisis of the Second Anglo-Dutch War,
           invites an admiring portrait of de Ruyter, outstripped only by
           AM's Baroque memorial to 'the loyal Scot' Archibald Douglas,
           burnt in the firing of the *Royal Oak*. The final injunction 'Paint
           last the King ...' issues in a bravura portrait of Charles II caught
           between conscience, lust and policy, with the concluding apostro-
           phe to him demanding royal disavowal of 'scratching courtiers' in
           favour of better counsel.

16   Pepys encounters 'The Fourth Advice to the Painter' ('Draw
           England ruin'd ...'), which makes his 'heart ake to read, it being
           too sharp and so true' (Pepys 8:439). The 'Fourth Advice' in par-
           allel with AM's 'Last Instructions' handles the Dutch success at
           Chatham and the end of the Second Anglo-Dutch War; with a
           linked 'Fifth Advice' ('Painter, where was't thy former work did
           cease?') that covers the fall of Clarendon, this soon finds publi-
           cation in *Directions to a Painter* (1667). Some or all of these are
           met with *The Answer of Mr. Wallers Painter, To His many new
           Advisers* (1667; also Lord, ed., *POAS*, 1:140–56)

October

3   (Thursday) LHC: with the session a week away, AM (London) asks for any directions from his constituency, especially since 'there never appeared a fairer season for men to obtain what their own hearts could wish either as to redresse of any former grievances or the constituting of good order and justice for the future'. (*PL* 2:57)

10   Parliament meets in a session that will last until 9 May 1668, with adjournments from 19 December 1667 to 6 February 1668, and then successively from 9 May to 11 August to 10 November 1668 to 1 March 1669, when prorogued.
        LHC: AM (London) sends parliamentary news at beginning of session. (*PL* 2:57–8)

14   AM speaks in the House of Commons in debate whether thanks should be given to the King for 'laying him [Clarendon] aside': 'many excellent speeches were made against it: by Sir Robert Atkins Sir John Maynard, Mr. Marvim [*sic*], Mr. dowdswell and the two good ricks and Colonel Birch, intimating that it was a precondemning him before any crime was layd to his charge' (BL, Add. MS 33413, 30ʳ [also printed in Milward 86]). The speech of 'Mr Marven pro' the Earl of Clarendon is reported also by Henry Capel: 'The raising and destroying of favoritts and creatures is Kings sport not to be medled with by us Kings in their choise of their Ministers move in a spheare distinkt from us. Its sayed because the people rejoysed at his fall wee must thanks the King. The people allsoe rejoyse at the restoration of the Duke of Buckingam the other day obnoxtious. Shall we not thank the King for that too? Its sayed we hat[e] him not, Should any man in this house be willing to have such a vote passe upon him? / Wee are to thank the King for the matter of his Speech This is not in particular any part of it and comes regularly before us.' (BL, Add. MS 35865, 25ʳ⁻ᵛ, also 10ʳ corrected version now attrib. to 'Mr. Marvell') [also printed in Milward 328])

17   AM named to committee of inquiry into the miscarriages of the late war. (*CJ* 9:4)
        AM named to committee of inquiry into the reasons of the sale of Dunkirk. (*CJ* 9:4–5)

22   Yorkshire MPs enlisted for committee for bill for the Bishop of Durham's leases of lead mines. (*CJ* 9:6)

2[4?]   LHC: AM (London) sends parliamentary news in brief. (*PL* 2:58)

26   LHC: AM (London) sends parliamentary news, including impeachment beginning against the Earl of Clarendon. (*PL* 2:59)

29   AM speaks in the House of Commons in debate over impeach-
            ment of Clarendon: 'Would have the faults hunt the persons –
            Would not have a sudden impeachment by reason of the
            greatness of the person or danger of escape, Lord Clarendon
            not being likely to ride away post [!] – Witnesses of that
            quality not to be had.' This last comment speaks to whether
            witnesses needed calling (if so, might in this case need to be of
            the highest rank) and whether parliamentary impeachments
            required as much. (Grey, *Debates*, 1:14).

31   Peter Pett now having been brought before the House of Com-
            mons to answer for negligence in defence of the fleet at
            Chatham, 'Marven' among the 'sectaries' (with John Swinfen
            and Edward Boscawen) who 'spoke for him and against sending
            him to the tower'. (BL, Add. MS 33413, 37ᵛ [also printed in
            Milward 108])

November

6   (Wednesday) Impeachment of Clarendon begins in House of
            Commons.

7   AM accorded a barrel of ale by the Hull Corporation as one of
            'the Townes Friends'. (BRB 5:111)

7 or 11   In the debates over the impeachment of Clarendon, 'After all
            the Articles of the charge had bin debated Mr. Mervin pressed
            that the words that were said to be spoken against the King
            should not be passed over in silence but be declared, the words
            as it sayd are these (The Chancellor should say that the King
            was an unactive person and indisposed for government.'
            Sir Robert Howard points to Edward Seymour who points to
            Sir John Denham, who 'affirmed that he had it from another
            who would Justifie that the Chancellor sayd so' (BL, Add. MS
            33413, 40ʳ [also printed in Milward 116]). Milward dates this to
            7 November; moreover, *Proceedings* (1700) 27 has something
            similar (6 November or so, and definitely before the resump-
            tion of the matter on the 11 Nov.): 'Mr. Marvel Chargeth
            Mr. Seymour with saying in his Accusation, That the King was
            insufficient for Government, which is now omitted in the
            Charge, and desires he may declare where he had it'; Grey dates
            it to 11 November, reporting that AM 'Moves, that whoever
            brought in the article of "the King's being unfit for govern-
            ment," would publish the person that gave him that informa-
            tion', with Denham being called on to explain, and rejoinder
            also by Waller. Resolution follows that Clarendon be impeached
            (Grey, *Debates*, 1:36–7).

9   Yorkshire MPs among those enlisted for committee for bill to
            encourage the English clothing trade. (*CJ* 9:17)

11	AM named to committee to which the petition of Margaret Caron is referred. (*CJ* 9:18)
	AM named to committee for a bill against pluralities. (*CJ* 9:18)
12	Yorkshire MPs enlisted for committee for bill regarding Dr Wharton's estate (Durham). (*CJ* 9:19)
	Impeachment of the Earl of Clarendon to be taken up to the Lords.
14	LHC: AM (London) sends parliamentary news after many daily and long sittings, so that even now 'I lose my dinner to make sure of this Letter'. (*PL* 2:59–60)
18	Yorkshire MPs enlisted for bill regarding William Palmes's estate. (*CJ* 9:22)
22	Yorkshire MPs among those enlisted for bill regarding Henry Hilton's charities. (*CJ* 9:24)
23	LHC: AM (London) sends parliamentary news. (*PL* 2:60–1)
25	AM named to committee examining French merchants' corruption of an MP. (*CJ* 9:25)
26	LHC: AM [London?] sends parliamentary news and business. (*PL* 2:61–2)
	Gylby [London] to Hull Corporation: has shared its letter of 22 November with 'my Partner' which is the first they have heard of the business, but both will exert themselves so the town may be reimbursed for extraordinary garrison expenses during the Second Anglo-Dutch War. (BRL 770)
28	Yorkshire MPs among those enlisted for committee for bill settling the draining of the Lindsey Level fen (Lincs.). (*CJ* 9:27)

December

Shortly after Clarendon's flight to the continent (30 November) is printed *Directions to a Painter, for Describing our Naval Business: In Imitation of Mr. Waller. Being the Last Works of Sir John Denham. Whereunto is annexed, Clarindons House-Warming. By an Unknown Author* (1667), an octavo volume in fours (half-sheet imposition presumably for speed), including the Second, Third, Fourth and Fifth Advices to a Painter, as well as 'Clarindon's House-Warming' and the two epigrams 'Upon his House' and 'Upon his Grand-Children'. The wit of attributing the Advices to Denham followed in part from the present publication of his works, which had been in press since late July (Bodl. MS Carte 35, 567^{r-v}, 569^r). The 'Fifth Advice' alludes to Clarendon's escape. Bodl. MS Gough London 14 includes a copy of *Directions* (1667) with contemporary manuscript corrections from the errata, also a belated attribution of the work to AM which dates from ca. 1700 when this was bound with other miscellaneous octavo materials.

3	(Tuesday) Clarendon arrives in France, news of his flight spreads.

	LHC: AM (London) sends parliamentary news and brief business. (*PL* 2:62–3)
5	MPs for seaports among those enlisted for committee for bill looking into the repair of Dover pier. (*CJ* 9:32)
7	MPs for seaports among those enlisted for committee for bill looking into the repair of harbour and piers of Great Yarmouth. (*CJ* 9:33)
12	LHC: AM (London) sends parliamentary and political news. (*PL* 2:63–4)
13	Yorkshire MPs among those enlisted for committee for bill preventing the importation of Irish cattle. (*CJ* 9:37)
14	MPs for outports among those enlisted for committee for bill making prize ships free ships of trade. (*CJ* 9:38)
16	'Mr Marvin' named to committee for bill banishing the Earl of Clarendon. (*CJ* 9:40–1)
19	Parliament adjourned to 6 February 1668.
	LHC: AM (London) sends news of the adjournment; brief list of bills passed. (*PL* 2:64)
21	Hull: 'It is thought fitt that Mr Major doe pay by command unto the Burgesses of Parliament for this Corporacon for seaventy three dayes reackoned from the 10th of October to the 21 of December inclusive Vizt to Coll Gilby xxiiii ^{li} – vi ^{s} –viii ^{d} and to Mr Marvell xxiiii ^{li} – vi ^{s} –viii ^{d}.' (BRB 5:116)

1668

AM's 'The Garden' seems likely to have been written this year or next, if indeed it required the posthumous publication of *The Works of Mr Abraham Cowley* (1668) for AM so much to draw on Cowley's example in this poem, as well as on Katherine Philips' *Poems* (1667). Cowley and his literary executor Thomas Sprat were in the Duke of Buckingham's circle, in which AM had some part. 'The Garden' may take up the late Cowley's mantle as a hortulan poet, with AM perhaps given further occasion by his current association with the 'gardening' Lord Wharton; Buckingham was just getting underway with Cliveden. That AM may now have been emboldened to circulate other of his verses seems evidenced by a copy of 'To his Coy Mistress' that surfaces in a tranche of poems from the mid- to late 1660s. (Pritchard 1983; Smith 152–9; von Maltzahn 2003; see 1672 lead entry below for Bodl. MS Don.b.8, 283–4)

Sometime this year a Capt. John Seymour employs George Larkin in Southwark to print *Advice to a Painter* and *The Cobbler of Gloucester*. (*HMC 9th Report*, App. 2, 76a)

January

28   (Tuesday) AM [W?] with Gylby writes to Hull TH, giving thanks
       for 'your late friendly present of your towne liquour', and
       promising 'to deliver your message to the Speaker'; and supply-
       ing wardens with 'a Copy of the Act for Yarmouth', to be con-
       tested. (ATH47/1, FTH1/5; *PL* 2:256)

February

6   (Thursday) Parliament reconvenes.
       LHC: AM (W) sends parliamentary and political news in brief.
       (*PL* 2:64–5)
13   Yorkshire MPs among those enlisted for committee for bill
       allowing parliamentary representation to the county and city of
       Durham. (*CJ* 9:48)
14   Report from the committee inquiring into the miscarriages of
       the war, with further debate in days to follow. (*CJ* 9:51)
14 or 15 In the House of Commons, 'Mr Marvell, reflecting on Lord
       Arlington, somewhat transportedly said] We have had Bristols
       and Cecils Secretaries, and by them knew the King of Spain's
       Junto, and letters of the Pope's cabinet; and now such a strange
       account of things! The money allowed for intelligence so small,
       the intelligence was accordingly – A libidinous desire in men,
       for places, makes them think themselves fit for them – The
       place of Secretary ill gotten, when bought with 10,000 l. and a
       Barony – *He was called to explain himself; but said,* The thing was
       so plain, it needed it not.
       Mr Vaughan.] Matters as little what the one (Marvell) says by
       way of exception against him, as the other (Birkenhead) by way
       of defence of him.' (Grey, *Debates*, 1:70–71)
       Grey dates this to 14 February, which is consistent with
       the Commons Journal report that the miscarriage of intelli-
       gence was debated that day. Milward dates it to the 15 February,
       reporting that 'Mr. Marvin made a moste sharpe speech against
       some of the [privy] councell, and especially hinted at the Lord
       Orlington [Arlington] as that he had got £1000 and a barrony'.
       Pepys agrees with Milward on the date (15th) and with Grey on
       the figure of £10 000. (BL, Add. MS 33413, 58ᵛ [printed in
       Milward 184]; Pepys, *Diary* 9:74, 17 February 1668)
15   LHC: AM (W) sends parliamentary news, including beginnings
       of the 'report of the miscarriages of the late warre'; 'I have been
       so busy this weeke that I could not write before'. (*PL* 2:65)
17   AM moves the taking into consideration of the King's Speech.
       Reported in letter from Arlington to Sir William Temple, which
       also describes AM's speech two days before: 'The House of Com-
       mons are yet in their enquiry after miscarriages; I leave it to

your other Correspondents to tell you what Votes they have passed therein. But cannot forbear letting you know that Mr. Marvel hath struck hard at me, upon the Point of Intelligence, tho hitherto unsuccessfully, as to the doing of me any harm thereby. This Day he hath given me cause to forgive him, by being the first Man that, in the midst of this enquiry, moved the taking into Consideration the matter of his Majesty's Speech, which begat the resolution of doing it on Wednesday Morning.' (*The Right Honourable the Earl of Arlington's Letters to Sir W. Temple, Bar.*, ed. Thomas Bebington, 1702, 226)

21   'Mr Marvin' speaks in the House of Commons about paying seamen with tickets, under debate as a miscarriage: 'said, that although the Officers upon hearing may clear themselves, yet it was requisit that they should be desired to informe the house where the fault was, for there is no quetion [*sic*], but that they are able to do it'. (BL, Add. MS 33413, 62ʳ [printed in Milward 196])

22   LHC: AM (W) sends parliamentary news including the miscarriages of the late war. (*PL* 2:65–6)

26   MPs for ports among those enlisted for consideration of proposals for bringing down the price of timber for the reconstruction of London. (*CJ* 9:56)

27   LHC: AM (W) sends parliamentary news in brief. (*PL* 2:66)

29   LHC: AM (W) sends parliamentary news. (*PL* 2:66–7)

March

3   (Tuesday) Yorkshire MPs enlisted for bill enabling Sir Thomas Heblethwaite to settle his estate. (*CJ* 9:59)

7   LHC: AM (W) sends parliamentary news, including beginnings of fresh reaction against nonconformists; AM confident that Sir Jeremy Smith 'will come of with full reputation' against Sir Robert Holmes's accusations regarding naval failure the previous year. (*PL* 2:67–8)

9   AM named to committee for bill regulating the silk throwsters trade. (*CJ* 9:63)

11   AM named to committee to examine William Carr's petition. (*CJ* 9:64)

12   LHC: AM [W] sends parliamentary news. (*PL* 2:69)

13   'Mr Marvin' speaks in the House of Commons against the renewal of the Conventicles Act, on the losing side with Sir Thomas Littleton, Mr Swinfen, Sir Robert Carr, Mr Jones and others. (BL, Add. MS 33413, 71ʳ [printed in Milward 225])

14   LHC: AM (W) sends parliamentary news; Sir Jeremy Smith's defence successful; renewal of Conventicles Act preparing. (*PL* 2:69–70)

| 19 | 'It is thought fitt and Ordered that Mr Major doe pay by command unto the Burgesses of Parliament for this Corporation for foure and fortie dayes reckoned from the xxviii day of February last past to the Twentieth day of this instant Moneth of March inclusive ...' £14 13s.4d. each. (BRB 5:124) |

'It is thought fitt and Ordered that Mr Major doe pay by command unto the Burgesses of Parliament for this Corporation for foure and fortie dayes reckoned from the xxviii day of February last past to the Twentieth day of this instant Moneth of March inclusive ...' £14 13s.4d. each. (BRB 5:124)

LHC: AM (W) sends parliamentary news. (*PL* 2:70–1)

26 Yorkshire MPs among those enlisted to committee considering the success of the act concerning butter. (*CJ* 9:69)

'Mr Marvin' speaks in the House of Commons in the debate whether the commissioners for selling lands in Ireland should proceed there as appointed by the King, and is 'for adjourning their goeing untill the adventurers case was heard at the barr'. (BL, Add. MS 33413, 74ʳ [printed in Milward 233])

27 AM a teller with Sir Robert Carr for the successful Yeas (25, vs Noes 25: the speaker then declaring with the Yeas) on the main question putting off for a fortnight the hearing for the matter concerning Lindsey Level. (*CJ* 9:70)

28 Yorkshire MPs among those added to committee for the bill touching restraints on juries. (*CJ* 9:71)

LHC: AM (W) sends parliamentary news in brief. (*PL* 2:71)

30 'This day the bill was brought in for continuing the act against conventicles, it was opposed by Mr Marvin, but it was ordered to be read tomorrow.' (BL, Add. MS 33413, 75ᵛ [printed in Milward 238])

April

1 (Wednesday) Yorkshire MPs among those enlisted to committee for bill enclosing part of the common of Outwood (Yorks.). (*CJ* 9:72–3)

4 LHC: AM (W) sends parliamentary news. (*PL* 2:71–2)

7 AM named to committee for bill raising £6000 out of John Lenthall's estate for the Stonehouses' portions. (*CJ* 9:76)

11 LHC: AM (W) sends parliamentary news. (*PL* 2:72–3)

[18] LHC: AM [W] sends parliamentary news. (*PL* 2:73–4)

20 Yorkshire MPs enlisted for committee for bill securing Lady Frances Savile's portion

25 LHC: AM [W] sends parliamentary news, including adjournment in the offing. (*PL* 2:74)

29 Yorkshire MPs enlisted for committee for bill settling Sir Charles Stanley's estate. (*CJ* 9:91)

May

2 (Saturday) LHC: AM (W) sends parliamentary news, including [Thomas] Skinner's Case hotting up. (*PL* 2:74–5)

Treaty of Aix-la-Chapelle forced on France by the Triple Alliance of Britain, Sweden and the Netherlands, attempting to push back Louis XIV's encroachment on the Spanish Netherlands. (*MPW* 2:247)

5   In a letter to the Hull Corporation, Robert Stockdale [W?] excuses his not having written at the last post about Skinner's Case, but cites the account 'of that affaire which you had from a better hand'. (BRL 1194/114)

7–9?   AM writes a draft of an 'Addresse from the House of Peeres to the King to make use of his prerogative in Ecclesiasticall affayres for the better composure and union of the mindes of his protestant subjects in the intervall of the present adjournment.' Later (1680?) endorsed by Wharton as 'in the hand writing of a friend deceased'. (Bodl. MS Carte 77, 597–8; von Maltzahn 2003)

9   AM [W] sends note (after 5:00am) to Philip, Lord Wharton (in the Lords) detailing the Commons votes that night in connection with Skinner's Case. (Bodl. MS Carte 81, 37; von Maltzahn 2003)

Parliament adjourned until 10 November 1668.

LHC: AM (W) sends parliamentary news at some length, describing the end of the session. Has with Gylby been trying to sort out Hull postal concerns with Sir John Bennet, deputy Postmaster General. (*PL* 2:75–6; see also Gylby's letter of this day, BRL 774)

July

10   (Friday) Henry North (son of the Suffolk MP Sir Henry North) communicates to John Watson (vicar of Mildenhall, Suffolk) 'A Libell Taken out of the [Last Instructions to a] Painter, upon H[enry]. Jermyn E[arl] of St Albans', lines 29–48. (BL, Add. MS 18220, 23ʳ; reproduced in Kelliher 1978a, 99)

September

24   (Thursday) A lieutenant William Wise having abused the present mayor of Hull, 'Another letter [is] to be written to Mr Marvell and alsoe one to Mr Recorder to entreate their Assistance in presenting and prosecuting the same'. (BRB 5:146)

29   LHC: AM (London) sends brief acknowledgement of correspondence. (*PL* 2:77)

William Lister (The Strand, London) to Hull Corporation concerning the lieutenant Wise: 'My Lord Generall [Albemarle] is yet in the Countrey, I heare he will be in his lodgings at White Hall to morrow Mr Marvell and I, intend to wait uppon him there, when wee have each th'opportunity of presenting your letter to his Grace wee may then bee prepared to given an answer to yours.' (BRL 779)

October

1 (Thursday) LHC: AM (London) reports on business, concerning Hull town / garrison relations. (*PL* 2:77–8)

15 LHC: AM co-signs letter from William Lister [London] regarding Hull town / garrison relations. (*PL* 2:78–9)

27 LHC: AM (London) reports more on business of Hull town / garrison relations. (*PL* 2:79–80)

William Lister (The Strand, London) to Hull Corporation, reports that the Lord General Albemarle has discussed with the Duke of York, whose officer Wise is (Wise also a relation of Albemarle's but the latter continues firm on Hull's behalf), and not much doing there; but Albemarle 'was pleased to debate the matter in variance betwixt yow and Lieutenant Wise, which Mr Marvell and mee in the presence of a very good freind of yours, wee came with his L[ordships] concurrence to this result. That an Injunction should be laid uppon Lieutenant Wise' to apologize fully to Lambert (the late mayor) in the presence of the mayor and aldermen. Writes singly now because 'Mr Marvells lodging and myne are at some distance, soe as we have not th'opportunity of meeting together to signe a joynt letter.' Promises their service. (BRL 780)

November

10 (Tuesday) Parliament meets to be adjourned again to 1 March 1669.

12 AM accorded a barrel of ale as one of the friends of Hull. (BRB 5:158)

28 LHC: AM (London) reports on business of town / garrison relations. (*PL* 2:80–2)

1669

February

23 (Tuesday) Hull TH letter to AM about Spurn Light: 'After a long silence we give you the trouble of this ensueing narrative together with our requests thereupon begging both you patience and pardon for it .... Now we are credibly informed some are busie againe about itt.' Asking him to find out more; it is left 'to your consideracon whether you will speake to mr Cressett touching the buisness or not'. (NTH52/1; ATH 1/3)

27 AM (London) writes Hull TH with thanks for letter and with a proposal to forestall trouble with the Spurn Light by bribing Sir Philip Frowd, who is the Duchess of York's secretary and 'spring of that engine' but likely 'an hungry and needy man'. Hull TH draughts answer verso. (NTH52/1; *PL* 2:256–7)

? AM [London] 'in great hast' writes note to his 'Dear Brother' Edmond Popple (Hull TH), presumably about Spurn Light, the response to which Popple should 'for more privacy inclose under your cover'. (NTH52/1; *PL* 2:257)

March

1 (Monday) Parliament meets to be prorogued until 19 October.

2 LHC: AM (London) reports meeting and further prorogation of parliament. (*PL* 2:82)

5 Hull TH sends AM the Spurn Light documents he has requested; AM's address is 'att the Crowne over against the Greyhound Taverne neere Charing Crosse London'. (NTH52/1; *PL* 2:373)

16 LHC: AM (London) briefly notes their business with Mr South and Sir Robert Cary, which Cyriack Skinner has referred to him. (*PL* 2:83)

23 Letter from Cyriack Skinner (The Strand, London) to Hull Corporation citing business of Mr South and Sir Robert Cary: confident that 'Mr. Recorder [William Lister] and Mr. Marvell' will soon have the matter in hand. (BRL 795; *PL* 2:364)

30 AM [London] writes note to John Hill (Hull TH): asks Hill to pay to 'my Cosin Mr William Popple the 25^{li} which your father orderd you this Post to pay me.' (NTH52/1; *PL* 2:258)

April

15 (Thursday) LHC: AM [London] returns to business of South and Cary. (*PL* 2:83)

Robert Stockdale [London] to Hull Corporation: '... to morrow at 4 a clock I am to meet Sr Robert Cary, & to gett Mr Marvailes company if he been not otherwayes ingaged'. (BRL 1194/174)

17 LHC: AM (London) writes with more of the business of South and Cary. (*PL* 2:84–5)

Robert Stockdale [London] to Hull Corporation: 'Mr Marveile Mr Ashton and my selfe had this day a meeteinge with Sir Robert Carey and some other of his freinds in order [to] an accommodation of that difference betwixt you and Sr Robert and Mr South.' In Mr the Recorder William Lister's absence AM judges himself unable to conclude the matter, so Cary proposes that he 'and Mr South, will within six dayes after Mr Marveile shall receive your approbation theireunto pay unto your assignee the sume of 30 li, 10 li of which in consideracion of charges here and belowe, And the other 20 li to be disposed on accordinge to your discretion to your power and any other injured by them'. (BRL 1194/175)

Richard Aston (Furnivall's Inn, Holborn) to Hull Corporation: more on South and Cary, '... this day Mr Marvyn Mr Stockdale and my self met Sir Robert and two other of his freinds more civill then hee, who upon some controversy about the affair proposed that they would pay 10 li for charges 10 li to the Corporacion for the poore or otherwise And 10 li to the persons injured; or 30 li in generall termes for all'. (BRL 797)

Robert Cary's letter of submission, 'willing to make sattisfaction, both by acknowledgement, and otherewise To which purpose I have treated with Mr Marvelle, and proposed to him that which I hope Sir you will be please to accept'. (BRL 798)

21 'Andrew Marvell Gent.' named by Danby in a general 'list of parlament men' with Gylby, under Kingston upon Hull. (BL, MS Egerton 3345, 7^r)

27 LHC: AM (London) reports the business with South and Cary resolved. (*PL* 2:85)

May

ca. 4 (Tuesday) Robert Stockdale [London] to Hull Corporation begins: 'Understandinge from Mr Marveile that you had received 30 li from Mr Browne by the appointement of Sir Robert Carey and Mr South, I did goe to Mr Ashton, to desire him to take care to gett theire discharge that neither they nor the Towne might come to any dammage.' (BRL 1194/178)

June

15 (Tuesday) Robert Stockdale [London] to Hull Corporation begins: 'I received yours last night with the inclosed papers, which I showed this morning to Mr Marvaile and after that found Mr Rooksby at the King bench barr, to whome I gave them, and who did promise me by this post to make [ ] a returne to you as is desired.' Notes the arrest of Richard Baxter, 'it being the present opinion of the wise men, that if they nipp but the heads, the roots will wither'. (BRL 1194/187)

28 Publication advertised of Guy de Miège, *A Relation of Three Embassies*, a full narrative of the Carlisle embassies by a junior member of the entourage (*TC* 1:13). The text is approved by Carlisle 30 November 1668, and licensed by Roger L'Estrange, 26 March 1669 (A6^v). Miège designed this to be published in his native French from the outset (A6^r), issuing in the 1669 *La Relation de Trois Ambassades* (Amsterdam, 1669), republished in 1672 and 1700; the work is translated into German (1701, see Adelung 337) and republished in John Harris, *Navigantium atque Itinerantium Bibliotheca. Or, a Compleat Collection of Voyages and Travels* ... 2 vols (1705), 2: 177–213 (also reprinted in 1744 and 1764).

September

18   (Saturday) AM [London] writes to Hull TH: his lateness in
          response follows from 'some occasions of mine own & absence
          out of Towne'; frustration of best-laid plans, again owing to
          Frowd; difficulty of success with private members bills, and
          uncertainty about length of session; advises a petition to the
          House of Commons for Spurn Light, and perhaps to buy off
          Frowd. Hull TH soon draughts response to Gylby: 'we thinke by
          Act of Parliament is the surest way which if our interest be
          joined with Coll Froudes we hope may prevaile ... therefore
          when itt please God send you to London we intreate you
          consult with Mr Marvell.' (NTH52/1; *PL* 2:258–60)

October

7   (Thursday) LHC: AM (London) gives notice of imminent session
          of parliament. (*PL* 2:86)
          Hull TH drafts letter to AM: grateful for his care and ready now
          to deal with Frowd, 'in which we doubt not your prudence
          haveing had soe much experience', from whose cooperation an
          act in parliament may be hoped, preferable to a charter.
          (NTH52/1)

19   Parliament meets in session that will last until prorogation on
          11 December 1669. 'Mr. Marvin' again named to committee of
          elections and privileges. (*CJ* 9:98)
          Gylby has not yet met with AM 'but shall tomorrow consult
          him in the busines'. (NTH52/1; *PL* 2:373)
          LHC: AM (London) sends parliamentary news. (*PL* 2:86–7)

20   At the meeting of parliament, 'a Libell [was] scattered in
          Westminster Hall' called 'The Alarme', much later attributed to
          AM by Narcissus Luttrell (Oxford, All Souls MS 167, 10^r–16^v, ca.
          1700; compare the lack of attribution in the Okeover MS,
          University of Leeds, Brotherton MS Lt. 55, 22–30, and the copy
          once in Joseph Williamson's possession, PRO, SP29/266/152).
          Its truculent invective urging pariots to save the king from his
          ministry seems unlike AM's note and at odds with his greater
          kindness to the Cabal.

22   'Mr. Marvin' named to committee to consider the Poor Laws.
          (*CJ* 9:100)
          Hull TH drafts letter to Gylby asking him to consult further
          with AM in Spurn Light business. (NTH52/1)

26   LHC: AM (London) sends parliamentary news. (*PL* 2:87–8)
          Gylby to Hull TH, 'I was this morninge with Mr Mervaile before
          yours came to my hand, and I am confident he is secure that
          nothinge can passe without his knowledge'; it is Gylby's part to
          treat with Sir Philip Frowd as he and AM have agreed. (NTH52/1)

28 AM [London] to Hull TH: with Gylby he is conducting their business; a meeting with Sir Philip Frowd is to follow. (NTH52/1; *PL* 2:260)

Richard Lyndall and Thomas Coates (London) write to their brethren at Hull TH: have been with AM and Gylby who have been reassuring. (NTH52/1)

LHC: AM (London) includes brief cover note with newsletters. (*PL* 2:88)

30 'Mr. Marvin' named to committee to consider an excise bill. (*CJ* 9:101)

AM and Gylby (London) send note to Hull TH: their meeting with Sir Philip Frowd has been postponed to 3 November (NTH52/1; *PL* 2:261)

November

2 (Tuesday) Letter from AM (London) to Hull TH: meeting with Frowd tomorrow, but 'in discourse in the Hall he seemd willing to come to terms as indeed he hath reason'; explains 'what it was that made this noise about a light house on the Spurn-head', and difference of present from previous patents. (NTH52/1; *PL* 2:261-2)

4 Gylby writes to Hull TH that Frowd has again failed him and AM; also that AM reports the grants for the lights except Humber mouth 'are past the seales'. He and AM miss Frowd again the next day and the next day since 'he is out of towne, then delayes'. (NTH52/1; *PL* 2:373)

AM accorded a barrel of ale as one of the town's friends. (BRB 5:200)

LHC: AM (London) sends parliamentary news, with second Conventicles Act preparing. (*PL* 2:88-9)

9 AM added to committee reviewing 'the Petition of the Master and Fellows of St. Mary Magdalen's College, in Cambridge'. (*CJ* 9:104)

LHC: AM (W) sends parliamentary news. (*PL* 2:89-90)

11 AM [London] writes to Hull TH: reports on negotiation with Frowd the day before; the matter of Frowd's interest not concluded, but the higher the charges needed to generate annual profit from Spurn Light the less likelihood of success with the bill. Later that day Gylby writes to same: Frowd not yet heard back from but will want to know more about revenues; AM right about the other lights' grants being past the seals. Hull TH drafts encouraging letters back (14, 18, 23 November); on 15 November, Gylby writes that he has not spoken again with AM or Frowd; after a fortnight's illness still has not seen AM (3 December). (NTH52/1; *PL* 2:262)

MPs for out ports enlisted to examine custom-house officers and fees. (*CJ* 9:105)

13   AM's name added to committee of privileges and elections. (*CJ* 9:107)

LHC: AM [W?] sends parliamentary news. (*PL* 2:90–1)

18   AM named to committee for bill settling Lady Elizabeth Lee's estate. (*CJ* 9:108)

20   LHC: AM (W) sends parliamentary news, including report from committee for the Conventicles Bill; discussion in parliament of General Edmund Ludlow's reported return to England and that 'Commonwealths men flock about the town and there were meetings said to be where they talkt of new Modells of Government'. (*PL* 2:91–2)

22   The Church of England reaction to the lapse of the Conventicles Act includes the publication by Samuel Parker, chaplain to Archbishop Sheldon, of *A Discourse of Ecclesiastical Politie* (1670, but advertised already now, *TC* 1:21), one of the works to which AM will take sharp exception in *The Rehearsal Transpros'd*.

25   LHC: AM (W) sends parliamentary news, including further concern about the 'many old Army Common welths and Councill of States men and Outlaws and forainers about town', including Henry Neville. (*PL* 2:92–3)

27   AM named to committee for bill to account for moneys given to indigent officers. (*CJ* 9:113)

LHC: AM (W) sends parliamentary news. (*PL* 2:93–4)

December

2   (Thursday) AM added to committee for bill regulating jurors. (*CJ* 9:115)

4   LHC: AM [W] sends parliamentary news. (*PL* 2:94–5)

6   Hull TH drafts letters to Gylby and AM with further Spurn Light information; answered by Gylby (9 Dec.) 'wee have propos'd to him [Frowd] if you approv'd of it, to devide the profit, and the Charge betwixt you, and him, but he refus'd it' – he and AM want some private instruction on how much they can offer. (NTH52/1)

7   MPs for ports enlisted for bill for repair of Yarmouth harbour. (*CJ* 9:118)

AM named to committee for bill for rebuilding London. (*CJ* 9:118)

AM a teller with Henry Henley for the unsuccessful Noes (80, vs 167 Yeas) on question whether the churchman Peregrine Palmer was duly elected for Bridgewater. Palmer's rival

Sir Francis Rolle had been returned but too many of his voters proved to have been disqualified under the Corporations Act. Rolle's dissenting sympathies led to his conspicuous opposition to Cavalier interests after his later election to parliament in 1675. (*CJ* 9:118–19; Henning: Peregrine Palmer, Sir Francis Rolle)

11   Parliament prorogued until 14 February 1670.

12   LHC: AM [W?] sends parliamentary news, including proroga-tion, at which AM comes near to demurring: it makes 'all bills votes and proceedings of this session null and voyd as if nothing had bin don or said. God direct his M[ajes]ty further in so weighty resolutions'. (*PL* 2:95–6)

1670

AM seems to have written two letters this year to an unknown recipient (likely Thomas Rolt) 'complaining that no one could expect promotions, spiritual or temporal, unless he made his court to the king's mistress, the Duchess of Cleveland'. The letters have not come to light since once seen in a Hertfordshire law office; their description and date fit details from the letter to Rolt printed in Cooke. (Hine 7; Beal 1993, 21; *PL* 2:325; see also February 1671 below).

AM's 'Horatian Ode' may be recalled in Thomas Flatman, *On the Death of...* *Albemarle* (1670): note especially, 'Nor here did thy undaunted Valour cease, / Or wither with unactive peace ...' (4; also in Flatman, *Poems and Songs*, 1674, 25–6, and later editions).

It is this year that AM 'by chance' comes no longer to see John Milton for the next years leading up to the publication of *RT* (1672). (*MPW* 1: 417)

January
AM's nephew William Popple moves to Bordeaux about this time (wine trade), beginning their extant correspondence. AM's letters to Popple of 21 March 1669/70 and 14 April 1670 cite two previous letters AM (W) sent to him at Bordeaux. (*PL* 2:313, 384)

7   (Friday) Hull TH drafts letter to Gylby with copy to AM: urges further conference with Frowd during this interval of parlia-ment and asks for further communication from them as the session approaches. (NTH52/1)

February
Perhaps now in preparation for the session of parliament about to begin, AM writes some or most of 'The Loyal Scot', especially the sections that incorporate the Archibald Douglas passage taken over from 'Last Instructions' (lines 1–86?, 250?–301) but perhaps almost the whole (date

argued by Mathole). A fuller union of Scots and English was under consideration, which the poem favours; episcopal power was great, which it deplores. Moreover it alludes to Lauderdale kindly (line 100), so before his change of role into a persecutor of conventicles. Where John Cleveland had in the 1640s excoriated 'The Rebell Scot', AM now makes of Archibald Douglas's self-sacrifice the occasion for some possible reconciliation between England and Scotland, that eirenic purpose leading him, however, to scourge episcopacy as dividing these nations. The manuscript and early print witnesses to the text do not enough explain the stages of this satire's composition, but the most bitter antiprelatical passage (87–249?) may also date from this time, although its incorporation of the epigram on Blood's attempt to steal the crown dates from the summer of 1671 or later (see 9 May 1671 below); at one point it comes very near AM's 'Short Historical Essay' incorporated in *Mr. Smirke* (1676). Such is the animus of this passage that it may have been occasioned by some sharper disappointment, for example, the impending renewal of the Conventicles Act in this session, or withdrawal of the Declaration of Indulgence, 8 March 1673. (Compare *PL* 1:180–7, 384–94 and Smith 397–410, from which edition the present line numbers are taken; 'Loyal Scot', lines 166–9; Mathole, chapter 4)

1	(Tuesday) AM (W) writes to Hull TH: has not written owing to ongoing expectation of having more to report, and negotiation with Frowd wearing on; but Gylby's recent contact has not changed matters, and too much importunity disadvantageous to their cause; of Frowd, 'a litle matter makes him much businesse', but with parliament soon to sit more may be doing (NTH52/1; *PL* 2:262–3)
14	Parliament meets in session that, with an adjournment from 11 April to 24 October 1670, lasts until prorogation 22 April 1671.
15	LHC: AM (W) notes beginning of parliamentary session. (*PL* 2:96)
19	LHC: AM (W) sends parliamentary news. (*PL* 2:96–7)
22	LHC: AM (W) sends parliamentary news, including commendation of royal wisdom in seeking deletion of Lords and Commons journals' entries relating to Thomas Skinner's and Sir Samuel Barnardiston's cases. (*PL* 2:97–8)
25	MPs for out-ports enlisted for committee considering fees in out-ports. (*CJ* 9:126)
26	LHC: AM (W) sends parliamentary news, including details of 'the act for Wines', debates about union with Scotland and customs fees; Conventicles Bill expected. (*PL* 2:98–9)

March

1	(Tuesday) Letter from William Popple (Bordeaux) to AM, cited in AM's letter to Popple of 21 March 1670.

4	Yorkshire MPs among those enlisted to be added to committee for the bill concerning Lindsey Level. (*CJ* 9:132)
5	AM named to committee for bill for draining Deeping Fen. (*CJ* 9:133)
	LHC: AM (W) apologizes for brief note owing to 'some unavoydable occasions'; has given his notes to Robert Stockdale who will send parliamentary news. (*PL* 2:99)
7	MPs for ports enlisted for committee for bill enabling the construction of Falmouth Key. (*CJ* 9:134)
10	LHC: AM (W) sends parliamentary news at length, centring in the passage of the Conventicles Bill and its terms: 'I have bin more particular to you herein that inconveniencies might better and in time be prevented.' (*PL* 2:100–3)
11	AM named to committee for bill for repairing churches. (*CJ* 9:137)
12	Yorkshire MPs among those enlisted for committee further to consider bill regulating jurors. (*CJ* 9:138)
14	AM named to committee for bill against child-stealing. (*CJ* 9:138)
15	AM (W) writes to Hull TH: has from Gylby had their letter; issue of Sweden's attempts to control the Sound and how the Navigation Act has invited such imitation. (NTH52/1; *PL* 2:263–4)
19	LHC: AM [W] sends parliamentary news. (*PL* 2:103–4)
21	AM [W] writes to William Popple (Bordeaux), sent with Edward Nelthorpe. Much political news in summary, especially that Lauderdale is in favour owing to his success in controlling Scotland for Charles II; that during the prorogation of parliament there has been much 'Caballing among the Courtiers'; and then much more about the fortunes of the session perhaps with sympathy for 'the Garroway Party' and 'the Country Gentlemen', with bitter reflections on the Second Conventicles Act, and also noting the Roos divorce bill and Charles II's support for it and the Duke of York's opposition. Charles II more than ever 'absolutely powerful at Home': 'In such a Conjuncture, dear Will, what Probability is there of my doing any Thing to the Purpose?' (Cooke 2:50–5; *PL* 2:313–16)
22	Yorkshire MPs enlisted for bill for the sale of Firbeck Manor (Yorks.). (*CJ* 9:144)
	AM added to committee of privileges and elections 'to hear the Cause between the Lord Clifford and Mr. Ferrers, touching the Election for the Town of Tamworth'. 'A court cully' who eventually becomes 'an excellent patriot', the Lord Clifford (Charles Boyle) came from a prominent Yorkshire family and benefited

from the interest of his father Richard Boyle, the second Earl of Cork, in the East Riding; AM wrote memorial verses for the Lord Clifford's cousin Frances Jones two years later. (*CJ* 9:144; Henning: Charles Boyle; see 28 March 1672 below)

AM named to committee for bill recovering arrears to indigent officers. (*CJ* 9:145)

23   AM named to committee for bill enabling John Bill to settle his estate. (*CJ* 9:145)

26   LHC: AM (W) sends parliamentary news, including Lords' alterations proposed for the Conventicles Bill, among which 'a reserving clause for his Majestyes ancient prerogative in all Ecclesiasticall things'. (*PL* 2:104–5)

30   AM named to committee for bill protecting English shipping from pirates. (*CJ* 9:149)

Yorkshire MPs among those enlisted for bill authorizing English commissioners to treat with their Scots counterparts for a union of the two kingdoms. (*CJ* 9:150; compare 'The Loyal Scot')

April

2   (Saturday) LHC: AM (W) reports the session busy near its end, so writes very briefly promising that he has given his notes to Robert Stockdale for a newsletter. (*PL* 2:105)

7   LHC: AM (W) reports parliamentary business, end of session expected. (*PL* 2:105–6)

9   LHC: AM [W] reports parliamentary business, house thin and end of session expected. (*PL* 2:106–7)

12   LHC: AM (W) reports parliamentary adjournment the day before (until 24 October 1670) and acts passed, promises copies of which when printed. (*PL* 2:107–8)

14   AM [W] writes to William Popple (Bordeaux): reports parliamentary business, including the questionable but perhaps commendable arrival of the King in the Lords to diminish the Duke of York's influence. Again notes the Lord Roos divorce bill and royal interest in it. Royal claims to prerogative too little contested, 'We are all venal Cowards, except some few' (Cooke 2:61–4; *PL* 2:316–17). Has sent two previous letters from the posthouse at Westminster and another in the hand of (their common relation, Edward) Nelthorpe – it is this year that Nelthorpe and Richard Thompson meet with John Farrington (PRO, C7/581/73), the failure of whose joint bank so colours the last years of AM's life.

16   LHC: AM (W) includes cover note on mailing of acts already printed. (*PL* 2:108)

21   Hull: 'It is Ordered that Mr Major doe pay by command unto Andrew Marvell Esqr one of the Townes Burgesses of Parliament

the sum of Thirty Seaven pounds six shillings and eight pence being vi.ˢ viii.ᵈ per day for One hundred and tenn days attendance at the Parliament from the 19th of October 1669 untill the 11th of December 1669: and from the 14th of February: 1669. untill the 11th day of Aprill instant, which money Mr Marvell hath desired and ordered to be paid into the hands of Mr Edmond Popple for the use of the said Mr Marvell ...'. (BRB 5:213)
Entry in Hull Accounts Book for 'monies taken out and paid unto Mr Andrew Marvell for his service as Burgesse of Parliament': £37 6s.8d. (BRF 3/23/120)

May

5 (Thursday) Hull: 'Thirty seaven pound six shillings and eight pence is this day taken out of the Iron Chest and putt into the hands of Mr Mathew Hardy to pay unto Mr Edmond Popple for the use of Mr Andrew Marvell according to the Order of this Board made the 21th of Aprill last.' (BRB 5:214)

20 The satirical 'Kinges Vowes' circulates (lines 1–39 collected at this date by John Watson, vicar of Mildenhall, Suffolk), which poem is included in Bodl. MS Eng. poet. d. 49, 235–7, and would much later be attributed to AM when printed with some belated additions (1703); also known as 'Royal Resolutions'. (BL, Add. MS 18220, 44ᵛ–45ᵛ; Lord, ed., *POAS*, 1:159–67, 455–6)
Hull TH drafts letter to AM: 'your brother Mr Popple hath been pleased to Comunicate to us your good intencions toward this Scosciety of which we have had soe large experience'; urges further discussion with Frowd to discover what terms he might accept. On same day another Hull TH letter to John Harris (London) asks him 'to Comunicate to Mr Marvell att Mr Richard Hill's howse the Rhinish wine howse in Westminster' whatever he can find out about who has signed what certificates for lighthouses elsewhere. (NTH52/1)

June

10 (Friday) Hull TH drafts letter to AM, 'Worthy Sir / After the presentacion of our hearty love and respects to yourselfe with a grateful acknowledgement of your many freindshippes to this Scosciety we present you with a ˡⁱᵗᵗˡᵉ Salmon yet the best we could procure which we have sent in a little Cagge or Kitt by William Taylor of Hull whoe set saile from hence yesterday morneing and we hope ere this wilbe with you. itt is marked as in the margen ['AM'] we intreat it may purchase your acceptance which wilbe a further addition to your former favours, We make bold alsoe to give you some further trouble which is to

acquaint you that there are now all along upon the coast some persons whoe have gott many thowsands of hands to procure the lighthouses we have soe long looked after ... Good Sir put itt positively to Sir Phillipp what he will doe and that he will deale plainely with us that we may not thus fruitlessly labor in the darke ...'. (NTH52/1)

On or near this date, Hull TH pays 4s. for salmon and 1s.6d. 'for a Caske for salmon' to be sent to AM; the shipping cost another 2s. (paid in the first week of October 1670). (FTH1/5)

14   AM (London) writes to Hull TH with thanks for their previous letters and the salmon; delay owing to hard negotation with Frowd, who when pressed suggests alternatives unlikely of success (AM frustrated with this style of business): 'I wish what can may be done within 5 or 6 weeks. For longer I can not well attend though upon any good likelyhood of doing you service I shall willingly imploy the whole Vacation.' Problem for Hull of the revived interest in Dover pier. (NTH52/1; *PL* 2:264–6)

16   'Alderman Foxley this day presented to this Board a booke containing all the severall Acts of Parliament made at the last Sessions of Parliament, which Andrew Marvell Esqr one of the Burgesses of Parliament for this Town did present to the Bench.' (BRB 5:215)

LHC: AM (W) alerts Corporation to views expressed in London about public works in Hull that could be charged to the town's expense; AM advises electing a High Steward out of the Privy Council and recommends the Earl of Sandwich as an appropriate choice. (*PL* 2:108–9)

18   Sir Philip Frowd's letter to Hull TH, 'Sir I thought to have written to you by the last Post haveing maide a promis so to doe to Mr Mervaile, but I have beene hindred by some ill accidents that have taken up my thoughts as well as my time ...'. AM has proposed to him the perfecting of some treaty in this business, but he thinks not, since it would be imprudent to tie himself down and he thinks he has lots of support, not least from the Ipswich men. (NTH52/1, copy)

20   Hull: 'It is Ordered that a letter of thankfullnesse be written to Mr Marvell for his letter dated the 14th of June instant for giving notice of Sir Thomas Chichley the new Master of the Ordinance is to come downe to view the defects of repaires in the Garrison and for the other particulars in the same letter.' (BRB 5:216)

July

14   (Thursday) AM [London?] to Edmond Popple (Hull [TH]) in response to his of 6 July: Frowd's interest vital to success of 'any

Act of Parliament for that Light-house'; likewise Hull TH co-operation needed by Frowd; measures suggested to forestall possible legislation for other lighthouses. (NTH52/1; *PL* 2:266–7)

October

[12	(Wednesday) Letter from Thomas Rolt ('a Friend in Persia') to AM, reported in AM's response of 12 October 1671. (*PL* 2:323; Duncan-Jones 1957)]
[21	Letter from Hull TH to AM, cited in AM's reply of 8 November.]
22	Hull TH pays total of £6 8s.6d. for five barrels of ale shipped to London, including one for AM. (FTH1/5; ATH 1/3)
25	LHC: AM (W) sends news as parliament reconvenes (24 October) after the adjournment, with report of the King's and Lord Keeper's speeches, the latter of which he will send if printed. (*PL* 2:109–10)

November

Samuel Parker publishes *A Defence and Continuation of the Ecclesiastical Politie* (1671) against John Owen, to which sharp exception will be taken in *RT*. Dated 1670 by Parker himself (Bodl. MS Wood F46, f. 272^r) and advertised in the Michaelmas Term Catalogue, 1670 (*TC* 1:58).

1	(Tuesday) LHC: AM (W) sends parliamentary news; printing of King's and Lord Keeper's speeches forbidden, but will send 'a written copy'. (*PL* 2:111)
[4	Letter from Hull TH to Marvell, cited in AM's reply of 8 November.]
8	AM [W] writes to Hull TH: unlikely that Frowd 'doth at all thinke of bringing his businesse into Parliament this session: which is likely to be short and so attentive to the levying of great summes for the public occasions that it will probably be deafe to any private imposition'. (NTH52/1; *PL* 2:267)
	LHC: AM (W) sends parliamentary news at length, adding that he hopes his letters will only be read by the 'bench' of the Hull Corporation, since 'others might chance either not to understand or to put an ill construction upon this openesse of my writing and simplicity of my expression'. (*PL* 2:112–3)
10	AM named to committee for bill improving navigation between Boston and the River Trent. (*CJ* 9:161)
	AM named to committee for bill on behalf of Sir Phillip Howard and Francis Watson encouraging English manufactures for preservation of shipping, which list includes 'all the Merchants of the House, and all that serve for any Port Town: And that they do send for the Masters of Trinity House, or any other Persons skilled in the Affairs of this Nature.' (*CJ* 9:161)
	Hull Corporation moves 'A Letter to be written to Collonell Gilby and Mr Marvell to entreat them to advise whether Bakers

bakeing bread to sell haveing two ovens in One Chimney are to pay hearth-money for each oven and whether Smithes Forges ought to pay or noe.' (BRB 5:231)

Hull Corporation orders AM a barrel of ale as one of its friends. (BRB 5:232)

LHC: AM [W] sends parliamentary news, especially the proposed rates on foreign commodities; with Gylby intends to respond to Corporation's letter newly received. (*PL* 2:114)

11   AM added to committee for bill settling Henry Williams's estate. (*CJ* 9:162)

14   Yorkshire MPs among those enlisted for committee for bill regulating Kidderminster (Worcs.) stuffs. (*CJ* 9:163)

15   Yorkshire MPs among those enlisted for committee for bill improving Outwood (Yorks.) common. (*CJ* 9:164)

17   LHC: AM [W] sends parliamentary news, answers questions raised by Hull Corporation about hearth tax, tax on coal shipments – difficult to bring in private bill for these at this late date. (*PL* 2:115)

19   LHC: AM [W] gives long advice about the dubiousness of bringing in any private bill on Hull's account which will then open the town's finances to wide inspection; seriousness of such an attempt and worrisome expense and effort to secure any likelihood of success. (*PL* 2:115–7)

Gylby (London) to Hull Corporation: 'Mr Mervaile and my selfe have consider'd of your letters touchinge the Ovens, and the Smyth Forges, and we doe finde by all we speake with, that all Bakers Ovens are to pay for the forges, there was a Bill the last Session to have acquit them, but it was lost by the prorogation.' They agree this no fit time for private bill for tax on coals. (BRL 813)

21   AM speaks in the House of Commons on the Hayes and Jekyll question (seeking to forestall prosecution following from Conventicles Act). (Grey, *Debates*, 1:294)

[22]   LHC: AM [W] sends parliamentary news, including support for an attempt on the part of Boston to limit tax on shipping coals. (*PL* 2:117)

23   AM named to committee for bill for repairing Boston pier and harbour. (*CJ* 9:168)

26   LHC: AM (W) sends parliamentary news in brief. (*PL* 2:118)

28   AM [W] writes to William Popple [Bordeaux]: 'I need not tell you I am always thinking of you.' Political news: suppression of conventicles, Quaker patience under persecution, money forthcoming to the crown from nonconformists. (Cooke 2:65–7; *PL* 2:317–18)

29 AM a teller with Sir Nicholas Carew for the unsuccessful Yeas (60, vs 65 Noes) seeking to return to the committee of privilege the MP Christopher Jay's claims for a breach of privilege affecting his property; that is, the House decides partly and belatedly in favour of this placeman and recovers for him his sheep-walk. (*CJ* 9:174; Henning: Jay)

LHC / W. Parliamentary news; with Gylby intends to respond to Corporation's letter newly received. (*PL* 2:119)

December

3 (Saturday) LHC: AM (W) sends parliamentary news, including measures to encourage attendance in the Commons. (*PL* 2:119–20)

Gylby (London) writes Hull Corporation with more advice, 'if you differ from us, in our oppinion, we will follow yours, as you shall derect'. (BRL 814)

5 Indictment of Elizabeth Calvert cites her publication of the *Directions to a Painter* (1667). (Smith and Bell, 14–15; Smith 322–3)

8 LHC: AM [W] sends parliamentary news, including commitment of the Bill for Conventicles. (*PL* 2:120–1)

10 LHC: AM (W) sends parliamentary news. (*PL* 2:121)

[12? Letter from Edward Thompson (York) to AM, cited as 'yours of the former Post' by AM in his letter of 17 December.]

13 Yorkshire MPs among those enlisted for committee for bill settling Sir Clifford Clifton's estate. (*CJ* 9:182)

14 Yorkshire MPs among those enlisted for committee for bill settling Lord Irwin's estate. (*CJ* 9:183)

15 'A Letter to be written to Collonell Gilby and Mr Marvell to treate with the Burgesses of Yorke Pontefract and other neighbouring Burroughs, that the Act for regulating the Post-Office may be re-assumed.' (BRB 5:235)

LHC: AM (W) sends parliamentary news; his thanks for gift of ale. (*PL* 2:122)

17 AM [W] writes to 'mon tres cher ami' Edward Thompson (York), particularly concerning Thompson family business in connection with AM's sitting the day before on the Committee for tax of £4 per ton at the Custom House, and more generally about the £800,000 supply that has been voted the king and details of how these taxes are to be raised. (University of Leeds, Brotherton Collection, Misc. Letters 2 Marvell; *PL* 2:319–20)

LHC: AM (W) sends parliamentary news; asks for Corporation's view of a proposed bill for 'general naturalization of all forainers that shall take the oaths of allegeance and Supremacy'. (*PL* 2:122–3)

[–   Letter from Sir Henry Thompson to AM, cited in AM's response
           of 5 January 1671.]
20   Parliament takes a week's recess over Christmas, meets on 29th
           only to adjourn again to 3 January 1670/71.
           LHC: AM (W) sends parliamentary news (*PL* 2:123). Gylby too
           writes as from them both, concerning post-office business either
           to go to trial or arbitration. (BRL 816).
[21   Letter from Edward Thompson to AM cited in AM's response of
           29 December 1670.]
[24   Letter from Edward Thompson to AM cited in AM's response of
           29 December 1670.]
25   AM returns to Westminster [?] as noted in his letter to Sir Henry
           Thompson of 5 January 1671.
29   AM [W] to Edward Thompson (York): grateful to help the
           Thompsons, since 'the kindnesse betwixt you & Will [Popple] is
           enough to ingage me in all things to catch at the opportunityes
           to court and oblige you or any of your relations'. Reports the
           consequence of the taxation of £4 per ton on wines, and
           observes that 'The businesse of Sir J: Coventry [having his nose
           slit] is all discoverd', and that the House adjourned until the
           following Tuesday 'when the bill of Subsidy is to have its first
           reading' – the scandal of the violence against Coventry invited
           delay of this proposed taxation. (BL, Add. MS 78684, 69;
           Kelliher 1979, 148)

1671

January
Richard Thompson, Edward Nelthorpe, John Farrington, and Edmund Page
form partnership for banking and trade. The first two have worked together
before and are Hull relations of AM; it is with them that AM takes up the
house in Great Russell Street in June 1677. Of Thompson it is later complained that 'he was dayly at Coffee houses and other publick places ...
heareing and telling news and that he did not regard his duty and engagement to mind the said office or banck', with dire results by 1676; of
Nelthorpe that he was given to very speculative commercial projects; of
both that they helped themselves to the bank's stock while putting their
own property in their wives and children's names. Thompson's son Robert
clerked for William Popple in Bordeaux, who had business with Nelthorpe;
and AM's great intimacy with Nelthorpe and relatedness are later attested
by Mary Palmer (Tupper 368, citing *The Case of Richard Thompson and
Company* (1678), 3–4; Wall 1959; PRO, C7/581/73; C6/276/48, and
C6/526/178; *PL* 2:348, 394, 395).

5	(Thursday) AM (W) writes to Sir Henry Thompson (Escrick, Yorks.), whom he has vindicated in the Customs committee: 'so litle hath this been in discharge of what I reckon my selfe indebted to you and your brother upon my Nephew Wills account, that I ought rather to beg your excuse then own your thanks.' (Historical Society of Pennsylvania, Simon Gratz Collection, British Poets, Case 11, Box 1; *PL* 2:320–1)

With this letter, Marvell writes a covering note to Edward Thompson ('Jan: 5. 1670/71') about parliamentary business: 'Deare Monsieur Eduoart, Pray present this letter to Sir Henry. We have this week onely red Tuesday the 8000000^li bill first time – second [reading] to be Tuesday next. Yesterday Forain Excise second to be Thursday next. To day the Addition on beere – second to be this day fortnight. The bills of Salt and of law not brought in yet. So we adjornd till Munday when the House is to be calld. And then woe to the absent. My word we need no frost nor snow this winter. The Bills will pinch us enough. There will be noe sort of men in the nation but we shall make them tingle to the very fingers ends. The mony will goe hard but the ways of collecting are so severe that it will spend all mens patience. If Gentlemen would come up and attend we might have something a better market Not one word yet in mention of Sir John Cov[entry] the more remains behind. The Act of forain Excise is brought in with a retrospect and searching of all shops but I hope we shall correct that onely to give a daye forward. I am / Yours Andr: Marvell'. (Colorado College, Tutt Library, Alice Bemer Taylor Collection, MS 0145; Beal 1993, facsimile II)

	LHC: AM (W) sends parliamentary news. (*PL* 2:123–4)
10	LHC: AM (W) notifies mayor George Acklam 'and the other gentlemen' of parliamentary business 'concerning your Wines', in response a letter of theirs. (*PL* 2:124)
	LHC: AM (W) sends parliamentary news. (*PL* 2:125)
12	LHC: AM (W) sends parliamentary news (*PL* 2:125–6). Gylby speaks for both of them and cites notice given Hull Corporation by 'Mr Mervaile in his last' letter of tax on wines (BRL 818).
14	LHC: AM (W) sends parliamentary news. (*PL* 2:126–7)
19	LHC: AM (W) sends parliamentary news. (*PL* 2:127)
21	AM named to committee for bill making a parish of Paris Garden (Surrey) distinct from St Saviour's, Southwark. (*CJ* 9:192)
c.24	AM [W] writes to William Popple [Bordeaux], with parliamentary news, especially the story of the slitting Sir John Coventry's nose and its aftermath, which includes outrage in

the Commons and delays in voting taxation. On a personal note: 'George's father [Sir Jeremy Smith] obliges you much in Tangier'; more generally, 'The court is at the highest Pitch of Want and Luxury, and the People full of Discontent.' (Cooke 2:56–59; *PL* 2:321–2)

24	LHC: AM [W] sends parliamentary news. (*PL* 2:128)
26	AM named to committee for supply bill concerning wine licences, confirming agreement between Charles II and the Duke of York. (*CJ* 9:194)
31	LHC: AM [W] sends parliamentary news. (*PL* 2:128–9)

February

AM writes to Thomas Rolt (Persia), cited in his letter to Rolt later this year; there seems also to have been a previous letter from the same to the same miscarried 'by the Armenian' (9 August, *PL* 2:324).

The parliamentary session seems still in progress at the time of writing the 'Further Advice to a Painter' ('Painter once more thy pencil reassume'), questionably attributed to AM when printed in *POAS* 1697 (accepted also by Lord, ed., *POAS*, 1:163–7, 456–7; compare *PL* 2:176–7, 376–8; omitted in Smith).

1	(Wednesday) Hull TH draughts letter to the MPs Gylby and AM: Charles Whittington seems on the quiet to have gained the seale on a grant for the lighthouses at Humbermouth. What to do? (NTH52/1)
4	LHC: AM ([W] sends parliamentary news. (*PL* 2:129–30)
7	AM [W] writes to Hull TH: some encroachment from Whittington in matter of Spurn Light; lighthouses also in Ireland a grievance. (NTH52/1; *PL* 2:268)
	LHC: AM [W] sends parliamentary news, including concerns 'about the growth of Popery'. (*PL* 2:130–1)
8	AM named to committee for bill on behalf of indigent officers. (*CJ* 9:199)
9	LHC: AM (W) sends parliamentary news (*PL* 2:131). Gylby (London) writes Hull Corporation that getting to parliament late that day he missed seeing AM, 'with whome I thinke it fitt I should consult before I resolve on any thinge' of consequence (BRL 821).
11	[Letter from Hull TH to AM and Gylby, cited in AM's response of 18 February.]
	Gylby to Hull TH: has with AM decided it best to communicate lighthouse aims to MPs for northern ports. (ATH47/1)
[14	Letter from Hull TH to AM and Gylby, cited in AM's response of 18 February.]
16	LHC: AM (W) sends parliamentary news. (*PL* 2:131–2)

18	AM [W] writes to Hull TH: Frowd now stirred by Whittington's activity, and AM 'well pleasd to find him & Mr Whittington jealous of one another which shall not want fomentation ...'. (NTH52/1; *PL* 2:268–9)
21	AM [W] writes to Hull TH: has visited the Duke of Richmond on TH business, since Sir Philip Frowd has the Duke of York and the King's support; Whittington enjoys support because his 'father had been a great sufferer for the King'; the jealous Frowd has 'no mony to go thorow with the business' but 'is still upon joyning all those Lights in one Act' and it should be possible to set Frowd and Whittington against each other. (NTH52/1; *PL* 2:269–70)

Gylby (London) to Hull TH, is still indisposed; 'as I was writeinge this, Sir Phillip Frowd, and Mr Mervaile came to mee, and a long discourse we had with Sir Frowd, and finde him still full of delayes'; the King and Duke of York say Whittington will not get Humbermouth lights. (NTH52/1)

LHC: AM (W) sends parliamentary news, including address from Commons to King 'concerning the dangerous growth of Popery', copy of which AM will send. (*PL* 2:132–3)

23	MPs for ports among those enlisted for committee to examine accounts for the repair of Dover pier. (*CJ* 9:208)
24	Hull TH drafts letter to Gylby and AM: very grateful that they are taking care of business and that it begins to promise some conclusion. (NTH52/1)
28	LHC: AM (W) sends parliamentary and other brief news. (*PL* 2:133)

March

2	(Thursday) AM named to recently revived (23 Feb.) committee for 'The Bill to prevent the Growth of Popery.' (*CJ* 9:211) AM named among MPs to inspect the Hearth Money bill that had passed 'and to bring in such new additional Bill as they shall think fit'. (*CJ* 9:211)
3	AM added to committee considering the petition of Sir John Prettyman. (*CJ* 9:212)
4	LHC: AM [W] sends parliamentary news and a committee request for information about any money paid for repair of Dover Pier in the 1660s. (*PL* 2:133–4)
7	LHC: AM (W) sends parliamentary news in brief. (*PL* 2:134)
11	LHC: AM (W) sends parliamentary news. (*PL* 2:135)
13	MPs for ports added to committee for bill against the adulteration of wine. (*CJ* 9:218)
14	AM named to committee for bill regulating trade in cattle. (*CJ* 9:219)

15	Yorkshire MPs among those enlisted to committee for bill for the preservation of game. (*CJ* 9:219)
	The bookseller Thomas Palmer reported 'fined and pilloried for circulating the MS. of a pamphlet called *Advice to a Painter*', so presumably it is just before this date that he has petitioned for remission from the pillory and fine of 40 marks to which he had been sentenced at the Old Bailey, 'for selling of two Bookes the one Intituled Nehustan [1668] the other The directions to a Painter', which petition L'Estrange marks as not to be granted. (*PL* 1:376; PRO, SP29/142.2/68, misbound as from 1665)
16	LHC: AM (W) sends parliamentary news. (*PL* 2:135–6)
22	Yorkshire MPs among those enlisted to settle Nevill Yelverton's estate. (*CJ* 9:222)
	AM named to committee for bill for settling William Clarke's estate. (*CJ* 9:222)
	'Presumably for tactical reasons', AM a teller with Henry Powle for the successful Noes (66, vs 62 Yeas) denying a proviso to reduce liabilities of offenders against the Conventicles Bill. (*CJ* 9:223; Henning: Marvell)
23	LHC: AM [W] sends parliamentary news. (*PL* 2:136–7)
25	LHC: AM (W) sends parliamentary news. (*PL* 2:137–8)
29	AM added to committee for bill concerning the River Wey. (*CJ* 9:226)
30	AM named to committee for bill settling Thomas Harlakenden's estate. (*CJ* 9:227)
	AM named to committee for bill determining differences about houses destroyed by public authority in London (by fire or explosion). (*CJ* 9:227)

April

6	(Thursday) LHC: AM [W] sends parliamentary news, including from committee that 'We still stave of Dover Peere'. (*PL* 2:138)
7	AM named to committee for bill to settle Charles Howard and his wife Mary's estate. (*CJ* 9:231)
10	AM named to committee for bill for London paving. (*CJ* 9:232)
13	LHC: AM [W] sends parliamentary news. (*PL* 2:138–9)
14	AM named to committee for bill protecting naval stores. (*CJ* 9:235)
18	LHC: AM [W] sends parliamentary news. (*PL* 2:139–40)
22	Parliament prorogued until 16 April 1672. LHC: AM (W) sends parliamentary news at prorogation. (*PL* 2:140–1)
late	AM [W] writes to William Popple [Bordeaux], parliamentary news centring in Lord Lucas's speech against excessive taxation 'and the weak Looseness of the Government', and observing the French threat although AM avers that France 'will attempt

Nothing on Us, but leave Us to dy a natural Death. For indeed never had poor Nation so many complicated, mortal, incurable, Diseases ... I think it will be my Lot to go on an honest fair Employment into Ireland.' The English court stinks. (Cooke 2:59–60; *PL* 2:322–3)

May

9   (Tuesday) Date of Colonel Thomas Blood's attempt to steal the Crown jewels, indulgently memorialized in Marvell's anti-episcopal epigram 'Bludius et Corona', in Latin and in English (the latter finds attribution to Sir Fleetwood Sheppard in *POAS* 1707), which is also incorporated in most copies of 'The Loyal Scot', lines 192–9 [or 178–85]. The epigram claims that whatever Blood's violence, that of the intolerant bishops is worse. The epigram circulates widely and separately from 'The Loyal Scot': Beal lists 13 examples of the Latin version; 27 of the English, of which one is dated 5 August 1672 by John Watson (Beal 1993, 37–8, 49–51; BL, Add. MS 18220, f. 102^v). The epigram met with some hostile responses in Latin and English (Bodl. MS Douce 357, 81^{r-v}; Smith 411–12, quoting Arbury Hall, MS 185). In some part an agent of Buckingham's, Blood is already more personally associated with AM at this date and a few years later lived around the corner from him in the Great Almery, Westminster (see 21 September below; Marshall; Westminster RO, assessments 1675–76, for which my thanks to Nigel Smith).

25   Hull: 'Sixty pounds more is taken out of the iron Chest, which Mr Major is also desired to send to Mr Andrew Marvell the other Burgesse of this Town towards his charges in his attending the Parliament at the two last Sessions of Parliament: The Parliament was reckoned to continue 188 days.' (BRB 5:250)
     Entry for 'monies given to Mr Andrew Marvell for his Attendance at Parliament from the 16th: of October 1670: to the 12th: of April: 1671': £60. (BRF3/23/122)

June

Hull TH sends a salmon to AM, which with shipment costs 7s.2d. (FTH1/5)

July

Now or soon after, AM writes epigrams 'Inscribenda Luparae' among many such in response to Colbert's competition for an inscription on the Louvre. The first of these makes reference to the burning of the Escorial (17–20 June 1671), first reported in England 22 June 1671 (*CSPD 1671*, 333); the pediment was raised the next year with another's verses (*PL* 1:273–4; Smith 185).

22   (Saturday) Robert Stockdale [London] to Hull Corporation: he has a commitment in the offing that means he will be unable to

serve them any longer, recommends in his place one Mr Henry Dethicke 'who is a very ingenious gent, and such an one as by his acquaintenance and intrest in all places of busines, may be a very fitt person for your service, butt for further satisfaction I referr you to Mr Marveile who is well acquainted with him'. (BRL 1194/313)

August

9   (Wednesday) AM writes to Thomas Rolt ('a friend in Persia'), with sympathies, opining that 'in this World a good Cause signifys little, unless it be as well defended. A man may starve at the Feast of good Conscience'. Cites advice of his 'Fencing-master in Spain': 'there was yet one Secret, against which there was no Defence, and that was, to give the first Blow.' Parliamentary, national, and international news: 'We truckle to France in all Things, to the Prejudice of our Alliance and Honour.' Story that 'One Blud ... some Months ago seized the Crown and Sceptre in the Tower'. Rolt's brother Edward had like AM been a state-servant in the Protectorate. (Cooke 2:71–7; *PL* 2:323–6; Duncan-Jones 1957)

September

21   (Thursday) A source informs Williamson that 'Marvell with Blood from Bucks', seeming to indicate that AM has with Colonel Blood come from Buckinghamshire (or perhaps from the Duke of Buckingham). (PRO, SP29/293/31–2, and *CSPD 1671*, 496; see 27 December below for AM again in Buckinghamshire)

November

9   (Thursday) Hull: entry for 'money paid to Alderman Acklam: For money he paid to Alderman Duncalfe: for money ... Andrew Marvaile: disburst For Counsell, about the Minister Act and Sir John Listers hospitall' ('for Councell upon the Towns Charter concerning the Grammar Schoole and the Assistant of Trinity Church'): £3 5s. (BRB 5:269; BRF3/23/123; Lawson, 95)

12   Death of Thomas Lord Fairfax, the great parliamentary general and AM's employer in 1650–52.

13   Hull TH pays £1 to send a barrel and some bottles of ale to 'Mr Mai' [= AM?]. (FTH1/5)

23   AM among those for whom barrels of ale ordered by Hull Corporation. (BRB 5:270)

December

7   (Thursday) First performance of *The Rehearsal*, written by the Duke of Buckingham and others; copy was registered with the

Stationers 19 June 1672 and its publication advertised 24 June 1672 (*SR* 1:444; *TC* 1:111).

23   By this date AM has inquired of Benjamin Worsley about Mr Cabell's daughter in Devonshire, secretly under consideration as a possible wife for Philip, fourth Baron Wharton's elder son, Thomas. (Bodl. MS Rawl. letters 50, 123ᵛ)

27   Benjamin Worsley (W) writes to AM at one of the Buckinghamshire houses of Philip, fourth Baron Wharton (Winchendon): in response to AM's inquiry, Worsley fortunately proves to have access to good report about Miss Cabell and encloses letter from his west-country source confirming 'this young Ladyes fortune'. (Bodl. MS Rawl. letters 50, 123–4)

[29   AM (Winchendon) writes to Benjamin Worsley (W) about the proposed match, as acknowledged in Worsley's letter to AM of 2 January 1672 (Bodl. MS Rawl. letters 50, 129ʳ).]

1672

By this date, Sir William Haward transcribes into his great miscellany a version of 'To his Coy Mistress' (Bodl. MS Don.b.8, 283–4; without attribution or title and indexed as 'Poeme amorous'), which seems to have come to him as part of a tranche of earlier material 'the composition of most of which can be dated May 1665 to April 1670'. (Kelliher 1970, 254; compare Hammond 2001)

A likely date of 1672–73 has been proposed for the antiepiscopal 'third stratum' of 'The Loyal Scot' that includes the eight lines of 'Blood and the Crown' (lines 87–235 [or possibly 95–249, in Smith's numbering]; *PL* 1:385–7), but see February 1670 above.

Quarto republication of *The Character of Holland* (1672), again printed for Robert Horn following his earlier folio edition (see 13 June 1665; Barnard). Still not attributed to AM, this single-sheet quarto (t.-p., blank, 1–5, blank) seems unlikely to have been published by him at this date in view of his allegiance now to the Dutch at the time of the Third Anglo-Dutch War. Some time this year the presbyterian Dr William Bate seems to have said that 'Marvell was an Intelligencer to the King of France', according to AM's later letter to Harley, 1 July 1676 (*PL* 2:346). The satire 'Nostradamus Prophecy' of this year is attributed to AM in collections of much later date (1689, 1697): though it seems unlike his loyalties to fault Buckingham for 'sodomy ... the Prime Minister's sport' (Lord, ed., *POAS*, 1:185–9, 459).

January

1   (Monday) Letter from Benjamin Worsley (W) to AM (Winchendon), with more about his own discretion in investigating the prospective Wharton match. (Bodl. MS Rawl. letters 50, 126–7)

2   Letter from Benjamin Worsley (W) to AM (Winchendon), with
           more about the Wharton match, including notice of some rivals
           and his own efforts to promote the cause of Thomas Wharton,
           who is now to meet the young woman in question; no time to
           waste lest this 'great fortune' be lost. (Bodl. MS Rawl. letters 50,
           129–30)

3   AM sends on to Wharton [Wooburn, Bucks.?] the Worsley letter
           of 1 January (presumably on receipt), with brief comment of his
           own. (Bodl. MS Rawl. letters 50, 126ᵛ; *PL* 2:326)
           Letter from Benjamin Worsley (W) to AM (Winchendon), with
           more about the match and rivals to Thomas Wharton. Includes
           separate observation that 'The King hath by one Act of late haz-
           arded all Things that can be hazarded almost in this world'.
           (Bodl. MS Rawl. letters 50, 149–50)

4   AM receives and sends on to Wharton [Wooburn?] the Worsley
           letter of 2 January, with note promising that he will be in
           London the following week to conduct their business. (Bodl. MS
           Rawl. letters 50, 130ʳ; *PL* 2:326)
           [AM (Winchendon) writes to Worsley (Westminster), as AM
           notes to Wharton the next day.]

5   AM (Winchendon) sends on to Wharton [Wooburn?] the
           Worsley letter of 3 January, with note excusing himself for
           not joining Wharton, owing to the visit AM has promised to
           Sir Thomas Lee (at Hartwell House near Aylesbury) that and the
           next day, where there will be some company 'from whom I can
           [not] well be disentangled'. (Bodl. MS Rawl. Letters 50, 149ᵛ;
           PL 2:327)

5–7   AM visits his fellow-MP Sir Thomas Lee at Hartwell House,
           Bucks.: the tolerant Lee shared many of AM's political views,
           'kept a magnificent table at his country house' (Henning:
           Sir Thomas Lee), and had long been admired by AM as 'equal to
           obey or to command' ('Last Instructions', 299).

8   AM presumably visits the Lord Wharton (at Wooburn?), as
           promised in his note to him of 4 January.

ca. 10   AM presumably has returned from Wooburn to London, as
           promised in his note to Wharton of 4 January: 'I shall infallibly
           be at London.'

23   Letter from Benjamin Worsley (W) to Philip, fourth Baron
           Wharton (Winchendon), with more about Thomas Wharton's
           match in prospect, also questioning AM's judgement in seeking
           to dissuade Wharton from helping to release what looks a
           victim of religious persecution (AM already expects 'a generall
           Release of all, that are in Custody or Confinement of this
           kinde'). (Bodl. MS Rawl. letters 50, 132–3)

February
7 (Wednesday) *The History Of the Twelve Caesars, Emperors of Rome. Written in Latine by Caius Suetonius Tranquillus. Newly Translated into English, and Illustrated with all their Heads in Copper Plates* (1672, advertised this day in *TC* 1:96). Printed for John Starkey, this translation in one copy (Bodl. 8vo I 43 Art.) has an apparently early title-page inscription 'By Andr. Marvel'. If it is AM's translation, it seems odd he should have had it to hand only for *RT2* and not *RT* (compare Patterson 2000b; *MWP*, 1:xli). A second edition is published by Starkey in 1677.

March
15 (Friday) Charles II issues Declaration of Indulgence to Roman Catholics and Nonconformists.
17 England declares war against Holland.
28 Death of Frances Jones, who is commemorated in Marvell's tetrameter 'An Epitaph upon ——— ' (1681, 71–2); the memorial is in the crypt of St Martin-in-the-Fields, London. 'She dyed in the prime of her Age, haveing never been marryed', and was the 38-year-old daughter of Arthur Viscount Ranelagh and his wife Lady Ranelagh (Milton's friend), whom the tablet proclaims as 'the Lady KATHERINE BOYLE, who was daughter to RICHARD BOYLE Earl of Corke, and Lord high Tresuror of Ireland'. AM's memorial laments 'this age loose and all unlaced'. (Crypt: south wall of north room, beyond coffee-shop and brass-rubbing centre; Brogan and Donno; Smith 199)

April
13 (Saturday) Hull TH drafts letter to the two MPs AM and Gylby, addressed to 'Mr Marvell's howse in the little Amboy in Westminster' (the Little Armory): 'after a long silence and the matter of the lighthowses as it were wholly laide aside', [Justinian] Angell to whom the land belongs 'hath made some progresse to obteine the erecting of the lights to himselfe' and has many hands along the coast in his favour, in part because only aiming at a farthing a ton duty (NTH52/1). How long AM has been at this Westminster address is unclear: it corresponds to that of Mary Palmer who later claims AM had 'for severall yeares before' 1677 'dwelt with her (in truth as a [*sic*] her husband) though he might be generally lookt upon only as a Lodger at her house' (PRO, C6/241/13). See pp. 95–6 above.
16 Parliament meets only to be prorogued (as by prior proclamation) to 30 October 1672.
18 AM (W) writes to Hull TH in response to its letter of 13 April: in Gylby's absence, AM reports his own view 'that Mr Angells

pretense unlesse he unite with Sir Philip Frowd will prove, as other have formerly, unsuccessful', and so all the more worth cooperating with Angell, whose ownership of the site of Spurnhead is a good basis for progress. (NTH52/1; *PL* 2:270–1)

May

7   (Tuesday) Hull TH drafts letter to AM: he should approach Angell to see how good his title to the Spurnhead site really is and how far it extends; to take a lawyer if he needs. (NTH52/1)

14   AM (W) writes to Hull TH in response to its letter of 7 May: 'I have since been severall times with Mr Angell, and twice at the Rolls' and no need to hire a lawyer 'onely to examine the Records which I have done carefully'; the leases confirm Angell's ownership and, in venturing Hull TH support for his claim, AM has been bargaining with Angell for a better annual allowance out of the prospective lighthouse money for the poor of the Trinity House. (NTH52/1; ATH 1/3 *PL*; 2:271–2)

June

1   (Saturday) Justinian Angell to Hull TH: 'I gave Mr Marvin an account of my title and Butting and Bounding in whitch I Hope those that you apoynted did make noe mistake.' (NTH52/1)

4   Hull TH drafts letter to AM: 'we must still intreate your helpe in the buisines of the Lighthowses'; the challenge is to reconcile the competing interests of Frowd, Angell, and themselves. (NTH52/1)

11   Soon after this date, AM writes to William Popple [Bordeaux]: 'Men talk of a Peace with Holland ... and it is my Opinion it will be before Michaelmass, for some Reasons not fit to write.' International and national news: 'France is potent and subtle.' (Cooke 2:68–9; *PL* 2:327–8)

13   Justinian Angell (London) to Hull TH: has 'beene with Mr Marvin at His Lodging', who has been explaining things to him; Angell now sees the merit of working with Hull TH and Deptford TH against Frowd's interest. 'I have this day Likewise by the perswations of Mr Marvin and upon His account condiscended' on behalf of the poor of Hull TH. (For receiving this and the next letter the Hull TH pays 6d. on 16 June, FTH1/5.)

AM (W) writes to Hull TH in response to its letter of 4 June: Angell still determined to go it alone, based on his ownership of the only land suitable for the lighthouse and his readiness to charge as little as a farthing per ton of shipping, but, owing to the influence of the Hull with the Deptford TH, is ready now to promise 80 rather than 50 pounds per annum for their poor. AM does not wish in such an important matter to

22 AM (W) writes to Hull TH: responds to its letter of 18 June. Describes his separate encounters with Sir Philip Frowd and with Angell and readiness to negotiate with both. (NTH52/1; *PL* 2:273–4; 3d. for receipt of this letter paid 26 June, FTH1/5)

conclude the transaction without consultation. (NTH52/1; *PL* 2:272–3)

24 Advertisement of Samuel Parker's *A Preface Shewing what grounds there are of Fears and Jealousies of Popery*, prefixed to Bishop John Bramhall's *Vindication of himself and the Episcopal Clergy from the Presbyterian Charge of Popery*. (*TC* 1:109)

28 Hull TH drafts response to AM's letter to 22 June on verso of same, authorizing him 'if it take place to conclude with Sir Phillipp upon these heads': that Hull TH gets one third of the profit of the lighthouse, that Frowd seek an act of parliament 'in which act we are not to be named', and so forth. In this way, Frowd to do most of the pushing for the success of the lighthouse, including getting Angell's land for the purpose by act of parliament. (NTH52/1)

July
4 (Thursday) AM (W) writes to Hull TH in response to its letter of 28 June: describes meeting with Frowd and terms under review, reaching a satisfactory compromise although Frowd is 'neither too quick nor over certain even in affairs that tend to his own advantage'. (NTH52/1; *PL* 2:274–5)

8 On second leaf of AM's letter of 4 July, Hull TH drafts letter of further advice about what may be involved in securing such an agreement legally, with the postscript: 'Sir if you thinke of any other way of security on both sides be pleased to intimate it to us.' (NTH52/1)

15 Last will and testament proved of AM's sometime contemporary at Trinity College, Cambridge, Herbert Thorndike (1598–1672), with the epitaph he composes; the document itself seems the source for AM's mocking quotation of it in *RT* (*MPW* 1:14, 154).

August
16 (Friday) Hull TH again pays 3d. for receipt of a letter from AM. (FTH1/5)
Very late this month, Hull TH pays £10 'To Robt Wrights wife for money paid to Mr. Marvell at London'. (FTH1/5)

September
3 (Tuesday) £1.1s.6d. 'given to the Comon Sergeant about Ponder etc.' but apparently with reference to earlier of his infringements of copy rather than the publication of *RT*. (Stats Co. Wardens' Accts)

7   Parker's *Preface* to Bramhall, upon which AM is animadverting
           (see November 1672 below), entered in the Stationers' Register
           (*SR* 2:446).
17   Parliamentary session due to begin 30 October postponed to
           4 February 1673; this may have taken some of the urgency out
           of AM's completion of *RT*.

October
[25   (Friday) Hull TH writes AM, according to his response of
           2 November 1672 (*PL* 2:275).]
29   AM returns to Westminster from an unmentioned location
           (according to his own report to Hull TH, 2 November 1672,
           PL 2:275), presumably with most of *The Rehearsal Transpros'd*
           written.
30   Parliament meets only to be prorogued again to 4 February
           1672/73.

November
Publication of *The Rehearsal Transpros'd* (*RT*). Here AM lengthily opposes
episcopal pretensions and especially the claims of Samuel Parker, chaplain
to Gilbert Sheldon, Archbishop of Canterbury. In the first quarter and last
half of *RT*, AM animadverts Parker's 'Preface' to his edition of *Bishop
Bramhall's Vindication of Himself* (1672); in the second quarter of the work
he addresses Parker's *Discourse of Ecclesiastical Politie* (1670) and its *Defence
and Continuation* (1670) (*MPW* 1:7ff.). AM's gift for mockery attracted a
wide readership for a work that vividly transposes ecclesiological discussion
into a more literary-dramatic idiom: Anthony Wood notes in his almanac
that this year 'People [were] taken with folleries, playes, poems, buffooning
and drolling books; [John Eachard's] "Contempt of the clergy," Marvill's
"Rehearsal transprosed," Butler's "Hudibras"' (Wood, *Life and Times*, 2:240).
Publication seems to have been in November: AM had returned to London
on 29 October and dedicated press-work might well generate five to
six sheets per week per press of this $20\frac{1}{2}$-sheet octavo book (Darby is
running three presses at this date). AM the next year reports that Parker
became 'sick of *the Rehearsal Transpros'd*', 'a new Disease, which spread
much through the Nation about last Autumn'; some remarks in *RT* seem
influenced by the new edition of Davenant, advertised only in mid-
November (*MPW* 1:14, 201, 231) although AM may have consulted it
already in press. Of *RT*, L'Estrange later reports that 'the first Impression
[edition] was distributed' to booksellers before the second edition (see
2 December below) was begun, with a common sheet X linking the first
and second editions; that Ponder in December still held over half the
copies of the first edition is suggested by the proportion of extant copies
with the corrected title-page reflecting censorship of the work (*MPW* 1:23,
27, 29). Printed by John Darby, the first edition is octavo in 164 leaves

(pagination of 326); its first issue is distinguished by the mock-imprint 'LONDON, Printed by A.B. for the Assigns of John Calvin and Theodore Beza, at the sign of the Kings Indulgence, on the South-side of the Lake Lemane. 1672'. Perhaps to safeguard AM, the great nonconformist minister John Owen handles the work in proof. (*MPW* 1:13, 26, 27n, 34–6; compare 11 December, and see 23 and 25 January 1673 below)

2   (Saturday) AM (W) writes to Hull TH in response to its letter of 25 Oct.: with Frowd, it is almost time to be drawing up their agreement regarding the lighthouse and AM believes 'that we shall now shortly come to a good issue'. (NTH52/1; *PL* 2:275)

6   AM among those for whom Hull Corporation orders barrels of ale. (BRB 5:307)

8   In response to AM's of 2 November and on same page, the Hull TH drafts a letter thanking him for his care and vigilance and noting that Frowd has harmed himself by his delays because 'now our late opponent Mr Angell hath layd his printed papers and peticions not onely here in our custome howse but we perceive in other to gett hands and prevailes not a little in that project'. (NTH52/1)

14   AM (W) writes to Hull TH: describes Frowd's confidence about the arrangements in prospect for the lighthouse, owing to 'his businesse being already secured at Court', although AM explains the need for the patent also to pass in parliament (which he thinks probable) without Angell impeding it. (NTH52/1)

17   Anthony Ashley Cooper, Earl of Shaftesbury, is made Lord Chancellor.

27   AM dines at Trinity House, Deptford (see next entry).

28   AM (W) writes to Richard Lyndall (Hull [TH]): Frowd is so slow in business 'that I think any one almost but my selfe would be tired out with it', and in the meanwhile Angell has petitioned the king and 'interessed my Lord Buckhurst and my Lord Hawley in the matter', leading now to inquiries to be made by Trinity House in Deptford. AM has influence with the Deptford TH owing to his opposition to the Act for Dover Pier in the last session of parliament, 'And we have you know besides a very good friend there' (presumably Sir Jeremy Smith). So since he knows that Angell and Lord Buckhurst's agent will be there, AM has dined at that Trinity House, 'having been often invited', where 'a full debate' concludes that that House's previous decision in the matter should stand, to Angell's disgruntlement. (NTH52/1; *PL* 2:276–7)

December

2   (Monday) £1.5s. 'spent on a Search for the Rehearsall transposed [*sic*]' (Stats Co. Wardens' Accts). This raid by Samuel

Mearne seized two sheets of the second edition, now being printed by John Darby for Nathaniel Ponder. Ponder complains of this to his and John Owen's patron Arthur Annesley, Earl of Anglesey, a privy counsellor sympathetic to dissent and likely already a friend to AM; and then Ponder returns to Anglesey with Roger L'Estrange, Surveyor of the Press, who hears from Anglesey that 'the King says <u>he will not have it supprest, for Parker has done him, wrong, and this man has done him Right</u>'. L'Estrange resorts to negotiating changes to *RT* with Anglesey and asking for authorial consent to same, thus further to delay the publication and reveal its author; Anglesey replies 'he could not say any thing of the Author, but that such alterations might be made without him'. Now and/or the next day L'Estrange reads the book and changes or strikes out passages he thinks offensive before agreeing to license it 'for the saving of [Ponder's] Propriety, and not at all to Authorize the Publication of it'. (*MPW* 1:23–9; see below, 23 January 1673)

3   'The day after the raid, the licence [for *RT*] was signed by a warden [of the Stationers' Company] and delivered to the clerk, George Tokefield ... [but] Tokefield refused to make the entry, persisting even after L'Estrange wrote on Ponder's behalf'; nor does Anglesey's letter to the same effect achieve success. (*MPW* 1:24–5, 28, citing House of Lords RO, Committee Book, and see 6 April 1677 below)

11   Letter from Benjamin Woodroffe to Theophilus, seventh Earl of Huntingdon: '... If I knewe how to send to your Lordship I should sometimes interrupt your honours studies with some of the new-bookes which come out. there is at present a booke that I cannot recommend to your Lordship but because every one reades it, 'tis fitt your Lordship should not be ignorant of it, 'tis called the <u>Rehearsall transprosed</u>. it hath beene stopt from spreading, but is againe allowed to be bought.' (Huntington Library, MS HA13634)

The second issue of the first edition of *RT* features an altered title-page in which the imprint reads 'LONDON, Printed in the Year, 1672'; on the title-page of one copy of this issue is written: 'The Preface of this Book, or, Title of it, was altered, within one weeke after It was printed And The following words left out. Printed for the Assignes of John Calvin, And, Theodore Beza, And are to bee sold At the Signe of the Kings last Indulgence.' Further noted: 'It is supposed to bee written, by Mr Marvell, A Countrey Gentleman, and A Great Republican' with the rejoinder, 'In saying he is a great Republican you ar very much mistaken for he is one of this parlaiment and a conformist.' (Folger Library, copy 1 of *RT*, M878B, leaf facing title page)

16   'Ordered, That the Booke or Coppie Intituled the Rehersall Transprosed be not entered in the Register Booke of this Company to Mr Ponder, And that the Clerke to this Company be found harmless and Indempnified in his not entring the same [marg: 'The Rehersall Transprosed not to be entered.']' (Stats Co. Court Book D, 208ᵛ; *MPW* 1:29)

Late   Renewed work on Ponder's second corrected edition of *RT*, an octavo with the addition to the title of 'The second Impression, with Additions and Amendments' and a notice that 'This Book having wrought it self thorow many difficulties, it hath newly incountred with that of a Counterfeit Impression in 12° under the Title and pretence of *the 2d Edition Corrected.* Whereas in truth that Impression is so far from having been Corrected, that it doth grossly and frequently corrupt both the Sence and Words of the Coppy' (A2ᵛ). This refers to the pirated edition in duodecimo printed by John Winter, based on the uncensored first edition. Ponder seeks to protect his own corrected copy, licensed but not entered in the Stationers' register, so he turns to L'Estrange for support, leading to a raid in which sheets of the duodecimo edition are seized by Ponder, Richard Jefferys (L'Estrange's assistant), and John Darby (*MPW* 1:25, 31–2). The other pirated duodecimo edition with a 1673 imprint distinguishes itself as 'The second impression, with Additions and Amendments' – it also follows edition 1 (rather than Winter's pirated version).

[Henry Stubbe,] *Rosemary & Bayes: Or, Animadversions Upon A Treatise Called, The Rehersall Trans-prosed. In a Letter to a Friend in the Countrey* (1672): a notably rapid response in three sheets quarto (t.-p., blank, 1–22), disliking the 'Raillery' of *RT* as much as clerical indecorum, and doubting that concessions to Presbyterian ministers will win over that 'party' (1, 6, 11, 18–19, 22); as Thomas Barlow notes on his copy, 'Mr Henry Stubbe, Physician, formerly of Ch[ris]t-Church [Oxford], writt this, for neither, against both Rosemary [AM] and Bayes [Parker] too' (Bodl. C 9.8(9) Linc., t.-p.).

1673

Samuel Parker now, AM claims in *RT2*, having discovered himself the author of *Preface*, was advised by AM to avoid 'unjust and personal reflections' in any further response to *RT*, to which Parker responded 'That if any Answer were intended, 'twas more then he was acquainted with, or would concern himself about; and assured me, my private reputation, nor no mans else, should ever be injur'd in publick by his consent'. Even so, Parker before, during and after this was marshalling his '*Posse Archidia-*

conatus' of writers against AM and keeping a 'Calumny Office' open for all comers with evil reports of AM. AM claims that 'the License of my Book was recall'd, and the *Rehearsal Transprosed* was dubb'd a Theological Book, only to bring it under the verge of that Jurisdiction, on purpose that it might be prohibited'; moreover, Parker 'procured that I should be asked by good Authority whether the *Rehearsal Transpros'd* were of my doing, which I under my hand avowed'. (*MPW* 1:33, 247–51)

This yeàr, after the parliamentary session, AM sequesters himself in Highgate, five miles north of Westminster (see 3 May, 24 June below). Whether he had done so before is unknown. Kelliher supplies a photograph of the house associated with AM in the mid-nineteenth century, which in 1673 belonged to the London merchant George Pryor (Kelliher 1978a, 87–8). It may well be this summer that AM writes the 'private Letter' Cooke reports, 'written to a Friend from Highgate, in which he mentions the insuperable hatred of his Foes to him, and their Designs of murdering him, he has these Words, *Praeterea magis occidere metuo quam occidi; non quod Vitam tanti aestimem, sed ne imparatus moriar'* (Cooke 1:14; see also Kelliher 1979, 149). AM's translation of 'The Second Chorus from Seneca's Tragedy *Thyestes'* has also been associated with this place of retreat, a translation understood as a reaction to the politics of the 1670s, although a common enough theme and text in this period (Craze 308; Smith 190–1; *PL* 1:275–6). Highgate was on the road north taken by the mails.

Roger Palmer, Earl of Castlemaine, *A Full Answer and Confutation of a Scandalous Pamphlet , Called, A Seasonable Discourse* ([Antwerp], 1673): draws on 'that witty, Masculine and most judicious Author [AM], in his imcomparable [*sic*] *Rehearsal Transpros'd*' (10), from which this Roman Catholic apologist quotes (19) and derives polemical strategy (Dzelzainis, 303–4).

Because AM's masculinity is conspicuously questioned in attacks on *RT*, this year has been suggested as the date for his possibly self-referential 'Upon a Eunuch: a Poet', although it has also been claimed that this Latin epigram 'probably belongs to the period of reflection on the nature of poetry ... in the early 1650s'. (*PL* 1:274; Hammond 1996; Smith 187)

January

2   (Thursday) AM (W) writes Hull TH in response to letter of
         24 December: has consulted with Sir Jeremy Smith about
         arrangements for convoys of Hull shipping (owing to threat
         from privateers in Third Anglo-Dutch War), who has advised
         that it is best that they with other ports similarly affected now
         petition the Duke of York for naval protection. That Frowd's
         hopes are so pleasingly encountering frustration affords hope

that the two Trinity Houses of Deptford and Hull can set up 'those Lights to the advantage of both houses'. (NTH52/1; *PL* 2:277–8; 6d. paid for receipt of the letter and 'a boat to convey', FTH1/5)

6   On verso of AM's letter of 2 January, Hull TH drafts response to AM: Deptford TH has given its support to Angell who thinks he is in the clear, but AM's letter lets Hull TH think otherwise. 'And if an opportunity offer we know your prudence is such you know how to feele theire pulse But in this time of troubles rather then loose too much labour we thinke a delay would be as seasonable.' (NTH52/1)

15   The printer of *RT*, John Darby, is forced by the Stationers 'to take down one of his three presses'. (Stats Co. Court Book D, 210ᵛ)

16   With new session of parliament in the offing, Henry Bennet, Earl of Arlington, pressures the Stationers Company to control the presses: 'Item paid wᵗʰ Warden Roper Mʳ Roycroft to goe to the Lord Arlington about the Printers 000 12 06.' (Stats Co. Wardens' Accts; *MWP* 1:33)

21   Stationers: 16s. 'paid for Coach-hire three times to Whitehall and expences about the Rehearsall transposed'. (Stats Co. Wardens' Accts)
Ponder threatened by Stationers' Company with prosecution for debt and moneys owing from publishing English Stock (profitable books of which the Company had the copyright). (Stats Co. Court Book D, 211ʳ; *MWP* 1:33)
Stationers: 11s. 'paid the Serjeant about Ponder'. (Stats Co. Wardens' Accts)

23   Roger L'Estrange examined by Secretary of State Henry Coventry on the subject of *RT*. L'Estrange testifies to his negotiation with Ponder and Anglesey and the difficulties in licensing *RT* and entering it in the Stationers' Register. (Leicestershire RO, Finch MSS, DG7, Box 4985, Bundle IX, 9/2; published in *HMC 7th Report*, 517b–518a, and *MPW* 1:23–5)

24   Joan Darby, wife of John Darby (Ponder's printer), testifies 'that in December last her husband being Constable went with Mr Lestranges man & Mʳ Ponder to the house of [blank space] Winter a Printer in Cocklane in an Alley neare Sepulchres Church, and there seized upon some sheets of a book called the Rehearsall Transprosed which were printed by the said Printer'. (*MWP* 1:25; Longleat House, Coventry MSS, vol. 11, f. 10; *HMC 4th Report*, App. 234a)

25   Ponder examined about *RT*: he testifies that John Owen was the only one he knows to have had the proofs in his hands; also

that the Lord Chancellor (the Earl of Shaftesbury) and Anglesey 'liked the Book' and that Anglesey reported 'the King was well pleased with it, and found no fault with it'. (*MPW* 1:26; Leicestershire RO, Finch MSS, in *HMC*, vol. 2, p. 10a)

February

4   (Tuesday) Parliament meets in session that lasts until 29 March, when adjourned to 20 October 1673 when prorogued (parliament has effectively been prorogued since 22 April 1671).

7   AM named to committee of elections and privileges. (*CJ* 9:249–50)

A *Common-place-Book Out of the Rehearsal Transpros'd* (1673, advertised *TC* 1:128): cites *Rosemary and Bayes* (as too kind to *RT*) and knows the author of *RT* 'taken up in great and Important Affairs of State: The Parliament may sit in February, and then the Good Old Cause, and The Work of all the Faithful in the Land, require his Counsel in Cabals, and his Speeches in Publick, as the most sufficient States-man and exact Orator that their Party does afford' (A2^r–3^v, 12). Mocks the 'brave Merry Andrew' and his 'Client J.O.' and associates this 'Marcellinus' with the 'blind M. who teaches School about Morefields' (34–6). Outraged by the slurs against Laud in *RT*, this author questions whether it is becoming for 'the Son of a Vicar to prate thus of an Arch-bishop' and compares the still unnamed AM with 'Eutropius the Eunuch ... a busie Solicitor with the Civil Magistracy, to have a Law made against the Priviledges and Power of the Church ... [later] utterly ruin'd by the very same contrivance, which his malice against Ecclesiastical Politie had framed' (44, 56).

13   MPs for ports among those enlisted for committee for bill preventing child-stealing and export. (*CJ* 9:251)

MPs for ports among those enlisted for committee of inquiry into decay of Muscovy, Eastland and Greenland trade. (*CJ* 9:252)

17   AM [W?] writes to Edmond Popple (Hull), in part concerning Hull TH business with a statement from Frowd about his affairs; Hull TH appends a note: 'Sir John Clayton and partners will allow to the trinity howse of deptford strand one halfepenny a tunne and Sir Phill Froud out of his will performe his promise with Mr Marvell.' (Part of letter survives in NTH52/1; *PL* 2:278)

19   John Beale (Yeovil), denouncing the enemies of learning in a letter to Christopher Wase (Oxford), decries 'Marvell, who deservs to be brought on his Knees in that house where he sits; and from thence to be sent to O Cs quarters, since apparently he justifyes that foule cause. And, if the Universityes would

nowe bestirre themselves, as they ought to do, I doubt not, but they might make Mervell an Example, for a terror to others. But common fame doth promise nothing of Spirite, Resolution, or Activity, or yet of Conduct, from such men ...'. (Oxford, Corpus Christi College, MS 332, 22ᵛ–23ʳ; see now Poole 82)

27 AM named to committee for bill confirming John Woolrich's award (from Sir Orlando Bridgman). (*CJ* 9:258)

28 AM named to committee for bill for destroying houses to stop fire. (*CJ* 9:259)

March
Arrest of Abraham Vanden Bemde, a naturalized Dutchman of Yorkshire background and resident of Westminster, who 'useth dayly to walk in Westminster hall, Court of Requests, and is frequently in the Lobby of the house of Commons' lobbying MPs on behalf of the Dutch during the Third Anglo-Dutch War; his 'inviolable Friendship with Mr. Marvell' is later cited by the biographer Thomas Cooke. (PRO, SP29/334/357; Wall 1957; Cooke 1:9)

8 (Saturday) Charles II withdraws Declaration of Indulgence, convinced by the Commons that this is 'the Price of Money' (as AM had at another time put it, *PL* 2:315); that afternoon the Commons goes into a committee of the whole house for the supply bill.
Hull TH drafts letter to Gylby and AM, with emphasis on the importance of Spurn Light among other lighthouses that have been proposed and on the exorbitance of other charges when the Spurn Light the main one needed. (NTH52/1)

10 Yorkshire MPs among those enlisted for committee for bill allowing parliamentary representation to the county and city of Durham. (*CJ* 9:266)

15 With the bookseller James Collins, Samuel Parker registers his own 'A reproofe to the Rehersall Transprosed'. (*SR* 2:457; see 1 May below)

17 Yorkshire MPs among those enlisted for committee for bill against moor-burning in Yorkshire and northern counties. (*CJ* 9:269)
Petition from Hull merchants trading with France about the grievance that the farming of wine duties has led to monopolistic abuses; Hull Corporation orders letter written to Gylby and AM on the subject. York merchants then additionally lend their voices to the petition. (BRB 5:319–21)

24 AM named to committee for bill improving London streets and sewers. (*CJ* 9:274)

29 AM represents Hull Corporation and merchants disgruntled with their postal service to Col. Roger Whitley, deputy

Postmaster General, as reported in letters of this date from Whitley to George Mawson, Hull postmaster, and to the mayor of Hull [Thomas Johnson]; further discussion with AM to follow. (London, Post Office Archives, Post Class 94, item 12, for which see item 13, pp. 94, 350).

Charles II signs Test Act excluding Catholics from office in England. Parliament adjourned.

April

5   (Saturday) AM [W?] to Edmond Popple (Hull [TH]), in response to a letter from the Hull TH: the House should stall in the matter of the lighthouse, and AM furnishes Popple with likely excuses that might be used for that purpose, and "tis good that your letter be writ with such temper as that it may neither approve absolutely nor deny but admit a construction suitable every way to your advantage'. (NTH52/1; *PL* 2:278–9)

7   John Eachard, *A Free and Impartial Inquiry into the Causes of that very great Esteem and Honour that the Nonconforming Preachers are generally in with their Followers* (1673), 33–4: partisan sneer at AM (without quite naming him) notes of Samuel Parker, 'he that could not be disputed and argued out of his assertion, must now be laughed and jested out of it; what the grave Doctor [Owen] could not do, the Jester is set on to Essay ... From sober words it's come to downright raillery' (date from imprimatur).

11   AM is in some part the 'Merry Andrew' satirized in the general character of a town-wit in *The Character of A Coffee-House, with the Symptomes of a Town-wit* (4–6), published 'With Allowance, April 11th· 1673'. (Patterson 1979)

12   After high hopes of success, the negotiation has finally failed of a match between Thomas Wharton and Miss Cabell, ostensibly because the young Wharton's election to parliament leads the widow Mrs Cabell to fear (very rightly) that he will become a courtier and a rake, and she questions the sincerity of his regard for her daughter. (See 23 December 1671–23 January 1672 above; Wharton correspondence, Bodl. MS Rawl. letters 50, especially letters from 8 March to 12 April 1673, 243–74)

22   Letter from Thomas Blount [London] to Anthony Wood [Oxford]: 'Dr Parker assisted by Achard is at the Press against the Rehersal, but I doubt wil not reach him' (endorsement summarizes same). (Oxford, Bodleian, MS Wood F40, 161ʳ; Bongaerts 139, 266–7)

The Earl of Anglesey is elevated to Lord Privy Seal.

28   AM swears to the Test in the next months after this date, when the certificates for swearing the Test are first entered with the

Stationers (*SR* 2:459, 460–1); as he professes early in *RT2*, he is 'come not long since from swearing religiously to own that Supremacy' (*MPW* 1:276).

29   Parliament adjourned until 20 October. Over the next four days AM takes 'a sudden journy' to Stanton Harcourt (Oxfordshire) and back (letter of 3 May to Sir Edward Harley, *PL* 2:328), presumably for a very brief visit to his friend Sir Philip Harcourt.

May

S'too him Bayes (Oxford, 1673): hostile response to the style and argument of *RT*, which cites the neediness of its author while mocking its claims for conscience (63, and passim) and emphasizing its tactic of scorning Parker for not better anticipating the Declaration of Indulgence (44–5). The unnamed author ('of Ox. Will. Burton' according to Wood) remains uneasy about the unnamed author of *RT* and his ill-defined allegiances; for date, see 6 May below (82–3, 98–100; Bodl. MS Wood F40, 164^r).

1   (Thursday) License granted for Samuel Parker, *A Reproof to the Rehearsal Transprosed, in A Discourse to its Authour. By the Authour of the Ecclesiastical Politie* (1673; *RT2*, ed. 1, sig. *1^v; *MPW* 1:218) This lengthy reaction to *RT* renews Parker's earlier assaults on Dissent and on the 'Modern Orthodoxy' espoused by nonconformists and latitudinarian churchmen. It widely denounces AM including a biography of him in some part inferred from references in *RT*, which takes him from his breeding 'among Cabin-boys' to his gambling losses, while noting his having travelled overseas and long loitered 'up and down about Charing-Cross and in Lincolns-Inn-fields', and concluding 'is it not a sad thing that a well-bred and fashionable Gentleman, that has frequented Ordinaries, that has worn Perukes, and Muffs, and Pantaloons, and was once Master of a Watch, that has travell'd abroad [cites Switzerland, Italy, the Vatican] ... that has been employed in Embassies abroad, and acquainted with Intrigues of State at home, that has read Playes, and Histories, and Gazets; that (I say) a Gentleman thus accomplisht and embellisht within and without, and all over, should ever live to that unhappy dotage, as at last to dishonour his grey hairs, and his venerable Age with such childish and impotent endeavours at wit and buffoonry' (*Reproof*, 274–5). On his presentation copy from Parker, Thomas Barlow notes 'The Author of this <u>Reproofe</u> &c. was Dr. <u>Parker</u> Chaplaine to Dr. Sheldon Arch-bishop of Cant: and Arch-Deacon of Cant: And the <u>Rehearsall Transprosed</u> was writt by Mr. Marvill a Parliament-man, and Burgesse for Hull', with further marginalia cold to Parker's style – 'uncharitable

3   and raileing' – and to his argument (Bodl. 8° A.41 Linc.: flyleaves, sig. A2ʳ–4ᵛ, and *passim*, esp. 160–82).

AM (London) writes to Sir Edward Harley (Brampton Castle, near Ludlow): had sought to wait on him 'severall times after we rose but mist you' before himself leaving town. 'I find here at my returne a new booke against the Rehearsall', the insignificant *S'Too him Bayes*. Has seen in press 330 pages of Parker's *Reproof*: 'it is the rudest book ... that ever was publisht .... However I will for mine own private satisfaction forthwith draw up an answer that shall have as much of spirit and solidity in it as my ability will afford & the age we live in will endure.' 'I intend by the end of the next week to betake my selfe some five miles of to injoy the spring & my privacy.' Letters for him to be directed ('till you find that the Posts are cleare') to Richard Thompson in Woolchurch Market, London. (BL, Add. MS 70012, 58–9; *PL* 2:328–9)

6   Letter from Thomas Blount [London] to Anthony Wood [Oxford]: 'Mr Parkers Reproof to the Rehearsal transprosd [marg: '30 sheets'] is every day expected in public, what that wil prove I know not, but your Oxford St'oo him Bays has got but slender reputation here' (endorsement summarizes same). (Oxford, Bodleian, MS Wood F40, 164; Bongaerts 140)

[Samuel Butler,] *The Transproser Rehears'd: or the Fifth Act of Mr. Bayes's Play* (Oxford, 1673; sold in London by Thomas Sawbridge, who advertises it this day, *TC* 1:135; for attribution see von Maltzahn 1995a). Among the responses to *RT*, *The Transproser Rehears'd* stays most with the world of wit and what is internal to it – invention, sense, accuracy of cultural reference, poise – while disparaging the coffee-house world for which it is in some part intended; it also tries much more insistently to bring Milton into the fray. At issue stylistically is AM's having turned against the Church of England the kind of raillery that Butler himself had directed against the canting divines of an earlier generation and to the Presbyterians of this day (13–14); at issue in the argument is that AM has 'divested Princes of an *Unlimited and Uncontroulable Power*, and given it to a more Imperious and Arbitrary Tyrant, Conscience' (110). Without naming AM, Butler plays on the word *marvel* (25, 134, 135) and on AM's familiarity with Milton, in which connection AM is mocked as a lickspittle and sexually deviant; moreover, AM is by 'Nature, or Sinister Accident' not fully a man but perhaps 'a Gelding' (131–4). In addition to their association with Buckingham, Butler and AM may already have been neighbours in Covent Garden, and Butler perhaps knows whereof he speaks when he attributes to AM a mean household 'of a single Man and a Horse' (146).

Advertisement for Samuel Parker, *Reproof to the Rehearsal Transprosed*, and for [Samuel Butler,] *The Transproser Rehears'd*, sold in London by Thomas Sawbridge (*TC* 1:134–5).

15   Advertisement for Parker's *Reproof* in the *London Gazette*, no. 781. (Noted in *RT2*, *MPW* 1:225)

June

16   (Monday) Advertisement for Edmund Hickeringill, *Gregory, Father-Greybeard, with his Vizard off* (1673, *TC* 1:142). Lengthy response to *RT*, which like Parker's *Reproof* inveighs ongoingly against the 'Modern Orthodoxy' of which AM the representative, a Calvinist presbyterianism associated with 'the hypocritical Oliverian Crew' also 'J[ohn].O[wen]. and the confederates' (*passim*, and 48, 134–5, 300). Hickeringill very insistently plays on the word *marvel* (7, 13, 16, 28, 32, 37, etc.) and jokes about 'Merry Andrew' (204, 218), but proposes 'Gregory Greybeard' as a witty moniker for his antagonist (9 and *passim*). He derides the commonplace-book style of *RT* as evincing a schoolboy's 'Thesaurus Poeticus' (168–70, 190) and scoffs at how its author 'often ope's and gapes at Politick Lectures, like an Oyster, against the coming in of the Tide' (173); also reports that author's 'drooping spirits' now in need of a nonconformist church collection to attempt some fresh endeavor (269).

24   AM (Highgate) writes to Hull TH, refers to a preceding letter to Edmond Popple summarizing affairs, and 'that Angells project with the two Lords his Partners is utterly quashd', with thanks owed also to Sir Jeremy Smith. Some caution is needed before the Hull TH proceeds anew with the lighthouse, however, and AM encloses the royal report on that matter (dated 15 May), which he sends belatedly because he has been 'out of Town'. (NTH52/1; *PL* 2:279–80)

July

15   (Tuesday) Letter from Thomas Blount [London] to Anthony Wood [Oxford]: '... Here is ... great searching the Print-houses for Marvels Reply to Parker, but cannot beleeve he wil give it so light a title, as a Whip for the Lambeth Ape, as is reported .... Tis now reported that the Dutch Fleet is out.' (Bodl. MS Wood F40, 166ʳ; Bongaerts 140–1)

August

6   (Wednesday) Letter from Thomas Blount (Orleton) to Sir Edward Harley: 'We were put in hope of Mr Marvels Reply

	[to Parker], but it appeard not whilst I stayd in London.' (BL, Add MS 70012, 80–1; Bongaerts 141–2)
9	AM (W) writes to the Hull TH, in response to its letter of 6 August: although Angell has now speculatively begun building a lighthouse, AM reassures the Hull TH that this proceeds with no support from the Deptford TH, with which it should foster its association. (NTH52/1; *PL* 2:280–81)
14	Hull TH drafts letter to AM in response to his of the 9th: it has written to the Deptford TH but also seeks to learn what he has found out and advises. (NTH52/1)
18	Hull: Gylby and AM paid £17 13s.4d. for their attendance of 53 days at the last session of parliament, 4 February to 29 March inclusive; 'also 16.s viii.d more shalbe paid him [AM] for moneys he hath disbursed in the Towns service, which makes the whole xx.li to be paid to Mr Marvell.' (BRB 5:334)

September

1	(Monday) Henry Ball (Whitehall) to Joseph Williamson (Cologne), newsletter, concerning public opinion inflamed against the French and their miscarriages in [naval] war against the Dutch: 'This does indeed so inflame the people that every Apple Woman makes it a Proverbe, Will you fight like the french? And the Inclosed advice to a Painter ingeniously Writt, and Cryed up extreamly when but touching Gently upon that String, and bought up so fast that I could not gett 2. of them.' Enclosure of 'Advice to a Painter to draw a Duke by' ('Spread a large canvas ...'), attributed to AM in much later collections (1689, 1697), though now accepted as Henry Savile's. (PRO, SP29/337/1ᵛ–2ʳ, and Christie, ed., *Letters Addressed from London to Sir Joseph Williamson*, 2:2; *CSPD* 1673, 524; Lord, ed., *POAS*, 1: 213–19, 463; see 7 July 1679 below)
6	Deptford TH writes to Hull TH about opposing Angell's proposal for Spurn Light: '... Mr Marvell hath beene pleased frequently to Comunicate the Advice received from you on this account and hath promised his care in prefaring the Publique good, before any private persons Interest.' (Deptford TH, Select Entries, 1670–76, 92)
12	Hull TH drafts letter asking AM to forward an enclosed letter to Deptford TH with the request that the lighthouse not be built where Angell is preparing to build it, since his action is a slight to both Trinity Houses. (NTH52/1)

October

20	(Monday) Parliament reconvenes after adjournment, addresses against Duke of York's marriage to Mary of Modena, is pro-

rogued until 27 October. The heavily parodic 'The Lord Chancellour's [Shaftesbury's] Speech to the Parliament. 20th of October 1673' ('I am comanded by his Majestie to acquaint you ...') is only much later associated with AM (1705); its apparent knowledge of the Treaty of Dover may better associate it with Buckingham himself (Beal 1993, 24, 26–7; University of Leeds, Brotherton Collection, MS Lt 55 [Okeover MS], 50–3; Yardley 197–201).

27   Parliament meets in a session that ends with fresh prorogation to 4 November.

November

3   (Monday) Date of letter threatening AM and quoted on the title-page of *RT2*: it was 'left for me at a Friends House' and 'Subscribed J.G. and concluding with these words; If thou darest to Print or Publish any Lie or Libel against Doctor Parker, By the Eternal God I will cut thy Throat.' This may in turn have occasioned AM's letter with a Latin fragment (professing to fear to kill more than to be killed) quoted in Cooke's biography. (Cooke 1:14; *PL* 2:357, 396; see also Kelliher 1979, 149)

4   Parliament prorogued until 7 January 1673/74. These next weeks AM sees *RT2* through the press.

9   Anthony Ashley Cooper, Earl of Shaftesbury, dismissed as Lord Chancellor – 'It is only laying down my gown and putting on my sword', he claims. (Ogg 380)

12   Arrival of Mary of Modena in England, whose marriage to the Duke of York is satirized in 'Advice to a painter to Draw the Duke by' ('Spread a large Canvas ...'; see 1 September above).

13   AM among those to whom Hull Corporation orders barrels of ale sent. (BRB 5:352)

24   In *A Sober Enquiry Into The Nature, Measure, and Principle of Moral Virtue* (1673, advertised this day in *TC* 1:153–4), Robert Ferguson, a nonconformist associate of John Owen, takes up the present ecclesiological quarrel with special reference to Parker's *Ecclesiastical Polity*, its *Defence and Continuation*, and the *Reproof to the Rehearsal Transprosed*, supplying a closely reasoned response to Parker's pretensions and defending AM in passing: 'I do not interest my self in the Transproser's Quarrel, he is able himself, if he think it needful, to give the Reprover due correction for his Folly and Impudence. But suppose that (abating the unhandsome terms, which I am confident when his head is cooler the very Author cannot but condemn) something might be pleaded for his keeness against A.M. being a sacrifice to Revenge rather than Truth, for medling with his Comfortable Importance; yet I cannot imagine upon what Motives he hopes

to justifie his treating J[ohn].O[wen]. with so much Pride.... It is
a new way of securing our selves from Opponents, to over-look
the Cause, and spend our Indignation upon the Person of our
Adversary, and to fetch our Defence from the Dung-Cart and
Oyster-Boats, instead of the Stoa and Academy' (A6ᵛ–A7ʳ).
Raillerie a la Mode Consider'd: Or the Supercilious Detractor ...
(1673, advertised this day in *TC* 1:153; same duodecimo edition
appears with two different t.-p.): a conduct book that warns
against the 'Vitious sort of Buffoonry' now fashionable (3);
among the booksellers has been presented 'with another new
piece, called the *Rehearsal Transpros'd*, &c. a Title I understood
not I confess: But seeing it a thing that had twice troubled the
Press, and having the Booksellers word that it was worth
reading, I took it. But having spent my time and Money upon
it, all I could say was, I found my self very Wittily beguil'd of
both.' But *RT* unedifying: 'Wit there was in it, but like a Jewel in
the Dunghill of Detraction, not worth the Generous and
Ingenious Mans raking for ...' Also cites *The Transproser
Rehears'd* and *Gregory, Father-Greybeard* (30–6).
'William Lloyd, one of the king's chaplains, replying to
Castlemaine['s *Full Answer*], complained of this new way of
writing that "I cannot think our Religion and Laws, our
Liberties and Lives, are so trivial a Prize, as to be carried by a
Mastery in fooling."' (William Lloyd, *A Reasonable Defence of the
Seasonable Discourse* (1674), 46; *MPW* 1:21; *TC* 1:153–4)

December

Publication of *The Rehearsall Transpros'd: The Second Part* ... *by Andrew
Marvell* (*RT2*). Ponder to pre-empt piracy publishes octavo and duodecimo
editions in tandem: the latter features some authorial correction and is
dated 1674 in all known copies but one (which is dated 1673 = BL,
C.115.n.27; *MPW* 1:216–20, though this may reflect the booksellers' habit
of postdating works published near the end of the year). In further controverting Samuel Parker and especially his *Reproof to the Rehearsal Transprosed*,
AM sharpens his *ad hominem* attack while further asserting the importance
of the royal supremacy and impugning clerical ambition. Although the
style recalls that of *RT*, a more sober method and a greater weight of scholarly reference are now trained on his antagonist and his works. AM's
response to the attacks of the *Posse Archidiaconatus* includes some defence
of Milton. (*MPW* 1:208–13, 324–35, 417–19; compare Parkin)

2   (Tuesday) Hull TH orders barrel of ale for AM (ATH 1/3).

20   A copy of the octavo edition of *RT2* comes into the possession
           of a Dr William Grey. Thomas Blount (Orleton) who has eagerly
           awaited the work seems to have read his copy of *RT2* (format
           unknown) by 11 January 1674. (*MPW* 1:209)

1674

Hertfordshire RO, MSS D/EP F.37: 1673 or after, Lady Sarah Cowper's 'The Medley' includes passages from *RT*, with and without attribution to AM (25, 57; compare *MPW* 1:64, 55) and to 'A.M.' is attributed the observation that 'Hee who can write well and yet is of a dul conversation, it's a sign he is not rich himself, but has a good creditt and knows where too take up' (13). The last lines of AM's as yet unpublished 'A Poem upon the Death of his Late Highnesse the Lord Protector' resemble the verses here included under the heading of 'Affliction': 'Small ills to men kind heaven in mercy sends / And shews us that no greater it intends / So watry Rain-Bows that Produce a sho[w]re / Secure us from a deluge any more' (262).

Lady Sarah Cowper seems to have compiled such materials in considerable part with the assistance of Martin Clifford (d. 1677), who was part of the Duke of Buckingham's circle; these Marvellian entries, however, are not included in the Duke of Buckingham's commonplace book from which the Cowper volume draws heavily. In her miscellany 'Poems Collected at Several Times from the year 1670', 'Andrew Merveil' is credited with 'Oh the sad day' (first published in Thomas Flatman, *Poems and Songs*, 1674, 49–50 [volume dates itself 10 April, a5^r]) – however unlikely the attribution, it shows that those not far from AM might think him writing lyric poetry in the Restoration. (Hertfordshire RO, MSS D/EP F.36, p. 90; Harold Love 1997)

An Apology and Advice For some of the Clergy, Who Suffer under False, and Scandalous Reports. Written on Occasion of the Second Part Of the Rehearsal Transpros'd: In a Letter to a Friend: And by Him Publish'd (1674): concedes to his correspondent, who plainly thinks AM has the better of the argument with Parker, only that AM 'hath much the advantage in Reproaching part', in part because clergy need to be above all reproach (2), also because their zeal often attracts a calumny that finds a grateful audience (4); Parker encouraged to self-examination, however, and to stricter duties of holiness (9–10). Attributed to Joseph Glanvill in Collins (8).

AM's success against Samuel Parker cited respectfully by Roger Palmer, Earl of Castlemaine, in *The Catholique Apology with a Reply to the Answer ... By a Person of Honour. The Third Edition much augmented* (1674): sig a3^{r-v} (AM in *RT2* writes 'wittily, and judiciously'), pp. 80 ('ingenious Mr. Mervin'), 152 ('Mr: Marvel (a protestant of so much wit and note)'), 153–4, 437, 470 ('the witty Transproser'), 498–9, 536 (AM named), 590 (*RT* and *RT2* listed). (Dzelzainis 1999, 304–7)

Perhaps ca. mid-1674, John Wilmot, Earl of Rochester, refers to AM in satirizing Samuel Parker in 'Tunbridge Wells':

> Listning I found the Cob of all this Rabble,
> Pert Bays, with his Importance Comfortable:
> He being rais'd to an Archdeaconry
> By trampling on Religion's liberty,
> Was grown too great, and lookt too fatt and Jolly
> To be disturb'd with care, and Melancholly,
> Thô Marvell has enough Expos'd his folly.
> He drank to carry off some old remains
> His lazy dull distemper left in's veins. (lines 69–76)

Although omitted from the first printed version of the poem in *Proteus redivivus* (1675), this passage appears in almost all the manuscript versions of 'Tunbridge Wells' and belatedly in *State-poems* (1697), with republication in later such compilations. In addition to AM's joke about Parker's 'Importance Comfortable', Rochester's allusion to that cleric's 'lazy dull distemper' shows him familiar with at least page 1 of *RT2* (compare *MPW* 1: 223; Rochester, *Works*, ed. Harold Love, 50–1, 373, 377–8, 548–53)

The satire 'On the Statue Erected by Sir Robert Viner', perhaps from this year, is dubiously attributed to AM only by Edward Thompson (1776) and then later editors, owing to its presence in Bodl. MS Eng. poet. d. 49, 250–51b, and its likely resemblance to his views. (Lord, ed., *POAS*, 1:266–9; Smith 413–5)

January

7   (Wednesday) Parliament meets in session that lasts until prorogation 24 February 1673/4. A major issue is war and peace with Holland: the Dutch now have 'daily expresses from the principall Parliament men' (PRO, SP105/222/122ʳ, 4/14 May 1674) with AM later reported as having visited Holland during this session for consultation with William of Orange (see 5/15 May below).

11   Thomas Blount (Orleton) to Anthony Wood (Oxford): 'what say your Academics to Reh. Transpr[ose]d 2d Pt, is it not bold?' (Bodl. MS Wood F40, 178ʳ; Bongaerts 145)

14   Hull TH sends AM a barrel of ale, at a total cost of ca. £1 5s.7d. (FTH1/5)

15–20   Impeachment of the Earl of Arlington begins. [AM writes to constituency (cited in his letter of 24 January, not otherwise known).]

24   LHC: AM (W) sends parliamentary news, and proposed terms of the peace with Holland. (Pierpont Morgan Library, LHMS, Misc. English; *PL* 2:141–2)

29   Hull: 'The Letter of Andrew Marvell Esqr, One of the Burgesses of this Town in Parliament dated the 24 of January 1673 is putt into the hands of Alderman George Acklam, and he is entreated to desire the Wardens of the Trinity-house to call a house to

advice Whether if an Act of Parliament for the continuance of 3s Imposicon upon a Chaldron of Coales to be paid by the Shipps delivering the Coales at London, may be a prejudice to this Port or no: And to desire their Answer thereupon with their reasons, if they think fitt, the said Act should be imposed.' A letter is written to AM about same, an undated copy of which remains in the Corporation records: as well as the business of the coals, under review with the Hull TH, warm thanks for 'your continuall watchfullnesse and observance of all occurrents that either may tend to the benefitt or disadvantage of this place and giving us tymely notice thereof'. (BRB 5:359; BRL 674)

30   AM is excoriated in 'A Love Letter to the Author of the Rehearsall Transpos'd These – To his ever drolling Friend, The mery Gentleman that penn'd The Non Pariello for a Treatise Call'd the Transpos'd Rehearsall at his Dwelling in Hull', with dark reflections on his character and sexuality. 'The Royal Society text concludes with a paragraph in which the writer says that he has just heard of the publication of Part II, though he has not yet read it, and the satire is dated 30 Jan. 1674 ... It is possible that the poem was composed earlier in 1673, and the final lines added when Part II appeared.' (Commonplace book of George Ent, London, Royal Society, MS 32, 41–54; Hammond 2002, 198)

31   AM named to committee of examination into an attempt to corrupt an MP. (*CJ* 9:301)

February

3   (Tuesday) Yorkshire MPs among those enlisted for committee for bill against moor-burning in Yorkshire and northern counties. (*CJ* 9:302)

       AM among those appointed to prepare reasons for a conference with the Lords ('for the only time in his parliamentary career'), this about address for peace with Holland. (*CJ* 9:302; Henning sv Marvell; compare *Journal of the House of Lords* 12:625–6)

9/19   Treaty of Westminster, end of English part in Dutch war.

13   Yorkshire MPs among those enlisted for committee for bill establishing Sir Samuel Morland's water-engines. (*CJ* 9:308)

       AM named to committee for bill settling judges' patents. (*CJ* 9:308)

14   AM named to committee preparing a bill against abuses in the collection of aulnage duty. (*CJ* 9:309)

18   AM named to committee for bill for better collection of hearth-money. (*CJ* 9:311)

24   Parliament prorogued until 10 November.

March

10   (Tuesday) AM (W) writes Philip, fourth Baron Wharton, concerning the courtship of his second son Goodwin Wharton. (Bodleian MS Rawl. letters 51, 218; von Maltzahn 2003)

19   AM (W) writes Hull TH regarding payment of fee as retainer to Sir William Jones, with commendation of his counsel. (NTH52/1; *PL* 2:281–2;)

April

This month AM composes 'On Paradise Lost', published in the second edition of *Paradise Lost* (1674) and in *1681*. AM makes reference to Dryden's swift adaptation of *Paradise Lost*, licensed this month; in view of AM's impending departure for Hull in May, he seems unlikely to have left the commendatory poem too late. The Latin commendatory poem preceding this is by the royal doctor, Samuel Barrow, who had been AM's contemporary at Trinity College, Cambridge (Admissions and Admonitions, 1560–1759, 266, 268; von Maltzahn 1995b). Many later editions of *Paradise Lost* will include AM's poem, starting again with the 7th edition (1705) and on into the many post-Tonson editions of 1751–.

17   (Friday) Henry Herringman's entry with the Stationers of 'Theophilus Thorowthistle', *Sober Reflections, Or, A Solid Confutation of Mr. Andrew Marvel's Works, In a Letter Ab Ignoto ad Ignotum* (1674): brief tract facetiously faulting 'Merry Andrew' (9) for the raillery of *The Rehearsal Transpros'd* and mocking his readership; shows a familiarity also with *RT2* (t.-p., 7). AM is 'neither Flesh nor Fish, nor good Red-herring' but of 'Amphibious valour' (5). On the same day Herringman also enters John Dryden's 'Fall of Angells', which operatic version of *Paradise Lost* AM satirizes in 'On *Paradise Lost*'. (*SR* 2:479)

21   Hull TH drafts letter to AM: now that Angell presents a *fait accompli*, there is widening assent to it, but his choice of location is bad, whereas 'we shall finde a more fitting place and not exclude Mr Angell if they [Deptford TH] thinke fitt to take him in'. Edmond Popple appends: 'Deare Brother I have putt the howse upon this letter to you supposeing by yours and Mr Nelthorps to day that you are not come out [from London to Hull] and the busines of great consequence.' (NTH52/1)

25   Richard Lyndall (London) to Edmond Popple (Hull TH): Lyndall 'wente to Westminster early and Found Mr Marvell in his chamber and presented your letter to him and desired as from you his advise and assistance in the bussinesse' of the Spurn Light, with AM urging caution in the matter. 'I told him which also he knew that Sir Jeri Smith was att Chattam payinge some shipps of and that it would be towards the latter end of next weeke before he came home ... but when he comes home

26   AM (W) writes to Hull TH: the Deptford TH has confirmed its earlier opinion on the Spurn lighthouse 'against Angels whole designe', but will not venture any positive recommendation 'for some considerable time.' (NTH52/1; *PL* 2:283–4)

AM among those signing off on November moneys disbursed, Deptford TH Cash Book.

December

1   (Tuesday) AM (W) writes to Sir Henry Thompson (Escrick, c/o Edward Thompson, York), with national news and the continuing nuisance of Sir John Hewley. A note on the letter indicates that AM was 'att Capt Mills house in the Little Armory. Westm''. (BL, Add. MS 70949, 1–2; *PL* 2:333–4, 388)

4   Hull TH drafts letter to AM in response to his of 26 November. It sees the advantage of the new sand as a reason for pushing Spurn Light, but does not wish to retreat from its position against Angell. (Hull TH, NTH52/1)

12   AM (W) writes to Hull TH in response to its letter of 4 December: although 'It is indeed great pity' that such a charitable society not devote its every resource to the poor, it is best not to insist on that but instead to write again to the Deptford TH to promote their correspondence; moreover, 'Our House [Deptford TH] will not be wanting to oppose the passing [Angell's] patent.' (NTH52/1; *PL* 2:284)

        Hull TH sends AM a barrel of ale, among others thus favoured in London. (FTH1/5; ATH 1/3) [Letter from Sir Henry Thompson to AM, cited in AM's response of the 19th.]

15   AM (W) writes to Edward Thompson (York) explaining he has still not addressed Sir John Hewley about the contested election: 'I dare not entreat you to excuse me to Sir Henry. Time will wear out offences that are not malicious especialy with one of his candor.' Politics in London, with an eye on the gathering of bishops who have, however, 'not yet calved'. (Hull University Archives, DDFA39/27; *PL* 2:334)

19   AM (W) writes to Sir Henry Thompson (Escrick, c/o Edward Thompson, York), with more about Hewley, where he has again been diffident, but since he knows Hewley's solicitors – 'Hartlib [jr.] is a man of some ingenuity and Rushworth I thinke of much honesty: the first my acquaintance but this my Friend' – he will discuss it in person with Rushworth. 'Forain news' (France) as well as 'things at home' (about the bishops and the court). (University of Manchester, Rylands English MS 347/200; *PL* 2:335–6)

AM among those signing off on December moneys disbursed, Deptford TH Cash Book.

Soon after the 18 December presentation to Charles II of the freedom of the City of London appears the satire 'Upon his Majesty's being made Free of the City', which laments the city's enslavement to a profligate King and a dangerous Duke of York. Lord gives credence to its very dubious attribution to AM in the 1697 *POAS*, in part because of the poem's resemblance to 'The History of Insipids' which he also finds Marvellian. (Lord, ed., *POAS*, 1:237–42)

In manuscripts of a verse satire attacking the Commons' opposition to court policies, AM 'who yet wears his ears' is excoriated among other MPs (first published in 1697 as 'A Charge to the Grand Inquest of England, 1674' although this print version changes 'Marvell' to 'S——' – here too Milton's name will be suppressed). (Lord, ed., POAS 1:220–27, 222, 464)

1675

Oxford, Bodleian Library, MS Sancroft 146, Sancroft 'A Catalogue of my Bookes'. Under 'M', 'A. Marvells Rehearsall (8°) transprosed. 2 pts. 1672/73'.

The satire 'Britannia and Raleigh' likely from the first months of this year is attributed to AM in much later collections (1689, 1697; BL, Add. MSS 7315, 7317), though sufficiently unlike his note and like that of John Ayloffe to merit Thompson and Lord's later reattribution of it to the latter. (Lord, ed., *POAS*, 1:228–36, 464–5).

The longer version of 'A Dialogue between Thyrsis and Dorinda', set to music by Matthew Locke, published in John Playford, *Choice Ayres* (1675), 80–4. Thus republished now with attribution to AM in *The Bee*, 3 vols (1715), 3:21–3.

January

21   (Thursday) AM sits on the board of Deptford TH. (Court Minutes, 1670–76, 152)

28   AM sits on the board of Deptford TH. (Court Minutes, 1670–76, 154)

ca. 28 AM [W] writes to Sir Henry Thompson (Escrick, c/o Edward Thompson, York), again about Sir John Hewley, now with news of the indebted Samuel Hartlib [jr] hastening to Holland and of John Rushworth's assistance; news of the court and politics, and ongoing interest in the bishops' extended consultation with the Lord Keeper [Heneage Finch], Danby and Lauderdale (date from postmark). (Photograph: Bodl. facs. d. 119, 139–40; *PL* 2:337–8)

AM among those signing off on January moneys disbursed, Deptford TH Cash Book.

February

1   (Monday) 'Andr: Marvell' signs with 'JeSmyth' and others a letter from the Deptford to the Hull TH asking its judgement on the enclosed proposals of Sir John Clayton for north coast lighthouses; also signs two other Deptford TH letters this day. (NTH52/1; *PL* 2:374; Deptford TH, Select Entries, 1670–76, 149–51)

4   AM [W] to Sir Henry Thompson (Escrick, c/o Edward Thompson, York), excusing himself to Thompson by complaining that Mr [Robert] Steward, an associate of AM's nephew William Popple, has used AM's name in a way that leaves him awkwardly implicated in differences over the wine trade; also brief political news. (Yale, Beinecke Library, MS Osborn files, 9987; *PL* 2:339–40)

6   LHC: AM (W) sends thanks for letter and barrel of ale; political business in brief. (*PL* 2:144)

11   AM sits on the board of Deptford TH. (Court Minutes, 1670–76, 157)

18   AM sits on the board of Deptford TH. (Court Minutes, 1670–76, 159)

     Aldermen William Foxley and William Skinner (London) write to Hull Corporation: have met with AM at James Shaw's office in Gray's Inn who is ready to take the Clipsham brief. They also note that 'Sir J[eremy] Smith and Mr Marvell, havinge good acquaintance with Sir John King, one of Majesties Councell', they go to him, 'Mr Marvell havinge contracted the substance of the two letters into a narrow compasse, made knowne to him the occasion'. To attend Sir John King the Monday evening next (22 February) – 'A letter gratulatorie to Sir J: Smith, and Mr. Marvell, for theire so readie assistance, cannot be Amisse.' (BRL 842)

25   AM sits on the board of Deptford TH. (Court Minutes, 1670–76, 160)

Late this month appears 'A pretended Libellous Speech prepared for his Matie. in February. 1674/5. to be spoken to boeth Houses att the meeting of the Parliament on the 13th. of Aprill following', a witty parody of Charles II's style in speeches from the throne: 'My Lords and Gentlemen / I told you last meeting the Winter was the fittest time for business, and truly I thought so till my Lord Treasurer assur'd me that the Spring was the best season for sallads, and Subsidy's ...' Here he advises parliament that 'The Nation hates you already, for having given soe much [taxation to the crown], and I shall hate you now, if you doe not give mee more: Soe if you doe not sticke to mee, you will not have a freind left in England'; he insouciantly if implausibly also professes his 'Zeale for the Church of England'

(Bodl. MS Don. b.8, 499–501; *MPW* 1:460–4; also satirized here is the Lord Treasurer Danby, whose copy is BL, MS Egerton 3345, 21ʳ–22ʳ). Extant in many manuscripts (Beal 1993, 66–7), 'The King's Speech' only finds attribution to AM when first printed 30 years later and then amidst a proliferation of dubious attributions (*POAS* 1704; Cooke 2:38–43 [2nd pag.]). The parody's quality is such as would make one wish it AM's.

March

1   (Monday) Girolamo Alberti, Venetian Secretary in England, to the Doge and Senate: 'A mock discourse is circulating in the squares which purports to be the king's speech at the next session of parliament giving the mob ideas most prejudicial to the Court. The lads who hawk about the streets the order in Council and the proclamation have the audacity to shout "Declaration of his Majesty for sweetmeats for the parliament." … The more [Charles II] protests against the nonconformists and maltreats them, the less is the country pleased, declaring that the acts of severity are all feigned and a piece of statecraft devised by the ministers now in favour. Lauderdale and the treasurer [Danby], alarmed by this popular outcry, are seeking to gain the confederate peers over to their side, promising them to deceive the bishops and persuade them to consent to the fusion with the Presbyterians.' (*Calendar of State Papers, Venetian, 1673–75*, 366)

4   AM sits on the board of Deptford TH; he is chosen and sworn deputy assistant for Sir Thomas Allen. (Court Minutes, 1670–76, 163)

6   AM named among the commissioners for recusants in Yorkshire East Riding, empowered with any other two or more of them 'to take and seize into His Majesty's hands two third part of all the lands, tenements, hereditaments, leases and farms of the Recusants …'. (*Calendar of Treasury Books, 1672–1675*, 694–5)

8   AM sits on the board of Deptford TH. (Court Minutes, 1670–76, 164)

          AM's style in controversy expansively followed by the nonconformist minister Vincent Alsop in *Anti-Sozzo* (1675), his response to William Sherlock, including reference to 'comfortable Importance' (212) but also wit *passim* (publication date from Thomas Barlow, Bodl. 8° C470 Linc., flyleaf). The 1676 reissue appends an advertisement of books sold by Nathaniel Ponder including *RT* and *RT2* (under 'Large Octavo's'), both named as AM's.

9   Letter from the presbyterian T[homas?] J[acomb?] [London] to Sir Edward Harley, postscript: 'Mr. Marvell desires to be remembred to you.' (Calendared in *HMC, Portland, III*, 349)

18	AM sits on the board of Deptford TH. (Court Minutes, 1670–76, 165) 'Andr: Marvell' among the signatures on letter from the Deptford to the Hull TH with thanks for advice about lighthouses. (NTH52/1; *PL* 2:374)
25	AM sits on the board of Deptford TH. (Court Minutes, 1670–76, 167)

April

1	(Thursday) AM sits on the board of Deptford TH and signs its letters sent that day. (Court Minutes, 1670–76, 169; Select Entries, 1670–76, 201–4, 232–3)
8	AM sits on the board of Deptford TH. (Court Minutes, 1670–76, 170)
13	Parliament meets in session that lasts until prorogation 9 June. LHC: AM (W) sends parliamentary news at the beginning of the session, including report of King's speech of which he will send a full copy when printed (compare February / 1 March above). (*PL* 2:144–5)
15	LHC: AM (W) sends parliamentary news. (*PL* 2:145–6)
17	LHC: AM (W) sends parliamentary news. (*PL* 2:146–7)
19	MPs from ports enlisted for committee for bill preventing export of wool. (*CJ* 9:319)
20	LHC: AM (W) sends parliamentary news. (*PL* 2:147)
22	AM a teller with Sir Nicholas Carew for the successful Yeas (88, vs 74 Noes) for a second reading of a bill preventing MPs from taking public offices. (*CJ* 9:321) LHC: AM [W] sends parliamentary news, including the wording of the Test for which the bill from the Lords not yet committed. (*PL* 2:148–9)
23	AM named to committee for bill for better preservation of fishing in the Avon, Severn, and Tame. (*CJ* 9:322)
24	LHC: AM [W] sends parliamentary news centring in the examination of the Duke of Lauderdale. Evil report of Sir Robert Viner (at this date the mayor of London involved in animosities in city council with AM's relations, the bankers Thompson and Nelthorpe). (*PL* 2:149–50; Tupper 368–9)
26	AM sits on the board of Deptford TH. (Court Minutes, 1670–76, 173)
27	LHC: AM [W] sends brief parliamentary news covering enclosure. (*PL* 2:150–1)
29	LHC: AM [W] sends parliamentary news. (*PL* 2:151)

AM among those signing off on April moneys disbursed, Deptford TH Cash Book.

May

1   (Saturday) LHC: AM [W] sends parliamentary news. (*PL* 2:152)

3   AM sits on the board of Deptford TH. (Court Minutes, 1670–76, 176)

4   LHC: AM [W] sends parliamentary news in brief, writing ca. 10 pm. (*PL* 2:152)

6   LHC: AM [W], 'having writ to you every Post since the Parliaments meeting', sends more parliamentary news. (*PL* 2:153)

7   AM the first MP named to committee for bill suppressing of pedlars, hawkers and petty chapmen. (*CJ* 9:332)

8   AM named to committee for bill naturalizing Theodore Russell and others. (*CJ* 9:333)

        LHC: AM (W) sends parliamentary news (*PL* 2:153–4). Gylby writes too that both he and AM on the committee for bill suppressing pedlars and the like, 'which some of your Corporation has inform'd us, is very much to their prejudice'. (BRL 849)

11   LHC: AM (W) sends parliamentary news. (*PL* 2:154–5)

13   AM sits on the board of Deptford TH. (Court Minutes, 1670–76, 178)

        LHC: AM [W] sends parliamentary news, acknowledgement of letters. (*PL* 2:155–6)

15   LHC: AM [W] sends parliamentary news; beginnings of contest between Commons and Lords over Shirley vs Fagg. (*PL* 2:156)

18   AM was to have supplied the biography of Milton eventually supplied instead by Cyriack Skinner, according to letter from John Aubrey (London) to Anthony Wood (Oxford): 'Mr Marvell has promisd me to write <u>minutes</u> for you of Mr Jo: Milton who lyes buryed in St Giles Cripplegate ch: —— I shall tell you where.' (Bodl. MS Wood F39, 296ʳ)

        LHC: AM (W) sends parliamentary news. (*PL* 2:156–7)

19   AM added to committee for bill settling Kellshall (Suffolk) charities. (*CJ* 9:341)

20   Yorkshire MPs among those enlisted for committee for bill preventing moor-burning in several northern counties. (*CJ* 9:342)

        LHC: AM [W] sends parliamentary news. (*PL* 2:157–8)

22   LHC: AM (W) sends parliamentary news; 'It is expected now daily to heare of some great Action of the French king in Flanders.' (*PL* 2:158)

27   LHC: AM [W] sends parliamentary news, as contest between the houses of parliament continues. (*PL* 2:158–9)

29   LHC: AM [W] sends parliamentary news, with enclosure of what may be a counterfeit letter, mysterious to AM, about the Spurn Light and thus of concern to Hull. (*PL* 2:159)

AM among those signing off on May moneys disbursed, Deptford TH Cash Book.

June

1   (Tuesday) AM named to committee for bill enabling Charles Cotten to settle his estate. (*CJ* 9:349)

        LHC: AM [W] sends parliamentary news. (*PL* 2:160)

3   Yorkshire MPs among those added to committee for bill abolishing the writ *de haeretico comburendo* (for burning heretics). (*CJ* 9:352)

        Deptford TH (with AM not present) determines to 'Attend Mr Secretary Pepys and Mr Marvill about the letter wherein the [Corton Lights] Report is to bee inclosed'; also reads again reads [George] Trewman's 'letter of 31 May Concerning Angell light that they are kindled', with decision to 'acquaint Mr Secretary Pepys and Mr Marvill of it'. (Court Minutes, 1670–76, 184)

        LHC: AM [W] sends parliamentary news; has sent 'a Catalogue of the publick Bills in our House ... Twere great damage should they all miscarry by the present differences'. (*PL* 2:161)

5   LHC: AM [W] sends parliamentary news. (*PL* 2:161–2)

8   LHC: AM (W) sends parliamentary news in brief. (*Works of Andrew Marvell*, ed. Thompson, 1:246–7; *PL* 2:162)

9   Parliament prorogued until 13 October, this just as Herbert Croft's *The Naked Truth* 'was delivering out' in an edition of 400 copies for MPs. (*Mr Smirke*, in *MPW* 2:50–1)

10   LHC: AM (W) sends brief note: 'I thinke it unnecessary and indecent to give you any other account of the Prorogation of the Parliament then what you will find in his Majestyes Speech, yesterday, here inclosed.' (*PL* 2:163)

17   AM sits on the board of Deptford TH. (Court Minutes, 1670–76, 185)

21   Hull TH [Edmond Popple]: 'Sent per Peter Thompson to my brother Marvell one salmon 4s.8d. / Paid for vinegar salt tub and carrying aboard etc.' 3s.10d. (FTH1/5)

22   AM sits on the board of Deptford TH. (Court Minutes, 1670–76, 187)

AM among those signing off on June moneys disbursed, Deptford TH Cash Book.

July

The satire 'The Statue at Charing Cross', perhaps from this month, is attributed to AM only belatedly (only the table of contents in *POAS*, 1698, A4ʳ), and then by Edward Thompson (1776) and modern editors owing to its presence in Bodl. MS Eng. poet. d. 49, 255–7, and its resemblance to the

views he expresses in his letter this month to William Popple (24 July).
(Lord, ed., *POAS*, 1:270–3; Smith 416–7)

6   (Tuesday) AM [W?] writes to Sir Henry Thompson (Escrick, c/o Postmaster, York), glad of safe return of King from a rough crossing of the Channel, and with news illustrative of the French ingratitude for English military support. (Maggs Sale Catalogues 445 (no. 2704) and 451 (no. 1190); *PL* 2:340)

15   AM sits on the board of Deptford TH. (Court Minutes, 1670–76, 189)

[17   Letter from William Popple [Bordeaux] to AM, cited in AM's letter of the 24 July.]

24   AM (Highgate) writes to William Popple [Bordeaux]: 'Being resolved now to sequester my self one whole Day at Highgate, I shall write four whole Sides if my Spirit will hold out.) in Answer to your kind Letter ...' Parliamentary news. 'Dear Will, present my kind Love and Service to your Wife. O when will you have arrived at what is necessary?' Satisfaction at the death of the persecuting Strangways, 'a flagrant Churchman'. (Cooke 2:44–9; *PL* 2:341–3)

[31   Hull Corporation writes AM, cited in AM's response, 14 August.]
AM among those signing off on July moneys disbursed, Deptford TH Cash Book.

August

10   (Tuesday) AM sits on the board of Deptford TH. (Court Minutes, 1670–76, 195)

14   LHC: AM (W) reports business of Spurn Light in response to the Corporation's letter of 31 July (received 11 August), insists on his loyal service and the advantage in advising Sir Jeremy Smith of their determination. (NTH52/1; *PL* 2:163–4)

17   AM sits on the board of Deptford TH; meeting devoted to Spurn Light. (Court Minutes, 1670–76, 196)

19   Hull Corporation reads AM's letter (14 August) about Spurnhead lighthouses; mayor to discuss matter with Sir Jeremy Smith 'as Mr Marvell directs'. Group to go see Smith and AM then to be sent a reply. (BRB 5:434)

21   AM sits on the board of Deptford TH. Spurn Light still the question: AM observes 'that Sir Jeremy Smith was daly expected up whoe will take Cognizance of the said lights and geive more fuller account thereof'. (In the next days the Deptford TH determines that the lights there of use only to locals and otherwise dangerous, but there is much more of this matter in the weeks and months to come.) (Court Minutes, 1670–76, 197)

23   Hull Corporation drafts letter to AM in response to his of the 14 August: Sir Jeremy Smith 'hath informed us, that you are a member for the Trinity-house at Detford and therefore inca-

pable to sollicit in this business, as we desired. till the Trinity-house at Detford be better satisfyed ...' (BRB 5:434)

25   AM sits on the board of Deptford TH. (Court Minutes, 1670–76, 200)

27   Performance of Thomas Duffet, *Psyche Debauch'd* (printed 1678): in this travesty of Shadwell's *Psyche*, the disreputable Bruin sings of 'My Importance comfortable' in praising his princess-mistress None-so-fair. (Act IV, sc. ii, p. 60; date in Van Lennep 235)

29   AM sits on the board of Deptford TH. (Court Minutes, 1670–76, 202)

AM among those signing off on August moneys disbursed, Deptford TH Cash Book.

September
6   (Monday) AM sits on the board of Deptford TH. (Court Minutes, 1670–76, 205)

8   AM sits on the board of Deptford TH. (Court Minutes, 1670–76, 206)

AM among those signing off on September moneys disbursed, Deptford TH Cash Book.

October
12   (Tuesday) AM sits on the board of Deptford TH. (Court Minutes, 1670–76, 212)

13   Parliament meets until prorogued 22 November.

16   LHC: AM (W) sends King's and Lord Keeper's speeches at the beginning of the session of parliament, with the briefest of cover-notes. (*PL* 2:164)

18   MPs for out-ports among those enlisted for committee considering trade with France. (*CJ* 9:359)

        AM sits on the board of Deptford TH. (Court Minutes, 1670–76, 214)

        AM (W) writes to his 'much honoured friend Sr William Petty' [London], wishing him success in the new Irish 'Farm' (a colonial venture) and recommending one Joseph Watson and his brother (who bring this letter) for Petty's employment in Ireland. AM signs himself as 'being of a long date, Sir, Your most humble Servant'. (BL, Add. MS 72850, 145; Beal 1993, 20)

        Hull: AM and Gylby paid £19 13s.4d. each for 59 days at last session of parliament. (BRB 5:443; BRF3/24/35ʳ; BRF3/25/9ʳ)

19   LHC: AM [W] sends parliamentary news, including vote against supplying the king. (*PL* 2:164–5)

21   LHC: AM [W] sends parliamentary news, including bills 'To Prevent the growth of Popery' and 'That the children of the

Royal family should be educated in the Protestant Religion and no Popish Priest to come neare them'. Asks for their discretion with his letters, since 'the times are something criticall beside that I am naturally and now more by my Age inclined to keep my thoughts private'. (*PL* 2:165–6)

23   AM named to committee for bill preventing Roman Catholics from sitting in either House of Parliament. (*CJ* 9:362–3)

LHC: AM [W] sends parliamentary news, including ships to be built but perhaps of too large construction for Hull port. (*PL* 2:166–7)

25   Hull Corporation records: 'A Letter is this day written to Mr Marvell, to Certify him, that there was no such letter written to Captain Cressett, as Mr Marvell Letter expresses.' (BRB 5:446)

26   LHC: AM [W] sends parliamentary news and asks whether Hull might build one or two ships of the third rate. (*PL* 2:167–8)

November
Creditors begin run on the London bank of Richard Thompson and Edward Nelthorpe, AM's relations. (Tupper 369 citing *Case of Richard Thompson*, 5–6; Wall 1959)

2   (Tuesday) LHC: AM (W) sends parliamentary news in brief, centring in ships to be built. (*PL* 2:168)

3   AM named to committee for bill settling Leonard Robinson's estate (Kirby Hall, Yorks.). (*CJ* 9:366)

Attends the failing Sir Jeremy Smith, who dies 11 p.m. (*PL* 2:169)

4   LHC: AM [W] reports death of Sir Jeremy Smith, friend to Hull and to AM. AM grateful for the warmth of their support; having checked on the unwanted circulation of his correspondence, concludes 'there is some sentinell set both upon you and me'. Parliamentary news. (*PL* 2:169–70)

6   LHC: AM (W) sends brief parliamentary news. (*PL* 2:171)

8   AM named to committee for bill for making the River Darwent (Derbyshire) navigable. (*CJ* 9:368)

9   AM named to committee for bill preventing wool exports and for petition complaining of the East India Company. (*CJ* 9:371)

LHC: AM (W) sends parliamentary news. Also 'There being a late printed book containing a narrative of the Test carryed on in the Lords house last session, they yesterday voted it a Libell: and to be burnt by the hands of the Hangman and to inquire out the Printer and Author.' (*PL* 2:171–2)

10   AM named to committee examining instructions for the excise and hearth tax. (*CJ* 9:372)

11   AM named to committee for bill preventing pedlars, hawkers and petty chapmen. (*CJ* 9:373)

LHC: AM (W) sends parliamentary news in brief. (*PL* 2:172)

15 Yorkshire MPs among those enlisted for committee for bill preventing moor-burning in several counties. (*CJ* 9:376)

AM attends the corpse of Sir Jeremy Smith as it is conveyed out of London for burial on 20 November in Hemingbrough, East Yorks. (on the Ouse near Selby).

16 AM named to committee for bill naturalizing Jacob David and others. (*CJ* 9:377)

LHC: AM [W] writes 'I am run something in arreare to you by reason of the long sittings of the House together with some avocation I have had by business relating to Sir Jeremyes estate and his funerall'; sends fuller parliamentary news now. (*PL* 2:173–4)

18 LHC: AM [W] sends parliamentary news. (*PL* 2:174–5)

20 Yorkshire MPs among those enlisted for bills preventing theft and rapine on the northern borders and for draining Lindsey Level. (*CJ* 9:381)

LHC: AM (W) sends parliamentary news, including Commons' attempt to have public bills passed before returning to the contention with Lords over Shirley vs Fagg; Lords moving toward addressing for a prorogation. (*PL* 2:175–6)

22 Parliament prorogued until 15 February 1676/7. Prorogation occasions the satire 'The Royal Buss' ('As in the daies of Yore odds ...'), rough verse but attributed to AM by [Milton's nephew] John Phillips. (PRO, SP29/381/89; Lord, ed., *POAS* 1:263–5; Phillips, *Secret History*, 85)

30 AM sits on the board of Deptford TH. (Court Minutes, 1670–76, 220)

December

ca. 7 (Tuesday) Letter from Sir Henry Thompson [Escrick or York] to AM [London], effusively thanking him for his 'protection and repeated favors'. He and Sir John Hotham have nightly drunk AM's health on their way home to Yorkshire; he also informs AM of local political news and alerts him to a recently widowed rich nonconformist in York – 'if she were worthy of you I wish you had her. I have not yet seen your friend Dr Witty'. (Hull University Archives DDFA39/26; Robbins 1964, 51; *PL* 2:392)

9 AM [W] to Sir Henry Thompson (c/o Postmaster, York), concerning parliamentary and national news, with much about banking interests including, it seems, those of 'our friends', the bankers Edward Nelthorpe and Richard Thompson. (University of Leeds, Brotherton Collection, Misc. Letters 2 Marvell; *PL* 2:343–4)

16 AM [W] writes to Sir Henry Thompson (Escrick) more personally, responding now to warmth of thanks in Sir Henry's letter

of ca. 7 December. In brief political news observes likely
changes in Commissioners of the Customs; some hope of
Shaftesbury in this connection, but this now less likely owing to
the publication of a speech under Shaftesbury's name 'as spoke
in the Lords house, which makes angers'; no meeting of parliament to be expected; 'Nell [Gwyn] in the meane time is said to
have obtained lodgings at Whitehall.' (BL, Add. MS 60391,
33–34; Kelliher 1979, 145–7, with facsimile)

28   AM (W) writes to Edward Thompson (York), with brief news.
(Harvard bMS Eng 870 (18); *PL* 2:344)

29   AM [W] writes to Sir Henry Thompson (Escrick): 'Sir I hope You
have had a good journy down I sent the Vote to a friende at
Hull with order to send You a Copy. The daily contrary rumors
concerning Parliament are not worth taking notice of. Truly
that of the Selling of Tangier I should think as litle. Goldsmith
Banquiers in Lombard Streete have been for now more then a
weeke been laid at by their Creditours and so much mony
drawn from them that I believe it will never more find the same
Chanell. And all as far as I can perceive upon unnecessary
Surmises or upon an intention of some persons wholy to breake
all credit of that nature. It skirted upon our friends at Wooll-
church market: but they proved Cock-sure. People talke as if
there were some neare probability of a peace and that we and
the Hollanders &c shall impose it upon the Confederates. I
heare that two ugly distichs have been pasted up at the Kings'
Bedchamber doore. I am sory that they should have so much
effect as to make the King distrust his safety and walk with
guards Mr Skelton is going to fetch over Count Furstenberg to
be deposited in his Majestys hands. The Dutchesse Mazarin is
either arrived or expected here. Sir Rich[ard] Grimes's brother
has marryd himselfe to Mrs Doll Howard one of the Maids of
Honour. I am Sir Your most humble servant Andr: Marvell.'
(Photocopy in Hull University Archives, DDMM28/1)

1676

Parliament does not meet owing to the long prorogation from 22 November
1675 to 15 February 1676/77.

January
The satire 'A Dialogue between the Two Horses', from the first week of this
month, is very dubiously attributed to AM only in print collections of 1689
and 1697 where doubtful attributions proliferate; it is much more awkward
and violent than other work better attributed to AM. (Lord, ed., *POAS*,
1:274–83, 469–70, who more plausibly proposes John Ayloffe the author)

4   (Tuesday) Earthquake experienced in West Midlands, to which AM refers in *Mr. Smirke* (*A true Relation Of the Terrible Earthquake, 1676; A Brief Account, and seasonable Improvement of the late Earthquake, 1676* [printed for Nathaniel Ponder]; *MPW* 2:164–5).

20   Hull TH pays for carriage to London of Gylby and AM's barrels of ale. (FTH1/5)

24   Date for which the torture is ordered (Edinburgh) of James Mitchell for his attempt on the life of Archbishop Sharp in 1668 (Mathole, chapter 5, citing Hume Brown, 4:500–1). It is very likely AM who writes the scathing Latin epigram on episcopal cruelties '*Scaevola Scoto-Brittannus*' when news of the torture comes south; in particular, this attacks the Duke of Lauderdale's agent Archbishop James Sharp. The poem seems written before Mitchell's execution, 18 January 1677/78, to which it makes no reference (Smith 418–20; and compare George Hickes, *Ravillac Redivivus*, 1678, 54–6). '*Scaevola Scoto-Brittannus*' is among the manuscript additions in Bodl. MS Eng. poet. d. 49, 264–5, and appears with a belated attribution to AM in BL, Add. MS 34362, 43^{r-v}, anonymously in Yale, Beinecke Library, MS Osborn b 54, 1225–6 (ca. 1681). George Hickes in 1678 seems aware of a Scaevolan reading of Mitchell's torment (Mathole, citing *Ravillac Redivivus*, 52).

February

7   (Monday) *London Gazette*, no. 1066 (3–7 February) advertises Turner's *Animadversions*: Evelyn's *Diary* notes Turner's work in the past tense by 20 February, although this may be a later interpolation (*MPW* 2:5, 40; Evelyn 4:ix, 83).

17   AM sits on the board of Deptford TH. (Court Minutes, 1670–76, 225)

20   Peter Gunning, Bishop of Ely, preaches before the king against Croft's *The Naked Truth*. (Evelyn 4:83; Lynch 53)

23   Imprimatur of Bishop of London for [Francis Turner], *Animadversions Upon a Late Pamphlet Entituled the Naked Truth* (1676), the work to which AM responds in *Mr. Smirke* and parts of *A Short Historical Essay*. Not advertised in the Term Catalogue until 5 May, *Animadversions* is printed now since William Fall has read it by the end of the month. (Claydon House letters, William Fall to Sir Ralph Verney, 28 February; Sir Ralph prefers *The Naked Truth*, 6 March).

March

3   (Friday) Stationers: 13s.10d. 'Paid and laid out about another Search for Naked Truth.' (Stats Co. Wardens' Accts)

4   Stationers: 9s. 'Paid Mr Warren for [ ] daies attendance searching for Naked Truth.' (Stats Co. Wardens' Accts)

10	Sir Joseph Williamson is alerted that Thompson and his fellow bankers have 'Lost there reputacons ... wee shall now I hope bee quiett in the Comon-councell the Leaders faileing'. (Tupper 369, quoting *HMC* 7:1, 1879, 468a)
11	Opening of George Etherege's *The Man of Mode* at Dorset Garden, source of the eponym and related references in *Mr. Smirke* (4ff.). Licensed for publ. 3 June 1676; entered with Stationers 15 June 1676. (*MPW* 2:6, 13; *SR* 3:22)
22	Stationers: 12s.6d. 'Paid Mr Garrett for his Brother Simmons what he laid out for Naked Truths horsehire and other expences.' (Stats Co. Wardens' Accts)
[29	L'Estrange granted warrant to search for 'unlicensed pamphlets or books', in some part with a view to discovering more about the publication of *The Naked Truth*.]

April

AM has in press *Mr. Smirke; Or, the Divine in Mode: Being Certain Annotations, upon the Animadversions on the Naked Truth. Together with a Short Historical Essay, concerning General Councils, Creeds, and Impositions, in Matters of Religion ... By Andreas Rivetus, Junior ...* (1676). Defending the bishop Herbert Croft from the harsh *Animadversions* of Francis Turner, AM publishes a two-part tract impugning High Church pretensions. The first half, *Mr. Smirke*, controverts Turner in an only somewhat jocoserious mode; *ad hominem* attacks and wide cultural reference add colour to the argument that Croft's moderation is plainly more Christian than Turner's overcertainties, the former's modesty preferable to the latter's callow work as 'the Churches Jester'. The second half, *A Short Historical Essay*, develops the historical argument that episcopal self-promotion has long bedevilled church and state, not least in the formative period of the Nicene Council, with the worldly ambition of priests too often overrunning their spiritual obligations. The king should secure himself and the nation against clerical self-interest. *A Short Historical Essay* may be an earlier composition turned to present account – AM in shifting to it styles it 'this following Essay of mine own' – with some topical rewriting now of this more deliberate work, whereas AM is plainly writing *Mr. Smirke* between the mid-March production of Etherege's *Man of Mode*, source for the eponymous clergyman Smirke, and the week(s) in April when his tract is going through the press. For publication he turns again to the bookseller Nathaniel Ponder and the printers John Darby, Thomas Ratcliffe and Nathaniel Thompson to publish this quarto in 11 sheets (much mispaginated), with censorship in the press complicating the production of two editions published in close succession. In a letter to Sir Edward Harley (see 1 July below), AM jokes (?) that he 'had better have taken a rich Presbyterians mony that before the book came out would have bought the whole Impression to burne it' (*PL* 2:346). (*MPW* 2:3–33, 28, 40, 113 and entries below)

29   (Saturday) Resignation from licensing the press of Henry Oldenburg, to whom Marvell still refers as licenser in *Mr. Smirke* (*MPW* 2:6, 52).

May

In this month (?) AM sends 'quatre fueille [*sic*] letter' and separately books (perhaps Croft's *Naked Truth* and Turner's *Animadversions*, in addition to *Mr. Smirke*?) to William Popple in Bordeaux (as noted in his letter to Popple of 15 and 17 July, *PL* 2:346). This may well be the date too of his poem 'Illustrissimo Viro Domino Lanceloto Josepho de Maniban Grammatomanti', or 'To a Gentleman that only upon the sight of the Author's writing, had given a Character of his Person and Judgment of his Fortune', owing to the reference to the abbot in the same letter to Popple of this summer; but the abbot's advice on the Nelthorpe bankruptcy the following year (see 26 June 1677 below) suggests there may have been other occasions for AM to question his presence in William and Mary Popple's life.

5   (Friday) Advertisement of Turner's *Animadversions upon ... The Naked Truth* in the Easter Term Catalogue: this may well have occasioned the reissue of the first edition with only a new title-page puffing it as 'The Second Edition'. (*TC* 1:238)

8   Wardens of Stationers' Company (Roger Norton and John Macock) 'Paid and spent [17s.] with our Master Mr Norton etc. on a Search, and coach hire to Mr Secretary Coventry etc. about Darby and Ponders Pamphlet being part of Mr Smirk.' (Stats Co. Wardens' Accts)

9   Wardens of Stationers' Company 'Paid and laid out [5s.6d.] in another Search for the residue of Mr Ponders Pamphlett with our Master and others.' (Stats Co. Wardens' Accts)

10   Wardens of Stationers' Company 'Paid [7s.] for goeing to Whitehall to the Councell about Ponders business in Coach-hire and other expences.' (Stats Co. Wardens' Accts)

Case under consideration of 'Ponder for printing Marvells Booke [Ponder] owned to have had those papers from Mr Marvell with direcions from him to print them. That he Ponder gave them out to bee printed. That he had no licence for the Booke. Ordered to be committed. Lord Privy Seale [Anglesey] opposed it. because the Cause is bailable. by the Statute. Lord Chancellor [Heneage Finch]. That for contempt of the Order of the Board late made against printing without licence for the seditiousness of the matter of it etc. That he may be committed for it.' From Secretary Joseph Williamson's notebook, document endorsed 'Marvel's Book'. (PRO, SP29/366/80)

'A Warrant to committ Nathaniell Ponder to the Gatehouse for carrying to the Prese to be printed an unlicenced Pamphlett tending to Sedition and Defamation of the Christian Religion

Dated the 10th of May 1676.' (PRO, PC2/65/217) Also 'A Warrant to Edward White to deliver him to the Keeper of the
Gatehouse signed as the other.'

11   AM sits on the board of Deptford TH. (Court Minutes, 1670–76,
231)

17s.6d. 'Paid and laid out upon a Search with our Master
Mr Mearn Mr Wright etc at Thompsons and elsewhere in the
Morneing And the Messengers and others in the afternoon.'
(Stats Co. Wardens' Accts)

13   Sir Christopher Hatton to William Longueville: 'One Ponder,
a stationer in Chancery Lane, is taken into custody about
an offensive discourse hee was printing for Naked Truth,
and hee is like to name Mr A. Marvell as the author.' (*Hatton
Correspondence* 1:125)

17   AM sits on the board of Deptford TH. (Court Minutes, 1670–76,
232)

18   Wardens of Stationers' Company 'Paid and spent [5s.] upon a
Search at Ratcliffs and Ponders by my Lord of Londons order.'
(Lynch 56; Stats Co. Wardens' Accts)

John Darby deposes 'that Ponder had approached him to print a
book, that he had a partner he would not name, that they
intended an impression of 1500 copies, and that Marvell was
the author'; Darby 'had composed only one sheet and printed
none'. (Longleat House, Coventry MSS vol 11, f. 128; *MPW*
1:36)

Sir Christopher Hatton to his brother Charles Hatton: 'Some
sheets of a booke, writ by Andrew Marvel against Dʳ Turner's
Animadversions on Naked Truth, have been taken at the presse;
wherin, it is said, he did much more sharply and scurilously
abuse Dʳ Turner and the Bᴾ of London then ever he did
Dr Parker.' (*Hatton Correspondence* 1:127)

23   Sir Christopher Hatton to [his brother], having cited Henry
Savile's being turned out of court for rudeness to Duke of York,
adds: 'I hope Andrew Marvel will likewise be made an example
for his insolence in calling Dʳ Turner, Chaplain to His Royal
Highness, Chaplaine to Sir Fopling Busy, as he terms him in his
scurrilous satyrical answer to his Animadversions on Naked
Truth.' (*Hatton Correspondence*, 1:128; *PL* 2:394)

Date cited for Gilbert Burnet's epistolary *A Modest Survey of the
Most Considerable Things in a Discourse Lately published, Entitled
Naked Truth* (1676), 29.

26   Nathaniel Ponder, who had been 'committed prisoner to the
Gatehouse Westminster for causing to be printed an unlicenced
Pamplet [*sic*] tending to Sedition and defamation of the

Christian Religion', discharged from the Gatehouse upon his petition and on promise of good conduct and a £500 bond. (PRO, PC2/65/242)

Date of imprimatur of [Gilbert Burnet], *A Modest Survey of the Most Considerable Things in a Discourse Lately published, Entitled Naked Truth* (1676).

30   Date of Edward Stillingfleet's epistle dedicatory to Henry Compton in *A Defence of the Discourse Concerning the Idolatry Practised in the Church of Rome, In Answer to a Book Entituled, Catholicks no Idolaters* (1676, imprimatur 3 June), A7ʳ–a1ʳ, which may have *Mr. Smirke* in view where it defends the early church and councils against 'whatever men of ill minds may suggest to the disparagement of those times'; in a letter to William Popple (see 15 July below), AM notes this response of Stillingfleet's to a 'sheet so seditious and defamatory to Christian Religion' (compare *PL* 2:346, 393).

June

1   (Thursday) Date of imprimatur of second edition of [Gilbert Burnet], *A Modest Survey of the Most Considerable Things in a Discourse Lately published, Entitled Naked Truth* (1676), in which final gathering D is from the same printing as the first edition.

4   Publication of *Mr. Smirke* (cited as 'ten days since', 14 June below), although private distribution of copies may well precede this (see 30 May above and next entry).

6   Letter from Thomas Blount [London] to Anthony Wood [Oxford]: '... but above all what say you to <u>Mr Smerk or the divine in mode</u>, if yon Churchmen put up so great a Joque – it wilbe no hard thing to prophecy, what wil become of [it] – it is sold for half crowns a peece and 15 non con[formist]s took off the whole Impress to disperse' (endorsement notes same, Oxford, Bodl. MS Wood F40, 214; Bongaerts 166). Edition B is that dispersed by nonconformists, one copy of which the rev. John Gray (1646–1717) attributes to 'Mr. Merveill' styled 'an English presbyterian Member of the House of Comouns, Droll Enough; and Satyr Too much'. (*MPW* 2:27, 33, 36)

ca.7   Goes 'for neare three weeks in the Country' to 'air' himself and 'make the Town new to me' (as noted in his letter to Harley of 1 July).

9   Wardens of Stats Co. spend a shilling to go 'To Whitehall and back to speak to my Lord of London', Bishop Henry Compton. (*MPW* 2:8; Stats. Co. Wardens' Accounts)

12   Advertisements of responses to *The Naked Truth* in the Term Catalogue: [Burnet's] *Modest Survey* and [Peter Gunning or Philip

Fell?] *Lex Talionis: Or, The Author of Naked Truth Stript Naked* (1676). (*TC* 1:246, 247)

13   Letter from Thomas Blount [London] to Anthony Wood [Oxford]: 'There wilbe an Answer if not two to Mr Smerks.' (Oxford, Bodl. MS Wood F40, 216ʳ; Bongaerts 167)

14   Anthony Wood (Oxford) to William Fulman (Hampton Meysey [near Fairford, Glouc.]): 'Last yeare a book intit. Naked truth was published by the Bishop of Hereford as tis said, to which an answer was writ by Dr Franc. Turner formerly of New Coll. but Marvell taking him up in a book which he published 10 dayes since, is for it clapt up prisoner (in the Tower they say). The title of the book is Mr Smirk or the Divine in mode, full of roguery and girds against the church and clergy. The book though suppress'd and call'd in, yet it makes a shift to come to Oxon: there are but yet two, of which I have one, sent me from London by I know not whome.' (Oxford, Corpus Christi College, MS 310, 17r)

19   Letter from William Fulman to Anthony Wood, 'I suppose Mr Smirk is not so large, but that you may bring it with you: Otherwise I know not how to see it.' (Oxford, Bodl. MS Wood F41, 300ʳ)

27   AM returns from country to London (as noted in his letter to Harley of 1 July).

July

1   (Saturday) AM (London) writes unsigned letter to Sir Edward Harley (Brampton Castle, near Ludlow), with news, including scandal of Rochester and a fatal episode at Epsom, political developments relating to the hopes of a new parliament, and recent publications relating to *The Naked Truth*, including that 'the book said to be Marvels makes what shift it can in the world but the Author walks negligently up & down as unconcerned. The Divines of our Church say it is not in the merry part so good as the Rehearsall Transpros'd ... the Essay they confesse is writ well enough to the purpose he intended it but that was a very ill purpose', and further comment on *Mr. Smirke* and the *Essay* (endorsed as from AM and in his hand). (BL, Add. MS 70120, Andrew Marvell folder; *PL* 2:344–6)

4   Hull TH pays for two salmon of which one and a half to AM, together with vinegar, salmon kitt (a small tub), carrying aboard, 9s.1d. (FTH1/5)

        Either this Tuesday or the next, AM receives letter of warm thanks from Herbert Croft, Bishop of Hereford, for the 'humane civility and christian charity' AM has shown in defending *The Naked Truth*, and with dark reflections on those who have attacked that work; soon after AM writes back to the bishop with further compliments and those in a vein of politeness so fine that it may seem a reproof to the harsher note in the bishop's letter. (Both letters quoted in AM's letter to William Popple of 15 July, *PL* 2:347–8)

15   AM sits on the board of Deptford TH. (Court Minutes, 1676–80, 7)

15/17   AM [London] writes to William Popple (Bordeaux, sent with Robert Thompson), on four leaves. Wishes not to offend the abbot [Maniban] or Popple's wife, whose regard he values, but is unimpressed by the book that has been sent him, and instead recommends the skeptical Cornelius Agrippa and Pico della Mirandola against astrologers (these sentences in Latin). About *Mr. Smirke*: it is a work slight and superficial but not unuseful ('inutilis'), and he doubts that 'they will or can answer him according to his folly'; AM quotes the letter of lavish thanks to him from Herbert Croft, bishop of Hereford and his own reply. He also expresses his curiosity about Popple's finances (in Latin again), owing to Marvell's ardent desire that Popple soon return to England so that he can enjoy his company before it is too late. (Early copy in Lambeth Palace MS 933, no. 88; *PL* 2:346–8)

18   AM sits on the board of Deptford TH. (Court Minutes, 1676–80, 8)

20   Letter from ? [London] to William Fulman: '... Had I thought it worth my while to have reflected upon the late Pamphlets that have made a noyse here, I could with ease have given yow an account of them: I suppose yow have seen the Naked Truth which made the first bustle, and set so many on work. The Animadversions upon it by the Revd Dr Turner, have been severely reflected upon by the right worshipfull Mr. Mervel who has placd the Dr in the very same Praedicament with the Archdeacon of Cant. Lex Talionis or the Author of Naked Truth stript naked, is they say the Ch. Church Answer, and I partly believe it. The modest Survey is done by the Scotch Burnet, who appears a great Hector for the Church, and fights with a two edged Sword, and slays all before him.' (Oxford, Corpus Christi College, MS 310, 127ᵛ)

August

4   (Friday) Report of the Committee on Trade, 4 August 1676, complaining of French depredations and the difficulty of winning reparations. On the same day, 'taeking a Coppy of the affidavits of such Masters whose ships were taken by the French, [John Harrington] read and show'd them to as many as he cold upon and about the Exchange in reflecion upon the Goverment'. This is later published as *A List of Several Ships*

Belonging to English Merchants Taken by French Privateers, referred to in the *Account*, from the same press, and printed with it in the 1679 edition of the *Account*. On 8 August Harrington's action was reported by Secretary Williamson's informer, Captain Elsdon. (PRO, SP29/392/21)

23   Hull: 'This day Six and Twenty pounds is taken out of the iron Chest to be paid unto Coll Anthony Gilbie and Andrew Marvell Esqr the Towns Burgesses of Parliament for their wages of Parliament for Thirty Nine days apeece attending at the last sitting of Parliament Thirteene pounds whereof Mr Hardy is to pay unto Coll Anthony Gilbie And the other Thirteene pounds he is to pay unto Alderman Duncalf who will undertake to returne the said Thirteene pounds to Mr Marvell.' (BRB 5:746; thus also BRF3/25/10^r)

September

Arthur Annesley, Earl of Anglesey, *The Truth Unvailed, In behalf of the Church of England ... Being a Vindication of Mr. Standish's Sermon Preached before the King, and published by His Majesties especial Command* (1676), 34: against Arminian innovation, 'If things stand thus (or rather if things totter at this rate; for the Corner-stone being removed, the whole building must shake, and no wonder if we all turn Quakers), why might not the facetious and candid Marvel, why might not judicious Polehill, why might not acute Dr. Tully, why might not honest Mr. Standish; nay, why may not this well-meaning Scribler (whatever Dr. Owen, Mr. Jenkins, or that shrewd man Antizozo ought to have done), set pen to paper, without such groveling Out-cries as are made ...'

21   (Thursday) AM sits on the board of Deptford TH. (Court Minutes, 1676–80, 12)

27   AM sits on the board of Deptford TH. (Court Minutes, 1676–80, 15)

October

17   (Tuesday) AM sits on the board of Deptford TH. (Court Minutes, 1676–80, 16)

20   Date given for Simon Patrick, *Falshood Unmaskt, In Answer to a Book, Called, Truth Unveil'd* (1676), 1, 25 – Patrick seems to have seen Anglesey's *Truth Unveil'd* close to its date of publication. He views the kindness of the 'Person of Quality' for AM as especially reprehensible, and attacks the *Short Historical Essay* (especially its pp. 58, 73) and *Rehearsal Transpros'd* (its p. 10) with some penetration (22–4). Licensed 3 November 1676 and advertised 12 February 1676/7 (*TC* 1:267).

31   In sale of library of Lazarus Seaman, the Lord Wharton's sometime chaplain, is included an octavo copy of *The Rehearsal*

Transpros'd (1672). (*Catalogus Variorum & Insignium Librorum ...
Lazari Seaman, S.T.D.*, 1676, Y4ᵛ).

November

14   (Tuesday) AM [London] writes to Sir Henry Thompson (Escrick, c/o Edward Thompson, York), thanking him for a promised barrel of ale, and joking at the expense of Nathaniel Bacon's failed rebellion in Virginia, and adding other international and national news. (Huntington Library, MS HM 21813; *PL* 2:348–9)

23   AM receives the barrel of ale promised from Sir Henry Thompson, some of which has gone missing in transit (as noted in his letter to Edward Thompson of 2 December).

28   AM [London] writes to George Acklam (alderman of Hull), in response to a letter from the Hull Trinity House: has presented their concern in the Clipsham claim against them to Sir Francis Pemberton, who has now written to them directly, with Marvell having been 'out of Town' the last few days; assures them of his eagerness to serve them, and thanks them also for their kind present of ale. (NTH57/1; *PL* 2:285, 375)

December

2   (Saturday) AM (London) writes to Edward Thompson (York), with thanks to Sir Henry Thompson for ale and with political news, including Shaftesbury's return to London, publications prosecuted, successful nonconformity, and dubiousness of tracts claiming that parliament has been dissolved owing to its long prorogation. (Princeton University Library, Robert H. Taylor Collection; *PL* 2:349–50)

16   The Warden of the Trinity House Thomas Coates (London) to the lawyer George Trewman (Hull): has seen 'Mr Marvill once since I came to London who acquainted mee hee hath received your token off ale and retournes yow thankes. and that he had some Conference with Councells about the Provisoe you advise me off' with reference to duties payable in the Clipsham case. (NTH57/1)

19   Thomas Coates (Porters key, London) to George Acklam (Hull TH): has received his letter that afternoon 'and very oportunely mett with Mr Marvill here dyneing that day with Sir Thomas Allein'; 'the Tedious season' makes everything go slowly; has 'offered Mr Marvill the Money butt hee pleased rather to accept itt Thirsday morneinge'. (NTH57/1)

21   AM (London) writes to Hull TH in response to their letter: is grateful to be entrusted 'so farre in so great a concerne of your worthy Society' and reports the legal advice that they take the Clipsham case to the Exchequer, which is more expensive but

in the likely event of success costs would be awarded against Clipsham. (NTH57/1; *PL* 2:285–6; Hull TH pays 3d. postage for this letter, FTH1/5)

AM [London] writes to Edmond Popple (Hull) a note enclosing his letter of the same day to the wardens of the Hull TH: further counsel about bringing Clipsham case to the Exchequer, and asks to be remembered 'to all friends and Katy beside'. (NTH57/1; *PL* 2:286–7)

Thomas Coates (Porters key, London) to George Acklam (Hull TH): 'These are to acquaint yow I was this day with Mr Marvill and paid him ten poundes I received off Mr. Harrison.' (NTH57/1)

26   Hull TH drafts letter to AM in response to his of 21 December: expressions of gratitude and discussion of primage. AM is sent £20 for expenditures at his discretion and is to leave no stone unturned. (NTH57/1)

29   AM mentioned in letter from Thomas Coates (London) to Hull TH as having been met with, dining with the (Court MP) Sir Thomas Allen; Coates 'had left a letter for Marvell with Francis Mitchell'. (NTH57/1; *PL* 2:375)]

30   AM [London] to Edmond Popple (Hull): has on the 28th sent 'what I forgot to inclose' in his former, and on the 29th received a letter from the Trinity House, 'all very well'; has thrown the bill for £20 'into my study' since it will not be needed until the lawyers' term. Has consulted with Robert Sawyer, 'the best at the [Exchequer] bar', and a sub poena must be submitted in good time to Clipsham; counsels prudence and regrets that Trinity House had taken advice to go in this matter to Common Law, but 'Country Counsell like ill Tinkers make work for those at London'. (NTH57/1; *PL* 2:287–8)

1677

Robert McWard, 'Preface to the Christian Reader', in John Brown, *Christ, the Way, and the Truth, and the Life* (Rotterdam, 1677), c[6]ʳ: denouncing Samuel Parker observes 'how when the devil raised up Parker, that Monster, to barke and blaspheme, the Lord raised up a Merveil to fight him at his own weapon, who did so cudgel and quell that boasting Bravo, as I know not if he be dead of his wound, but for any thing I know, he had laid his speech'.

By the beginning of this year, AM 'also had a lodging for his privacy in Mayden lane in Covent Garden where he kept his money bonds bills Jewells writeings and other goods and chattles' or also 'mony truncks and Hampers wherein were great summes of money in Gold and silver besides bonds bills books Jewells and other goods of value' (PRO, C6/276/48). This lodging AM may have had before although only now do references to it proliferate (see 'my study', 30 December 1676 above); the wealth later supposed by Mary Palmer to have been kept there may in some part be attributed to the case she was then pleading, though some longer fascination with this Bluebeard's Closet may be supposed.

January

ca. 4   (Thursday) AM (London) responds to Hull TH: has retained Robert Sawyer as their counsel, consulted with other lawyers, and employed a solicitor too, but will himself 'nevertheless constantly look after the whole transaction'. Their Bill in the Exchequer and the sub poena for Clipsham are almost ready; he instructs them how to serve the latter. (NTH57/1; *PL* 2:288)

6   AM (London) writes to Edmond Popple (Hull), disputing the advice of the country solicitor Trewman; emphasizing the urgency, he reproves Popple for allowing Trewman's counsel to make him 'wamble' – 'Surely, Brother, it is the best to steer steddy and having once set saile to follow ones course' – but also apologizes that he writes 'it by advice'. (NTH57/1; *PL* 2:289–90)

[11]   AM [London] writes to Edmond Popple (Hull), with more about serving the sub poena on Clipsham and also a draught of the Bill for the Exchequer for Popple's 'supervision', this written on the margins of a letter dated 9 January from John Fisher to AM, addressed to him 'at his Lodgings at Mr James Shawes house in Maiden Lane in Covent Garden'. (NTH57/1; *PL* 2:290, 375)

11   John Fisher [London] to George Trewman (Hull): ... 'Mr Marvell calld on me even now and desires to be remembred to you and hopes things are now upon a right bottome.' (NTH57/1)

17   G[eorge] T[rewman] drafts letter to AM bringing him up to date about the Hull end of the Clipsham business. (NTH57/1)

18   LHC: AM (London) asks for private bills the Corporation might wish to propose, although the slow progress of public bills amid so many prorogations may frustrate any private ones. AM hopes 'in the more generall concerns of the nation [that he] shall God willing maintaine the same incorrupt mind and cleare Conscience, free from Faction or any selfe-ends, which I have by his Grace hitherto preserved'. (*PL* 2:176–7)

ca. 20   George Trewman [Hull] writing John Fisher [London] adds postscript, 'Pray present my humble service to Mr Marvell'. (NTH57/1)

ca. 30   Hull TH drafts letter to AM with more on Clipsham affair. (NTH57/1)

February

Ca. February 1677 ('aboute a yeare & a halfe before he the said Andrew died') AM's debt to the Nathaniel Ponder of some £14 (for books) becomes due (Kavanagh 2002, 210; PRO, C24/1069.2/36, Ponder deposition).

1	(Thursday) Thomas Long, *The History of the Donatists* (1677 [dated 1 February, 1676/7, A5ᵛ]): cites 'Apologists' who [like AM] 'make their Pamphlets swell with the frequent mention of the Indulgence of some of the Emperors to peaceable Christians, but pass by the many strict Edicts of the most Christian and pious Emperors' (A3ᵛ–A4ʳ). Advertised 28 May 1677 (*TC* 1:272–3).
3	(Saturday) AM (London) writes to Hull TH in response to its letter: is glad to oblige 'in the Prosecution of your businesse' and reassures them about the good progress of the Clipsham affair. (NTH57/1; *PL* 2:290–1)
12	George Trewman [Hull] drafts letter to John Fisher [London] asking that AM be able to see same letter about Clipsham affair. (NTH57/1)
13	AM (London) writes to Hull TH: was 'yesterday at the Exchequer to heare your Counsell give cause why your Injunction [against Clipsham] should be continued', and continued it is; recommends that for the next legal term they supply someone well-versed in the business to support the lawyers working on the case. (NTH57/1; *PL* 2:291–2)
	George Trewman [Hull] drafts letter to John Fisher [London] including reference to AM's good opinion. (NTH57/1)
15	Parliament meets after long prorogation in session that lasts until 13 May 1678 (but with adjournments from 16 April to 21 May 1677, from 28 May to 16 July 1677, and from 16 July to 3 December 1677, and from 3 December 1677 to 15 January 1678).
	LHC: AM (W) sends parliamentary news as session begins, with question of long prorogation raised, especially in the Lords. (*PL* 2:177–8)
16	The Lords Buckingham, Shaftesbury, Wharton, and Salisbury are committed to the Tower by the House of Lords for insisting that the long prorogation marks a dissolution of the Cavalier Parliament, and perhaps more generally 'for writing pamphlets and moving the city to sedition and rebellion'. (Bodl., MS Wood Diaries 1677, 9ʳ)
17	LHC: AM (W) sends parliamentary news, including the Lords' commitment of the Earls of Salisbury and of Shaftesbury and the Lords Wharton to the Tower, also now the Duke of Buckingham (for insisting that parliament was dissolved *de facto* owing to its prorogation for more than a year). (*PL* 2:178–9)

19	House of Lords Libels Committee (appointed 16 February) meets today and is ongoing until 9 April.
20	LHC: AM [W] sends parliamentary news. (*PL* 2:179–80)
21	AM a teller with William Sacheverell for the unsuccessful Noes (104, vs 127 Yeas) on the question of Sir Richard Temple's chairing the committee of the whole house considering supply (Temple very much in the court interest). (*CJ* 9:386)
22	LHC: AM [W] sends parliamentary news. (*PL* 2:180–81)
24	LHC: AM [W] responds gratefully to mayor's letter of 20 February and sends parliamentary news. (*PL* 2:181)
26	AM a teller with William Sacheverell for the unsuccessful Noes (98, vs 147 Yeas) questioning the right of Newark to send burgesses to serve in parliament (Henry Savile having been elected there, who is as yet perceived as being much in the Duke of York's interest). (*CJ* 9:388–9)
27	LHC: AM [W] sends parliamentary news including report of Lords also preparing 'Bill against Popery with severall provisions for Education of the Royall Children, for nominating of vacant Bishops &c: in case of a Popish King'. Lords committee near discovering the author of a libel against parliament. (*PL* 2:181–2) George Trewman [Hull] drafts letter to John Fisher [London] about Clipsham affair: '... But we have wholly left it to Mr Marvell and what he and you concluded But seeme rather to be instruments to perswaders at his request then to offer for what we writt wilbe certainely proved ...' Hull TH also drafts letter to AM [W] with high praise for his handling of things; Clipsham inclines to peace so in negotiation 'we need not instruct you that it be drawne on soe as to seame his seeking rather then ours'. (NTH57/1)

March

1	(Thursday) LHC: AM (W) sends parliamentary news, including Dr Cary fined £1000 for carrying 'the Booke concerning Parliament' to print and not revealing its author. (*PL* 2:182–3)
3	AM (W) writes to Hull TH: after some reverse in the Clipsham case, is nonetheless confident that they should not settle 'too cheaply ... if you find your selves so firmly founded as we imagine you'. (NTH57/1; *PL* 2:292–3) LHC: AM (W) sends parliamentary news, including Denzil Lord Holles contesting in the Lords the rumour that he is author of the *Grand Question*; it is very cold, also in the Commons owing to a broken window. (*PL* 2:183–4)
5	AM named to committee for bill settling Lord Maynard's estate. (*CJ* 9:392)

6   LHC: AM (W) sends parliamentary news, including fears of French power. (*PL* 2:184–5)
         Debates on this subject and the resulting addresses and royal speeches from 6 March–16 April are summarized in AM's *Account*, drawing on a 'Journall touching the Engageing the King to joyne with the Confederates in a Warr against France' (BL, Add. MS 35865, 135–56, or more likely a common source; *MPW* 2:211–12, 323–41).

7   MPs for ports among those named to committee examining grievances about passes for ships. (*CJ* 9:394)
         John Warly, *The Reasoning Apostate: Or Modern Latitude-Man Consider'd* (1677), A4^v, listing 'Names of some Treatises more Obscurely mentioned in the following Considerations', includes 'The Author of Smyrk, p. 43.'; alludes to *Mr. Smirke* (7, 48, 88) and a *Short Historical Essay* (42–3, 106); maintains 'there is no use of a Petulant Splene in Religious Debates' (14). (Dated from episcopal imprimatur; compare *MPW* 2:159)

8   LHC: AM [W] sends parliamentary news despite the late hour since 'I have taken a habit of writing every Post' and the Hull Corporation might otherwise imagine something extraordinary to have happened. (*PL* 2:186)

9   Bill of John Fisher to 'Trinity House in Hull against Clipsham' £10 19s. 'Received then of Andrew Marvell Esqr the Summe of Tenn pounds Nineteen shillings in full of this bill by me John Fisher.' (NTH57/1)

10   LHC: AM (W) sends parliamentary news including the Lords' judgements against the prorogation tracts; enclosure of Commons address warning king of danger 'of the growth and power of the French King' (in AM's hand). (Enclosure bound out of order in Hull CA, Andrew Marvell Letters 2:233; *PL* 2:186–7)

12   AM second named to committee for bill settling Mr. Awbrey's estate. (*CJ* 9:397)

13   LHC: AM (W) sends parliamentary news including the Commons' strong endorsement of Sir Henry Thompson's election, long contested. (*PL* 2:187–8)

15   AM named to committee for bill suppressing pedlars, hawkers and petty chapmen; the only bill for which committee he volunteers on three occasions (Hull was proverbially tough on beggars, Fuller, *History of English Worthies* [1662], p. 189). Lords send to Commons 'An Act for securing the Protestant Religion, by educating the Children of the Royal Family therein' (the 'Bishops' Bill' printed in AM's *Account*). (*CJ* 9:399–400)
         LHC: AM (W) sends parliamentary news including the Lords' sending down the Bishops' Bill. Encloses transcripts in his hand

of Commons address and further Commons response to royal answer. (Hull CA, AM Letters, 2:215 (1–3); *PL* 2:188–9)

16   Yorkshire MPs among those added to committee considering the imports of Irish cattle. Commons hears John Harrington's petition about soldiers impressed into French service. (*CJ* 9:400–01)

17   LHC: AM (W) sends parliamentary news, including Harrington's petition. (*PL* 2:189)

19   AM sits on the board of Deptford TH. (Court Minutes, 1676–80, 27)

20   The House of Lords Libel Committee orders the witnesses brought in who have sworn proofs that some eminent stationers have printed libels, including *Mr. Smirke* among other earlier publications. (*HMC 9th Report*, App. 2, 76b)

22   LHC: AM [W] sends parliamentary news. (*PL* 2:189–90)

24   AM named to committee for bill naturalizing children of English subjects born abroad 'during the late Troubles'. (*CJ* 9:405)

      AM (W) writes to Edmond Popple (Hull): sends accounts of his business for TH and hopes that Clipsham will reimburse them. (NTH57/1; *PL* 2:293)

      LHC: AM (W) sends parliamentary news, including passage of 'the Bill for Habeas Corpus, so necessary for the subject'. (*PL* 2:190–91)

26   AM named to committee for bill taking away the writ *De haeretico comburendo* (for burning heretics). (*CJ* 9:406)

27   'The Engrossed bill sent downe from the lords about Popery and settleing the Choise of Bishops and breeding the Royall Children in case the Succeeding King should refuse to take a teste was read a second tyme'; Sir Eliab Harvey 'As an expedient to keep our Bishops from Popery moved that they should all be obliged to Marry'. Then Sir Tho. Meeres 'moved for the Comittment of the Bill'. Then 'Mr Marvell, That the King being in health, and the hearts of Prince in the almighty he might turne them before they came to the Crowne, and against goeing about to prevent things att soe great a distance as this seemed to bee' (from report of Thomas Neale for Danby). (BL, MS Egerton 3345, 41; Henning 1:xxiv)

      See also the headings reported by Daniel Finch (Leicestershire RO, Finch Papers, P.P. 43), which confirm in outline the very full report of Marvell's speech in Grey, *Debates*: 'Mr Marvell.] He wonders to see this Bill so ready to be committed, that the consequence may be no likelihood of the King's consent – But 'tis an ill thing, and let us be rid of it as soon as we can. He could have wished it had perished at the first reading rather than have been revived by a second. He is sorry the matter has occasioned so much mirth. He thinks there was never so solemn and sad an occasion, as this Bill before you; but he is glad the House is returned into that temper, which the gravity of the matter requires. The Bill seems very unseasonable; the beginning is of two things not of mature consideration. First, it supposes "the death" of the King – It might have had a more modest word to have disguised it from the imagination ("Demise.") Secondly, it supposes "that possibly the Crown may devolve on a Popish Government;" which ought not to be supposed, easily and readily. God be thanked for the King's age and constitution of body! The King is not in a declining age; and if we intermeddle in things of this consequence, we are not to look into it so early, as if it was the King's last Will and Testament. The Law makes it Treason, "to imagine the death of the King that is – " A word more in it – The true and proper sense is not to imagine the King's death – His age may confirm you in no danger suddenly of the consequences of the Bill, but as for that of "a Popish Successor," he hopes 'tis a matter remote in the event, and would not precipitate that evil, no, not in a supposition. For some reason, without doubt, this matter has been thought of in the House of Lords, and next to the King living, he would cast as little umbrage on the Successor, as might be. There is none yet in sight, but whose minds are in the hands of God, *who turns them like the rivers of water.* Whilst there is time there is life, and whilst life, time for information, and the nearer the prospect is to the Crown, information of Judgment will be much easier. When God *takes him on high, and shows him the glory of the World, and tells him, "All these things will I give thee, if thou wilt fall down and worship me,"* he thinks these will be no temptation – Those who change for conscience-sake will have so much self-denial, that the Crown will not make them alter the thing – 'Tis unseasonable; it may be proper some other time, but not now. This Bill is a great invasion on Prerogative – To whom ever God shall dispose the Kingdom, 'tis entire to the King. He does not love to reflect on the persons of those who represent the Protestant Religion – (the Bishops.) But 'tis said, "This Invasion is not made by the Prelates; they were but passive in it." But he will not speak of such reverend persons, with any thing of severe reflection, but will only suppose this power of the Bishops given to any other order of men; to nine Physicians, and they administer the Test to the King – Having altered the property of the persons, to speak with a little more freedom, he knows no body of men, if the Parliament please, but may do it as well as they. The College of Physicians have a Charter from the King, and are his sworn servants; let these come to the King to administer the Oath. 'Tis a pretty experiment. Just a tryal, whether the Loadstone will attract the iron, or the Iron the Loadstone ... [etc.] ... But whether this Bill will prevent Popery, or not, this will secure the Promotions of the Bishops; 'twill make them certain. He is not used to speak here, and therefore speaks with abruptness. Closes all with his Motion that the Bill may have the same fate other have moved for, "not to be committed".' AM's position then finds support from John Maynard and Sir Robert Howard. (Grey, *Debates*, 4:321–5)

Bill committed, with qualification, with 127 for commitment, 88 against; AM named to committee for the bill, where 'it dyed away, the Committee disdaining, or not daring publickly to enter upon it, some indeed having, as is said, once attempted it in private, and provided R[obert]. S[awyer]. a fit Lawyer for the Chairman, but were discovered'. (*CJ* 9:407; *MPW* 2:323)

LHC: AM (W) sends parliamentary news (*PL* 2:192). Gylby also writes though very ill, 'but I tould my Partner as much and I hope he will not faile you'; expects war to follow from Commons address, 'the rest I leave to my Partner' (BRL 879).

House of Lords Libels Committee hears from bookseller Thomas Burrell that he knows nothing about *Mr. Smirke*. (*HMC 9th Report*, App. 2, 78b)

28   In AM's absence from the House, the Speaker Edward Seymour 'cast a severe reflection upon him' – 'if the Gentleman (Marvell) spoke irreverently of "the Physicians," he would have done the same of "the Bishops"' – and contrasts such anti-episcopal slurs with stouter defences of the national interest. (Grey, *Debates*, 4:326–7, 329)

29   'Mr Marvell, coming up the House to his place, stumbling at Sir Philip Harcourt's foot, in recovering himself, seemed to give Sir Philip a box on the ear. The Speaker acquainting the House, "that he saw a box on the ear given, and 'twas his duty to inform the House of it," this Debate ensued.

Mr Marvell] What passed was through great acquaintance and familiarity betwixt us. he neither gave him an affront, nor intended him any. But the Speaker cast a severe reflection upon him yesterday, when he was out of the House, and he hopes, that, as the Speaker keeps us in Order, he will keep himself in Order for the future.' Subsequent speakers express their dismay – one 'never knew before a blow given in the House of Commons', Sir Job Charlton insists on the Speaker's honour and 'moves to have Marvell sent to the Tower', Joseph Williamson insists 'that the action for that time was in some heat' – but with Harcourt excusing it ('Marvell had some kind of a stumble, and mine was only a thrust; and the thing was accidental') AM can make his apologies: he 'Has so great a respect to the Privilege, Order, and decency of the House, that he is content to be a sacrifice for it. As to the casualty that happened, he saw a seat empty, and going to sit in it, his friend put him by, in a jocular manner, and what he did was of the same nature. So much familiarity had ever been between them, that there was not heat in the thing. He is sorry he gave offence to the House. He seldom speaks to the House, and if he commit an error, in the manner of his Speech, being not so well tuned, he hopes it is not an Offence. Whether out, or in, the House, he has a respect to the Speaker ...'. Sir Henry Capel further palliating Marvell's action encounters Sir Robert Holmes's attempt to aggravate the matter, and although the Speaker observes that 'Marvell struck Harcourt so home, that his fist, as well as his hat, hit him, other 'Country' members, Sir Robert Howard, William Garroway, and Sir Thomas Meeres join in putting the matter to rest. (Grey *Debates*, 4:328–31; also BL, MS Egerton 3345, 41, and Reresby, *Memoirs*, 115)

LHC: AM (W) sends parliamentary news. (*PL* 2:193)

30   MPs for ports enlisted for committee for bill taxing rough diamonds and other commodities. (*CJ* 9:409)

AM sits on the board of Deptford TH. (Court Minutes, 1676–80, 29)

31   LHC: AM [W] sends parliamentary news; hopes for success for the Bill against Hawkers and Pedlers, so that 'the Country will not long be infested with those people'; notes darkly of the Lords' 'Bill for the speedier Conviction of Popish Recusants' that 'That is the Title'. (*PL* 2:193–4)

April

2   (Monday) AM named to committees for bills naturalizing Peter Renew and others, erecting a court of conscience in Westminster, and confirming Cirencester writs. (*CJ* 9:411–12)

3   LHC: AM [W] sends parliamentary news including attempt to curb excessive election spending; skeptical summary of the Lords' 'extraordinary' bill against 'Popish Recusants' which seems more

nearly in favour of the same (*PL* 2:194–5). Gylby also writes despite indisposition, so has not been to the House of Commons for the four days past and 'must wholy relye upon my Partner for giveinge you an Accompt of what has past in our house'. Alerts them to some fee that should have been paid Hull's Lord High Steward (BRL 848).

5   AM named among those to prepare a foreign cattle bill, modelled on the Irish cattle bill. (*CJ* 9:415)

LHC: AM [W] reports that the House has sat without intermission so writes fasting; parliamentary news, including Commons' outright rejection of the 'bill against popish recusants' as having contents quite at odds with its title. (*PL* 2:195; *MPW* 2:311–12)

6?   Hull TH drafts letter to Gylby and AM with claim that too great a burden will be imposed on navigation if Angell's increase of duty and Sir John Clayton's further lights are granted. (NTH52/1)

6   Samuel Mearne tells the House of Lords Libels Committee that L'Estrange had claimed to have the King's order for publishing *RT* and that 'The next day after I had seized the Rehearsall Transprosed Mr Le Estrange licensed it'; Mearne also produces the letter 'to Mr Tokesfield from Mr L Estrange concerning licensing the said Booke' (*HMC 9th Report*, App. 2, 78b; *MPW* 1:28, citing House of Lords RO, Committee Book, H.L., 6 April 1677, 197)

10   LHC: AM [W] sends parliamentary news. (*PL* 2:196)

Gylby to Hull TH: has shown their letter to AM; nothing yet about any lighthouses has come into the House of Commons. (NTH52/1)

12   LHC: AM [W] sends parliamentary news, including the king's message of the previous day regarding readier supply, adjournments in prospect. (*PL* 2:196–7)

14   LHC: AM (W) sends parliamentary and other news, including that the French have taken St Omer and that, with the French king at Calais, there has been an exchange of dignitaries of which 'God send us an happy Conclusion'. This is enclosed in a second letter of same date and place with further parliamentary news. (*PL* 2:198)

15   AM sits on the board of Deptford TH ('Forenoon'). (Court Minutes, 1676–80, 31)

16   Parliament adjourned until 21 May.

17   LHC: AM [W] sends parliamentary news at the adjournment of the session, with the king to Newmarket. Encloses royal message of 16 April (angry to have been stinted of supply) and

Commons response same day saying thanks but house now too thin to vote moneys [not in AM's hand]. (Hull CA, AM Letters, 2:228^{r-v}; *PL* 2:199)

21   LHC: AM ('Maiden-lane', London) sends cover letter with enclosure of AM's copy of 'The Lords Addresse [of 16 April] about the Bill for Shipps'. (Hull CA, AM Letters, 2:228a^{r}; *PL* 2:199–200)

25   AM (W) writes to Sir Henry Thompson (Escrick, c/o postmaster, York) with political news including the French embassy at Newmarket; the Lord Wharton's petition to the Lords and his being granted liberty until the next sitting of parliament, which is expected 21 May. Citing the comet that has been seen, AM alerts Thompson to a forthcoming eclipse of the sun on the morning of 21 May, with some innuendo against the French. (Hull Univ. Archives, DDFA39/29; *PL* 2:350–1; compare *HMC, 13 Report*, App. 6, p. 7).

27   Hull TH drafts letter to AM [W] with full explanation of what has been done in the Clipsham affair to date. (NTH57/1)

May
AM listed as thrice worthy in Shaftesbury's list of MPs, with later emendation noting his death and replacement as MP by Alderman Ramsden. (Haley 1970, 103)

Perhaps now already AM begins the first and main stage of the composition of the *Account*, which publishes the debates of the preceding parliamentary session and also a summary of the brief session later this May. AM at one point notes 'the progress made in so few weeks' and, since the second half of the work draws heavily on extant summaries of debates, it may have been largely complete long before going to press later in 1677. (*MPW* 2:185–6, 209–10, 241)

1   (Tuesday) LHC: AM (W) notes that the bulky Money Act is printed and sent out; will send the rest of the acts when printed. (*PL* 2:200)

3   LHC: AM (London) sends notice of reassembly of parliament 21 May and political news in brief. (*PL* 2:200–1)

10   AM and Col. Gylby paid their parliamentary salary of £20 6s.8d. each for 61 days. (BRB 5:511; BRF3/24/37^{r}; BRF3/25/11^{r})

16   AM sits on the board of Deptford TH ('4 afternoone'). (Court Minutes, 1676–80, 33)

17   AM sits on the board of Deptford TH ('3 afternoone'). (Court Minutes, 1676–80, 34)

21   Parliament reconvenes for a week after the month's adjournment, chiefly to debate whether to go to war with France. The debates are summarized in manuscript, on which source AM depends for his very similar version in the *Account* (BL, Add. MS

72603, 48–59, and BL, MS Stowe 182, 56–66; *MPW* 2:212, 343–67).

22   LHC: AM [W] sends parliamentary news after the adjournment: 'As farre as a man many guesse there will be no mony given this sitting but upon very visible and effectuall termes' of the King making alliances against France. (*PL* 2:201)

24   LHC: AM (W) sends parliamentary news including the King's speech and the Commons hardened insistence on alliances, especially with the Dutch, before any supply to be granted. (*PL* 2:201–2)

26   LHC: AM (W) sends parliamentary news, as well as enclosure of full copy of the Commons' address to the King. (*PL* 2:203)

    Geo[rge] Trewman [London] writes to Hull TH that 'Mr Marvell is soe busie the parliament sitting close that I could not get to speake with him or if I had it could not have helped us in the case' of Clipsham. (NTH57/1)

28   Parliament adjourned until 16 July.

    John Fisher (London) to George Trewman [London]: AM has brought him the letter AM had received from Hull TH. (NTH57/1)

29   LHC: AM (W) sends parliamentary news including the King's speech in response to the Commons' address, adjournment follows. (*PL* 2:203–4)

June

AM requests Mary Palmer to 'putt off the house they dwelt in at Westminster' and take a house in Great Russell Street 'in her owne name' on lease from Mr and Mrs Morris (PRO, C6/242/13, Mary Marvell answer). AM does not reveal the lodgers' names although they will be paying the rent, housekeeping charges and £10 a year to Mary Palmer 'for her Trouble'. Secrecy includes Nelthorpe being known as Mr White to the neighbours and hiding his whereabouts from his own wife (PRO, C6/242/13; C10/216/74; Tupper 371–2). Over an undetermined period AM incurs ca. £150 debt to Nelthorpe according to later depositions (Kavanagh 2002, 211; PRO, C24/1069.2/36). The location of this Great Russell Street property is described in Kelliher 1978b, 139–43.

2   (Saturday) AM sits on the board of Deptford TH (afternoon). (Court Minutes, 1676–80, 38)

7   AM sits on the board of Deptford TH. (Court Minutes, 1676–80, 41)

9   Edward Nelthorpe deposits £500 with the goldsmith Charles Wallis, with the bill payable to AM. It is later alleged that other like 'bonds bills or noates' had before and after this been taken in AM's name in trust for Nelthorpe and his partners as they sought to protect assets from their bankruptcy. (PRO, C7/589/82, answer of Farrington; C6/275/120; C6/276/48)

ca. 11	('midsomer') Edward Nelthorpe and Richard Thompson go into hiding with most of the cash and instruments of the bank they had partnered with Farrington and Page; Farrington is soon imprisoned, where he long remains, with the creditors initially persuaded by Thompson and his wife that Farrington holds the books except that he is alleged to have burnt them. (PRO C7/581/73; C6/275/120; Tupper 370)
11	AM sits on the board of Deptford TH at annual Trinity Monday meeting at Trinity House, Deptford. (Court Minutes, 1676–80, 44)
26	Letter from Mary Popple [Bordeaux] to Edward and Mary Nelthorpe ('Deare brother and sister'): relays advice on financial matters from 'the Abby' (surely the same 'abbé' her evil genius as in AM's letter to his nephew of 15/17 July 1676 and his witty poem on Maniban) but needs to know more, not least since the [astrological] figure for Sir William Cowper can only reveal so much. Surprised that [François Mercure] van Helmont should wish not to 'be known to be the author of the Zo[h]ar' since his involvement is well-known on the continent where there is regular information on the progress through the press of that kabbalistic work. Postscript in which William Popple reverts to Sir William Cowper and his family's fortunes according to their 'figures', and business news (Hertfordshire RO, MSS D/EP F.81, penultimate item). In another note, Mrs Richard Thompson also cites a letter from her 'sister pople' (30 March 1677, PRO, SP29/402/166; Tupper 368).
30	AM [London] writes unsigned letter to Sir Edward Harley (Brampton Castle), news of progress of French armies, city elections, trial of Brown for publishing prorogation tracts, and fortunes of the four lords imprisoned in the Tower, especially now 'Shaftsbury at the Kings Bench upon his Habeas Corpus', where the courtroom was full by four in the morning. (BL, Add. MS 70120, Andrew Marvell folder; *PL* 2:353–4)

July

16	(Monday) Parliament meets only to be adjourned to 3 December.
17	AM [London] writes unsigned letter to Sir Edward Harley (Brampton Castle), with news of the brief and thinly attended meeting of parliament for its further adjournment to 3 December, with court MPs calling for adjournment before the question was even put, thus drowning out William Cavendish's motion that the order be read by which the Commons had last been adjourned. (BL, Add. MS 70012, 247–8; *PL* 2:353–4)
	LHC: AM (London) has come back to 'Town' for the meeting of parliament appointed for the 16th, on which day the

expected further adjournment to 3 December was commanded by the King; Commons not much disposed to follow up the irregularities in the previous adjournment of the session. Business and political news; AM also reports the sexual crimes prosecuted at the last sessions – the first by a Frenchman 'I thinke' – despite two of these meeting with acquittals owing 'to the difficult Proofe that the Law requires' and despite 'the ill relish of such horrid wickednesse at the end of my Letter'. (*PL* 2:205–6)

August

5   (Sunday) George Trewman (Hull) writes letter to John Fisher (London) noting: 'The [Trinity] howse present theire humble service to Mr Marvell and your selfe.' (NTH57/1)

7   AM [London] writes in unsigned reply to Sir Edward Harley (Brampton Castle, c/o Postmaster, Ludlow), with news, chiefly political, about the four Lords (Salisbury, Wharton and Buckingham released upon petitions, Shaftesbury holding out), English involvement in the war between Holland and France, and the violent suppression of conventicles in Scotland. Has been 'much out of Towne' by his own report. (BL, Add. MS 70012, 249–50; *PL* 2:354–6)

9   The 'Lord Wharton appear'd most, but my Lord Shaftsbury was in the Bottom of it too' as some Presbyterian 'private presses' are reported to be printing clandestine pamphlets, for which [Francis] Smith is 'the principall Agent'; among these are prorogation tracts (arguing the invalidity of parliament after the recess of more than a year, 1675–77), tracts arguing the case of the Lords committed to the Tower (for claiming the present parliament invalid), and a 'Discourse reflecting upon the Duke of York, and the Lord Treasurer concerning a design to bring in Popery', which may be AM's *Account*. (Information taken ca. 28 July, now reported by Roger L'Estrange to Secretary Joseph Williamson, PRO, SP29/401/321, and *CSPD 1677–1678*, 691–2; *MPW* 2:185; compare *HMC 9th Report*, App. 2, 75a)

AM signs off on August moneys disbursed, Deptford TH Cash Book.

September

1   (Saturday) AM sits on the board of Deptford TH. (Court Minutes, 1676–80, 59)

5   Hull TH reckons £30 in AM's hand for Clipsham lawsuit (ATH 1/3).

7   Death of AM's friend and Westminster neighbour the political philosopher James Harrington: 'Mr. Andrew Marvell made a good epitaph for him: but [it] would have given offence' – Aubrey has a

'quaere' about this, so has not seen it; Aubrey's notes list AM second after Henry Neville among Harrington's friends. Aubrey (London) later reports to Wood (Oxford) the innocuous epitaph for Harrington at St Margaret's, Westminster 6 June 1678). (Bodl. MS Aubrey 6, 98ᵛ, MS Wood F39, 308ʳ; Aubrey, *Brief Lives*, 291)

12	John Fisher (London) writes to George Trewman (Hull): 'I received your kind letter and imparted it to Mr Marvell allsoe who was glad to heare from you.' (NTH57/1)
14	AM sits on the board of Deptford TH. (Court Minutes, 1676–80, 60)
15	Warden Thomas Coates (London) writes to Hull TH: met yesterday with AM at Deptford TH to arrange a second meeting at Elm Court (Middle Temple) and will go with AM to meet counsel in the Temple. (NTH57/1)
	AM (London) writes to Hull TH: discounts Clipsham's 'vaunts' as not 'to be much valued', with the only uncertainty in the case being whether costs payable by Clipsham. (NTH57/1; *PL* 2:293–4)
22	Warden Coates (London) writes to Hull TH: met with various persons including AM on Wednesday last regarding TH business. (NTH57/1)

AM among those signing off on September moneys disbursed, Deptford TH Cash Book.

October

15	(Monday) AM sits on the board of Deptford TH. (Court Minutes, 1676–80, 65)
25	Marriage of William of Orange and Mary: 'The marriage and the new understanding between Charles and William were regarded as part of a great international conspiracy to subject the Dutch to William, the English to Charles, and both peoples to Catholicism' (Haley 1958, 648).
28	Royal proclamation postponing the sitting of parliament still further to 4 April 1678; this took the urgency out of finishing and publishing AM's *Account* until nearer the beginning of that session. For presswork on the *Account*, AM and/or his associates turned again to the Baptist printer John Darby (*MPW* 2:187–9). The delay may well have invited AM's turning to the controversion of Danson's divisive *De Causa Dei* after that work's appearance late in November.
30	Hull TH drafts long letter to AM [London] expressing profound gratitude and emphasizing the charities supported by the TH and its fees; Lechmere and Sawyer are the lawyers to retain. (NTH57/1)

AM among those signing off on October moneys disbursed, Deptford TH Cash Book.

November

3   (Saturday) AM (London) responds to the letter of Hull TH dated
         30 October: grateful for its consideration, he notes the advance
         to him not yet drawn down by the expenses incurred to date,
         despite his now being sent a further £30. (NTH57/1; *PL* 2:294–5)

15   AM (London) to Hull TH: he sends news of the entire success of
         their case against Clipsham, even if they must still pay their
         costs in it. AM's account for his expenses (£6 10s.7d.) in the
         Clipsham affair is entered into the Hull TH file on 19 November
         (NTH57/1; *PL* 2:295, 375)

         George Trewman (London) writes to Hull TH: 'Though I question
         not but Mr Marvell hath given you an account of this dayes
         action', reports 'This morneing Mr Marvell spoke with my Lord
         Cheife Barron and gave him a hint of the matter whoe gave him a
         very civill respect I was with him, I went alsoe with him to Barron
         Littleton whoe asked how his maisters at Hull did and Marvell
         told him he was likely to heare of some of them and gave him
         alsoe a touch of the matter which I alsoe spoke of and he was
         pleased take notice of itt and of me ... Sir Robert Sawyer failed us
         and came not at all' and other lawyers were stiff with them. PS:
         'Mr Marvell desires the account he sent downe may be sent up to
         me ...'. 'And as for Mr Marvell the howse is much ingaged to him
         which I leave to further discourse and consultacion.' (NTH57/1)

         LHC: AM (London) reports his successful meeting with the Duke of
         Monmouth on Hull's behalf, with expressions of esteem on every
         part, and proposes their letter of thanks to the Duke. (*PL* 2:206)

17   AM [London] writes unsigned letter to Sir Edward Harley
         (Brampton Castle, c/o Postmaster, Ludlow), apologizing for
         having written at too great length about himself before; now
         relays brief news, and refers to his having no instalment to send
         (of what may be 'An Account of the Growth of Popery and
         Arbitrary Government'?); has dined with Denzil Lord Holles
         that day with their discussion turning in some part on fears of
         France; postscript at top of page 'I am afraid they burne Popes
         to night'. (BL, Add. MS 70012, 254; *PL* 2:356–7)

[26   T[homas] D[anson], *De Causa Dei: or, a Vindication Of the
         Common Doctrine of Protestant Divines, Concerning Predetermina-
         tion* (1678) on this day registered with the Stationers: this is the
         work that AM controverts in *Remarks*. Danson's preface is dated
         31 October 1677; the work likely appears near this registry since
         four weeks for eight sheets is a normal for presswork. Danson's
         work responded to John Howe's *The Reconcileableness of God's
         Prescience of the Sins of Men, with the Wisdom and Sincerity of his
         Counsels, Exhortations, and Whatsoever Other Means He Uses to*

Prevent Them (1677), which had been written as if a letter to Robert Boyle – this had appeared ca. May (imprimatur 19 April; registered 4 May; and *TC* 1:272). (*MPW* 2:382ff.; *SR* 3:36, 48)

27 AM (London) writes to Hull TH with reassurance that the decree in their favour has been registered, also with thanks 'particularly for your Ale which came up in very good condition and is excellent Liquor'. The carriage of two barrels of ale for AM and Gylby is itemized in the Hull TH list of disbursements. (NTH52/1, and FTH1/5; *PL* 2:296, 375)

AM among those signing off on November moneys disbursed, Deptford TH Cash Book.

December

1 (Saturday) LHC: AM (London) reports that as messenger on Hull's behalf has had two further meetings with the Duke of Monmouth; AM's gratitude to the Corporation for its 'great civilityes' to him. (*PL* 2:207)

3 Parliament meets only to be adjourned, but now next session brought up to 15 January 1678, which now requires the rapid completion and publication of the *Account*. The conclusion of the *Account* refers to this call for a January session, summarizes the argument of the work as a whole, and alludes to evidence given in the present trial of AM's associate John Harrington. (*MPW* 2:187, 213)

4 LHC: AM (Covent Garden) reports on the brief meeting of parliament noting that, whereas an earlier royal proclamation had promised a further adjournment to 4 April 1678, the King requests adjournment now only until 15 January 1677/78. (*PL* 2:207-8)

8 LHC: AM (Covent Garden) expects war with France. (*PL* 2:208)
AM signs on letter from Deptford TH to John Wright (Ipswich) about Wintertonness light. (Deptford TH, Select Entries, 1677-81, 46)

13 AM sits on the board of Deptford TH. (Court Minutes, 1676-80, 71)

20 AM sits on the board of Deptford TH. (Court Minutes, 1676-80, 67)
Hull Corporation orders: 'that a letter be written to Mr Marvell to procure Six Jacobus peeces of Gold with a litle silke purse and about Newyears tyde to present them to his Grace James Duke of Monmouth the Towns High Steward as his annuall honorary from the Town. And Mr Marvell is to have allowance for what he shall soe disburse out of that xx ^{li} the Duke was pleased to give for bringing two Children of Alexander Byers Scotch man.' (BRB 5:546)

21 Around this date, Hull TH spends at least £1 12s. on Warden Coates and George Trewman's meeting and dining with AM in London. (FTH1/5)

AM among those signing off on December moneys disbursed, Deptford TH Cash Book.

1678

'On Paradise Lost' by 'A.M.' republished in the third edition of *Paradise Lost* (1678), A3^{r-v}.

[Vincent Alsop,] *Melius Inquirendum. Or A Sober Inquirie, Into the Reasonings of the Serious Inquirie* (1678) recalls phrases from the *RT* controversy (A4^v, 67, 292).

John Oldham, 'Sardanapalus', line 9 includes phrase 'Undershrievalties of Life', drawn from AM's *RT2* (*MPW* 1:347; Oldham lxxiii–lxxv, xcii, 344). Published in many MS copies before modern printing.

January
Early this month, it seems, is published AM's *An Account of the Growth of Popery and Arbitrary Government*, 'about Christmass last' as AM later reports to his nephew (see 10 June below). The first edition (quarto, 156 pp.) printed by John Darby is followed by a second quarto edition of uncertain date and printer (144 pp.) and many later editions (see below; *MPW* 2:188–9, 214–20); some copies feature early MS attribution to AM (e.g. Chicago, Newberry Library, Case J 5454.55, t.-p.). The first edition seems to have been finished in a hurry in time now for the mid-January session of parliament, which is then delayed; the distribution too may have been delayed since the earliest notice of it comes in February (see below).

The first half of the *Account* supplies a character of 'popery' and then narrates the political history of the ten years leading into the parliamentary sessions of 1677, drawing out the pro-French policies of 'Conspirators' associated with the Court. The second half completes the story of those sessions, publishing in full 'the Bishops Bill' for the Protestant education of royal children and then supplying extended summaries of the debates about war with France in March–April and May 1677, these taken from several sources (*MPW* 2:209–13). Though in part an assembly of materials, and those somewhat raggedly joined, the work is shot through with Marvellian ironies and turns of phrase, if in a less exuberant vein than earlier of his prose works. The whole is designed to draw suspicion on royal demands for supply without first declaring war on France, even as it professes to blame the conspiracy it implies between Danby and the bishops and a pro-Catholic Court interest centring in the Duke of York (see below; von Maltzahn 2005; and *MPW* 2:196–207).

1   (Tuesday) LHC: AM [Covent Garden] has this day presented 6 jacobuses to the Duke of Monmouth on Hull's behalf; preparations for war with France; AM commends the choice of William Sancroft as Archbishop of Canterbury; New Year's greeting. (*PL* 2:208–9)

2   On Edward Nelthorpe's bill for £500 (in AM's name) is now
           paid the £15 half-year interest, according to an endorsement on
           the bill later cited. (PRO, C6/275/120, answer of John Greene;
           C7/589/82, answer of John Farrington)
7   AM cited in further bill to Hull TH from John Fisher [London]
           in the Clipsham affair: has been paid £10 before and now
           the last £5 to complete the bill (NTH57/1). A letter from
           Mrs Richard Thompson to Major Braman indicates her husband
           is in Chichester (Tupper 371).
8   AM (Covent Garden) writes to Hull TH, again commending its
           London solicitor Fisher's honesty and usefulness, very well
           worth their £5 and deserving of 'a little vessell of your Ale'.
           (NTH57/1; *PL* 2:296)
12   Hull TH orders 10 guineas given to AM when Thomas Coates
           goes to London. (ATH 1/3)
15   Parliament meets only to be adjourned until 28 January in a
           session that then lasts, with further adjournments for much of
           April, until prorogation 13 May.
           LHC: AM (Covent Garden) reports meeting of parliament only
           to encounter further adjournment to 28 January with the
           Speaker having again adjourned the Commons 'without putting
           the Question' which will raise debate when House does meet
           again. Business in brief. (*PL* 2:209)
19   John Fisher [London] writes letter thanking Hull TH for payment,
           cites having received the rest owing from AM. (NTH57/1)
28   Parliament reconvenes.
29   LHC: AM [Covent Garden] sends parliamentary news after
           the adjournment, including debate over irregularities at the
           successive adjournments. (*PL* 2:210)
31   LHC: AM (Covent Garden) sends parliamentary news, and
           encloses hasty transcript of Commons address to the King about
           alliances (*PL* 2:211). *London Gazette* advertises for the discovery
           of Thompson, Nelthorpe, Page or Farrington (Tupper 370).

February
Marchamont Nedham, *Christianissimus Christianandus* (1678) in the press,
which seems to refer to AM (likely a friend of Nedham's in the 1650s) when
late in the work are deplored those 'Authors' of discontents (73–4), who
revive after intervals of parliament against the new meeting, and who speak
in terms of the 'Confederates' (76). (Registered 25 January, *SR* 3:56, and
advertised 28 February, *TC* 1:302)

Hull TH late this month (?) records 3s. spent on carriage of ale for Gylby
and AM. (FTH1/5)
2   (Saturday) LHC (W) sends parliamentary news. (*PL* 2:211–12)

4	AM is visited in Westminster by Warden Coates on behalf of the Hull TH with a token for his services and reimbursement for his payment to the lawyer John Fisher on their business. Coates's letter to the Hull TH the next day notes AM's modesty and gratitude for their favour (see also AM's letter of the 25th of this month). (ATH47/1; *PL* 2:375–6)
5	LHC: AM [W] sends parliamentary news, with ongoing debate about alliances. (*PL* 2:212–13)
7	Yorkshire MPs among those enlisted for committee for bill preventing theft and rapine on the northern borders. (*CJ* 9:434)
	LHC: AM [W] sends parliamentary news, including the submissions of the Lord Wharton, the Earl of Salisbury, and the Duke of Buckingham; John Harrington's fine. (*PL* 2:213–14)
ca. 8	Loose sheets of the *Account* being taken for stitching.
9	LHC: AM [W] sends parliamentary news. (*PL* 2:214–15)
12	AM named to committee for bill for better discovery of the estates of Richard Thompson, Edward Nelthorpe, and others, bankrupts, with privilege of the house to extend to the parties to be heard, in their coming and going (*CJ* 9:437). As Farrington later has it, Thompson and his wife reported such 'untruths to some members of Parliament that they procured or occasioned a bill to be brought in the then house of Commons in order to be passed into an Act of Parliament for the putting your orator to an Ignominious death for burning the said books and defrauding the said Creditors' (Tupper 372, quoting PRO, C7/581/73).
	LHC: AM (W) sends parliamentary news, including second reading and commitment of the bill against Thompson, Nelthorpe and Company. (*PL* 2:215)
14	LHC: AM (W) sends parliamentary news, including Shaftesbury's petition. (*PL* 2:216)
18	Yorkshire MPs among those enlisted for committee for bill discharging Winestead Manor from an entailment. (*CJ* 9:440–1)
19	Warrant to Samuel Mearne, the King's Stationer, 'to make strict and diligent Search in any house, Shop, printing roome, warehouse or other place (where you shall suspect there are any seditious scandalous or unlicensed books or pamphlets) for a certain Scandalous Pamphlet called [An Account of the growth of Popery and Arbitrary Government in England] and in case you find any Copies of the Same, to seize and bring them away together with the Offender or Offenders before one or some one of his Majesties Justices of the Peace ...' Whitehall. (PRO, SP44/334/457)
	LHC: AM [W] sends parliamentary news, including supply of a million pounds voted 'to inable his M[ajes]ty to enter into

actuall warre with the French King; postscript with parliamentary business relating to Hull. (*PL* 2:216–7)

21 The Stationer William Whitwood seizes copies of AM's *Account* 'in the hands of Samuell Packer in Cornhil, who afterward dyed in the Kings Bench' (British Library, C. 55 d. 20; also Oxford, Queen's College, Z.b.17 (1)) and the wardens of the Stationers' Company pay 19s.8d. for 'Seizing a Porter with 12 Growth of Popery and carrying him to White hall' (Stats Co Wardens' Accts). See 13 April below.

LHC: AM (W) sends parliamentary news, including Shaftesbury's plea of habeas corpus at the King's Bench held against him. (*PL* 2:217–18; cited as sold at Sotheby's 14 March 1979, Beal 1993, 18)

22 The bookbinder Thomas Bedwell committed to Newgate 'for dispersing Treasonable and Seditious Libells' (including AM's *Account* among others). (PRO PC2/66/248)

Wardens of Stationers' Company spend 15s. 'Attending King and Councell next day' after the initial seizure of the *Account*, which must be subject of some of the many unspecified searches in the next few months. (Stats Co. Wardens' Accts)

23 LHC: AM (W) sends parliamentary news. (*PL* 2:218–9)

Hull TH drafts letter to AM to alert him that Angell, fearing opposition in parliament, is trying instead to augment his patent by getting very many names to it; AM to seek to frustrate any such stratagem and to warn Gylby of the attempt. (NTH52/1)

25 The Lord Treasurer Danby asks the House of Lords: 'That, in order to the Discovery of the Author of a dangerous Libel now abroad, Mr. Roger le Strange (who believes that he shall be able to discover the Author of it) may have Liberty to see the Manuscripts of the Libels condemned by this House in March last, which remain sealed up in the Custody of the Clerk of the Parliaments, and are not to be seen but by Order of this House.' The Lords therefore directed the Clerk to show 'the said Manuscript Libels' to L'Estrange under supervision. (*Journal of the House of Lords* 13:161; PRO, SP29/401/232')

AM (W) writes to Hull TH and professes his deep obligation for its generous gift, this is 10 guineas 'for all his labour and paines and writeing letters in the business' of the Spurn Light; Hull TH also pays the Warden Coates's wife £11 17s.6d. for monies given AM. (NTH52/1, FTH1/5; *PL* 2:296–7, 375; also entered in final listing ca. end 1678 of disbursements in opposing Angell, end of NTH52/1)

26 LHC: AM (W) sends parliamentary news and reports Shaftesbury's release. (*PL* 2:219)

28   AM (W) writes to Hull TH about Angell's renewed efforts to
            promote his patent; AM has an assurance from the Lord
            Chancellor (with whom he has placed a caveat) and also from
            the Deptford TH that it will not pass; he is again grateful for the
            present to him. (NTH52/1; *PL* 2:297)
            Sir Robert Southwell [London] to Duke of Ormond [Dublin]:
            'There are two wicked libels come out. The one is a book shew-
            ing (or pretending to shew) the growth of Popery in the man-
            agement of the late Councils; and the other is to persuade all
            the Grand Juries in England to petition for a new Parliament by
            giving a list of all those who vote for the Court as labourers in
            the great design of Popery and arbitrary power, by shewing
            what gifts or benefits they receive from the Crown, with all the
            scandalous reflections on their persons that could be devised.
            If I can light on either, your Grace shall see the prognostics
            that always bode evil – I mean the boldness of these.' (*HMC*
            Ormonde, NS 4:408)
            LHC: AM [W] sends parliamentary news; progress of Louis
            XIV's campaign such that 'there is great apprehension even to
            consternation among prudent persons'; Duke of Monmouth at
            the head of 3000 men to ship to Ostend, 'So that all things
            compared it lookes like warre.' (*PL* 2:220)

March
Either late in February or early March, AM meets James Yonge, a naval
surgeon from Plymouth visiting London, who later lists AM among the
'famous men and women I have seen in my travels'. (Yonge 24, 155–7)

Marchamont Nedham, *Honesty's best Policy; or, Penitence the Sum of Prudence*
([1678], two editions, one of 16 and one of 18 pp.): impugning Shaftesbury
in particular, and calling him to some fuller repentance of his ways,
Nedham supplies a counternarrative to that of AM's *Account*, seen as a
Shaftesburian production and styled 'the new *Directory for Petty States-men*'
(7) and 'a Treasonous Libellous Pamphlet, industriously now spred and dispersed into all hands about the Kingdom, to rail down both Houses of
Parliament, his Royal Highness, all the high Officers of State, the Kings
Privy Council, the Principal Secretaries, all the Judges, all other Officers of
the Government, and the Court it self', which 'then concludes all with a
vile jeering Caress of His Majesty Himself'. The references on pp. 17–18 to
the *Account* show Nedham using the first quarto edition; he notes the book
is 'now in the hands of the house of Peers, [and] desserves their most severe
inquisition'.

1   (Friday) The stationer William Leach informs Secretary William-
            son that: 'Mr. Samuel Packer one of the Clerkes of the poultry
            Counter about three weeks since came to [Leach's] shop and

brought a booke or pamphlet intitled the growth of popery and of Arbitrary governement in England, to stitch up for him, and to the best of his remembrance the said Packer tould him that it was presented him that morning, and was very unwilling this Informant should see the title, that the said Packer hath since absented himselfe from his Employment in the Poultry Compter.' (PRO, SP29/401/337)

The following undated messages from Samuel Packer in hiding to his wife Ann (in Masons Alley) come in a sequence before those dated 15 and 21 March 1678:

First, answering her 'resentment of my Absence', Packer explains: 'it is better to be where I can send to thee then where I can neither send to any nor any to me for I now easily see no lesse severe will be my usage if I am taken they apprehend and imprison some every day on this occasion even upon the most frivoulous suppositions Love I thanke you that you cautioned me to be well advised You must thinke in so weighty an Affaire as this I want not Advise And all agree for me to appeare is voluntarily to destroy my selfe.' But he makes arrangement so that she may visit him. (PRO, SP29/405/190)

Samuel Packer to his wife Ann: 'I could not be satisfied untill I sent thee A Line or two to satisfie thee of my health, butt since I am in this Circumstance [?] under this trouble itt is utterly inconveient [*sic*] to come home while this trouble is over and as inconvient I think att present to see thee prethee doe not trouble thy selfe butt be cheerfull .... I hope thou wouldst rather have me be absent then in A prison.' (PRO, SP 29/405/191)

Samuel Packer to his wife Ann: he 'would have appoynted some where to have seen thee Butt they prosecute att present so violently thatt I dare nott stir out of doores unlesse by stealth. If I should I should be inevitably taken and miserably used which I hope thou desirest nott I dare nott come to any Freind nor they to me butt by Notes and Letters there is A Thousand Pounde bidd for me as soone as their Rage is A little over I will send for thee God willing to meet me.' Again sends money for her and for their child. (PRO, SP29/405/192)

2   Sir Robert Southwell [London] to Duke of Ormond [Dublin]: 'There is much discourse here of two bitter libels that are out; the one is of bulk. I can never believe that the lord Halifax his pen is in it; many also do guess at Mr. Mervin [*sic*], who surely knows how to employ his time much better. If I can light on them your Grace shall know it.' (*HMC* Ormonde, NS 4:411)

LHC: AM (W) sends parliamentary news; news from continent better than feared; 'It seems that now we are ingaged in an actuall warre which if so will necessarily ingage his M[ajes]ty in a much greater expense and will I hope be chearfully supplyed by all his good Subjects.' (*PL* 2:220–1)

5   AM named to committee for a bill against delays in lawsuits. (*CJ* 9:449)

LHC: AM [W] sends parliamentary and brief foreign news. (*PL* 2:221–2)

9   LHC: AM (W) sends parliamentary and brief foreign news. (*PL* 2:222–3)

12   LHC: AM (W) sends parliamentary and brief foreign news. (*PL* 2:223–4)

14   Parliamentary debate on the state of the nation includes speeches that seem to follow the lead of the *Account* against the king's ministers; a newsletter reports the speeches against the king's ministers, which include complaint about the prorogation the previous May, when 'they were sent home with shame & reproaches for their boldnes, and put into the Gazet ignominiously, with run away servants, and lost Dogs' (Bodleian, MS Carte 72, 359^r–62^v, esp. 361^v; *MPW* 2:197; see also Grey, *Debates*, 5:223–47).

LHC: AM (W) sends parliamentary news, especially Commons in committee of the whole house determining on address to the king asking for immediate war with France. (*PL* 2:224–5)

15   London: the fugitive Samuel Packer to his wife Ann: 'I longe to heare from thee how thou doest and the Childe and every Body and I would as willingly see thee in order to which I would have thee find out Edmund if possible this Afternoon and lett him meet me att seaven this Evening' to arrange their meeting. (PRO, SP29/405/193)

16   LHC: AM (W) sends parliamentary and foreign news in brief; renewed parliamentary concern about 'the dangers from the Growth of Popery'. (*PL* 2:225)

19   LHC: AM [W] sends parliamentary news and reports preparations for war with France. (*PL* 2:225–6)

21   AM sits on the board of Deptford TH; Angell's claim under review. (Court Minutes, 1676–80, 80)

AM (W) writes to Hull TH with report of Angell's renewed progress owing to an application to the King in Privy Council, who in turn is 'satisfied concerning the usefulnesse of those Lights'; Deptford TH to determine the matter and AM's membership at Deptford precludes his reporting their resolutions. In parliament AM and Gylby at the 'ready to pursue your directions'. AM encloses a document largely in his own hand describing Angell's proposals and the 18 January order of council relating to them. (NTH52/1; *PL* 2:298, 376)

Samuel Packer to his wife Ann: she has failed to meet him the night before, proposes new time and place for their meeting. (PRO, SP29/405/194)

ca. 21   Goodman Atwood, deputy marshal of the King's Bench, writes to the Lord Treasurer Danby: 'Haveing lately apprehended one Samuell Packer whoe fled for dispersing a Libell entituled the Growth of Popery, I thought my self obleiged to accquaint your Honour with my proceedings; after I had secured Packer I searched on Jenckes Howse a Linnen Draper by the Royall Exchange where I found behind a great Looking Glass severall pampletts [sic] perticulary Harringtons Case, and in his Clossett Browns Case dureing his Confinement in the Kings Bench all which with some other things I delivered to Mr Secretary Williamson; All my most humble request is that I may be discharged of the prisoner for I am att great charge and trouble in the keeping of him; and beg your Lordships favour that I may be reimbursed and receave his Majesties Reward mentioned in the Gazett.' (PRO, SP29/405/189)

22   AM named to committee for bill for enriching and repairing St Asaph's Cathedral. (*CJ* 9:460)

23   LHC: AM (W) sends parliamentary news. (*PL* 2:226–7)

25   AM sits on the board of Deptford TH. (Court Minutes, 1676–80, 82)

Hull TH drafts letter to AM with summary of the position against Angell and who is supporting him. (NTH52/1)

London Gazette, no. 1288 (21–25 March) notice of award (reproduced in Kelliher 1978a, 113): 'Whereas there have been lately Printed, and Published several Seditious, and Scandalous Libels against the Proceedings of Both Houses of Parliament, and other His Majesties Courts of Justice, to the Dishonour of His Majesties Government, and the Hazard of the Publick Peace: These are to give Notice, That what Person soever shall Discover unto one of the Secretaries of State, the Printer, Publisher, Author, or Hander to the Press of any of the said Libels, so that full Evidence may be made thereof to a Jury, without mentioning the Informer; especially one Libel, Intituled, An Account of the Growth of Popery, &c. And another call'd, A Seasonable Argument to all the Grand Juries, &c. the Discoverer shall be rewarded as follows: He shall have Fifty Pounds for such Discovery, as aforesaid, of the Printer, or the Publisher of it from the Press; and for the Hander of it to the Press one hundred Pounds. And if it fall out that the Discoverer be a Master, or a Journyman-Printer, he shall be Authorized (in case of tracing the Proof up to the Author) to Set up a Printing-

House for himself; and no Agent either in the Printing, Publishing, or Dispersing of the said Libels, shall be Punished for so
doing, in case he shall contribute toward the Discovery of the
Author of any such Libel.' The next advertisement is for John
Dryden's *All for Love*, which as if to correct the *Account* instead
commends Danby and the present government as one achiev-
ing 'all the Advantages of Liberty beyond a Commonwealth,
and all the Marks of Kingly Sovereignty without the danger of a
Tyranny' (Dryden, *Works*, 13:5–6).

26   Stationer Joseph Leigh's affidavit that the scrivener William
Paxton and one Webb had in January alerted him to an unau-
thorized press at 'Cartwrights'; that 'Soone after this, Came
forth a Book entituled An Account of the growth of Popery etc.
Whereupon this Deponent had Recourse to the said Paxton and
Webb thinking them fitt to doe service in discovering of the
Presse which Printed it'; that frequent meeting and disburse-
ment lead nowhere; that on 13 March 'among'st other discourses Paxton told this Deponent that [John] Harrington
was in this business of the Growth of Popery' but that visit to
house with the Stationers' Warden has yielded nothing. (PRO,
SP29/402/192)

27   Parliament adjourns to 11 April.
28   AM [W] responds to Hull TH's letters of 23 and 25 March:
Angell's business has been brought to the Deptford TH, where
AM a member and hence unable much to report on their business, but royal support for the Spurnhead lights suggests the
need for a petition to the king in council against the extra
imposition. (NTH52/1; *PL* 2:299)
AM [W] writes Edmond Popple (Hull [TH]): advises how to forestall Angell's success. (NTH52/1; *PL* 2:296–7)
LHC: AM (W) sends parliamentary news including fuller debate
concerning the growth of 'Popery'; adjournment to 11 April.
(*PL* 2:227–8)

29   Hull TH drafts letter to AM to inform him fully so that he can
in turn inform Deptford TH of the burden Angell will be laying
on navigation; also a subscription of the many Hull worthies
who oppose Angell's plan. (NTH52/1)
AM among those signing off on March moneys disbursed, Deptford TH
Cash Book.

April
Roger L'Estrange, *An Account of the Growth of Knavery, Under The Pretended Fears
of Arbitrary Government and Popery* (1678): L'Estrange condemns the *Account* at
length, dwelling on the author's seditious purpose and uncertain identity;

associating the publication with that of the list of Court MPs in *A Seasonable Argument*; complaining that this 'Merry-Andrew' is 'a great Master of Words' (but not of business) and 'a Mercenary Pen'; and noting that 'By his Vein of improving the Invective Humour, it looks in some places as if he were *Transprosing* the *First Painter*' (3–7). L'Estrange appends an extract from the *Account's* 'Declamation against Popery' to illustrate that the author has 'taken more Pains to Shew his Skill, than Care to Deliver his Opinion' (65–72).

1	(Monday) Hull TH drafts letter to Gylby in response to AM's letter about Gylby's representations to Charles II. (NTH52/1)
6	AM with Gylby (London) write to Hull TH with assurances of their assiduity on its behalf, and that the Duke of Monmouth, high steward of Hull, is to be approached to interpose in Privy Council; they send a draught of a petition about the Spurn Light for the masters and wardens' correction and signatures. (NTH52/1; *PL* 2:300)
	Warrant for seizing 'a certain Scandalous and sedition Pamphlet entituled A Seasonable Argument to all Grand Juries &c and for the Auther Printer or Dispersers of the Same ... having found to take into your custody'. Whitehall. (PRO, SP44/334/475)
11	Parliament meets after brief adjournment to select new speaker, Sir Robert Sawyer, only to be alerted to fresh adjournment forthcoming from 15–29 April.
	LHC: AM [W] sends parliamentary news, with Sir Robert Sawyer replacing Edward Seymour as Speaker, owing to the latter's reported illness. (*PL* 2:228)
	Hull Accounts Book entry for 'Cash remitted to Andrew Marvel Esquire to disburse about Towns Occasions': £35. (BRF3/24/140ᵛ; BRF3/25/13ʳ)
13	Thomas Vere, Warden of the Stationers' Company, certifies to Secretary Williamson 'that on the 21th: of February last William Whitwood of London Staconer did apprehend One Thomas Bedwell who was by his Majesty in Councell Comitted to Newgate for Publishing and Offering to Sale a Seditious booke Entituled Consideracions of the Growth of Popery and Arbitrary Government in England Twelve of the said Bookes he did likewise seize from the said Bedwell Which Bookes were left in your Honours Custody and that the said Whitwood hath been at much charge and loss of time in prosecuting that affayre, and hath since beene very dilligent in making a further discovery' (PRO, SP29/403/39 and 40). This document is certified in turn by Williamson, endorsed 'Certificate William Whitwood for apprehending the disperser of the Libell called An Accompt of the Growth of Popery' (PRO, SP29/403/38; another copy is PRO, SP44/334/479).

[N.N], *A Letter from a Protestant Gentleman to a Lady Revolted to the Church of Rome* (1678, advertisement this day in *TC* 1:310), p. 180: in the number of Church of England publications advertised at the end by James Collins, is 'Dr. Parkers answer to Mr. Andrew Marvels book, called the Rehearsel Transpros'd.' Advertisement of L'Estrange's *An Account of the Growth of Knavery.* (*TC* 1:313)

AM sits on the board of Deptford TH. (Court Minutes, 1676–80, 34)

Edmund Bohun notes in his diary: 'This day I ended the reading of a most infamous libell intitled "An Account of the growth of popery and arbitrary government in England": Amsterdam, 1677. An excellent character of which booke appears in another small booke writ about that time', namely Nedham's *Honestys Best Policy* which he quotes at length with citation. (Bohun, *Diary*, 40–1)

Parliament meets in session that lasts until prorogation 15 July. AM named to committee of elections and privileges. (*CJ* 9:481)

HC: AM (W) sends news of fresh session of parliament: 'What I remarke in the house is that it is much fuller then ordinary and more are still upon the Road and there seems a more then usuall concernment among all men as if some great and I hope good thing were to be expected.' Encloses King's Speech (copy in AM's hand). (Hull CA, AM Letters 273; *PL* 2:234–5)

AM named to committee considering expiring laws and which to be revived. (*CJ* 9:482)

HC: AM [W] sends parliamentary news, including striking of a committee to bring in 'a Bill or Bills to hinder the growth of popery'; debate whether Commons should again address the King for war with France; 'In generall what I learne by information both within and without doors is that both Holland and Spaine appeare to be agreed upon termes with France.' Copies for them the Commons addresses and excerpt from the Commons Journal, 15, 16 March. (Hull CA, AM Letters, 275–6; *PL* 2:235–6)

AM sits on the board of Deptford TH, where he with Sir Joseph Jordan is on this Trinity Monday meeting at Trinity House, Deptford, '(according to their seniority) choosen younger wardens for the succeeding yeare'. (Court Minutes, 1676–80, ; *PL* 2:374)

HC: AM (W) sends parliamentary news, with many of the bills from the previous session now moved anew. (*PL* 2:236)

AM (London) writes to Hull TH with a copy of the order of the Privy Council, and advising about further preparations against Angell's project; the Hull TH's further advice to AM, promised in a letter to him of 8 April, has not yet been received by him. (NTH52/1; *PL* 2:300–1)

Hull TH drafts letter to AM and Gylby noting what has been sent from Hull and with fuller list of subscribed names against Angel's claim. (NTH52/1)

15 Parliament adjourned for another fortnight.

16 Sir Robert Southwell [London] to Duke of Ormond [Dublin]: 'The answer to *The Growth of Popery*, called *The Growth of Knavery*, is writ by a good smart pen.' (*HMC* Ormonde, NS 4:423)

LHC: AM [W] sends parliamentary news including adjournment until 29 April (*PL* 2:229)

Hull TH drafts letter to AM and Gylby with expressions of deep gratitude. (NTH52/1)

17 Anonymous imprimatur licensing *Remarks Upon a Late Disingenuous Discourse, Writ by one T.D* (sig. [*]3ᵛ).

18 *A Letter from Amsterdam to a friend in England*: the seditious persona of this tract advises 'Bring on new *Accounts of Growth of Popery and Arbitrary Government:* Charge them upon *evil Counsellers*.... Nevertheless, write on still: I am sorry we have lost the *Prime* Pen; therefore make sure of *Andrew*. Hee's a shrewd man against *Popery*, though for his Religion, you may place him, as *Pasquin* at *Rome* placed *Harry the Eighth*, betwixt *Moses*, the *Messiah*, and *Mahomet*, with this *Motto* in his Mouth, *quò me vertam nescio.* [where to turn I know not] 'Tis well he is now *Transprosed* into Politicks; they say he had much ado to live upon Poetry' (4–5; dated from SPD, Car. II, Case G, as noted *CSPD 1678*, 121–3). John Verney sends a copy to his father Sir Ralph Verney (2 May) who responds 'I was glad to see the letter printed at Amsterdame, for I love those things' (6 May).

18 AM with Anthony Gylby [London] to the Hull TH, in response to theirs of 13 April: urges them to persist in collecting representations from neighbouring towns against the impositions projected by Angell and to gather all information that may be used against him; names the names of those Hull shipmasters who have subscribed to Angell's proposal and notes how well informed Angell is about 'all that passes at Hull about his businesse'; indeed Angell is full of 'shift and trick'. (NTH52/1; *PL* 2:301–2)

19 Stationers' Register, entry for AM's *Remarks* to James Astwood, under hands of William Jane and Macock. The imprint of this

work, however, will have it 'Printed and are to be sold by Christopher Hussey' (see May below).

AM (Covent Garden) acknowledges £10 he has received on account for Hull TH business against Angell or Philip Edwards. (NTH52/1; *PL* 2:303)

25   LHC: AM (Covent Garden) reports he has visited the Duke of Monmouth on Hull's behalf and their message was well-received; this two days before but did not write that day because 'I was unexpectedly diverted'. (*PL* 2:229)

29   Parliament reconvenes for a fortnight until its prorogation 13 May, meets with profession of compliance from the crown in attempting alliances against France to preserve the Spanish Netherlands, despite difficulties with the Dutch; Commons' report given of the 'danger from popery'. (*CJ* 9:464–71)

30   AM named to committee to prepare abstract of the alliances presented to the Commons, under treaty at Nimeguen. (*CJ* 9:472)

     LHC: AM [W] sends parliamentary news at the fresh meeting. (*PL* 2:230)

     Hull TH drafts letter to AM and Gylby with warning of all that Angell has been getting up to, including bribes not least of 'one William Fugill a bookbinder in Hull whoe was his instrument in getting hands and affidavits'; cites documents to expect also from York and Hull TH's gratitude again. (NTH52/1)

AM among those signing off on April moneys disbursed, Deptford TH Cash Book.

May

[AM,] *Remarks Upon a Late Disingenuous Discourse, Writ by one T.D. Under the pretence De Causa Dei, And of Answering Mr. John How's Letter and Postscript Of God's Prescience, &c. Affirming, as the Protestant Doctrine, That God doth by Efficacious Influence universally move and determine Men to all their Actions, even to those that are most Wicked. By a Protestant.* (London: Printed and are to be sold by Christopher Hussey, at the Flower-de-luce in Little-Brittain. 1678.) Octavo in 156 pp.; advertisement this day in *TC* 1:308. AM's authorship is attested by his contemporary James Yonge (who had met AM and Robert Boyle), by the knowledgeable Edmund Calamy (1671–1732), and by implication in the library listings of John Locke and John Owen (also in what seems an early MS attribution 'viz: Andrew Marvel', perhaps by one MH, on Bodl. 8° N.193). The nonconformist minister John Howe, the embodiment of an earlier Cromwellian conservatism, had ties to the Boyles and to Wharton; moreover, his promotion of the Baxterian 'middle way' seems to have accorded with AM's efforts to build a more moderate consensus between High Church and Calvinist extremes. Stylistically *Remarks*

shares many traits with other of AM's prose
for Howe's work express a deeper suspicion of
determination' and attendant arrogations of s
2:381–411, 398–9, 446; Harrison and Laslett, 185

2   (Thursday) Abstract of alliances repor
Charles II refuses to concede. (*CJ* 472

3   Thomas Bedwell discharged upon hi
styled a porter: he 'was about nyne V
Newgate for carrying certain Scan
Sellers Shop, Where he is like to peri
PC2/66/319)

4   LHC: AM (W) sends parliamentary
votes about alliance with Holland;
'have already made their condition
has with the third vote scanted
Prince.' (*PL* 2:230–1)

7   LHC: AM [W] sends parliamentary
King's rebuke, seeking further
Holland before the Dutch conc
(*PL* 2:231)

[9]   LHC: AM [W] sends parliamentar
Sawyer pleading illness, so restorin
of the Commons.

11   LHC: AM [W] sends news of a se
very full house (one tallying 350
address on which the Commons

13   Supply still not granted, parliame
In the auction of the library of th
associate, are advertised two
Transpros'd with its *Second Par*
on Dr. Turners Animadversion
[= *Mr. Smirke*] and another duo
two volumes ('1673–74'); also r
published on 20 March 167
Dunmore and Richard Chis
D. Doctoris Benjaminis Worsley,
Ee4ᵛ, Ff3ᵛ,Gg4ᵛ, Bbb4ᵛ)

14   LHC: AM (W) sends parliame
legislation lost as a result; so
and 'God in mercy direct his N
most conduce to his own a
(*PL* 2:233–4)

     Advertisement of AM's anonym
Discourse (*TC* 1:308)

16

18

23

24

25

27

28

June

?   Memorandum from stationer William Whitwood to Secretary Williamson: 'as you were pleased to give me leave to Remember you of speakeing to Mr Bartie in the House, about my Reward promised in the Gazett for discovering the Publisher of the Growth of popery etc, soe I Intreate your Honour that you would continue your favourable assistance In It to / Your Honours Most Humble and Obliged Servant William Whitwood.' (PRO, SP29/404/297)

1   (Saturday) LHC: AM (W) sends parliamentary news, including costs of demobilization. (*PL* 2:236–7)

3   MPs for ports among those named to committee for bill for measuring colliers [boats carrying coals]. (*CJ* 9:486–7)

4   LHC: AM [W] sends parliamentary news, including demobilization; 'And from Holland there are severall rumours as if now they are in probability of a Peace, they were grown very factious among themselves to the diminution of the Princes Authority.' (*PL* 2:237–8)

5   Yorkshire MPs among those enlisted for committee considering creditors' petition against Hamburg Company. (*CJ* 9:489)
     AM sits on the board of Deptford TH where he is sworn a warden with Captain Isaac Woodgreen sworn his deputy. (Court Minutes, 1676–80, 88)

6   LHC: AM (W) sends parliamentary news. (*PL* 2:238)

8   LHC: AM [W] sends parliamentary news, with enclosure of Henry Coventry's message of the day before from the King seeking supply (in AM's hand). (Hull CA, Marvell letters 2:274; *PL* 2:239)

10   AM [London] writes to William Popple [Bordeaux], noting that: 'The Patience of the Scots, under their Oppressions, is not to be paralelled in any History. They still continue their extraordinary and numerous, but peaceable, Field Conventicles.' Cites publication 'about Christmas last' of the *Account*: 'There have been great Rewards offered in private, and considerable in the Gazette, to any who could inform of the Author or Printer, but not yet discovered. Three or four printed Books since have described, as near as it was proper to go, the Man being a Member of Parliament, Mr. Marvell to have been the Author; but if he had, surely he should not have escaped being questioned in Parliament or some other Place.' (Cooke 2:70–71; *PL* 2:357)

11   LHC: AM [W] sends parliamentary news. (*PL* 2:239–40)

15   LHC: AM (W) sends parliamentary news, including hopes of the country gentlemen that their long attendance in parliament

may soon meet with respite, and with enclosure of a paper presented against Hamburg Company proposals. (*PL* 2:240–1)

19   AM named to committee for bill for executing John Fortescue's trusts. (*CJ* 9:501)

22   LHC: AM [W] sends parliamentary news, including dwindling attendance. (*PL* 2:242–3)

Hull TH in letter to Warden Coates refers to a [missing] letter from AM, presumably of mid-June. (NTH52/1)

25   LHC: AM [W] sends parliamentary news. (*PL* 2:243–4)

26   Hull TH drafts letter to AM and Gylby: Popple has shown the House 'your letter' and verso another communication cites 'a letter from Mr Mervill' (now missing). (NTH52/1)

27   MPs for out-ports enlisted for committee for bill prohibiting French commodities. (*CJ* 9:507)

LHC: AM [W] sends parliamentary news and brief foreign news. (*PL* 2:244)

31   Treaty of Nimeguen signed between Holland and France.

July

1   (Monday) *An Abstract of the Patent Granted by His Majesty, For Erecting a Corporation for Relief of the Poor Widows and Children of Clergy-men. Dat. Jul. I. A.D. 1678.* The list of governors' names includes 'Andrew Mervil, Esquire' (but not starred as one of the Court of Assistants): claim is that 'the late Yearly Meetings of Clergy-men's sons in London' have yielded revenues previously and that the aim now is to formalize the accumulation and distribution of wealth for this charity 'in all parts of the Nation'. List features chiefly gentry, and appended note indicates that principle of selection in some part at least is 'Gentlemen of worth and quality ... known to be sons of clergymen'. (Bodl. Wood 276A (38), also PRO, SP29/405/8)

AM added to the revived committee for the bill concerning champerty and maintenance. (*CJ* 9:509)

4   LHC: AM (W) sends parliamentary news and, despite some setback, AM expects it 'most probable that some kind of peace will rather take place'. (*PL* 2:244–5)

6   Warrant from Sir Joseph Williamson (Whitehall) to John Bradley and/or Thomas Ashby to bring 'Samuel Packer lately of the Poultry Counter' who 'had a hand in publishing or dispersing a certaine scandalous and seditious pamphlet entituled an account of the growth of popery and Arbitrary Governement ... in safe custody before [Sir Joseph Williamson] to answer such matters as shall be objected against him'. (PRO, SP44/334/514)

LHC: AM (W) sends parliamentary news from a thin house (in one division tallying 139 MPs): 'Things tend toward an end of the Session.' This is the last of AM's almost 300 surviving constituency letters. (*PL* 2:245-6)

8   Warrant from Sir Joseph Williamson (Whitehall) to Goodman Atwood, deputy marshal of the King's Bench, and to Thomas Ashby to search Samuel Packer's abode and seize 'all treasonable and seditious Pamphlets, Books, Papers, and Writings'. (PRO, SP44/334/518)

12 Order in Privy Council for examination of Samuel Packer and Thomas Bedwell: 'And the Examinations so taken to transmit to his Majesties Attorny Generall to be made use of for the effectual prosecution of the said Packer, or any others who shalbe found guilty of the Offence aforesaid.' Signed by John Nicholas. (PRO, SP29/405/96; PC2/66/370)

Order in Privy Council to search Francis Smith's warehouse, stationers to 'enter into any the Shops or Warehousees of the said Francis Smith and particularly the Warehouse aforesaid ['on the Top of the Leads of the Globe Taverne in Cornwall'], and seize all such unlicenced Bookes and Pamphlets as shalbe ther found and to bring them to one of his Majesties Principall Secretarys of State to be disposed of as the Law directs'. (PRO, PC2/66/370)

13 The Stationer Samuel Mearne misinforms (?) the Bishop of London that Francis Smith 'had a private Warehouse wherein might be great numbers of the Book called *The growth of Popery*, and *Advice to Grand Juries in order to the Election of a New Parliament*, discovering the many Grievances the Nation groaned under by the mis-proceedings of the late long Parliament ... [the] Warehouse, so suggested for private and dangerous, was in the open Street at the Globe Tavern near the Royal Exchange'. So 'on a Saturday in July, 1678' Mearne conducts a search a week after L'Estrange had done the same, makes off with £200 worth of books, and obtains a damasking order, and in a couple of days £50 worth are destroyed. 'Their seizure was made on a Saturday towards evening, and the Wednesday following, by the mediation of a Person of Honour that hath known me for twenty years, I made my Application to the present Lord of London, that a stop might be put to further spoil ...', this with damages of over £100. (Francis Smith, *An Account of the Injurious Proceedings*, 1681, 19)

15 Parliament prorogued until 1 August.

16 L'Estrange's application for two warrants to search Axtel's house in Newington and his warehouse at one Drake's in Tokenhouse Yard: 'I find under D'Anvers his hand to him an Accompt

concerning Books: And being yesterday to hunt him out, I am inform'd that he deales in Stockings, and Papers. His Lodging in Town and his Warehouse are so Private, that his next Neighbours could give no Accompt of them. He is son to that Axtel that was executed with other of the Kings Judges ...'. (PRO, SP29/405/116)

Warrant to Richard Baker or any other messenger, on information that Axtel had had a hand in publishing and dispersing several scandalous and seditious libels, to search Axtel's house at Newington for the treasonable and seditious libel *An account of the growth of popery*, and to seize that or any other such seditious material and Axtel himself to be brought in. Noted that a like warrant is given to search Axtel's lodgings at Drake's in Tokenhouse Yard. (PRO, SP44/334/522)

The Bishop of London (Henry Compton) issues 'Order to Damask Francis Smith's Stock, 1678' following 13 July seizure 'at the Warehouse of one Francis Smith Staconer [of] severall scandalous seditious and unlicensed Bookes.' (Rivington 6g)

17   Thomas Rymer, *The Tragedies of The last Age* (1678 [licensed 17 July]; reissued 1692): in denouncing Seneca's Phaedra, scoffs at her nurse's expounding to Hippolytus 'that a City-life and Women are a comfortable importance' (93–4).

19?   Examination of Samuel Packer by Secretary of State Joseph Williamson, signed by both: Packer claims to have found 'the Growth of Poverty [sic] ... in his seat upon the Table. That he onely read the Title Page of it, without haveing heard any thing of it before, or without knowing the contents thereof. That as he went to dinner he called at Leach's the citty Stationer, and threw it downe upon the Counter, behind which Leach stood, desireing him to have it sticht up'; Packer unconcernedly going on to the Kings Head Tavern 'with one Webb an Excise man', Leach then delivered the book there without comment. Packer made himself scarce once the search was on for him, but also because he did not wish to be arrested for debt; he defends himself against other inferences drawn from his notes to his wife (see above March). Dated and endorsed 19 July, but overwritten as 22 July. (PRO, SP29/405/168)

23   Sir Joseph Williamson (Whitehall) certifies that Goodman Atwood, deputy marshal of the King's Bench, following a warrant to him and Thomas Ashby, tipstaff of the King's Bench, apprehended Samuel Packer, now prosecuted for dispersing and publishing a scandalous and seditious libel, *An Account of the Growth of Popery*, and that he has been diligent in further discovering the matter. (PRO, SP44/334/525)

26	Before Samuel Packer is to be bailed, the condition of the persons who will be his 'Security' needs to be checked by the Attorney General. (PRO, PC2/66/378)
29	Visiting Yorkshire, AM meets with the Hull Corporation to discuss the towns affairs: 'This day the Court being mett with Andrew Marvell Esqr one of the Burgesses of Parliament for this Borough came into Court, And the Court and Mr Marvell held severall discourses about the Towns affaires.' (BRB 5:576)

August

At the very end of July or in the first days of August, Hull TH gives a dinner for Gylby and AM costing £1 14s.9d., with a further 11s.8d. 'spent at George Mawson ['s] with Mr Marvell' and a further £1 5s.6d. 'paid Mr Marvell to ballance his account'. (FTH 1/5)

1	(Thursday) Parliament meets only to be prorogued again to 29 August, when it will be prorogued again to 1 October, and then again by prior proclamation to 21 October. (PRO, PC2/66/381 and 385).
ca. 9	AM leaves for London.
10	Hull TH drafts letter to AM addressed 'To Howse in Hull': sends 'deed granted by Mr Angell' which AM to take to Chancery for Angell to acknowledge, and so forth. 'But we leave all to your prudent management of which we have had such large experience.' In same mailing another letter is drafted to Angell ('We have by Coll Gilbye and Mr Marvell received yor deed of the grant of the annuity to the poore of this howse whoe returne you theire prayers And we the hearty thankes of this howse ...') and another to Dr Robert Witty: 'Worthy Doctor, Upon the account we have received from Mr Marvell our warden of the good service you have done in the helping forward an end to the difference betwixt this howse and Mr Angell As the makeing of peace is acceptable worke to all men Soe the howse kindely attests your endeavors therein and returnes you theire hearty thankes and when things are setled and confirmed as they ought to be they will neither be forgetfull nor ungratefull.' (NTH52/1; *PL* 2:376)
ca. 13	AM arrives in London. Having contracted a tertian ague and now on the verge of a third fit of fever, he summons a doctor, who bleeds him. (Kelliher 1978a, 118–19, drawing on Morton 96–7)
15?	AM seized by another fit of fever, but rather than giving him quinine (ounce of Peruvian bark) his doctor administers 'a draught of Venice treacle' and has him heavily covered with blankets, which leads him to be 'seized with the profoundest

	sleep [while] sweating profusely'. (Kelliher 1978a, 118–19, translating Morton 96–7)
16	Andrew Marvell dies comatose (*Apoplecticè*) in the house in Great Russell Street (Morton 97; Kelliher 1978a, 119); 'suddenly of an Appoplexy' (PRO, C6/242/13, answer of Mary Marvell; see also 17 and 20 August below). That he had been poisoned was a rumour that later Whigs long circulated.
17	Colonel E. Grosvenor [London] reports in letter to MP George Treby (Plympton, West Devon) 'that Mr Marvell died yesterday, of an Appoplex'. (Derbyshire RO, D239 M/01068)
18	'Andrew Mervill. Esqr.' buried in St Giles-in-the-Fields and thus named in the burial register there. (Kelliher 1978a, 119)
ca. 18	A 'Mr Furloe' gains keys to AM's lodgings in Maiden Lane from Mary Palmer (by her account), taking advantage of her 'great Sorrow and Distracion of Mind'; pretending to get some writings belonging to Edward Nelthorpe (absent in France, apparently seeking to collect money from William Popple in Bordeaux), he 'removed all ... hampers trunks bonds bills and other goods without [her] ever going thither to see what was in them or what belonged to her Said husband' – she herself later finding little there 'but a few Bookes and papers of a small value' (PRO, C6/274/48; C6/242/13; Tupper 371n, 374). Mary Palmer later claims what was taken included the £500 bond from the goldsmith Charles Wallis that comes into dispute (C7/587/95); Farrington later insists that it was neither 'he [n]or his agent' who acted thus (Tupper 375, C8/252/9).
	Not long after this, John Aubrey notes on the back of a letter from Anthony Wood dated 11 July [1678] that 'Mr Andrew Marvell sepult St. Giles – Fields Aug. 18 1678 in South aisle neer the Pulpit', with Wood noting in his diary: 'Andrew Marvell, a ministers son – q[uaere]. Fullers Worthies – bred up in Cambridge – A Burgess in this present parl[iament], for Hull authour of The Rehearsall transprosed – Mr Smirk – buried in S. Giles Church in the Feilds in the south Isle – by the pulpit 18 Aug. 1678.' (Bodl. MS Wood Diaries 22 (1678), 22ʳ)
19	Deptford TH: 'Mr. Andr. Marvill Burgess in Parliament for Hull, and an Elder brother of this Corporation, lately dying the Corporation proceeded to the choice of another in his room.' Sir Richard Haddock chosen Warden in AM's place (sworn 12 September). (Court Minutes, 1676–80, 97, 99)
20	Roger L'Estrange writes to Henry Compton, bishop of London, and, having warned him of a conventicle of the Family of Love, adds: 'It may Possibly be Newes to your Lordship that Mr Marvell is Dead, (sodainly) and was bury'd on Sunday night

at St Giles as in the Fields.' Eager to retain his own privilege of licensing almanacs. (Bodleian, MS Rawl. C983, 18ʳ)

Hull TH drafts letter to Dr Robert Witty (London) with report of AM's death: 'the Messenger missinge of him, att his former Lodgeing made further Inquiry and on Fryday by Mrs Nelthorpe had Certaine notice of his death for which wee are all very sorry and as unhappy in our losse off soe Fathfull a Frende to our Society.' Added is a note from the Hull TH to the messenger John Gunby (Beverley) who has now been delegated the same errand: 'wee are all very sory to heare sad newse off Mr Marvill's death which hath deprived us off a Fathefull Friende to our Corporation'; he is to take the 'writeinges directed to Mr Marvell, unto Doctor Robert Witty who Lodges att the Crosse Keayes in fleetstreet over against the w[hi]t[e] horse ... you will best finde him about six or seaven in the morneinge', with £5 for Witty. (NTH52/1; *PL* 2:376)

23 Roger L'Estrange to Joseph Williamson: has with difficulty discovered Ann Brewster's lodging and 'can prove against her the bringing of three libells to the Presse in Manuscript: viz. The Letter about the Test; The Two Speeches of the D: of Buck: and the Ld Shaftesbury; and Jenks his Speech; upon which Accompt, she hath so long conceald her selfe. She is in the House of a person formerly an officer under Cromwell [Henry Danvers?]: one that writes Three or Foure very good Hands, and owns to have been Employd in Transcribing things for a Counsellor in the Temple [Joseph Browne?]. From which Circumstances one may fayrly presume that all those Delicate Copyes, which Brewster carryed to the Presse, were written by Brewsters Landlord, and Copyd by him, from the Authour. Beside that it is very probable, that the late Libells concerning the Growth of Popery, and the List of the Members of Parliament past through the same hands .... If she be questiond, probably shee will cast the whole, upon Mr Marvell, who is lately dead; and there the enquiry ends. I was twice to attend upon you Sir, with this Enformation, but you were the 1st time abroad, and the 2d In Kent.' (PRO, SP29/406/49)

Also James, Duke of Monmouth to the mayor and aldermen: 'Upon my arrivall att London I mett with the report of Mr Marvells death one of the Burgesses for your Towne which gives me occasion to become a Suitor to you in behalfe of Mr Shales that you would elect him to supply that vacancy in parliament ...' (marked as read 29 August). (BRL 893; also *CSPD 1678*, Chas II, SP Dom., Entry Book 52, p. 46)

24   Enclosing letter from James, Duke of Monmouth, a letter from John Shales to the Mayor of Hull with offer 'to succeed Mr. Marvell' and asking for a response 'to my Lord Treasurers at Whitehall'. (BRL 894)
29   Letter from Dr Robert Witty (London) to Hull TH concludes: 'if there be any thing now upon the losse of our dear Friend Mr M. for whome I am a syncere mourner, with you all, wherin I may be thought able to serve you here, you know where you may command...' In a letter to the Hull TH of the same day, Justinian Angell cites 'the prudent modderation of ouer good friend Dockter Witte; to whom and both Mr Marvin in your behalfe I were content to refer the hole afayr' of the Spurn Light. (NTH52/1; ATH 1/3; *PL* 2:376)
          Note from James, Duke of York (Windsor) recommending John Shales to succeed AM as MP. (ATH47/1)

September
Only posthumously does Mary Marvell claim AM her husband: 'after the death of the said Andrew Marvell ... she the said Mary did pretend herselfe to be the widow and relict of the said Andrew Marvell and did severall times with tears bewaile the mean and low condicion the said Mr Marvell had left her [ ] by such her cunning obteined several summes of money from several persons towards the charge of his funerall.' (PRO, C6/242/13; C8/252/9; C7/587/95; Tupper 371, 375)

Reimbursement now of Warden Coates for London trip includes 'spent at seve[rall] times with Mr Marvell and Dr Witty and for Coach higher and wherry higher 19s.6d.' and 'for a dinner with Mr Marvell', 5s.6d. (FTH 1/5)
2   (Monday) 'There is alsoe a great Mortallity in divers parts of England as well as in London and weekly Bill Parishes, in which dyed the last weeke about 500 ... Mr Andrew Marvell a Member of Parliament for the towne of Hull and a famous Sticler about the French Popish & Court interest is lately deceased.' (Newsletter from Southwell [London] to Ormond [Dublin], Bodl. MS Carte 103, 225ʳ)
18   Edward Nelthorpe dies. Richard Thompson is with him and takes on the Great Russell Street house, keeping Mary Palmer at her salary of £10 a year. (PRO, C6/276/48; Tupper 373).
22   T. Barnes to [?Joseph Williamson], saying that 'since the death of our frind Mr. uxhmbz [Marvel, it seems] the Wrighting of that booke of the growth of etc was said to be donne by him'. (PRO, SP29/406/189)
26   Hull Corporation votes £50 'towards the discharge of Mr Marvells funeralls': 'In Consideracon of the kindnesse the Town and Borough had for Andrew Marvell Esqr one of the

Burgesses of Parliament for the same Borough (lately deceased) And for his great merritts from the Corporacon, It is this day ordered by the Court that Fifty pounds be paid out of the Towns Chest towards the discharge of his funeralls And to per-petuate his memory by a Grave-stone.' (BRB 5:585)

30   Hull Accounts Book entry for 'Cash given to Administrators of Andrew Marvel Esquire towards his Interrment': £50 (BRF3/24/ 76ʳ; 3/24/140ᵛ; BRF3/25/14ʳ). The Popples never accept the claims of AM's 'widow', Mary Palmer, that she was married to him (Cooke, 1:36). 'Fifty Pounds is taken out of the Iron Chest which Mr Hardy is to carry unto Mr Majors who is desired to see to the Disposall of the same for Mr Marvells funerall according to the Order of the grant thereof made the Twenty Sixth day of September instant.' (BRB 5:587)

October

12   (Saturday) Sir Edmund Berry Godfrey goes missing, discovered murdered late the next week. This further propels the Popish Plot, discovered late in September, into the central piece of national news in the months to follow.

21   Parliament meets. 'New Writs to be issued' include: 'for the Electing of a Member to serve in this present Parliament, for the Town and County of Kingston upon Hull in the County of York, in the room of Andrew Marvell Esquire, deceased.' (*CJ* 9:517)

25   Hull Corporation writes a letter 'to Mr Robert Stockdale approv-ing what he hath done concerning the procuring of the writt for elecion of a new Burgesses of Parliament in the stead of Mr Marvell lately deceased ...'. (BRB 5:594)

28   A manuscript of 'A Combat between Soul and Sense' (a version of AM's 'A Dialogue between the Resolved Soul and Created Pleasure') seized among papers taken from the lodgings of Colonel John Scott in Canning Street; this is the first poem in *1681*. (Bodl. MS Rawl. A176, 80–1; Duncan-Jones 1975, 290; Smith 33–8)

31   John Farrington takes out administration of Edward Nelthorpe's estate. (PRO, PROB6/53/88ᵛ)

November

2   (Saturday) Hull: 'This day Mr Sheriffe brought in the Kings Majesties Writt for the Electing of a new Burgesse of Parliament in the place of Mr Andrew Marvell lately deceased.' (BRB 5:594)

25   William Ramsden elected in AM's place as MP for Hull; will be re-elected with the Duke of Monmouth's candidate, Lemuel Kingdon, in the general election, 24 February 1679.

29–30   Death of Marchamont Nedham, reported by Aubrey (London) to Wood (Oxford), 5 December 1678. (Bodl. MS Wood F39, 312^r)

30   Parliament prorogued, and is at last dissolved 24 January 1678/79.

John Aubrey's notes on 'Mr Andrew Marvell' date from soon after AM's death: 'He was a great master of the Latin tongue: an excellent poet in Latin and English: for Latin verses there was no man could come into competition with him. The verses called the Advice to the Painter were of his making…. He was of a middling stature, pretty strong sett, roundish faced, cherry cheek't, hazell eie, browne haire; he was in his conversation very modest and of very few words. Though he loved wine he would never drinke hard in company: and was wont to say <u>that he would not play the good-fellow in any mans company, he would not trust his life in whose hands</u>. He kept bottles of wine at his lodgeing, and many times he would drinke liberally by himself: to refresh his spirits, and exalt his Muse.' James Harrington 'his intimate friend'; John Pell 'was one of his acquaintance. He had not a generall acquaintance…. I heard him say that the Earle of Rochester was the only man in England that had the true veine of Satyre.' Dates death to 18 August and, having later checked with 'the Sexton, that made his grave' locates it 'under the Pewes in the south side of Saint Giles church in the fields' (Bodl. MS Aubrey 6, 104^r; see Kelliher 1978a, 94–5). In notes on the cleric Herbert Thorndike, Aubrey cites AM's reference in the *Rehearsal Transpros'd* to Thorndike's epitaph; and in his notes on Rochester that 'Mr Andrew Marvell (who was a good Judge of Witt) was wont to say that he was the best English Satyrist and had the right veine' (Bodl. MS Aubrey 6, 50^v, 55^v).

1679

Perhaps already now, John Ayloffe writes the bruising anti-Stuart satire 'Marvell's Ghost' ('From the dark Stygian banks I come'), which features prominently in manuscript and print collections of state poetry (especially *Third Collection* 1689; *POAS* 1697). Ayloffe and AM had been in service to the Dutch in 1674; Ayloffe's involvement in the Rye House Plot (1683) led to his execution, 30 October 1685. (Lord, ed., *POAS*, 1:284–6, 470)

31 March: Mary 'Marvell' and the lawyer John Greene take out administration of AM's estate (PRO, PROB6/54/25ᵛ): Greene claims on oath to be AM's creditor but later admits to working for John Farrington, who will claim to have done Mary Palmer this 'great kindnesse because she did often with teares bewaile to him this Defendant her owne poverty and that of her pretended husbands', but more especially because Farrington in turn will claim to be AM's creditor as administrator of Nelthorpe's estate, seeking to get from the goldsmith Wallis the money from the £500 bond in AM's name which Nelthorpe's name alone could not release (PRO, C6/275/120, Greene's answer; C7/589/82, Mary Marvell and Farrington's answers; C8/252/9, Farrington's answer).

April to June 1679? John Oldham, 'Satyr II', lines 15–18, 89–90, and especially 110–11 recall AM's 'The Loyal Scot' ('Instead of all the Plagues had Bishops come, / Pharaoh at first would have sent Israell home', lines 108–9 [122–3]) and the Blood epigram, lines 178–85 [192–9]). First printed in *Satyrs Upon the Jesuits* (1681) and often republished thereafter on its own and in collections of Oldham's works. (Oldham, 18, 20, 21, 366, 368)

30 April: John Farrington recognized as administrator of Nelthorpe's estate, after which he enters a caveat on the administration of AM's estate (PRO, PROB6/53/88ᵛ; C6/276/48, Mary Marvell answer; C7/587/95).

5 June: John Aubrey (London) reports to Anthony Wood (Oxford) that 'Andrew Marvell sepult in St Giles Ch: in the Fields 18 Aug. 1678'. Wood's endorsement notes AM's biography is to be entered in *Athenae Oxonienses* under the life of Samuel Parker (in keeping with his method of including persons not of Oxford in the biographies of alumni associated with them). (Bodl. MS Wood F39, 324ʳ, 325ᵛ)

10 June: The Press Act of 1662 expires, which leads in the next months to a proliferation of publications. Control of the press is then attempted by various means, especially through court actions for seditious libel; not until after the Oxford Parliament in 1681 is a more effective censorship imposed. (Crist 1978)

7 July: *Advice to a Painter, &c.* ('Spread a large canvas, Painter, to contain ...', folio sheet [4 pp.]) puts into print a 1673 attack on the Duke of York's

Catholicism (Lord, ed., *POAS* 1:213–19). Attributed to AM in a later manuscript with many other questionable attributions to AM (National Library of Scotland, Advocates MS 19.1.12, 84ᵛ) but this has been better attributed to Henry Savile (see *Savile Correspondence*, 107, 108–9).

30 September: The Prerogative Court of Canterbury grants joint administration of AM's estate to 'Mariae Marvell' and the lawyer John Greene (PRO, PROB6/54/25ᵛ; Tupper 367). The goldsmith Wallis later explains that 'The wife and relict of the said Nelthorpe had been put into the said Letters of Admnistracon together with the said Mary Marvell instead of the said Greene but that they contrived the same the better to conceale it from anie suspition that the said bill or bond did belong unto the estate of the said Edward Nelthorpe'; Greene was much involved in business with Richard Thompson and his partners (PRO, C6/275/120; C7/581/73; Tupper 377).

October: Publication of the folio edition of *An Account of the Growth of Popery and Arbitrary Government ... By Andrew Marvel, Esq;* 'Printed at Amsterdam, And Recommended to the Reading of | all English Protestants.' This integrates *A List of Several Ships* into the *Account*, on sig. P2–S2. Bishop Thomas Barlow notes on his copy (Oxford, Queen's College, 6 B. 17 [11]) that "Tis certaine Mr Marvell neither did, nor could compose this booke. My Ld. Shaftesbury is beleived, and (as 'tis said) knowne to be the Author of it'. Not dated but listed as 1679 in *A Compleat Catalogue of all the Stitch'd Books and Single Sheets Printed since the First Discovery of The Popish Plot ...* (1680), p. 5, and likewise in the ordering of Luttrell's folio 'Popish plot vol. 1. Narrative & Tracts relating to it' where his list of the contents includes (Cambridge UL, Sel.3.239) no. '21. And. Marvell Growth of popery in England. 78'; also Florence, Archivio di Stato, F.M. Filze 4248–52 binds it with other 1679 tracts in folio: as nos. 5–6, between no. 4. *A True Narrative of the Horrid Plot and Conspiracy ...*, and no. 7, *The Parallel or an Account of the Growth of Knavery ...*, L'Estrange's republication answering the republication of AM's work. (*MPW* 2:216–7)

18 October: Newsletter reports that: 'severall printers and dispersers of books are Complained Against for divers books lately Come forth one Called the growth of Popery, another Called the Countrey Appeale About which and severall other matter one mr Ray and other persons are Committed to Newgate and will be severely handled Indictments being order to be drawne up Against them.' (Folger Library MS L.c. 850, 18 October, 1679)

20 October: Narcissus Luttrell records that: 'The [Privy] Councell hath taken into Consideration the many Seditious books & pamphletts that dayly come abroad and have Adjudged the Appeal from the Country to the Citty, the Growth of Popery, and Weighty Considerations to have Treasonable matter in them, and will endeavour to prevent the comeing forth of any such for the future, by punishing those already in Custody,

and putting the Laws in full execution against those that shall presume to publish such for the future.' This is 'a new edition of the Growth of Popery'. (Oxford, All Souls, MS 171, 76^r; Luttrell, *Brief Historical Relation*, 1:23)

November: Roger L'Estrange publishes *The Parallel or, An Account of the Growth of Knavery* (1679), a revised folio edition of his *Account of the Growth of Knavery* of the previous year (advertisement in November, *TC* 1:374). This now begins 'There came forth about two years since, a Couple of Seditious Pamphlets in quarto; The one, just upon the heel of the other: The former was entitled, *An Account of the Growth of Popery and Arbitrary Government in England, &c.* which was followed by *A Seasonable Argument to perswade all the Grand Juries in England, &c.* the latter being only an abstract and explication of the designe of the other'; L'Estrange now complains of 'the other side having reviv'd the occasion of it, since the death of Andrew Marvell, by a Posthumous Impression, with his name at length to it', the motive being 'to Canonize Mr. Marvell (now in his grave) if not for a Saint, yet for a Prophet, in shewing how pat the Popish Plot falls out to his conjecture' – 'it is no wonder, that the Secretary to a Commonwealth should write with the Spirit of a Re-publican' (A2^{r-v}).

8 November: Francis Gwyn (Spring Garden, London) to Lord Conway: has supplied 'the most considerable pamphlets I can pick up, that caled the Growth of Popery is only a new eddition of the Former without any additions to it'. (PRO, SP29/412/77)

AM may be the poet 'of scandalous memory' John Dryden cites in his dedication of *The Kind Keeper* (1680), rather than Richard Flecknoe; the play itself uses the catchphrase 'my comfortable Importance' in its Marvellian sense (V.i.618). Performed 11 March 1678 and publication advertised in the November 1679 Term Catalogue, with a few later editions. (Dryden, *Works*, 14:3, 94, 380, 425; *TC* 1:370; Macdonald 121–3)

Louis du Moulin, in deriding excesses of the Church of England, has learnt from 'the Book of that great man, M. Andrew Marvel, against Dr. Parker' (*RT2*, [1:420]) that at the Savoy conference 'after a long Contest and warm Dispute between the Non-conformists and the Conformists, and these last having got the better, one of them cryed aloud, with a great transport of joy, at his going out, *Well, now the Cause of Bell and the Dragon has carryed it*'. (du Moulin, *A Short and True Account of the Several Advances ...*, 1680, including *A True Report ...*, 1679, 87–8)

1680

A Short Historical Essay Touching {General Councils, Creeds, and Impositions in Matters of Religion. Very Seasonable for Allaying the Heats of the Church.

Written by that Ingenious and Worthy Gentleman Mr. Andrew Marvell, Who died a Member of Parliament (1680). Wing M888. Some revision for present quarto republication, especially deletion of the late references to Francis Turner and other respondents to Croft, and final redirection of the work from the 'Animadverter' to 'Enemies of the Peace and Tranquillity of the Religion of England' (38). AM's name is in prominent font on title-page; the tract is advertised in Hilary Term Catalogue, February, costing 6d. and printed for T[homas] Fox, Westminster Hall (*TC* 1:382). (Lynch 55, 69–70; *MPW* 2:22–24)

[Andrew Marvell], *Relation de l'Accroissement de la Papauté Et du Gouvernement Absolu en Angleterre, Particulierement Depuis la longue Prorogation de Novembre 1675. laquelle a fini le 15 Fevrier 1676. jusques à present. Traduit en François de la Copie Angloise* ('A Hambourgh, Chez Pierre Pladt, Libraire, 1680'). A translation into French of AM's *Account* (based on the first quarto edition) in a duodecimo of 245 pages, of which 228 for the translation of the *Account*, and 15 for that of *Mr Harringtons Case*.

John Oldham, 'Counterpart to the Satyr against Vertue', line 178, includes phrase 'the Under-shrievalties of Life', taken from AM's *RT2* (*MPW* 1:347; Oldham lxxv, 273, 504). Composition dated ca. 1679–80; first printed in *Remains of Mr John Oldham* (1684), often republished thereafter.

The Lively Picture of Lewis du Moulin, Drawn by an incomparable Hand. Together with his Last Words: Being His Retractation (1680 [Luttrell: 20 January 1679/ 80]). In materials framing Jean Daillé's disparagement of du Moulin, the tract condemns du Moulin's partiality in letting 'Mr. Andrew Marvell pass quietly for an innocent Writer' because 'one of his own gang', and observes that he 'extols and admires him so much, as to call him (pag. 88) *that Great man*; though he hath in a most scurrilous manner abused the Venerable Council of Nice, and expressed therein the very dregs of Socinianisme, or something else no less Heretical ... and in plain terms represents those Fathers who were there assembled, as a company of pitiful Dunces; who gave sentence as their Chaplains directed them'. AM would have been condemned 'had he been of our side', but is thus indulged because he was ready 'to rail at the Church of England' (9–10).

Republication of 1667 *Directions to a Painter* with '1667' imprint designed to conceal the new edition, in regular octavo format (A–C8), Wing M869B. This new edition is listed in *A Continuation of the Compleat Catalogue of ... The Popish Plot* (1680) as 'Directions to a Painter for describing our Naval business in imitation of Mr. Waller', and is dated by Narcissus Luttrell to 19 February 1679/80; he notes it 'was seis'd by the messenger; it was formerly printed in 166 odd; a notable thing in verse' (*Narcissus Luttrell's Popish Plot Catalogues* 1956, 16–16a). The Privy Council called it in, 23 February 1679/80: 'Directions for a Painter to be burn't' (PRO, PC2/68/401).

The Litany of the D. of B. Publication of satirical litany praying that the Duke of Buckingham will keep from many sins, including 'From Changing Old Friends for Rascally New ones, / From taking Wildman and Marvil for True Ones, / From Wearing Green Ribbons 'gainst him gave Blew ones.' This print version is dated in Bodl. Wood 417 [39] to 1679/80, but the satire may have been in manuscript circulation previously. (*POAS*, ed. Lord, 2:192–9, 526)

31 March: Confirmation of administration of AM's estate. (PRO, PROB6/54/25ᵛ; Tupper 367)

19 April: *Bibliotheca Digbeiana* (1680), sale of books in which the following seem to be from the collection of George Digby, Earl of Bristol: p. 103, 'Rehearsal Transpros'd: First Part: Second Edition. 1673' [AM unnamed]; 104, 'Andrew Marvell's Character of Holland', first in a volume of quarto pamphlets of poetry (so 1672 ed., not yet attributed to AM in any other source); 109, 'Mr. Smirk, or the Divine in Mode', first in a quarto volume of ecclesiastical controversy; and in another, 110, 'Marvell's defence of Naked Truth against Dr. Turner' (112, octavo bound volumes include one with *A Common Place-Book Out of the Rehearsal Transpros'd*).

A Letter to the Earl of Shaftesbury this 9th. of July, 1680. From Tom Tell-Troth a Downright Englishman [1680]: advises Shaftesbury to desist from his machinations and to root out 'Fears of Popery and Arbitrary Government' for the 'quiet and welfare of the Nation'; the author condemns the 'abundance of such ware, as little Andrew Marvel's Unhoopable *Wit and Polity*, and the *Independent Commons* amongst it, together with the *Growth of Popery, &c.* as also the *Naked Truth, Treatises about French Interests*, and the *Succession of the Crown*, and all this bustle they have made amongst us' (4).

Tell-Truth's Answer to Tell-Troth's Letter to Shaftesbury, in Vindication of his Lordship ([Luttrell 9 August]). In response to the previous tract, observes that: "tis no wonder you should fling a stone at Mr. Marvel's Grave, for any whiffling Cur will venture to beard a dead Lion: 'tis well known, that little Andrew (as you contemptibly call him) had Wit and Policy enough to silence the greatest Droll and Scribler that ever troubled the Nation' (3).

15 October: Date of Mary Marvell's certification to 'every Ingenious Reader, that all these Poems, as also the other things in this Book contained, are Printed according to the exact Copies of my late dear Husband, under his own Hand-Writing, being found since his Death among his other Papers, Witness my Hand this 15th day of October, 1680.' (*1681*, [A2ʳ])

[S. Amy], *A Praefatory Discourse to A late Pamphlet* … (1681 [Luttrell: 3 November 1680]), 18–19: in additionally charging L'Estrange with popery in this second edition of 'The Preface' to *A Memento for English Protestants* (1680), Amy hopes 'some new Marvell will rise, to bridle the Intemperance

of his Mercenary Pen, and put his poor prostitute wit out of counte-
nance.... I shall leave him then to the Fate of Bayes, which he cannot long
escape' (Raymond 2003, 335).

'Philolaus', *A Character of Popery and Arbitrary Government, With a Timely
Caveat and Advice to all the Freeholders, Citizens and Burgesses, how they may
prevent the same, By choosing Good Members To Serve in this New Parliament*
(1680?): one instance of the very many that might be cited of the old
catch-phrase 'popery and arbitrary government' having gained a currency
with no necessary debt to AM's *Account.*

1681

*Miscellaneous Poems. By Andrew Marvell, Esq; Late Member of the Honourable
House of Commons* ('London, Printed for Robert Boulter, at the Turks-Head
in Cornhill. M.DC.LXXXI.')

This collection is the chief authority for Marvell's poems, most of which
have no other independent witness. For the poetical organization of the
volume, see Introduction above, pp. 5–6. The frontispiece supplies a head-
and-shoulders portrait of AM, apparently drawn from the 'Hollis' portrait, in
octagonal frame. The text was corrected and apparently abridged in the press,
presumably between the time of Mary Marvell's certification (15 October
1680) and Luttrell's record and other advertisements of its appearing in
mid-January 1680/81 (Luttrell, 18 January 1680/81, in 'Poetry Long Waies
1678.79.80' [= Chicago, Newberry Library, M872]; *The City Mercury*, 264 (20
January 1680/1); Hilary Term Catalogue, *TC* 1:432). For his copy Luttrell paid
3s. For the bookseller Boulter, see von Maltzahn 1999, 53–4.

The major changes in press involve the deletion of the Cromwell poems,
'An Horation Ode upon Cromwel's Return from Ireland', 'The First Anniversary Of the Government under O.C.', and 'A Poem upon the Death of
O.C.' These cancellations have been assumed to follow from growing apprehensions about printing such materials during the course of the second
Exclusion parliament. Although the otherwise suppressed materials may from
the outset have been meant for limited circulation in only some copies, the
pattern of printing does suggest that boldness gave way to caution as parliament met with signs of its eventual prorogation (10 January 1680/81). The
folio format is mostly in fours and collates as follows in all known copies
(except BL, C.59.i.8, Huntington Library 79660, and Bodl. MS Eng. poet. d.
49): [frontispiece portrait (often missing)], [A1–2 (= t.-p. and 'To the Reader')],
B1–2, C1–2, D1–4 through to Q1–4, R1, S1, T2–4, U1, X1. Both BL, C.59.i.8
and Huntington Library 79660 have the original R2–4, S1–4, and T1 (115–29),
where 'The Character of Holland' is followed by 'An Horation Ode upon
Cromwel's Return from Ireland' (115–18) and 'The First Anniversary Of the
Government under O.C.' (119–29); here all other known copies feature an

interruption in pagination (p. 116 is followed by 131) and signatures (in a folio chiefly in fours, R1, S1, T2 [cancelling R2–T1]). Only BL C.59.i.8 includes U2–4, cancelled elsewhere and replaced with X1 (with the end of the now final 'Second Song'): in BL C.59.i.8, U4^v ends with a catchword and a further final sheet [X1–2] would have accommodated the rest of 'A Poem upon the Death of O.C.' (140 lines, at 38 lines per page in print, yielding pp. [145–8]), although it may never have been set.

John Aubrey records of Milton that 'His familiar learned Acquaintance were Mr Andrew Marvell, Mr. Skinner, Dr Pagett M.D.' (Bodl. MS Aubrey 8, 63^v). His notes on James Harrington include a marginal query about 'Mr. Marvell's epitaph on him' (Bodl. MS Aubrey 8, 11^r).

Sir Peter Pett, *The Happy Future State of England: or, A Discourse by way of Letter to the late Earl of Anglesey, Vindicating Him from the Reflections of an Affidavit Published by the House of Commons, A^o. 1680 ...* (1688), composition ca. 1681 inferred from sig. *2^v and the prefatory dating as from Devon, 27 January 1680[/81] (1). Pett observes that Roman Catholic 'Numbers did considerably decrease after the fermentation in peoples minds relating to Religion followed the Declaration of Indulgence, and after the severity of the Parliament to Papists thereby occasion'd, a convincing Argument may be had from the Letters of Mr. Coleman, the which did confute several imputations of it in Mr. Marvel's Growth of Popery to the King's Ministers, better than any Apologies could have done' (150). Defends English Catholics from blame for the Fire of London, as also proven by AM's hostile testimony in the *Account*, which Pett quotes (180); also quotes from the Lord Keeper Bridgeman's speech to parliament, October 1670, which he presumably has from AM's *Account* (185).

5 February: Richard Thompson still with 'Mrs Palmer', as per his letter to Major Braman. (PRO, SP29/417/234)

A 'Letany' with harsh reflections on 'the Lawless Dominion of Mitre and Crowne', and Samuel Parker in particular, begs to be freed 'From a Comfortable Importance Divine ...', so using that Marvellian catchphrase in its original sense. (Reproduced from 'Derby MS' in Beal 1998, 27; see also Bodl. MS Don. b. 8, 696 and BL, Add MS 34362, 124^r–125^r)

[John Nalson], *The Complaint of Liberty & Property against Arbitrary Government* (1681 [Luttrell 31 March]), 5: this tract against Shaftesbury deplores those 'that now make the outcry against Arbitrary Government, Andrew Marvel, Oliver's Latin Secretary leads the Van, in a Libel, which wore that Name, and I need not tell you who they are that prosecute the out-cry'.

Roger L'Estrange, *An Account Of the Growth of Knavery, under the Pretended Fears of Arbitrary Government, and Popery. With A Parallel betwixt the Reformers of 1677. and those of 1641. in their Methods, and Designs. The*

Second Edition (1681). Republishes the first edition without its appended extract from AM's *Account*.

[George Savile, Marquis of Halifax?], *A Seasonable Address To both Houses of Parliament Concerning the Succession; The Fears of Popery, and Arbitrary Government* (1681), 10: 'Before the discovery of the Plot our Ministers were reflected on, as designing Popery and Arbitrary Government, by many scandalous Pamphlets, and one in particular call'd, *an Account of the Growth of Popery*, &c. as if the people were to be prepar'd to believe the whole Court were Popish; that while they were alarm'd against that party, they might be unprovided to defend themselves against the other [the Presbyterian party].' Attribution in Wing STC but does not feature in Brown's edition of Halifax's works (Savile). Ca. March 1681.

[John Dryden], *His Majesties Declaration Defended ... Being an Answer to ... A Letter from a Person of Quality to his Friend* (1681 [Luttrell: 15 June]), 3, 13: now 'a certain person of Quality' has been 'chosen like a new Matthias, to succeed in the place of their deceas'd Judas', presumably AM. Later adds: 'And when Papists are to be banished, I warrant you all Protestants in Masquerade must go for company; and when none but a pack of Sectaries and Commonwealths-men are left in England, where indeed will be the danger of a War, in a Nation unanimous? After this, why does not some resenting Friend of Marvel's, put up a Petition to the Soveraigns of his party, that his Pension of four hundred pounds per annum, may be transferred to some one amongst them, who will not so notoriously betray their cause by dullness and insufficiency?' (Dryden, *Works*, 17:195, 213, 425, 427)

1 June: this Trinity Term the legal battle begins in which Edward Nelthorpe and Richard Thompson's former banking partner John Farrington file a bill of complaint in the Court of Chancery against the lawyer John Greene, the goldsmith Charles Wallis, and Mary Marvell alleging that a bond for £500 lent to Wallis is payable not to AM's estate but to that of Nelthorpe, who held the bill since AM had taken the bond only in trust, being himself incapable of lending so much money but instead indebted to Nelthorpe; after AM's death, his legacy was legally 'granted unto Mary Marvell his relict and John Greene of London Gent', whom Farrington has asked for authority, 'which they refuse to doe and pretend that the said five hundred pounds was the proper mony of the said Andrew Marvell although they know or believe the Contrary', and hence their present confederacy with Wallis (PRO, C6/276/48; Tupper 367, 378).
Attached is Mary Marvell's answer [undated]: she agrees with Farrington about the bill in the name of AM, 'this defendants late husband', only to disagree that AM was doing this on Nelthorp's behalf rather than his own (she later claims to have known nothing of the bond until the legal proceedings this term, PRO, C7/587/95). She describes Nelthorpe's acquir-

ing all contents of value from AM's Maiden Lane lodgings after his death, even though Nelthorpe had been 'then in France as this defendant hath been informed'; and that about half a year before AM's death Nelthorpe had told 'that her husband need not streighten himselfe in any thing for that he the said Marvell had money'. She reports that AM's sister Mrs Blaydes knew nothing of Farrington's caveat in her name on AM's estate; moreover, Farrington had pretended great kindness to her but had initially concealed the matter of the Wallis bond only later to press her repeatedly to give him power of attorney for its recovery.

Thomas Shadwell, *The Lancashire Witches* (1681), features a chaplain 'Smerk' as bitter comment on High Church ministers: chaplain to the lower-church Sir Edward Hartfort (recalling Sir Edward Harley), Smerk is 'Foolish, Knavish, Popish, Arrogant, Insolent: yet for his Interest, Slavish' (A2^v, A4^v and *passim*). First performed in September [?], the play suffers at the hands of the Master of the Revels because reputed an attack on the Church of England. A new edition in 1691 is reissued, also as item 11 in the composite *Works of Tho. Shadwell, Esq* (1693), reprinted in 1721; the play was revived in the 1690s and after (Van Lennep 301, 387, 432, 479).

[John Dryden], *Absalom and Achitophel* (1681 [Luttrell: 17 November]), seems to echo AM's 'An Horatian Ode' in a number of lines, as when the Duke of York is, 'though Oppressed with Vulgar Spight, / Yet Dauntless and Secure of Native Right' (353–4, compare 'Horatian Ode' 61–2); or when Achitophel asks 'when should People strive their Bonds to break, / If not when Kings are Negligent or Weak?' (387–8, compare 'Horatian Ode' 39–40); or when it is noted of Jotham's intervention, 'So much the weight of one brave man can do' (887, compare 'Horatian Ode' 75–6); lines 805–8 may recall 'Horatian Ode', lines 34–6. Appears in very many editions thereafter, both individually and in collections of Dryden's poems and works. (Dryden, *Poems*, ed. Hammond, 1:445–6, 482, 491, 518, 524; Macdonald, 18–26)

William Disney, 'an ejected Nonconformist minister, who was convicted of high treason and executed for printing and publishing Monmouth's *Declaration* in June 1685', publishes *Nil dictum quod non dictum prius ...* (two issues 1681, with altered title-page), which 2–3 'silently adapts a long passage from Marvell's central argument in *RT2*' (*MPW* 1:213–14, 331–2, noting also that Disney 3–4 adapts *RT2* 343–4; Hetet 1987, 52–4). Disney also borrows confidently (6) from the opening of AM's *Short Historical Essay*; the same bookseller, Thomas Fox, sold Disney's work as well as the 1680 edition of *SHE*, so Disney may well have been responsible for the alterations to the latter – he had been a contemporary of AM's at Trinity College, Cambridge (Admissions and Admonitions, 1560–1759, 268).

7 November: bill of complaint by Charles Wallis against John Greene, Richard Thompson, John Farrington, Edward Page, and Mrs Marvell. Wallis

claims to have repaid Edward Nelthorpe in guineas within a few days of the loan and alleges Farrington behind the conspiracy now to take more of his money, with Mary Marvell imposed upon (at first unwillingly) and Greene employed to conceal the connection to Nelthorpe's encumbered estate. (PRO, C6/275/120)

16 November: Greene answers Wallis that only a year after letters of administration were granted did he and Farrington become aware of the £500 bond in question. Greene says if Wallis pays the principal, interest and reasonable legal costs, the bond will be returned. (PRO, C6/275/120)

9 December: Farrington answers Wallis that Nelthorpe alone had taken the £500 to Wallis with the bond naming AM, 9 June 1677; doubts that AM knew anything of it; a goldsmith like Wallis would never have failed to take a receipt for money paid out. Farrington wishes to recover the money because he remains in jail for debt and wants creditors off his back. (PRO, C7/589/82)

? Echoes of 'A Dialogue between Thyrsis and Dorinda' (and 'To his Coy Mistress'?) in epitaph by Daniel Scargill for his first wife Sarah Scargill, in the church of St Mary Magdalene, Mulbarton, Norfolk. (Davidson 1986)

Francis Smith, *An Account of the Injurious Proceedings of Sir George Jeffreys ... Against Francis Smith, Bookseller* (1681), 19: describes the Stationer Samuel Mearne's oppression in July 1678.

1682

AM's 'On Paradise Lost' translated into German by Ernst Gottlieb von Berge, in *Das Verlustigte Paradeis* (Zerbst [Saxony-Anhalt], 1682), *6^v–7^v.

Ca. 1682, Andrew Allam sends Anthony Wood a summary of the Parker–AM controversy, including a bibliography of works responding to *The Rehearsal Transpros'd*, Wood endorsing the document 'Andr. Marvell, rehearsall and its answer [marg: 'p[arts]. 1.2.'] – to be brought in into Dr Sam. Parker' with more AM references from Allam in reporting on Parker himself (Bodl. MS Wood F47, 672, 673^{r-v}, 692^r). This will provide the substance of the entry for AM in Wood's *Athenae Oxonienses*, including Allam's judgement that: 'The pen combat exercis'd between D^{or} Sam: Parker & Mr And: Marvel was briskly manag'd wth as much smart, cutting & satyrical wit on both sides, as any other perhaps of late hath been.... it was generally thought nay even by many of those who were otherwise favourers of D^{or} Parker's cause, that he thro a too loose & unwary handling of the debate tho in a brave, flourishing, & lofty stile laid himself too open to the severer strokes of his snearing adversary, & that the odds & victory lay on Marvel's side; Yet it wrought this good effect upon the D^{or}, that for ever after it toke down somewhat the high spirit of this braving defying writer, in so much that tho Marvel in a 2^d part reply'd upon the D$^{or's}$ reproof, yet he judg'd it more prudent rather to lay down the cudgells, than to enter the lists again with an untowardly combatant so hugely well vers'd & experienc'd in the then but newly refin'd art (tho much in mode & fashion almost ever since) of sportive, jeering buffoonry.... This Marvel was a very celebrat'd wit among the Fanaticks, & thought to have been the only one truly soe for these pretty many years last past, wch they have had. Benjamin Alsop now a Conventicling Parson about Westminster, hath put in very eagerly to succeed Marvel in his Antisozzo against D^{or} Sherlock.' (678b^r)

About this time Allam also sends Wood a briefer summary of the *Naked Truth* / *Mr. Smirke* controversy with quotation from the preface to the latter and further bibliographical detail (699^r).

11 January: Mary Marvell's answer to the goldsmith Charles Wallis's bill of complaint (PRO, C7/589/82): tells her side of the story of the Nelthorpe and Thompson bankruptcy; cites her very belated discovery of the existence of the bond now in dispute; claims that Nelthorpe had in AM's lifetime told her that AM had money and insists that the closeness of AM's relation with Nelthorpe makes it necessary for the other side to prove that AM's bill was indeed Nelthorpe's and not AM gaining Nelthorpe's assistance in his own affair.

23 January: Mary Marvell now files her own bill of complaint against John Farrington, John Greene, and Charles Wallis, at which point her claims to have been married to AM begin to come into question (PRO, C7/587/95; Tupper 378–9). At issue is what at AM's death (dated 'on or around' 10 August 1678) was taken from his 'lodgings in Mayden Lane in Covent Garden where he kept his moneys bonds books writings and other goods and chattles and where hee frequently lodged for his privacy and other conveniences' which she claims to have included his bill for £1000 for payment of £500 with interest. She charges the banker, the lawyer, and the goldsmith with collusion in seeking to defraud her of the same.

3 February: Greene's answer to Mary Marvell disputes her claim to have been AM's wife. (PRO, C8/252/9)

6 February: Farrington's answer to Mary Marvell disputes her claim to have been AM's wife and also her valuation of AM's assets: she and AM 'did not lodge togeather as man and wife nor dyett togeather' but rather this housekeeper ate her meals after AM and Nelthorpe 'as servants use to doe'; she always went by the name of Mary Palmer; moreover, the whole of what AM had at his death not worth £30. Nelthorpe and then Thompson had paid the £26 yearly rent for the house in Great Russell Street (PRO, C8/252/9; Tupper 379).

18 February: Farrington files a bill of complaint against Mary Marvell, John Greene, and John Morris and his wife (these last the owners of the house in Great Russell Street): Mrs Palmer, he declares, stole from Nelthorpe and defrauded him with the connivance of the Morrises; she also contributed to Thompson's arrest. He adds 'nor is it probable that the said Andrew Marvell who was a Member of the house of Commons for many year together and a very learned man would undervalue himselfe to intermarry with so mean a person as shee the said Mary then was being the widdow of a Tennis Court Keeper in or near the Citty of Westminster who died in a mean condicion'; nor did AM ever 'own or confess that he was married to the said Mary'. (PRO, C6/242/13; Tupper 379)

[John Dryden,] *The Medall. A Satyre Against Sedition. By the Authour of Absalom and Achitophel* (1682 [Luttrell: 16 March 1681/2]), A3^v: 'I have perus'd many of your Papers; and to show you that I have, the third part of your *No-protestant Plot* is much of it stolen, from your dead Authour's Pamphlet call'd, the *Growth of Popery*; as manifestly as Milton's defence of the English People, is from Buchanan, *De jure regni apud Scotos*: or your first Covenant, and new Association, from the holy League of the French Guisards.' Dryden's preface and poem appear in further editions in 1682–84, and in successive editions of his poems and works in the 1690s and after. (Dryden, *Works*, 2:40, 291, 424–5; Macdonald 26–8)

7 April: Mary Marvell and the Morrises answer Farrington's bill of complaint (C6/242/13; Tupper 380). Claiming herself 'the Widdow and Relict of Andrew Marvell Gentleman', whom she married 13 May 1667 at the church of the Holy Minories, 'As by the Register book of the said church may appeare', Mary Marvell cites AM's having long been with her at lodgings in Westminster and describes the midsummer 1677 move to Great Russell Street, also AM's keeping the lodgings in Maiden Lane from which Farrington or one Mr. Furloe stole much of value. Defending herself against all charges, she also argues that just because AM 'was a Parliament man and a Learned man, Yet it doth not follow but he might marry this Defendant as in truth he did'; moreover, 'the difference of their Conditions' was a 'reason why the said Mr Marvell was pleased to have the Marriage kept private'. Hence her secrecy until after his death and her playing her housekeeperly role, though with AM and Nelthorpe 'shee did very often and soe often as she pleased set downe with them at Meales and Eat her Meat with them'. She did not exploit her situation as Farrington claims, particularly in the matter of 'Moneyes towards her Husbands Funeralls', which burial had been at Hull's charge, with the money for 'Erecting the Monument ... in a London Doctours hands' (Dr Robert Witty).
Same day, White Kennett notes 'Elizabeth Hampton lived in Holywell Oxon: in the late times much admired for her gift of prayer resorted to by

most of the Puritan Doctours and Fellows of houses among the rest by Dr Parker: whereupon Marvell jeers him as bred up at the feet of Elizabeth Hampton She lies buried in Holywell churchyard within ground and this inscription by Mr Hickman of Christchurch ...'. (BL, MS Lansdowne 937, 8ᵛ; *RT2* in *MPW* 1:385, 261)

26 May: John Greene answers Farrington (PRO, C6/242/13; Tupper 381). He can believe that AM's name was used in trust for Nelthorpe, whose money it was that was lent to Wallis and not AM's.

Trinity Term: The interrogatories in Farrington vs Marvell and Greene lead to some consensus that AM was indebted for ca. £150 to Nelthorpe, who sought to protect AM from Nelthorpe's creditors (PRO, C24/1069.2/ 36; Kavanagh 2002). Since these responses closely follow the questions, the emphasis here on AM's poverty in the 'severall years before' his death does not imply that it had been otherwise earlier. Answering are Thomas Speed (Nelthorpe's servant, 24 June); Nathaniel Ponder (AM's bookseller who could never reclaim from AM a debt of £14 5s.9d., 28 June), Edmond Portman (cashier and bookkeeper to Nelthorpe and partners, 1 July); Gershom Proud (servant to Nelthorpe and partners, 4 July); and Charles Wallis (the goldsmith, 11 July), who now maintains AM not capable of lending the £500 at issue.

Edmund Bohun, *An Address to the Free-men and Free-holders of the Nation* (1682, advertisement in June, *TC* 1:496), 38–9: recalls the *'Boutefeus'* who had 'printed a damnable Libel under the Title of *The Growth of Popery*, wherein they Libell'd the whole Government', and more still about the *Seasonable Argument*.

Roger L'Estrange's *Observator*, in developing the parallel between 1641 and the present, notes among the similarities that: 'The Late Discourse upon the *Growth of Popery* answers the First Remonstrance of Dec. 15. 1641. Which Discourse was only intended for the Disposing of Peoples minds to Entertain a great many Stories that we have heard of since, how much soever against the grain.' (*The Observator*, vol. 1, no. 188, 14 August 1682)

L'Estrange's *Observator*, with current events in Hungary in view (Protestant and Catholic against the Turk), can score off those too harsh on popery: 'And has not Our Reverend Julian Copyed that humour to the Heighth: (as Honest Andrew Marvell did before him) making Popery, even worse then Paganism itself.' (*The Observator*, vol. 1, no. 189, 15 August 1682)

20 August: Letter from Samuel Parker to Anthony Wood, '... As for my scribles their order is this'; list includes 'Sixtly A Reproof to the rehearsal transprosed 1673'. (Bodl. MS Wood F46, 272ʳ)

[Thomas Shadwell], *The Tory-Poets: A Satyr* (1682 [Luttrell 4 September])
begins with an 'Epistle to the Tories' in which the pamphleteer scorns the
Tory claim that 'all are Traytors … that speak against Arbitrary Government' and especially with Dryden in his sights deplores 'This Mercenary
party couler'd Muse' to whom 'a few Guinies' are 'as delicious as the reverend Doctors Comfortable Importance is to a languishing Divine' (A3^{r-v},
5). Ben Jonson invoked as standard of excellence, whose ghost might well
now 'bid adieu to th'Elysian Field' and return to earth a satirist (9).

L'Estrange's *Observator* returns to the extravagance of claims against popery,
having his credulous Whig note that 'The Emperour is a Papist; And Mr.
Marvel tells ye, that [Popery is such a thing, as if it were either Open
Judaism, or Plain Turkery, or Honest Paganism, there is yet a Certain Bona
Fides, in the most Extravagant Belief; And the sincerity of an Erroneous
Profession may render it more Pardonable. Growth of Popery, P. 5. 1. Edit.]
And the Author of *Julian*, in his Comparison betwixt Paganism, and Popery,
gives it clearly to the Pagan, from the Christian.' (*The Observator*, vol. 1,
no. 204, 13 September 1682)

The Hypocritical Christian (1682 [Luttrell; 29 September]): a Tory attack
on the 'Godly, zealous, Whiggish Cit' includes a final injunction to the
disaffected Cit to be loyal, and

> 'Ne're read a Factious Pamphlet with delight.
> Ne're feed on Horse flesh; read Discourses
> 'Twixt Charing-Cross and your Wool-Church-Horses.' (pp. 1, 4)

[Robert Ferguson and/or John Culliford?] 'Philo-Veritas', *The Second Part
of the Growth of Popery and Arbitrary Government: Beginning Where the Former
left, viz. From the Year 1677. unto the Year 1682* ('Cologne: Printed for
Philliotus', 1682). The pagination of this tract follows from that of the first
quarto edition (so here begins 157–); the author begins his narration
choosing to 'omit any farther remarks of the Conspirators actions, against
our Religion and Liberties, which hath so well been handled by the Author
of the first part of the groth [*sic*] of Popery and Arbitrary Power, which
ended with the Adjournment of the Parliament at the pleasure and will,
not only of the King, but by the Authority and Prerogative of Speaker
Seymor in the House of Commons, where again he exerted his Prerogative,
and without the Vote of the House, Adjourned to the 15th. of January
1677[/8]' (165).

13 November: an informant (King) writes to Secretary Jenkins that 'There
was a booke presented to the Duke [of Monmouth] by one Smith a bookseller, it is cald the Second part of the Groweth of popery from seventy two
…'; Smith has left 'sealls or tickets with the duke to give to other persons
that he may know who and what they are that come for the Booke. I shall
have a booke this Day which I shall send to you'. (PRO, SP29/421.2/16)

15 November: A trial is ordered in Chancery to decide John Farrington's dispute with Mary Palmer and John Greene over whether the bond had been AM's proper or Nelthorpe's using AM's name in trust. (PRO, C78/1133/33–34; Tupper 381)

John Dryden, *Religio Laici* (1682 [Luttrell 28 November]), 7: Martin Marprelate cited as 'the Marvel of those times', 'the first Presbyterian Scribler, who Sanctify'd Libels and Scurrility to the use of the Good Old Cause'. Appears in further editions in 1682 and 1683, and in successive editions of Dryden's *Works* in the 1690s and after. (Dryden, *Works*, 2:106, 340, 357, 447–8; Macdonald 33–5)

John Dryden, *The Duke of Guise*, first performed 28 November: complaining of Whigs its prologue may well recall AM's *Account* in observing that 'A noise was made of Arbitrary Sway' (line 35). Prologue separately published 4 December (Luttrell) and with play as a whole ca. 13 February 1683 and severally thereafter. (Dryden, *Works*, 14:211, 476, 515; Macdonald 124–7, 143)

L'Estrange's *Observator*, vol. 1, no. 251 (1 December): in discussion of the newly published *Second Part of the Growth of Popery and Arbitrary Government*, Observator notes that "tis a Hard Book to come at', with Trimmer admitting that he had his copy by token, and that from friends newly removed to Holland. Eventually discussion of it yields Trimmer's observation that it has something Scottish in the diction – pointing to Robert Ferguson as the author – as confirmed by Observator's sneer about 'Scotch Liberty', citing pp. 256, 259, 283, 297, 319.

L'Estrange's *Observator*, vol. 1, no. 252 (4 December): when Trimmer laments that 'this same [*Growth of Popery* [sic]] lays open such a History, it makes my very heart bleed to think on't', Observator responds that he has now glanced over it and finds it full of falsities and impostures, and by its Scotticisms almost certainly the work of 'R.F.'. Decrying how 'It runs all the way, you see, upon the Style of Conspiracies, Confederacies, and Conspirators', Observator thinks it worth a point by point refutation.

6 December: L'Estrange to Secretary Jenkins, describes the practice of clandestine printing, especially the initial dispersion to the country of publications only then circulated in London itself. Hence 'This Second Part of the Growth of Popery has been abroad in Confiding Hands for some time before it was taken Notice of at Whitehall'; it is 'Undoubtedly' by Ferguson, and Shaftesbury is involved with it too. (PRO, SP29/421.2/84)

L'Estrange's *Observator*, vol. 1, no. 253 (6 December): skeptically observes that: 'This *Second Part of the Growth of Popery* is only a Continuation of Marvells Design, and History; and the Conspirators are the same, I presume, in Both: That is to say; Men of the same Party, and Principle, though not the same Persons ... Marvell tells ye, fol. 9. That they are neither Old Cavaliers, nor Avow'd Papists: But in short; Whatever they are; they are Conspirators.'

The Observator, vol. 1, no. 254 (7 December): more on *The Second Part*, the issue now being the 'Notorious Falsity, and Malice' of the work, lengthily controverted.

The Observator, vol. 1, no. 256 (11 December): against the claim that L'Estrange's notice of seditious books increases their sale, Observator maintains that his responses are too belated for that, since: 'it is the Common Practice of the Faction; upon the setting of any Dangerous Libell afoot, to Furnish, and Stock the countries with an Impression of them or two, before it appears about the Town; And that to Answer both the Ends, of Profit to the Stationer, and Design to the Faction; it is Dispers'd with all the Industry Imaginable, by Tickets, Recommendations, &c. So that the Pamphlet has wrought the Effect before many an Honest Man comes to know that there is such a Book in Being.'

19 December: Robert Ferguson (Amsterdam) writing to his wife is confident of his position since the government in its 'unjust wrath' is 'forced to charge the 2d Part of the Growth of popery and a vindication of the Association upon me, which I had no hand in, nor knew any thing of'. Ferguson's disclaimer may have been meant for more than his wife's eyes. (PRO, SP 29/421.2/124)

Undated paper from late 1682 in Justice Warcup's hand: 'In the Treasonable Pamphlett lately putt forth, called the Second Part of the growth of Popery and Arbitrary Government His Majesty and all his Ministers and Officers, are termed Conspirators, and more vilifyed then in all former Libells, and all Accions for the preservacion of his Majesty and His Governement rendred most infamous.... the said Pamphlett makes it appeare, that the Party keepe a Journall of all publick Accions, perverteing the truth, and reserveing the same, for disturbance in a future Parliament.' (PRO, SP29/421.3/41, *CSPD* 1682, 607)

Thomas Atterbury uses a form-letter investigating the circulation in bookshops of *Doleman* and *The Second Part of the Growth of Popery and Arbitrary Government*. (PRO, SP29/421.3/42, *CSPD* 1682, 607–8)

1683

J[ohn] A[dams], of King's College, Cambridge, writing 'To Mr. Creech on his Translation of Lucretius' (1 January), explains he had thought, before encountering the Oxonian Creech's work, that Cambridge was the Muses' haunt, since Chaucer and Cowley had been there and that was 'Where Milton first his wondrous Vision saw, / And Marvel taught the Painter how to Draw'. These commendatory materials first appear in the second edition of *T. Lucretius Carus. The Epicurean Philosopher, His Six Books* De Natura Rerum *Done into English Verse, With Notes,* trans. Thomas Creech (1683), C2ᵛ, and in subsequent editions and issues (1683, 1699, 1700).

17 January 1683? (dated 1681/82, but follows on previous): L'Estrange to Jenkins: 'if Mr. Atterbury may be sent to mee, (and assoon as possible) I make no doubt of a discovery of this Late Growth of Popery. But he must take my Direction, and Advice along with him, or All will be spoyled.' (PRO, SP29/418.1/52, and *CSPD 1682*, 32)

The Third Part of the Growth of Popery and Arbitrary Government in England (1683): the Whig catch-phrase in the title of AM's *Account* is here under Tory correction; in a plea for non-resistance, more support is sought for the ecclesiastical ministry (A3ᵛ–A4ʳ, ff.) and the contempt of magistracy is held to lead 'to Arbitrary Government, when Men will cast off the Yoke of lawful obedience, and be governed only by their own Arbitrary Wills' (A4ᵛ).

16 April: Robert Stephens (London) to Secretary Jenkins: at the sessions at Guidhall that day, 'Eleanor Smith the Daughter of old Francis Smith for the 2d part of the Ignoramus Justices was fined ten pounds, and her Brother, Francis Smith and her self both bound to their good Behavior and to give Bail to Answer an Indictment for the Second Part of the Growth of Popery they being both charged in Court for being the Publishers thereof ...'. (PRO, SP29/423.2/36)

21 May: the Stationers' Wardens go 'twice to Whitehall about the 2d. Part of the Growth of Poperie and for discoverie of who dispersed the Lenton dialogue', spending 6s. 9d. (Stats. Co. Wardens' Accts)

22 May: the Stationers' Wardens buy 'the 3d. Part of the Growth of Popery' and go to Whitehall about it, spending 4s.6d. (Stats. Co. Wardens' Accts)

24 May: the Stationers' Wardens further attempt 'the discoverie of the author and Printer of the 2d. Part of the Growth of Popery', spending 12s.6d. (Stats. Co. Wardens' Accts). On the same day, L'Estrange writes to Secretary Jenkins to say that he is not surprised to find Bradyll (alleged printer of some sheets of *The Second Part of the Growth of Popery and Arbitrary Government*) at liberty, since 'The Printer [is] commonly out of Distance of a full discovery where the Coppy is divided into severall Houses; and hard to prosecute. Better still, however, Bradyll informs of being in the company of 'Ferguson, Darby and Starkey' and expects to find 'the woman that delivered the Coppy. / the M.S. of this Libel, he is positive in, to be Whitakers hand. / I intend to examine all the Written hands he has by him, and what others he can get, of the Ordinary Writers.' L'Estrange wishes for a commission of the peace so he could 'do this whole busynesse of Libells throughly'. (PRO, SP29/424.1/154)

'There having been a severe libell lately writt, called The Second Part of the Growth of Popery and Arbitrary Government, reflecting on the late proceedings of affairs, inquiry has been made for the author thereof, and one Bradley, a printer, and another, are putt into Newgate about it.' (Luttrell, *Brief Historical Relation*, 1:260)

25 May: the Stationers' Wardens take 'the author [John Cullivant] waiting on the Lord Major and on Secretarie Jenkins', spending 6s.6d. (Stats. Co. Wardens' Accts)

26 May: a newsletter reports that: 'Yesterday one John Cullivant was seized and charged before Lord Major for handing a treasonable paper to the press Entitled the 2d part of the Growth of popery and his pocket being also searched there were found divers Unaccomptable papers whereupon his Ldpp committed him close prisoner to Newgate without haveing pen ink and paper.' (Folger Library MS L.c. 1381)

26–31 May: the Stationers' Wardens are much engaged with the printer Thomas Braddyll and his examination, also with Langley Curtis (which latter dealings continue in June). (Stats. Co. Wardens' Accts)

27 May: L'Estrange to Secretary Jenkins: 'Yesterday one Braddyl a Printer came to mee begging my Advice, and Intercession for him about a piece of the Growth of Popery (3 sheets) that was printed by his Wife for Francis Smith, in his absence, with Protestations that he knew nothing of the doing it.' Says he cannot interfere and pressures Braddyl 'to shew the original M.S. from whence it was Printed, and to discover the Hand, and the Authour of it, if he could. He promised so to do …'. Robert Stephens (messenger of the Press) implicated in the sale of same. (PRO, SP29/424.2/25)

29 May: a newsletter reports: 'In my last I told you that one John Culliford was by my Lord Major committed for treason to Newgate for handing to the Presse a Booke intituled the Second Part of The Growth of Popery since which the Printer is seized and Comitted for the like Crimes to the said place and that which is observable Francis Smith Junior whoo a long season has published those sort of Bookes without Authorityes being able to find out the Author is now become the Evidence against them and tis believed will impeach divers others.' (Folger Library MS L.c. 1382)

1 June: the Stationers' Wardens go 'with Mr Smith to the Attorney Generall', spending 3s.2d. (Stats. Co. Wardens' Accts)

7 June: L'Estrange to Secretary Jenkins concerning Stephens's malpractice: 'I know a Printer will give it upon his Oath that Stephens lately told him that Astwood Printed part of the Growth of Popery too; And yet no Notice taken of him.' (PRO, SP29/424.2/95)

The Observator, vol. 1, no. 355 (12 June): L'Estrange notes with venom of his rival Stephens, that 'when he was upon the Hunt (as he Pretended) after [the Second Part of the Growth of Popery] has himself Declar'd, that Astwood Printed Part of it; And that he himself met Astwood (as one Assures me that speaks upon knowledge) and told him, [There was a Black Cloud Hanging over Him] or to that Effect: Whereupon, Astwood went out of the way.'

The Observator, vol. 1, no. 368 (3 July): L'Estrange scathingly notes: '*Fiat Justitia*, says he? Why Astwood would be Hang'd then, for his Unrepented *Growth of Popery*, & his Authour, for Twenty other Things beside.'

19 July: The Earl of Abingdon writes to Secretary Jenkins: 'Since my last Sir George Pudsey and two more Justices examined Alderman Wright and took an account of his papers and books .... His books were a collection of the most scandalous libels as *The Growth of Popery*, *No Protestant Plot* and a *Life of Lord Shaftesbury* dedicated to the protesting lords, which I never heard of before.' (PRO, SP29/429.1/38ʳ as per *CSPD 1683, July to September*, 161)

30 August: Report to Secretary Jenkins of the examination of Samuel Starkey, who claims 'that Sir Roger Hill payd the mony to him and Hartshorn: which now he charges them to have stolen, because they should not ill represent his resistance nor take away a book of the Growth of Popery sent him by one Andrew Johnson and some other Papers'. (PRO, SP29/431/62–3)

1 September: Newsletter to John Squier, Newcastle, 'It was omitted in my last to let you know that Cullyford was tried at the Old Bailey for contriving and publishing two as base and villainous libels as have come out of the press since the liberty of it, one entitled The Second Part of the Growth of Popery and the other, The Ignoramus Justices. They proved by the printer, bookseller and messenger of the press that he had brought several sheets and corrected them. He was found guilty and sentenced to stand in the pillory, to be fined 200 marks with imprisonment and to give security till the fine be paid.' (*CSPD 1683, July to September*, 352)

On 5 September 'one Cullivant (Convicted last Sessions for printing the 2nd part of the growth of Popery) stood his first time in the Pillory by Leadenhall Markett and to day at the Royall Exchange'. (Folger MS L.c. 1429 and again noted in L.c. 1430, both dated 6 September)

6 September: L'Estrange's Observator asks 'why not help the Pope then, to Destroy the Turk, as well as the Turk to Destroy the Pope?' only for Trimmer to respond: 'Because Mr Marvel in his [*Growth of Popery*] makes this same Popery to be a Great deal worse, then either [Open Judaism, Plain Turkery, or Honest Paganism. Fol. 4.] There came a Report into a House in Covent-Garden t'other day, of Vienna's being Taken; and somebody was Lamenting the Loss: [Well! (says Another) I don't care for my part, if it be Taken: for I had rather the Turk had it then the Papists.' (*The Observator*, vol. 1, no. 399, 6 September)

Same date: 'Mr. Cullyford stood to-day in the pillory before the Royal Exchange and his books were burnt by the common hangman, Mr. Peck, who has been some time in the messenger's hand, was last night by an order of Council committed to Newgate, as was also a printer for the same crime.' (Newsletter to John Squier, Newcastle, *CSPD 1683 July, September*, 374)

Same date: 'One S[a]m[ue]ll Packer (formerly in trouble for the first part of the growth of Popery and as Assistant to Richard Goodenough the Conspirator during his being under Sherriff of Midlesex, is seized and Committed to Newgate for high treason.' (Folger Library MS L.c. 1429)

11 November: 'John Culliford, who printed the 2d Part of the Growth of Popery, was charg'd with an action of scandalum magnatum at the duke of Yorks suit' (Luttrell, *Brief Historical Relation*, 1:288)

After the discovery of the Rye-House Plot against the crown, AM and Ferguson singled out as especially pernicious with reference to the *Account* and its *Second Part*, and AM cited as 'sometime one of Oliver Cromwell's Latin Secretaries', by [John Nalson] *The Present Interest of England* (1683), 17, part of a larger complaint about 'All the Tongues and the most virulent Pens of the Faction' (13).

Grateful for the escape from the Rye-House Plot, and echoing Dryden's *Religio Laici*, Miles Barne observes 'They have always had Martin-mar-prelats and Marvels to sanctifie Lies, Scurrility and Railing to the service of the Good Old Cause'. (*A Sermon Preach'd before the University of Cambridge* [9 September], Cambridge, 1683, 15)

The Saints Liberty of Conscience in the New Kingdom of Poland ('Warsaw', 1683), 3: a mocking Tory list of rewards to Whigs for services to the state includes 'For the Author of the Growth of Popery. 100.00.00.'

The Earl of Anglesey notes Sir Peter Pett's tactic of quoting 'the Testimony of an adversary, I mean of Marvil, in his growth of Popery' in favour of English Catholics: *Memoirs of the Right Honourable Arthur Earl of Anglesey* (1693), 110 (citing Pett 180; here A4ʳ dates Anglesey's letter to 18 July 1683 and he can look back to Pett's 'Discourse' as having been sent to him when he was Lord Privy Seal). (Patterson and Dzelzainis 2001, 726)

1684

28 January: The Court of Chancery intervenes because so little doing in the case of John Farrington vs Mary Marvell; Sir John Cole to settle the issue so trial can proceed. (PRO, C33/261/308ʳ; quoted in Tupper 381)

L'Estrange's *Observator*, vol. 2, no. 13 (6 February): '*Obs.* There was found in my Ld Shaftsburys Study ... The Book I have severall Times mention'd, of [Men-Worthy, and Worthy-Men,] together with the Treasonous Paper of

Association; which (no Doubt of it) So far Corresponded One with the Other, that the Book Mark'd out the Men that were Design'd for Slavery, or Massacre; And the Other Provided for the Putting of That Resolve in Execution. / *Trim.* But This was since Otes's Discovery. / *Obs.* But the Book was of an Older Date; as Appears by Andrew Marvels Name upon the Roll of Worthy-Men there; who (as I take it) was Dead before. But whoever Compares His Growth of Popery, &c. with Otes'es Plot, will find so Near a Resemblance betwixt the Lines of the One, and of the Other, that it looks liker a Scheme, and Project of the Plot it self, then a Political Calculation of such a Thing to Come.'

The Observator, vol. 2, no. 14 (9 February): expands the discussion in the previous issue of the faction and 'the Mercenary Reprobated Pens that they Employ'd, as Marvel, Ferguson, Hunt', and repeats the point that Marvell's death before Oates's revelations shows that Shaftesbury's plot preceded that discovery, with L'Estrange claiming now that the *Account* was part of this Presbyterian conspiracy, so pat is its description of the Popish Plot to come.

The Observator, vol. 2, no. 15 (13 February 1683/4): again claims of AM's *Account* that 'here is the Scheme of a Popish Plot, already Erected; the Common People Prepar'd by Dismal Visions, and Apprehensions of Things for the Emprovement of the invention, and without any Other Foundation (upon the Main) then Malice, and Imposture'; L'Estrange explains further that the Shaftesburian conspiracy of 1682–83 had been in preparation long before, as is evident from the *Account*'s 'Positions, Opinions, and Reports, not only Derogatory to the Kings Honour, and Government, but contrary to the very Foundations of the Monarchy; and Manifestly Desinging upon the Sacred Life of his Majesty Himself'.

The Observator, vol. 2, no. 16 (16 February): in his larger attack on fanatics, and counter-attack on Oates in particular, who achieve something worse than popery in their war on popery, L'Estrange insists that 'Marvel Dreamt of a Popish Plot, and Otes Expounded it'; so that rather than confirming AM's predictions, the Popish Plot is part of the same Presbyterian misrepresentation.

The Observator, vol. 2, no. 17 (20 February): more on 'how Marvels Project, and Otes'es Discovery came to call Cozens'.

March?: Francis Smith, junior, petitions the King to forgive the petitioner's father (seized 3 March) 'who is unfeignedly sorry, and resolved not to offend your Majestye in future': the Petitioner did some time since discover, Apprehend, and convict, one Cullyford the Author of A Scandalous Libell, entituled, the second Part of the Growth of Popery. And ... hath since given Evidence against the said Cullyford in an Action brought by your Majesties Royall Brother, On which his Royall Highnesse hath had a Verdict of One hundred Thousand pounds Damages', but to the petitioner's detriment. (PRO, SP29/437.1/93–4; *CSPD* October 1683–April 1684, 304–5, 352; Luttrell, *Brief Historical Relation*, 1:288)

Roger L'Estrange, *The Observator in Dialogue. The First Volume* (1684): prefatory cover pages of collected edition list Marvell in index of persons (A2ʳ).

7/17 March: There may be a reference to AM's *Account* or its *Second Part* when John Locke (Amsterdam) writes to Edward Clarke [Chipley, nr Taunton]: 'People are writing against one another as hot as may be, and there are every day pamphlets published here that deserve as well to be burnt as the *History of the Growth of Popery*, or *No Protestant Plot*, or the like ...'. For the book-burning compare 6 September 1683 above and the entry for Francis Smith, 1689 below. (Locke, *Correspondence*, 2:612)

13 March: Sir John Cole reports 'to Chancery that he had drafted the issue in a manner satisfactory to all the contestants' in the case of Farrington vs Mary Marvell. (Tupper 381; PRO, C38/1683/A-G)

26 May: *Bibliotheca Oweniana, sive Catalogus Librorum* ... (1684), 13–14 (2nd pagination): under divinity in octavo, items 124–5 are 'Andr.Marvell's Rehearsal transpros'd' with 'Another of the same, (fillited and gilt)' (both 1672); item 166 is 'Rehearsal transpros'd, 2 vol. compleat, by And. Marvell (gilt back)' (1672); item 168 is 'Remarques on a Discourse, de causa Dei, by Burthog.' (1678); and item 203, 'Transproser rehears'd.'.

2 June: The trial in Farrington vs Mary Marvell has been held, since the Court of Chancery now orders 'that, since the verdict had been passed in favor of Farrington, the contestants should return to Chancery for judgment on the equity reserved'. (Tupper 381; PRO, C33/261/560v)

13 June: Chancery decrees: 'that the Defendant [Mary] Marvel doe permit the Complainant to make use of her name in sueing for and recovering the said five hundred pounds and Interest and doe give the said Complainante a full Authority for that purpose but the Complainante is to indempnifie the said Defendant from any charges that shee shall be put unto by reason thereof.' (PRO, C78/1133/2; Tupper 381)

7 July: Complaint of John Farrington, who has been in prison since June 1677 (whereas Richard Thompson now lives in 'a very good house in the rules of the Kings Bench' where his fellow prisoners guard him well against the marshall and any creditors), that first Nelthorpe and now Richard Thompson have held much of the bankrupts' money; that after Farrington's arrest Thompson and his wife had persuaded the creditors that Farrington had held the books but burnt them, for which an act in parliament had been attempted to punish him with death, although this had been dropped as the creditors have come to understand the matter better. (PRO, C7/581/73; Tupper 370)

8 November: Echoing John Farrington's claims, Mary Nelthorpe in answer to a complaint by Richard Thompson attests Edward Nelthorpe's secrecy in disappearing in 1677 and her having been kept away from him at the time

of his death; she and her children have been defrauded by Thompson of a great part of Nelthorpe's estate, since over three years only £600 disbursed to her on her children's account, with Thompson and his family now safely 'in the rules of the Kings bench prison'. (PRO, C10/216/74)

J.H. Esq. [styled John Harington in Newberry Library catalogue], *The Grecian Story: being an Historical Poem, in Five Books. To which is Annex'd The Grove: Consisting of Divers Shorter Poems upon several Subjects* (1684), includes, second pagination, 13–14: 'One to his Fair, coy Mistress'.

1685

W. C., *The Siege of Vienna, A Poem* (1685 [Luttrell 26 January]), A3^v: 'I confess Poverty an epidemical Distemper amongst the Poets, their Fortunes in a large inheritance in fairy Ground. Ben. Johnson, the meritorious Cowley, and my incomparable Country-man Mr. Marvell, died poor.'

John Dryden, *Threnodia Augustalis* (1685 [Luttrell 9 March]), lines 230–5 may recall AM's 'An Horatian Ode', lines 79–84, 119–20. Charles II had died on 6 February; Dryden's elegy was republished in 1685 and in his *Poems* (1701). (Dryden, *Poems*, ed. Hammond, 2:389–405; Macdonald 39–41)

In Elias Ashmole's list of Popish Plot pamphlets (1685 seems latest date) are bound volumes or collocations of works including *Mr. Smirke* (1676) and 'Historicall Essay touching Councills, Creeds & Impositions by Andr. Marvell' (1680); also 'Growth of Popery and Arbitrary Government' (1677) with related works. (Bodl. MS Ashm. 1506, 68^v, 69^r [see Ashm. 733], 73^v)

Oxford, Queens College, Sel. b. 163: a copy of *1681* given to the Queens undergraduate library already 8 October 1685 by William Lowther.

1686

Samuel Parker seems now to have been working on the passage in his autobiography excoriating AM, Shaftesbury and the Shaftesburians, *De Rebus sui Temporis* (1726), 227. See below under 1726, 1727.

Bibliotheca Angleseiana, sive Catalogus Variorum Librorum (1686, auction beginning 25 October): sale of the Earl of Anglesey's library, which wide holdings include the '2 parts compleat' of *RT*, dated 1673, and Parker's *Reproof*, dated 1675 (under large octavo); three copies of *Mr. Smirke* bound in compilations separate from that with *The Naked Truth* and responses to it; *Account* 'both parts'. (In 2nd pagination, 36, 60, 61 [*bis*], 62, 64; Patterson and Dzelzainis 2001, 712–13, 725; for an important annotated copy, see London, Lambeth Palace Library, Z999)

1687

A Short Historical Essay Touching [General Councils, Creeds, and Impositions in Matters of Religion. Very Seasonable at this Time. Written by Andrew Marvel, Esq; (1687). Wing M889. This quarto (38 pp.) printed for the great Whig bookseller Richard Baldwin follows the 1680 edition's revisions away from immediate context of the original (Lynch 55, 70; *MPW* 2:24). This quarto is reissued by Baldwin as *A Seasonable Discourse, Shewing the Unreasonableness and Mischeifs of Impositions In Matters of Religion, Recommended to Serious Consideration. By a Learned Pen* (1687), with the title-page and sig. A2 reset (Wing S2229). Baldwin advertises the publication as 'By Mr. Andrew Marvel, late Member of Parliament' in 'Books Printed for Richard Baldwin', a page appended to a copy (Bodl. Firth e.23 [2]) of *An Historical Account of the Most Remarkable Transactions* (1690), which book is licensed 3 October 1690.

Notes upon Mr Dryden's Poems in Four Letters. By M. Clifford ... To which are annex'd some Reflections upon the Hind and Panther. By another Hand [that of Thomas Brown] (1687), 17–19, 23, 25, 32, 33–5, 37, 38: 'for long stretches Brown's text is virtually a cento of quotations from *RT*', restoring to Dryden the name 'Bayes' that had been borrowed by AM from *The Rehearsal* for application to Samuel Parker; the influence of *RT2* also appears (e.g. list of headings, 24). (*MPW* 1:21–2)

'A Prologue to the University of Cambridge' celebrates the university where 'Marvel too enrichd his Godlike mind / With Flame & vigorous thoughts beyond mankind', and where Milton, Cowley, and Spenser also spent formative years; the prologue is dated to 1687 or soon thereafter. (Princeton University Library, MS Taylor 5, 31–2; Hammond 2003)

In the manuscript of his 'Secret History', Gilbert Burnet impugns Bishop Samuel Parker and observes that Parker's 'extravagant way of writing gave occasion to the wittiest Books that have appeared in this age, for Mr. Marvell undertook him and treated him in ridicule in the Severest but pleasantest manner possible, and by this one Character one may Judge how pleasant these Books were, for the last King that was not a great Reader of Books read them over and over againe'. When later published as *History of My Own Time*, AM's name is replaced by the phrase 'the liveliest'. (BL, Harl. MS 6584, 221ʳ, and Foxcroft, 216).

24 November: Burial of Mary Palmer, thus named in register at St Giles in the Fields, her address '.gᵗ. Russell Str:'. (Tupper 382)

1688

William Popple composes 'An Epitaph intended for my Uncle Marvell who lies buried in St Giles's Church in the Fields'. 'Near unto this Place / Lyeth the Body of Andrew Marvell Esq; / A Man so endowd by Nature, / So improv'd by Education, Study and Travel, / So consummated by Practice and Experience; / That joining the most peculiar Graces of Wit and Learning, / With a singular Penetration and strength of Judgement; / And exercising all these, in the whole Course of his Life, / With an unalterable Steadiness in the ways of Virtue, / He became the Ornament and Example of his Age; / Belov'd by Good Men, fear'd by Bad, admir'd by All; / Though imitated, alas, by few, and scarse fully parallel'd by any ...'. (BL, Add. MS 8888, 86ʳ; first published in Cooke, 1726, 1:41; erected in 1764)

Gilbert Burnet, *An Enquiry into the Reasons for Abrogating the Test imposed on all Members of Parliament. Offered by Sa. Oxon.* (1688): cites Samuel Parker's hatred of Charles II for not promoting him, but 'the Late King being so true a Judge of Wit, could not but be much taken with the best Satyr of our Time; and saw that Bays's Wit, when measured with anothers, was of a piece with his Verse, and therefore judged in favour of the *Rehearsal Transpros'd.*' (Reprinted in Burnet's *A Collection of Eighteen Papers, Relating to the Affairs of Church & State, During the Reign of King James the Second*, 1689, 202)

AM's 'Eyes and Tears' included without attribution and abbreviated in the second part of *Poetical Recreations Consisting of Original Poems, Songs, Odes, &c.* (1688), 26–8, among poems 'By several Gentlemen of the Universities, and Others'.

Six copies of 'The Rehersall Transprosed, the second part, in 8ᵒ' included in the stock of Nathaniel Ponder in 1688 (appropriated in November that year) as per exhibition in 'Chancery case brought by Nathaniel Ponder against Edmund Dixon and others (PRO, C8/377/55, 31 May 1692)'. (Mandelbrote 48)

1689

5 January: *A Collection of The Newest and Most Ingenious Poems ... Against Popery* (1689 [Luttrell date, but Anthony Wood dates his to 'the latter end of Dec. 1688', Bodl. Wood 382 (4)]): this lacks any Marvellian satires or attributions (so too *A Second Collection of the Newest ...*, 16 February 1688/9, and *The Fourth (and Last) Collection of Poems, Satyrs, Songs, &c*, 1689), but is first in the bookseller Richard Baldwin's sequence of such volumes, which he later advertises as 'A Collection of Poems, Satyrs, and Songs, against Popery and Tyranny. In four Parts. Most of them writ by the late Duke of Buckingham, Mr. Andrew Marvel, Mr. John Aylof, and Mr. Stephen College' (in 'Books Printed for Richard Baldwin', a page appended to a copy [Bodl. Firth e.23 (2)] of *An Historical Account of the Most Remarkable Transactions*, 1690 – licensed 3 October 1690; this corrects von Maltzahn 1999, 60).

17 January: Date of license granted by Robert Midgley on t.-p. of *Mr. Andrew Marvell's Character of Popery* (1689). Printed for Richard Baldwin. Wing M866. This single-sheet quarto pamphlet extracts the anti-Catholic prologue to AM's argument in order now to wish good riddance to the last of the Stuart kings. The preface here commends 'the Author of this ensuing Paper, a Person of no less Piety and Learning then Sharpness of Wit and Soundness of Judgment', who 'laboured to set it ["popery"] forth in its proper Colours, as if he had intended it as his last Legacy to this Nation, to shew how ruinous it would be to us, should we be again compell'd to imbrace it ... And as it were prophetically to let us understand what a Deliverance God has bin pleased to bless us withal, in so lately freeing the Kingdom from that Inundation of Antichristian Pomp and Vanity, and Cheats of Romish Superstition, which was about to have overwhelmed it. 'Tis true, the touches are bold ...'. (3–4).

26 February: *A Collection of Poems on Affairs of State; Viz. Advice to a Painter. Hodge's Vision. Britain and Raleigh. Statue at Stocks-M— Young Stateman. To the K—. Nostradamus Prophecy. Sir Edmondbury Godfrey's Ghost. On the King's Voyage to Chattam. Poems on Oliver, by Mr. Driden, Mr. Sprat, and Mr. Waller. By A— M—l Esq; and other Eminent Wits. Most whereof never before Printed* (1689 [Anthony Wood buys his in Oxford at this date, Bodl. Wood 382 (6)]): the first in the second series this year of 'Collections' of poems on affairs of state. This attributes to AM some Restoration political satires: 'Advice to a Painter, by A. M. Esq;' (3–5) – this is the 'Advice to a Painter to draw a Duke by' ('Spread a large canvas ...') of 1673; 'Britannia and Raleigh. / By A. M.' (7–12); and 'Nosterdamus's Prophecy. / By A. M.' (15–16). Not attributed to AM are the anonymous 'Hodge' (5–7) and 'On the Statue at Stocks-Market' (12–13). This appears in another edition from the same year with very erratic pagination and in a smaller font.

12 March: *A Third Collection of the The Newest and Most Ingenious Poems, Satyrs, Songs, &c. Against Popery and Tyranny, Relating to the Times. Most of which never before Printed* (1689 [dated Luttrell; Wood 382 (7)]): first publishes John Ayloffe's 'Marvill's Ghost' with emphatic title on first page of collection proper (5); reprints *Directions to a Painter* (including the Second and Third Advices to a Painter) as Denham's (9–20).

The Second Part of the Collection of Poems on Affairs of State [etc. = titles, in double column] *By A— M—l and other eminent Wits. None whereof ever before Printed* (1689), 1–6: 'A Dialogue Between two Horses' attributed to 'A. M—l, Esq;'.

The Third Part of the Collection of Poems on Affairs of State. Containing, Esquire Marvel's further Instructions to a Painter. And The late Lord Rochester's Farewel (1689): pages 1–25 publish AM's 'Last Instructions' for the first time in print (this book in four sheets quarto omits any signature B, without, however, interrupting AM's poem). Cambridge University Library, Keynes T.5.10 is an early gathering of the three Collections of *POAS* with the four 'Collections of Poems, Satyrs, Songs, &c.': not unusually, an early reader has filled in Andrew Marvell's name when confronted with his initials; moreover, where the poems leave blanks for names this reader has been especially assiduous in filling those in too, except that with 'Last Instructions' only about half are thus completed, as if this were a peculiarly challenging text in this respect.

Of uncertain date is the printed copy of *Last Instructions to a Painter, 1667* (two sheets octavo, n.d.) at the Library Company of Philadelphia (Rare Wing, 935 Q [6]), but this seems to have been published in the 1680s or more likely the 1690s, judging from its font, the half-title, and its self-conscious juxtaposition of 'Last Instructions' with 'The Loyal Scot' (17, 27). Each poem is subscribed 'By A.M.'. This copy was bound into a volume of tracts owned by Benjamin Franklin's uncle (1650–1727, also named Benjamin Franklin), who began collecting books in earnest ca. 1681/82; it is his hand on a flyleaf that lists the tracts bound into this volume and their prices, and notes *Last Instructions* 'by Andrew Marvell Esq'; (compare Library Company of Philadelphia, 'Folio Accessions 1–4999', items 923–58, and 'A Numerical Catalogue of the Books in Quarto', items 599–607; Green 11; Franklin 48–50).

Directions to a Painter, For Describing our Naval Business in Imitation of Mr. Waller. Being the last Works of Sir John Denham. Whereunto is annexed, Clarindon's Housewarming, By an Unknown Author. ([Edinburgh?] 'Re-Printed in the Year 1689'). M869C. A new octavo edition of the *Directions* (1667), in 46 pp. (A1–8, B1–4, C1–8, D1–4).

State Tracts: Being a Collection of Several Treatises Relating to the Government. Privately Printed in the Reign of K. Charles II (1689): in this compilation of 'Shaftesburian' publications, AM's *Account* is the sixth tract (69–123, followed by *A List of Several Ships*, 124–35), which text follows from the folio edition of 1679. AM's is much the longest piece here in a work notably directed against Stuart rule generally and not just against the Catholic James II; it is soon republished by Richard Baldwin (1693 below).

Yet another edition of *Londons Flames* (1689) includes AM's name in the report of the parliamentary committee into the Fire of London (4, 12; see 20 December 1666).

The Speech of A Noble Peer of this Realm (1689), 2: the bookseller Francis Smith recalls among his grievances, that 'He had of the Books called, The Growth of Popery and Arbitrary Government, as many burnt by the Common Hangman, as would have yielded above 150 l.' (also BL, Add MS 71446, 107^r–105^v) – this may well have been the *Second Part of the Growth of Popery and Arbitrary Government*, in the prosecution of which he was implicated.

AM's 'On Paradise Lost' is echoed by Charles Goodall in 'A Propitiatory Sacrifice, To the Ghost of J—M— by way of Pastoral ...'. Writing about

Milton's rising above rhyme, Goodall observes: 'But I offend – and whilst I praise his Stile, / Do in Apostate Rhimes his Worth defile.' (*Poems and Translations Written Upon several Occasions, and To several Persons. By a late Scholar of Eaton*, 1689, 116)

In a legal commonplace book of the barrister Sir William Longueville (1639–1721), under the heading 'Dispensation', 'Rehersall transposed [*sic*] 2. pt. p. 200. a prince that goes to the Top of his power, is like him that shall goe to the Bottom of his Treasure' (entered 14 August 1689). (BL, Add MS 50117, 10^r)

1690

A Seasonable Discourse (see 1687) advertised by Baldwin in 1690, in 'Books Printed for Richard Baldwin', recto of quarto page appended to a copy of *An Historical Account of the Most Remarkable Transactions* (1690), which work is licensed 3 October 1690 (Bodl. Firth e.23 [2]). Gives title and adds 'By Mr. Andr. Marvel, late Member of Parliament'; verso advertises 'A Collection of Poems, Satyrs, and Songs, against Popery and Tyranny. In four Parts. Most of them writ by the late Duke of Buckingham, Mr. Andrew Marvel, Mr. John Aylof, and Mr. Stephen Colledge.'

[John Phillips,] *The Secret History of the Reigns of K. Charles II. and K. James II.* (1690, in two editions at least, also 1697). Bitter indictment of Charles II and James II, which historical account of 1665–77 (45–78, 80–2) freely incorporates without acknowledgement long passages from the *Account* (*MPW* 2:241–66, 293–4, 341–2, 373–4), and embellishes AM's story of the 'Conspirators' into one of Stuart misrule. Only then does this author cite AM when quoting 'The Royal Buss' on Charles's preference for 'the Caresses of the expanded Nakedness of a French Harlot, before the preservation of Three Nations. For then it was as Mr. Andrew Marvel, with a Satyrical Indignation expresses it,

> That Carwel, that Incestuous Punk,
> Made our most Sacred Sovereign Drunk,
> And Drunk she let him give the Buss,
> Which still the Kingdom's bound to Curse.' (85)

Likely from the 1690s is the commendatory poem on 'Mr Andrew Marvells character' in a Yorkshire manuscript compilation, perhaps authored by Richard Graham: 'Tho' faith in Oracles be long since ceas'd, / And Truth in Miracles be much decreas'd / Yet all true wonders did not vanish quite /While Marvels tongue could speak or pen could write. / Marvell whose Name was for his Nature fitt, / Mirrour of Mirth, and Prodigie of Witt ...'. (*HMC* 6th Report 342a–343b; Davies)

1691

Ca. 1691 John Locke's cataloguing of his library lists all of AM's prose works, including *Remarks*. (Patterson and Dzelzainis 2001, 721; Harrison and Laslett, 32, 185–6 [items 1931–6])

4 February: Letter from John Aubrey to Anthony Wood (4 February 1690/91): 'Mr Marvel in his Poëms upon Tom May's death, falls very severe upon him.' (Bodl. MS Wood F39, 414^r)

[Thomas Brown,] *The Reasons of the New Convert's Taking the Oaths to the Present Government* (1691), A2^{r-v}: 'I have no reason as yet to be so weary of my life, as to desire to be deified after Andrew Marvel's manner.' (Satire at Dryden's expense; *TC* 2:349)

A second political satire entitled 'Marvell's Ghost' dates from this year: it reflects the reaction against non-jurors, and William Sancroft in particular, after the discovery 1 January 1690/91 of Preston's Plot against William III. First published in print in 1707, the title may reflect some belated development of AM's reputation as an anticlerical patriot, nonetheless loyal to the crown. (Lord, ed., *POAS* 5:275–80, 574)

Significant early marginalia, likely by a John Lands, in annotations throughout AM's *Account* in the copy BL, C. 55 d. 20; date supposed from a marginal note in *The Second Part*, 319 (C. 55 d. 20*): 'To the Truth of this, I subscribe my name (having heard this at Justice Hall, at his [Shaftesbury's] Tryal) In° Lands Xbr. 22. 1691.'

[John Toland?] *A Letter from Major General Ludlow to Sir E.S.* (Amsterdam, 1691), 8: Charles I's lenity for 'Romish Idolatry, and Spanish Tyranny', quotes *Mr. Smirke* without acknowledgement: 'To publish a good book, was made then a Sin, (by this Bishop of London [Laud]) and an ill one a Vertue; and while one came out with Authority, the other could not have a Dispensation; So that we seemed to have got an Expurgatory Press, though not an index; and the most Religious Truth must be expunged and suppressed, in order to the false and secular interest of some of the Clergy.' (See *Mr. Smirke, MPW* 2:51–2)

1692

Richard Morton, *Pyretologia* [Gr.] (1692), 96–7: in discussion of treatment of fevers, describes the fatal mistreatment of 'celeberrimus ille vir Andreas Mervill cum magno Reipub. (praesertim literariae) detrimento' ('that most celebrated man Andrew Marvell with great loss to the commonwealth, especially of letters'), in whose cure Morton was unable to intervene (for Morton see Matthews, 357).

[John Toland?] *A Letter from General Ludlow to Dr. Hollingworth* (Amsterdam, 1692) [dated 30 January 1691/2, p. 70], iii: opens with quotation from *Mr. Smirke*, "Twas a great Man's Saying, That EVERY CLERGY-MAN is not qualified to sustain the Dignity of the Church's Jester. That therefore before Men be admitted to so important an Employment, it were fit that they underwent a severe Examination' (see *MPW* 2:40). The author also draws on *Mr. Smirke* to impugn Hollingworth as resolving to be troublesome 'rather than lose the Lechery of his Scribling, and the vain Glory of his Pedantry, [so] 'tis fit that such an arrogant Levite, who seats himself in a Juncto with their Majesties, to consult wisely how to preserve them from a People who mean them no Harm, should be a little animadverted upon; which task I undertook, after I found that Persons of better Ability, would not trouble themselves with such contemptible Pamphlets' (iv; see *Mr. Smirke*, *MPW* 2:100, 176).

[John Toland?] *Ludlow No Lyar* (Amsterdam, 1692 [Luttrell, 24 June]), 7: quotes from *Mr. Smirke* to discuss the decorum of the present controversy, '... I will adventure to borrow again, from my Old Lay-Friend, the most ingenious Mr. Andrew Marvell. "Albeit (saith he) Wit be not inconsistent and incompatible with a Clergy-Man; yet neither is it inseparable from them: So that it is of concernment to my Lords the Bishops, henceforward to repress those of 'em who have not Wit, from Writing; and to take care that even those that have it, do husband it better, as not knowing to what Exigency they may be reduced"' (see *MPW* 2:38).

Richard Hollingworth, *The Character of King Charles I ... To which is Annex'd Some Short Remarks upon a Vile Book, call'd Ludlow no Lyar* (1692 [Luttrell, 1 August]), 22: mistakenly supposes Ludlow tract to draw on AM's work against Parker: 'As for what he repeats out of Manvel [*sic*], which were made against Dr. Parker, I pray God forgive him, it is a Description that belongs not at all to me, as all those know, who have been acquainted with the course of my life.'

Anthony Wood, *Athenae ... Fasti Oxonienses*, 2 vols (1691–92): drawing chiefly on information from Andrew Allam and John Aubrey [see above], Wood supplies a fuller notice for AM in the life of Samuel Parker (2:619–20) and refers to AM in other biographical entries (1:864, 2:126, 303, 470, 489, 561, 838). The brief biography of AM centres in his role as the nonconformists' 'buffooning Champion', notes him 'somtimes one of John Miltons companions', supplies the bibliography of the Parker controversy and the verdict that 'it was generally thought, nay even by many of those who were otherwise favourers of Parkers cause, that he (Parker) thro a too loose and unwary handling of the debate (tho in a brave, flourishing and lofty stile) laid himself too open to the severe strokes of his snearing Adversary, and that the odds and victory lay on Marvell's side'. Briefer mention follows of *Mr. Smirke* and the *Short*

Historical Essay, of the *Account,* and of *1681.* In his life of Denham, Wood notes of the *Directions to a Painter* that although 'Sir John Denhams name is set [to them], yet they were then thought by many to have been written by Andrew Marvell Esq. ... The Printer that printed them, being discovered, stood in the pillory for the same'. (See also additional references to AM in later editions of Wood, *Athenae,* ed. Bliss, 4:312–13, 546, 718.)

1693

In a new edition of *State Tracts* (see 1689), Richard Baldwin republishes AM's *Account* once more; under a fresh title, *State-Tracts. In Two Parts* (1693; advertised May, *TC* 2:457–8), this is sometimes bound with *State Tracts: Being a Farther Collection* (1692; advertised February 1691/92, *TC* 2:394).

[John Toland?] *Truth brought to Light* (1693 [Luttrell, 28 January 1692/93]), 11: 'I must tell you (Sir) An Ounce of Mother-Wit is worth a Pound of Clergy' (see *Mr. Smirke, MPW* 2:39).

Sir Peter Pett, *Memoirs of the Right Honourable Arthur Earl of Anglesey* (1693, advertisement in November, *TC* 2:476), 110: Anglesey refers to Pett's citation in *The Happy Future State of England,* 180, of Marvell's *Account* on the Fire of London (see also above 1681, 1683).

1694

Charles Gildon, ed. *Chorus Poetarum* (1694) includes much of 'The Loyal Scot ... By Andrew Marvell, Esq.' (65–74); also the eight-line Latin epigram 'To Christina, Queen of Sweden', as 'By Mr. Marvel', with the same 'English't by Sir F[leetwood] S[heppard]' ('Bright Martial Maid ...'), to whom Gildon dedicates this volume (19–20); and attributes to 'Andrew Marvel, Esq;' the satire 'Britannia and Raleigh', here styled 'Rawleigh's Ghost in Darkness: Or Truth cover'd with a Veil' (53–64).

AM's *Account* much influences Roger Coke, *A Detection of the Court and State of England during The Four Last Reigns, and the Inter-Regnum. Consisting of Private Memoirs &c.,* 2 vols (1694). Coke draws heavily on the *Account,* in *Detection,* vol. 2, 168–212 [Mmm1, ff.] *passim,* and particularly directs his reader to the *Account* for Orlando Bridgeman's speech, 24 October 1670 (173); and finally notes 'Mr. Marvel, at the End of his Growth of Popery, gives an Account of sixty three of these [ships] with the Masters Names, their Burden, Lading and the Ports they belonged to, from the Beginning of 1674, to the latter End of 1676' (212) – so is using 1679 edition or later. Coke's work is much reprinted (1696, 1697 and a 'Fourth Edition' in 1719 but advertised as newly out in 1729 [*The Knight-Errant,* no. 2 (4 March 1728/29), verso]).

Sir Robert Howard, *The History of Religion* (1694), 84–7: draws on AM's quotation of Hilary and Gregory Nazianzen in the *Short Historical Essay*. (*MPW* 2:25, 153, 158–9)

Letter from Sir Peter Pett (London) to Arthur Charlett (Oxford), 21 January [1694]: citing the Earl of Anglesey's unfortunate venture into wit in *Truth Unveiled* (1676), notes that the answering *Letter to the Author of the Vindication of Mr Standish* [= *Falshood Unmaskt*, 1676] 'triumphs over his Lordshipps book with as much witt and Sharpnes as Marvell did over Parker'. (Bodl. MS Ballard 11, 30^v, and thus entered into further editions of Wood's *Athenae*, ed. Bliss, 4:183)

Nahum Tate, *In Memory of Joseph Washington, Esq; Late of the Middle Temple, an Elegy* (1694 – licensed 7 November), 4: commending Washington's 'Roman Virtue at the needful Hour', Tate cites his 'brandish'd Pen, in Liberty's Support': 'Scarcely in Marvel's keen Remarks we find / Such Energy of Wit and Reason join'd. / Great Milton's Shade with pleasure oft look'd down, / A Genius to applaud so like his Own.'

Edward Phillips in 'The Life of Mr. John Milton' cites AM among Milton's 'particular Friends that had a high esteem for him' and visited him in the 1650s (including also Lady Ranelagh, Marchamont Needham, and 'above all, Cyriack Skinner'); also notes that at the Restoration 'Mr. Andrew Marvell, a Member for Hull, acted vigorously in his behalf, and made a considerable party for him'. (*Letters of State, Written By Mr. John Milton* (1694), xxxvii, xxxviii)

Richard Franck, *Northern Memoirs, Calculated for the Meridian of Scotland* (1694), 214–5: cites 'one marvelous Andrew, or Andrew Marvel' among 'the six great Patriots of the English Nation' (along with the 'four great Harries (viz.) Ireton, Vane, Nevill and Martin', and Cromwell).

1695

William Popple, 'Instructions to A Painter, To draw the History of the Good Samaritane. Luke. Chap: 10th Ver: 25th etc.': an interesting provenance for what may seem an unlikely adaptation of this Marvellian genre to a holier subject, if still against priestcraft. (BL, Add. MS 8888, 94^v–99^v)

1696

Poems on Several Occasions. By The Duke of Buckingham. The late Lord Rochester. Sir John Denham. Sir George Etheridge. Andrew Marvel, Esq; The Famous Spencer. Madam Behn. And several other Eminent Poets of this Age (1696; advertised in June, *TC* 2:590): reissue of Charles Gildon's *Chorus Poetarum* (1694).

Richard Baxter, *Reliquiae Baxterianae: Or, Mr. Richard Baxter's Narrative of The most Memorable Passages of his Life and Times*, ed. Matthew Sylvester (1696), Part III, 102, sect. 221: cites AM's victory over Parker in connection with Baxter's own work as a controversialist; also Part III, 103, sect. [2]33, Parker's response to AM.

1697

Poems on Affairs of State: From The Time of Oliver Cromwell, to the Abdication of K. James the Second. Written by the greatest Wits of the Age. Viz. Duke of Buckingham, Earl of Rochester, Lord Bu[ckhur]st, Sir John Denham, Andrew Marvell, Esq; Mr. Milton, Mr. Dryden, Mr. Sprat, Mr. Waller, Mr. Ayloffe, &c. (1697), two editions (hence the double page references that follow): the Preface cites AM with Milton as exemplifying 'the Spirit of Liberty' to be found in poets (A4ʳ/A2ᵛ). In this compilation, the opening Protector-poetry (Waller, Dryden, Sprat) leads directly to the painter poems, 'believed to be writ by Mr Milton', and to much more attributed to AM (in the table of contents, in the poems' headings, and often also in their subscription), ending with 'On His Excellent Friend Mr. Anth Marvell, 1677' (through to 132/123). Ayloffe's 'Marvil's Ghost' surfaces later (169/160) and then, in some copies of the first edition and in all of the second edition some extra poems are appended, including the unattributed 'Clarendon's House-Warming' and 'Royal Resolutions' attributed to AM (2nd pagination 1–7 / 247–53).

It is in great part owing to this editor's construction of a 'Marvellian' canon of state poetry that so many Restoration satires have come to be attributed to AM then and since (von Maltzahn 1999). The resulting gathering of Marvellian satires includes 'The last Instructions ... by A. Marvell, Esq;' (58/54) and 'To the King' (83/78); 'The Loyal Scot' (84/79); 'Britannia and Rawleigh, a Dialogue, by A. Marvell, Esq;' (89/84); 'Advice to a Painter, by A. Marvell, Esq;' ('Spread a large canvas ...' 95/89) and 'To the King' (98/92); 'Nostradamus's Prophecy. by A. Marvell, Esq.' (98/92); 'Sir Edmundbury Godfrey's Ghost' (unattributed, 100/94); 'An Historical Poem by A. Marvell, Esq;' ('Of a Tall Stature ...' 103/97); 'Hodge's Vision, from the Monument. Decem. 1675, by A. Marvell Esq;' (109/102); 'A Dialogue Between two Horses. by A. Marvell, Esq; 1674' (114/106); 'On the Lord Mayor and Court of Alderman, presenting the late King and the Duke of York each with a Copy of their Freedoms, Anno Dom. 1674' (120/112); 'On Blood's stealing the Crown. By A. Marvell, Esq;' ('When daring Blood ...' 123/115); 'Further instructions to a Painter, 1670. By A. Marvell Esq' ('Painter, once more thy pencil reassume ...' 124/115); 'Oceana. & Britannia. By. A. Marvell, Esq;' (125/117); and finally the commemorative 'On his Excellent Friend, Mr. Anth. Marvell, 1677 [sic]' (131/122) which appears only in *POAS* 1697 and related print and manuscript collections (its blank verse and Miltonic note suggest it a production of the 1690s designed to promote the Marvellian persona in these publications – Lord, ed., *POAS*, 1:436–7, 480; von Maltzahn 1999, 67). It is followed by Buckingham's 'An Epitaph on the Lord Fairfax' (132/123).

The '260'-page edition of *POAS* 1697 is the first, and can be distinguished from the '267'-page second edition published to accompany *State-Poems; Continued from the time of O. Cromwel, to this present year 1697* (see below) which running-head is mistakenly incorporated in this second edition of *POAS* 1697 (sheet G, 81–96).

State-Poems; Continued from the time of O. Cromwel, to this present Year 1697: cites AM among the poets gathered in the collection of poems on affairs of state that the present editor published 'About four Months ago' (A2^r), and again that more by 'Esquire Marvell' to be included in the present volume (A2^v), though not borne out by its contents (except the unattributed 'On the Statue at Stocks Market', 30–2) and perhaps 'The Second Advice to a Painter', 45–8. AM is only mentioned in Tate's poem for Washington (225; see 1694 above) and in Rochester's 'Tunbridge Wells' (218–23, see 1674 lead entries above), and his name is removed, with Milton's, from the manuscript version of 'A Charge to the Grand Inquest of England, 1674' (19; see December 1674 above).

AM listed under 'Poets and Great Wits' by John Evelyn, *Numismata. A Discourse of Medals, Antient and Modern* (1697), 262 (with Marlowe, Thomas May, and Milton under the M's).

1698

Poems on Affairs of State: From Oliver Cromwell, To this present time. Written by the greatest Wits of the Age, Viz. Lord Rochester [etc.] (1698), A4^r: Table of Contents includes (169) 'On King Charles the First, his Statue at Charing-Cross. By A M—vell', but with no such attribution in text itself (169–72).

John Toland, in 'The Life of Milton', notes that in the Protectorate 'Andrew Marvel, who by his Parts and probity made himself so much known since that time in England, us'd to frequent him the oftenest of any body; and whether it was he or Milton (for both are nam'd for it) that made the Verses sent with Cromwel's Picture to the Queen of Sweden, I am uncertain'; quotes the epigram ('*Bellipotens virgo* ...') in Latin and English. (*A Complete Collection of the ... Works of John Milton*, 'Amsterdam', 1698, 1:38–9)

Cotton Mather quotes approvingly from 'the Pen of a Conformist ... 'tis the Witty Marvel's' to castigate high-flying Church of England men, in

Eleutheria: Or, An Idea of the Reformation in England: and A History of Non-Conformity in and since that Reformation (1698 – with other issues that year for booksellers in Boston, Mass., and Edinburgh), 79–81: twice quotes *RT* at length, 'There are a particular Bran of Persons, who, in spite of Fate, will be accounted, The Church of England, and to shew they are Pluralists, never do write in a modester Style, than We, We ...'; also quotes from the same 'Conformist' to recall episcopalian intransigency when comprehension was attempted in the 1660s.

1699

Poems on Affairs of State: From The Time of Oliver Cromwell, to the Abdication of K. James the Second. Written by the greatest Wits of the Age. Viz. Duke of Buckingham, Earl of Rochester, Lord Bu[ckhur]st, Sir John Denham, Andrew Marvell, Esq; Mr. Milton, Mr. Dryden, Mr. Sprat, Mr. Waller, Mr. Ayloffe, &c. ... The Third Edition (1699): new edition of *POAS* 1697. Sometimes bound with the second edition of *State-Poems; Continued from the time of O. Cromwel, to this present year 1697. Written by the Greatest Wits of the Age, viz. The Lord Rochester* [etc.] (1699), which *POAS* 1699 advertises (268).

Separate republication of John Toland, *The Life of John Milton* (1699), 123–4, includes the laudatory reference to AM as Milton's most frequent visitor in the Protectorate and possible author of the epigram sent with Cromwell's portrait to Queen Christina, quoted in Latin and English.

1700

John Dryden, *Fables* (1700), 'Of the Pythagorean Philosophy' (from Ovid, *Metamorphoses* 15): in lines added to his source, Dryden describes Nature as 'Ever in motion; she destroys her old, / And casts new Figures in another Mold' (264–5), which may recall AM's 'An Horatian Ode', lines 34–6. Republished in 1713 and often thereafter. (Dryden, *Works*, 7:492, 881; Dryden, *Poems*, ed. Hammond, 1:518; Macdonald 62–3)

1701

Some recollection of AM's 'The Garden' has been detected in Ann Finch, Countess of Winchilsea's 'Petition for an Absolute Retreat', written about this time and published in her *Miscellany Poems* (1713). (Finch 68–77; Brower 72–4, 79; Moody)

1702

Private Debates in the House of Commons, In the Year 1677. In Relation to a War with France, and an Alliance with Holland, &c. (1702), draws at length on a common source for materials included in AM's *Account*. (*MPW* 2:212, 343–68)

An Abridgment of Mr Baxter's History of his Life and Times, ed. Edmund Calamy (1702), 590: abbreviates Baxter's reference to Parker being 'so handled by the ingenious Mr. Andrew Marvel, that he grew much tamer'. Also 595: 'Mr. Andrew Marvel mentions a Politick Engine, who about this Time was employ'd by some Oxonians, as a Missionary among the Nonconformists of the Adjacent Counties; and upon design, either gatherd a Congregation of his own, or Preach's amongst others, till having got all their Names, he threw off the Vizard, and appear'd in his Colours, an Honest Informer' (see *RT*, *MPW* 1:89).

1703

'A Short Historical Essay ... By A. Marvel Esq;' 'In 64 pages', included in *A Fifth Collection of Tracts, Relating to the Doctrine of the Trinity, &c.* [no imprint]: AM's is the last and latest of the tracts bound under this title (a number of which are double-column unitarian publications from the 1690s) as *A Short Historical Essay Touching General Councils, Synods, Convocations, Creeds, and Imposition in Religion. By Andrew Marvel Esq;* (1703) – note the addition to the title of synods and convocations. AM's *SHE* is a fresh publication with this present reissue of other earlier materials.

Daniel Defoe, *More Reformation. A Satyr upon Himself* (1703 [Luttrell 16 July]), lines 532–5: 'Now, Satyr, all thy Grievances rehearse, / And so retrieve the Honour of thy Verse. / No more shalt thou old Marvell's Ghost lament, / Who always rally'd Kings and Government.' Reprinted in *A Second Volume of the Writings of the Author of the True-Born Englishman* (1705). (Lord, ed., *POAS* 6:571, 788–9)

1704

Poems on Affairs of State , From 1640. to this present Year 1704. Written by the greatest Wits of the Age, viz. [list includes Buckingham, Rochester, Dorset, and 'Andrew Marvel, Esq;' among others] *Most of which were never before publish'd. Vol. III.* (1704): includes 'His M—y's most Gracious Speech to both Houses of P—t.' (84–8) which in 'The Index' (iv), is attributed to AM (see February 1675 above). Also included is 'A [mock] Catalogue of Books to be sold by Auction at the City Godmothers in Mincing-Lane, on the 29th of May next ...' featuring 'Passive Obedience kickt to the Devil ... In a letter written by Mr. John Toland to Andrew Marvel Esq, at his Mansion-house in Elysium' (435–6). This collection does not, however, take up other earlier attributions of 1670s satires to AM.

Jonathan Swift makes use of AM's *Rehearsal Transpros'd* and its *Second Part* (1672, 1673) in *A Tale of a Tub* (1704), both for local pieces of wit, perhaps including its title, and for wider satirical strategies; his annotated copy of 'Marvel, the Rehearsal transposed' (1672) is advertised in the sale catalogue of his library (8, item 302). Much of *A Tale of a Tub* had been written by 1697. Swift openly declares his admiration for AM's success in an 'Apology' added to the 5th edition (1710; this *Apology* is also published with a separate title in 1711): he observes the interest 'when any great Genius thinks it worth his while to expose a Foolish Piece; so we still read Marvel's Answer to Parker with Pleasure, tho' the Book it answers be sunk long ago ... but these are no Enterprises for common Hands, nor to be hoped for above once or twice in an Age'. Swift's work is soon much republished, both separately, in translation, and in successive editions of his miscellaneous and collected works. (Swift, *A Tale of a Tub*, ed. Guthkelch and Nichol Smith, esp. lix; Williams; Ehrenpreis; Paulson; Scouten and Teerink, esp. 165–87)

1705

The Second Volume of Miscellaneous Works, Written by George, Late Duke of Buckingham ... With ... Valuable Speeches, in both Houses of Parliament, by several Lords and Commons: Printed from Original Manuscripts, that give a light into the Secret History of the Times (1705), 248–54: 'Andrew Marvel's Speech made for Lord Chancellor Shaftsbury' spoofs what Shaftesbury might have said on behalf of the crown when Lord Chancellor in 1673, turning on Stuart mismanagement, and advocating parliamentary control over, rather than acquiescence in, such malfeasance (see 20 October 1673 above).

A New Collection of Poems Relating to State Affairs, From Oliver Cromwel To this present Time: By the Greatest Wits of the Age: Wherein, not only those that are Contain'd in the Three Volumes already Published are incerted, but also large Additions of chiefest Note, never before Published. The whole from their respective Originals, without Castration (1705). Follows *POAS* 1697: the difference now being that the table of contents and text alike simply attribute the four 'Directions to a Painter' to Sir John Denham and, among all the same AM attributions, credit 'Fleet[wood] Shepherd' with the English translation of 'On Blood's Stealing the Crown' (106). Alexander Pope's copy with his annotation is British Library C. 28. e. 15 (Boyce; Cameron).

Entry under 'Marvel' in Jeremy Collier, *A Supplement to the Great Historical, Geographical, Genealogical and Poetical Dictionary* [of Moreri] (1705), citing Wood's *Athenae* as his source: 'MARVEL (Andrew) Son of Andrew Marvel Minister of Kingstone upon Hull in Yorkshire, born in the XVIIth. Century, was Educated in Trinity College in Cambridge, and was afterwards an Assistant to John Milton Latin Secretary to Oliver Cromwell. He was Elected

Burgess for Hull in the Conventionary Parliament began at Westminster the 25th of April in 1660, for which Town he likewise served in the Parliament held in 1661. As to his Opinion, he was a Dissenter: And for the other part of his Character it must be granted, he had a lively Genius, Rallied with a good Grace, and when he pleas'd, with great keeness of Satyr. His Works are; *The Rehearsal Transpros'd* in two parts. Mr. *Smirk*, or the Divine in mode, being certain Annotations upon Animadversions on *Naked Truth*, together with a short Historical Essay concerning General Councils, Creeds, and Impositions in matters of Religion. The *Rise* and *growth* of *Popery. Miscellaneous Poems*, this last was publish'd after his Death, which happen'd in 1678.'

1706

Matthew Tindall, *The Rights of the Christian Church Asserted* (1706), 196: approvingly quotes AM's 'Historical Essay of Councils, &c.,' that even the Council of Nice, 'as Mr Marvel justly observes, was a pitiful human Business, attended with all the ill Circumstances of other worldly Affairs, conducted in a Spirit of Ambition and Contention; the first, and so the greatest Oecumenical blow, that by Christians was given to Christians ...'.

[John Hughes and] White Kennett, *A Complete History of England: With the Lives of All the Kings and Queens Thereof*, 3 vols (1706, another edition in 1719). Describing the parliamentary session of February 1676/7, Kennett shows his dependence on AM (or AM-dependent intermediary, like Coke); he cites 'Marvel's Account of the Growth of Popery' as a phenomenon in its own right, both in its freedom in representing 'The Dangers of Popery, and the Advances of the Popish Interest at Court' and in its having elicited a reward for the discovery of its printer or author (3:309–10, 312–13, 317 ['361']).

1707

Poems on Affairs of State, From 1620. to this present Year 1707. Many of them by the most eminent Hands [AM not listed] ... *Vol. IV* (1707, two issues). In criticizing the 1705 *New Collection of Poems Relating to State Affairs*, James Woodward complains of its omission of some of the best material from preceding volumes, which list includes 'Andrew Marvel to the King. / Poem on his Friend Mr. Marvel. / .... / Marvel's Ghost by Ayloffe. / .... [/vi] Clarendon's House-warming. / On Lord Chancellor Hyde's Banishment' (v–vi). The volume includes complete 'The first Anniversary of the Government under his Highness the Lord Protector: suppos'd to be written by Edmond Waller of Becconsfield Esq; and printed in 1655' (x, 245–56). It also publishes 'Marvel's Ghost: Being a true Copy of a Letter sent to the A. Bp. of Cant. upon his sudden Sickness, at the Prince of Orange's first Arrival into London, 1688/9' (xi, 318–21; see 1691 above).

George Hickes, *Two Treatises, One of Christian Priesthood* ... (1707) the pre-face questions 'whether the Reasonings of this Author [Matthew Tindall], (who hath licked up the Venom of Hobbes, Selden, and Marvel, and dis-gorged it upon the Church) can be of any force against the Testimony of such a cloud of Witnesses, against the joint Authority of so many holy Saints and Martyrs, even of all Christianity, from the time of the Apostles' (ix in the two editions of 1707 and the one of 1711); Hickes also complains that Tindall 'cites a most false, and malicious Character of the first General Council of Nice, out of Marvel's Historical Essay of Councils ...' (lxxii; 2nd edn lxxii–lxxiii; 3rd edn lxxxvi–lxxxvii) and laments that 'nothing will satisfie these Men, whose Reasons are perverted, and whose Souls are poi-soned to such a degree, with the Anti-Nicene Venom against Priesthood and Priests' (lxxiv; 3rd edn, lxxxviii).

1708

Dangerous Positions: or, Blasphemous, Profane, Immoral, and Jesuitical Asser-tions, Faithfully Discovered (1708): also writing against Tindall (and recalling George Hickes's judgement the year before), the present author complains that he 'has not only licked up the Vomit of those stigmatiz'd Authors of the last Age, Selden, Hobbs, and Marvel, and disgorg'd them against the Church of Christ: But likewise the whole History of Profaneness in the profane Age, is tack'd together, copied by this Assertor, and pretended to be the History of the Christian Religion, and the Rights of that Church, which God purchased with his own Blood' (B3^v–B4^r).

Letter from Robert Banks (Hull) to Ralph Thoresby (Leeds), dated 14 April 1708: correcting Thoresby on East Riding details pertaining to Hull; addenda include: 'Mr. Andrew Marvel, the poet and botanist, and some-time burgess in Parliament for this town, was born here; his father, Andrew Marvel, was never vicar, but a preacher here, and was unfortunately drowned in passing the Humber. I have spoken to Mr. William Skinner, who, I find, had not the curiosity to keep any of Mr. Marvel's valuable letters, but, as he tells me, gave them to the pastry-maid, to put under pie-bottoms.' (Hunter, 2:102)

Daniel Defoe, *A Review of the State of the British Nation*, vol. 5, no. 29 (3 June), 115–16: asks 'what shall we say to Andrew Marvel's old Proverb, that *he that Buyes must Sell*. I will not explain it as looking so here; but his Meaning he explain'd publickly to be, That he that would buy the Country to choose him, would sell the Country when they had chosen him: Nay he went further, he said they MUST do so, that is, *to get their Money again*. It is indeed an unaccountable thing, that a Man should spend a thousand Pound to get leave to go to London, where he must perhaps spend 500 more, meerly for the Service of his Country, and get nothing by it; and this too in an Age, when every Body knows they have long left off the Folly of being publick spirited, as a thing obsolete, and quite out of Fashion; but more of this in my next.'

Daniel Defoe, *A Review of the State of the British Nation*, vol. 5, no. 30 (5 June), 117: 'Our Last concluded with Andrew Marvel's old Proverb, *Viz. He that buys must sell*; which is explain'd thus; "That he that would buy the Country to choose him, would sell the Country when they had chosen him, &c." To which I shall add a Story of William Rufus ...'.

Daniel Defoe, *A Review of the State of the British Nation*, vol. 5, no. 62 (19 August 1708), 246: denouncing tyrants, Defoe demands 'Hear the Censure of a true Satyr on that Subject:

> To say such Kings, Lords, rule by thee,
> Is most prodigious Blasphemy;
> If such Kings are by GOD appointed,
> The DEVIL may be the Lord's anointed.
> Andr. Marvel.'

1709

An Account of the Growth of Deism in England. With other Tracts of the same Author. To which are Added, Sir Robert Howard's History of Religion. Mr. Marvels History of Councils. [etc.] (1709), vii: table of contents cites tract 'XII. A Short Historical Essay touching General Councils, Synods, Convocations, Creeds, and imposition in Religion. By Andrew Marvel, Esq; Pag. 339.' – again note the addition to the title of synods and convocations, as in 1703 edn above – with AM's tract on 339–401. The passage in Howard's *History of Religion* drawing on AM's *Short Historical Essay* appears here on 321–3. (*MPW* 2:25, see 1694 above)

A History of Insipids, A Lampoon, By the Lord Roch—r, With his Farewell. 1680. Together with Marvil's Ghost. By Mr. Ayloff (1709). Henry Hill's advertisement at end of *The Circus: or, British Olympicks* (1709) includes Rochester's *History of Insipids* and AM thus named from that title listing Ayloffe's 'Marvell's Ghost'.

Daniel Defoe, *A Review of the State of the British Nation*, vol. 5, no. 157 (29 March), 626: deriding any present offer of a peace with France, Defoe recalls how the French had raised their demands in negotiating the Treaty of Nimeguen: 'Which tho' call'd the Treaty of Nimeguen abroad, was in Burlesque call'd the *Petticoat-Peace*, as being clap'd up in Portsmouth's Closet, if Andrew Marvel is to be believ'd, and Sir William Temple almost acknowledg'd it.'

Daniel Defoe, *A Review of the State of the British Nation*, vol. 6, no. 73 (22 September), 292: moralizing about Louis's XIV's career of victory and defeat ('Ballance—Nothing'), Defoe's postscript quotes 'To say such Kings, LORD, rule by Thee, / Is most prodigious Blasphemy', which he attributes to 'And. Marvel's Sat.'

1710

The Limehouse Dream; Or the Churches Prop, by Andrew Marvell, Junior ... (1710): commenting on the trial of Henry Sacheverell, this tract favouring that cleric is deceptively signed as by a latter-day AM.

1711

Daniel Defoe, *A Review of the State of the British Nation*, vol. 8, no. 2 (29 March), 7: against censorship ('The Method of Suppressing fair Reasoning by Power ...'), Defoe claims that even if attempted it would not succeed, citing the example of 'the Days of King Charles II. when the License Tyranny Reign'd over the Press, whether that Age did not abound in Lampoons and Satyrs, that Wounded; and at last went far in Ruining the Parties they pointed at, more than has ever been practis'd since the Liberty of the Press – And he that does not know it, must be very Ignorant of those Times, and has heard very little of Andrew Marvel, Sir John Denham, Rochester, Buckhurst, and several others, whose Wit made the Court odious to the People, beyond what had been possible if the Press had been open'.

Joseph Addison, *The Spectator*, no. 89 (12 June): draws on AM's 'To his Coy Mistress' to caution the coquette. (Legouis 1934)

Already in the two-canto 'The Rape of the Locke', canto 2, lines 3–10, Alexander Pope imitates 'The Third Advice to a Painter', 97–104 ('Not virtuous men ... Not constant lovers ... Not ... Not ... Not ... Not ... Feel half the rage of gen'rals when they fly'). Published the next year in Lintott's *Miscellaneous Poems and Translation. By Several Hands*. (See 1705 above, 1714 below; Pope, *Rape of the Lock*, ed. Tillotson, 132)

1712

Occasional Poems on the Late Dutch War, and the Sale of Dunkirk. To which is added, A Satyr against the Dutch (1712): 24-page octavo volume offering abbreviated and reorganized versions of 'The Second Advice to a Painter' and 'The Third Advice' (also 'Fourth' and 'Fifth'), attributed still to Denham. The present volume includes also 'The last instructions to a Painter about the Dutch Wars, 1667. By A. Marvel, Esq;' supplying only the portrait of Charles (lines 885–944) and abruptly concluding 'Painter adieu: How well our Arts agree? / Poetick Picture, Painted Poetry' (16–17); then attributes to 'the same Hand' the satires 'Advice to a Painter to Draw the Duke by' ('Spread a large Canvas ...'), 'Nostradamus's Prophecy' (20–1), and 'To the King' ('So his bold Tube ...' by 'A.M.' = 'Last Instructions', lines 948–90); and last provides a more recent 'Satyr against the Dutch'.

[AM] *The History of the Peace with France and War with Holland In the Year 1672. & Seq. Containing the Secret Intreagues between the Courts of England and France, and the Debates in Parliament thereupon. The whole written by a Member of the then House of Commons. To which is added a Preface relating to the Present Times* (1712): this octavo pamphlet (t.-p., i– vii, 1–71) abridges much of AM's historical narrative in the *Account*, and especially the debate in 1677 about war with France, in order now to warn against present Tory compromises with that enemy; it may have been edited by John Oldmixon, who promotes it, and is sold by the Whig bookseller Ann Baldwin. The *History* runs from 'It is well known, were it as well remembred, what the provocation was, and what the success of the War begun by the English in the Year 1665 ...' to the end of AM's tract and amounts to about 40 per cent of AM's work.

[John Oldmixon], *The Secret History of Europe. Shewing That the late Greatness of the French Power was never so much owing to the number or Goodness of their Troops, and the Conduct of their Ministry at Home, as to the Treachery and Corruption of the Ministers Abroad* (1712): draws heavily on AM's *Account*, especially as the history of the early 1670s (107ff.) turns to the perfidy of the French in the Third Anglo-Dutch War and of the English Court later in the 1670s (150–1, 154, 160–2, 182–3, 184; Patterson 1997, 195–7).

Daniel Defoe, *A Review of the State of the British Nation*, vol. 8, no. 131 (24 January), 525: picking up on a passage about bribed writers in the *Spectator*, Defoe wonders about 'People that Rail because they are not Brib'd', noting 'the first kind we meet with of this sort in Modern Account, Mr. Marvel takes notice of very happily.

That Parliament Men should rail at the Court,
And get a Preferment immediately for't.'
[From 'A Dialogue between the Two Horses']

Thomas Newcomb, *Bibliotheca* (1712), 37: has Horace say of place of torment, 'to augment my last Despair / Place Ayloff's self, and Marvell there'.

The Proceedings in the House of Commons, Touching the Impeachment of Edward Late Earl of Clarendon (1712), 27: 'Mr. Marvel Chargeth Mr. Seymour with saying in his Accusation, That the King was insufficient for Government, which is now omitted in the Charge, and desires he may declare where he had it' (ca. 6 November 1667, or so, and definitely before the resumption of the matter on the 11 November 1667).

1713

Daniel Defoe, *Review*, vol. 1 [9], no. 76 (28 March), 151: citing the failings of the satires of the present age, Defoe harks back to 'that keenness of Satyr, the happy turns and brightness of Fancy ... that were seen in Andr. Marvel, Sir John Denham, Rochester, Buckingham, Buckhurst, Sidley, and others ...'; he cites Charles II's pleasure in 'The Dialogue between the two Horses', 'tho' it was the bitterest Satyr, upon him and his Father, that ever was made ...'.

1714

Again in the five-canto *The Rape of the Lock* (now canto 4, lines 3–10), Alexander Pope imitates 'The Third Advice to a Painter,' 97–104 ('Not virtuous men ... Not constant lovers ... Not ... Not ... Not ... Not ... Feel half the rage of gen'rals when they fly'). Published in three editions this year, one the next, and very often thereafter. (See 1705 and 1711 above; Pope, *Rape of the Lock*, ed. Tillotson, 140–1, 183)

John Lacy, *The Ecclesiastical and Political History of Whig-Land, of Late Years. To which are Prefix'd the Character of a Late Ecclesiastical Historian, and of the Author of this History* (1714), 50: denouncing Toland and his Calves-Head fellows, notes that their new edicts include 'That the Chief of their Heroes should be Oliver Cromwell, and the Doctrine of the Poets, Miltonick or Marvelous'.

Swift cites his *The Publick Spirit of the Whigs* as 'the most disgustful Task that ever I undertook: I could with more Ease have written three dull Pamphlets, than remarked upon the Falshoods and Absurdities of One', which suggests that to help himself he returned to *RT2*, which AM had cited as 'the odiousest task that ever I undertook'. Swift's work is soon republished, both separately, in translation, and in successive editions of his miscellaneous and collected works. (Swift, *Prose Works*, ed. Davis, 8:xvii, 66–7; *MPW* 1:266; Scouten and Teerink, esp. 299–302)

1716

Miscellany Poems [*The First Part of Miscellany Poems* etc.], 4th edn, 6 vols (1716). This latest edition of the John Dryden–Jacob Tonson miscellanies includes with attributions to 'Andrew Marvell, Esq.': 'The Nymph Complaining' (1:157–60), 'Young Love' (1:161–2), 'Daphnis and Chloe' (1:231–4), 'Damon the Mower' (2:177–9), 'Ametas and Thestylis making Hay-Ropes' (2:179–80), 'Musick's Empire' (2:185), 'The Garden' (2:186 – omitting stanzas 4 and 6), 'On Mr. Milton's Paradise Lost' (2:205), 'Senec. Tragoed. Thyeste Chor. 2. Translated by Andrew Marvell Esq.' (2:207). There is also reference to AM's *Account* in the reprinting here of Dryden's 'Epistle to the Whiggs' introducing *The Medall* (1:273).

1717

AM's 'First Anniversary' published in *Poems on Several Occasions: Viz. Waller's Anniversary on the Government of the Lord Protector, Anno 1655. A Pastoral Courtship, &c.* (1717), 1–25; attribution to Waller explained in the Preface, 'The Anniversary on the Government of Cromwell has too much the peculiar Air, and Features of the Great Man it challenges for its Parent, to leave any Room to question its being Legitimate; and whoever was formerly acquainted with Mr. Waller, will easily recollect him at Sight' (A2^r).

ca. 1717? The Country Tory Anthony Hammond, in sketching a fuller narrative of his life and times, cites 'Marvells Growth of Popery. 1677' in developing his chronology. (Bodl. MS Rawl. A245, 43^r)

1718

Laurence Echard, *The History of England*, 3 vols (1707–18, with a second edition this year and another in 1720): AM listed among chief sources for the 1670s, also noted is the attempted prosecution of AM's *Account* in 1678 with a brief biographical entry for his death that year, citing him with Marchamont Nedham as 'pestilent Wits, and noted Incendiaries', but ready to concede his 'having an Appearance of more Honesty and Steadiness' (3:247, 369, 388, 402, 409, 424ff., 439, 501).

1719

Francis Peck, *Sighs Upon the never enough Lamented Death of Queen Anne. In Imitation of Milton* (1719), xiv–xv: having quoted Milton at length on 'modern Bondage of Rhiming', adds 'Mr. Marvel concludes his commendatory Verses before *Paradise lost* with these four admirable Lines: I too, transported by the Mode, offend, / And while I meant to praise thee, must commend, / Thy Verse, created like thy Theme, sublime / In Number, Weight, and Measure, needs not Rhime.'

Pierre Desmaiseaux, *An Historical and Critical Account of the Life and Writings Of the Ever-memorable Mr. John Hales* (1719), 35–42n: quotes at length from Wood's *Athenae* on Parker–AM controversy, from *RT*, from Parker's *Reproof*, and from *RT2* to establish 'that Mr. Marvel, who glories in having had the Acquaintance and Conversation of Mr. Hales, calls Dr. Parker's account of our Author's pretended Socinianism and Conversion, *a fine story*, or a ridiculous Fable ...'.

1720

Ambrose Philips, *The Free-Thinker* 253 (22 August): cites AM's 'Latin Copy of Verses' on a French abbot's skill in 'entering into the prevailing Qualities and Dispositions of Persons, he never saw, as well as for prognosticating their good or ill Fortune, from the bare Inspection of their Hand writing, though in a Language unknown to him', thus missing AM's inflection in 'To ... Maniban'.

Jacob Giles, *An Historical Account of the Lives and Writings of Our most Considerable English Poets* (1720), 2:98–100: for 'Andrew Marvel, Esq;' notes 'A North-Country Gentleman, of a good Family, and Member of the long Parliament [*sic*]. He was a Person of Wit and Learning, and applying himself to Poetical Studies, he has given the World several performances: what is most to his Honour is, his being the first that found out the Beauties of Milton.' Lists AM's poems as: 'On Milton's Paradise Lost' ('This is an Excellent piece'), 'Damon the Mower', 'Young Love', 'Musick's Empire' ('one of the best of Mr. Marvel's Writing', first lines quoted), 'Instructions to a Painter relating to the Dutch-Wars. 1667', 'Britannia and Raleigh', 'Oceana and Britannia', 'An Historical Poem' (a satire on 'King Charles's Exile and Restauration'), 'Hodge's Vision from the Monument', 'A State Dialogue between the two Horses at Charing-Cross and Stocks Market' (final couplet against the Stuarts quoted), 'Nostradamus's Prophecies', 'Royal Resolutions', 'On Blood's Stealing the Crown' (English quoted in full).

1721

John Dennis, *Original Letters* (1721), 75: notes AM's having preceded Dryden in appreciating Milton's poetry.

Applebee's Original Weekly Journal (26 August): Defoe ('Jonathan Problematick') wishes to write 'the elaborate Historys of all the Secretaries of S—, for some Ages past, from the famous Walsingham in Queen Elizabeth's Reign, of whom a modern Poet says;

"Her Walsingham cou'd dark Councils unriddle,
"And Conjur'd by th'Help of his Book and his Fiddle.'
Andrew Marvel's Satyr ['A Dialogue between the Two Horses', 151–2]
(Legouis 1928, 430)

1722

On or before this date (the year of his death), Dr John Baron, Fellow and then Master of Balliol, adds AM to the list of Yorkshire writers in his copy of Fuller's *History of the Worthies* (1662), taking his information from Wood's *Athenae Oxonienses*. (Bodl. MS Rawl. Q.c.3, 205)

1724

The Works Of the Late Reverend and Learned John Howe, M.A., ed. Edmund Calamy, 2 vols (1724) 1:24; Edmund Calamy, *Memoirs of the Life Of the Late*

Revd. Mr. John Howe (1724), 68–9: 'In the year 1677, [Howe] publish'd a Tract, entitl'd, *The Reconcileableness of God's Prescience of the Sins of Men, with the Wisdom and Sincerity of his Counsels and Exhortations, and whatever other means he uses to prevent them*: Written by way of Letter to the honourable Robert Boyle Esq; This Treatise was exceedingly admir'd by some, and as much oppos'd by others. Mr. Theophilus Gale in particular, his old fellow Collegiate, publishing about this time his fourth part of *The Court of the Gentiles*, made some Animadversions upon it. Whereupon Mr. Howe added a Postscript, in Defence of the said Letter, in which he makes a return to Mr. Gale's Remarks. Mr. Danson also wrote against this Tract, but I know not that Mr. Howe took any notice of him; the ingenious Andrew Marvel Esq; made a very witty and entertaining Reply to him. Upon the account of this Performance of his, Mr. Wood represents Mr. Howe, as *a very great and strict Arminian*; but very wrongfully. For that which he mainly asserts in that Discourse, is no more than this, that *it is inconceivable, that the holy and good God should irresistably determine the Wills of Men to, and punish the same thing; that he should irresistably determine the Will of a Man to the hatred of his own most blessed self, and then exact severest Punishments for the Offence done*, which the strictest Calvinist has not the least occasion (as far as I can perceive) to scruple to acknowledge. This Notion widely differs from asserting the blessed God universally to have left his reasonable Creatures an indetermin'd Power, with respect to all Actions, Good as well as Evil, to the utter exclusion of *Efficacious Grace*, in reference even to the best Actions that are. 'Tis that, that is the true Arminian Principle ...'

Daniel Defoe, *Tour Thro' The Whole Island of Great Britain*, 3 vols (1724–27), 1:51, touches on AM's application of CABAL to the initials of the Clifford – Arlington – Buckingham – Ashley Cooper – Lauderdale ministry. (Collins 18)

1725

Laurence Eusden, *To Mr. John Saunders, On Seeing His Paintings in Cambridge* (dated Trinity College, Cambridge, 22 November 1725): 'Welcome, nice Artist, to these learn'd Retreats, / The Springs of Science, and Apollo's Seats! / Think not, my Numbers shall prescribe a Law, / And, like bold Marvel, teach Thee, how to draw: / I only would my Thoughts, sincere, impart, / And, without Flattery, praise a Sister-Art.'

Pierre Desmaiseaux, *An Historical and Critical Account of the Life and Writings of Wm. Chillingworth, Chancellor of the Church of Sarum* (1725), 255–6n (and index): quotes approvingly from AM's *Account*, as printed in the *State Tracts* (1689), for its hostile valuation of 'the Popish Religion ... [by] a very ingenious Author.'

George Vertue, *Vertue Note Books*, 2:22: 'Andrew Marvell his picture an Original in possession Mr Asheley. a relation of the Ld. Ashley Cooper. –

Lilly. p. Bedford Row near Grays Inn.' (also in table of contents to the note-book, 2:2). Date uncertain for another reference (2:53), where Vertue seems to draw on Wood for possible attribution of *Directions to a Painter* to AM.

1726

The Works of Andrew Marvell Esq., ed. Thomas Cooke, 2 vols (1726), duodec-imo published for Edmund Curll, with frontispiece portrait of AM adapted from that in the folio *Miscellaneous Poems* (1681). Thomas Cooke (1703–56) is a good classicist of dissenting background: his first publication is a poem on the death of the Duke of Marlborough (1722) and his Whig attack on Pope, Swift and others (1725) earns him harsh treatment in *The Dunciad*; his translation of Hesiod (1728) wins him a more lasting fame; and he becomes editor / author of *The Craftsman* in 1741. Cooke dedicates the present work to the duke of Devonshire, son of William Cavendish, first Duke of Devonshire, here styled a friend of AM (1:v–vii); the biography within the volumes is dedicated to John Bempde, son of AM's friend Abraham Vanden Bemde (1:1, 9; March 1673 above); the second volume is additionally dedicated to the Earl of Pembroke, citing his 'Zeal for the Revolution' (March). Cooke's influential biography and his publication of the letters to Popple (mistakenly presented as letters to Cavendish) much shape AM's Whig reputation; the letters Cooke has from AM's 'nieces' who also furnish him 'with some Materials for his life', presumably including the William Popple epitaph for AM (quoted in full), with other biographi-cal assistance from the Cambridge antiquary Thomas Baker (1:ix–xi, 36–7, 41). Since Cooke's 'Design in this is to draw a Pattern for all free-born English-men, in the Life of a worthy Patriot', he dwells on AM's Restoration career, supplying the story of Danby's failed bribe as well as notice of the Parker and Turner controversies and the *Account* (1:3, 8ff., 11–13, 21–34). Cooke characterizes AM as 'very reserved among those he did not well know, and a most delightful and improving Companion among Friends. He was always very temperate, and of a healthful and strong Constitution, to the last' (1:37).

First volume 'Consisting of Poems on several Occasions. To which is prefixed An Account of the Life and Writings of the Author'. Cooke is con-cerned to correct the English and especially the Latin of AM's poems, which preoccupation shows in his valuation of the poems: 'Most of them seem to be the Effect of a lively Genius and manly Sense, but at the same Time seem to want that Correctness he was capable of making. If we have any which may be properly said to come finished from his Hands, they are these, *On Milton's Paradise lost, On Blood's stealing the Crown*, and *A Dialogue between two Horses*' (1:ix–x, 18–19). The eighteenth-century ten-dency to render stanzas as continuous couplets is most conspicuous in 'Upon Appleton House', which with 'Upon the Hill and Grove at Billborow' is presented first, presumably in keeping with the estate-poem / loco-descriptive preferences of Country Whigs.

Second volume 'Consisting of Poems on Several Occasions, Latin and English; State Poems; And other Pieces, in Prose. To which are added, Some Explanatory Notes to the State Poems, and several Letters, never before printed'. After a few more 'Poems on Several Occasions' ('A Dialogue between the Resolved Soul, and Created Pleasure', 'On the Victory obtained by Blake', 'On Mr Milton's Paradise Lost'), the 'State Poems' that follow include quite a full complement of the 'Marvellian' Restoration satires as per attributions in *POAS*, with some sympathetic annotation (2:135–44). Cooke observes that AM's *State Poems* contain 'much of the secret History of the Reign of King Charles the second' but doubts whether AM the author of the *Directions to a Painter*, not included, although 'Last Instructions', 'Instructions to a Painter. Part II' ('Spread a large Canvas ...') and 'Instructions to a Painter. Part III' ('Painter, once more thy Pencil reassume') are kept (1:19–20, 2:88–133). The volume is completed by the final 'Carmina Miscellanea' (the Latin poetry with translations of 'A Drop of Dew' and 'The Garden') and 'Epistles' (chiefly those to Popple) (vol. 2, new pagination 1–77).

'Thomas Cooke, 5 l. for writing Marvel's 'Life,' &c (April).' (Roberts 240)

Samuel Parker, *De Rebus sui Temporis Commentariorum Libri Quatuor* (1726), 274–88 and 362, 363 (index): features a bitter attack on AM, Shaftesbury and the Shaftesburians, for details of which see below under Thomas Newlin's translation of this work in 1727. Parker seems to have written the work by 1686 (227); there is an interleaved large-paper copy of this edition (Bodl. 4° Rawl. 325) in which his second son, also Samuel Parker (d. 1730), enlarges the complaints against AM, especially 274a, 276c, 284c. In addition to the different English translations printed in 1727 and 1728, there is another in manuscript (BL, Harl. MS 4218).

Jonathan Swift makes some local use of AM's *Rehearsal Transpros'd* and its *Second Part* (1672, 1673) in *Gulliver's Travels*, notably AM's description of Parker's afflatus leading to dangerous levitation (Aeolists) and AM's Suetonian 'Hinnibility' (Houyhnhnms). Swift's work is soon much republished, both separately, in translation, and in successive editions of his miscellaneous and collected works. (*RT2*, in *MPW* 1:308; Swift, *Gulliver's Travels*; Pritchard 1990; Anselment; Scouten and Teerink, esp. 192–244)

1727

The First Part of Miscellany Poems. Containing Variety of New Translations of the Ancient Poets: Together with Several Original poems. By the Most Eminent Hands. Publish'd by Mr. Dryden ... 6 vols. (1727). In its gathering of seven-

teenth-century verse, this fifth 'edition' of the Dryden-Tonson miscellanies redistributes the same nine poems by AM from the edition of 1716, but in the same order (now 1:151, 154, 223; 2:173, 176, 181, 182, 201, 203).

Bishop Parker's History of His Own Time. In Four Books. Faithfully Translated from the Latin Original, by Thomas Newlin (1727): index, under Marvell – 'a scurrilous slanderer, publishes infamous libels'; under Milton – 'by his interest Marvel that resembled him in malignity of genius, is made Under-Secretary to Cromwell'. Parker decries the formation of the Green Ribbon Club of radical Whigs (330–1), amongst which 'lewd Revilers, the lewdest was one whose name was Marvel. As he had liv'd in all manner of wickedness from his youth, so being of a singular impudence and petulancy of nature, he exercised the province of a Satyrist, for the use of the Faction, being not so much a Satyrist thro' quickness of wit, as sowerness of temper; but of indifferent parts, except it were in the talent of railing and malignity. Being abandon'd by his father, and expell'd the university, he afterwards made his conscience more cheap than he had formerly made his reputation. A vagabond, ragged, hungry Poetaster, being beaten at every tavern, he daily receiv'd the rewards of his sawciness in kicks and blows' (332). More follows in this vein, with Parker knowing of AM's authorship of 'The First Anniversary' and scorning AM's later receipt of a constituency wage. Parker lengthily summarizes AM's *Account* and its context (336–47); at issue is how Shaftesbury disowned his former policies when he moved into opposition in 1674 and instead charged them to the crown, with AM's inconsistency on the Declaration of Indulgence between *RT* (pro) and the *Account* (contra) attributed to 'the treachery of this drunken buffoon' (348).

1728

Samuel Parker, Bp. *Parker's History of His Own Time*, trans. 'by another hand' (1728, reissued 1730): an unfriendly republication of this work (sold by Henry Curll). The prefatory materials quote Wood on AM's victory in controversy with Parker and how that discomfiture 'took down the insolence of [Parker's] high Spirit' (7); a more demotic note marks the passage where Parker attacks AM, Shaftesbury and the Shaftesburians (214–25, 237–8).

Daniel Defoe, *The Compleat English Gentleman*, quotes 'Dialogue between two horses', 53–4, 80–90? Daniel Defoe, *The Compleat English Gentleman*, ed. Karl Bülbring (1890), 25: 'The advancing men to honours without the merit, is abusing the honour and the man too.... see what Andrew Marve[ll] sayes upon something of this kind

> To see a <u>White staff</u> make a beggar <u>a Lord</u>,
> —Scarse a <u>Wise man</u> at a <u>Long</u> Councel Board.'
> [= BL, Add. MS 32555, f. 9]

Moreover, lamenting the misery of a nation 'represented by men who, in a body, are to be led by a few, if that few guide wrong!', Defoe adds (only then to delete): 'Of whom the famous Andrew Marvell sings merrily:

> But thanks to the w ... who made the King dogged,
> For giving no more the fools were prorogued.' (181, 285)

1730

Joseph Spence, *Literary Anecdotes*, ed. James M. Osborn, 2 vols (Oxford, 1966), 1:317: 'Marvell, rough like Oldham', reported as from Mr. Sc[ott], summer? 1730.

John Oldmixon, *History of England, During the Reigns of the Royal House of Stuart* (1730): in correcting Echard in particular, this Whig historian often quotes from AM's *Account* and the satires attributed to him, with a high regard for 'the immortal Milton, and the very witty Marvel' in addition to incidental references to AM (491, 532, 534, 551, 560, 565–6, 567, 580, 583, 589, 593, 601–2, 607–8).

1731

Edmund Calamy, *An Historical Account of My Own Life*, ed. J.T. Rutt, 2 vols (1829), 1:82: Calamy notes evidence from AM's *Account* of acute concern about 'the growth of popery' in years preceding the Popish Plot.

A Letter To the Reverend Subscribers To a late voluminous Libel, Entitled, The History of England, during the Royal House of Stuart (1731), 4: in this response to John Oldmixon's *History of England* (1730), AM is listed with Milton and Sir Anthony Welden as infamous 'for libelling and defaming'.

1732

Henrich Ludolff Benthem, *Engeländischer Kirch- und Schulen-Staat*, 2nd edn (Leipzig, 1732), 1134–5: AM now features in list 'Von den Gelehrten in Engeland', which cites his education at Trinity, Cambridge; his help to Milton, the famous Latin secretary to Oliver Cromwell; his having surely been a 'Dissenter' since his satires sought to bring king and church into disrepute; and AM's works, following Wood.

1733

Paul de Rapin de Thoyras, *The History of England*, trans. N. Tindal, 2nd edn, 2 vols (1732–33, folio): only now does the translation of Rapin make note of AM and echo him for the history of the 1670s, though this in great part by drawing on Coke, Kennett, and Echard, who were much indebted to the *Account* – for example, 2:682n in using Kennett takes words from AM ('They were adjourned by the Speaker, without the consent of the house, or so much a his putting the question, though Sir John Finch was, for the same thing, impeached of High-Treason in 1640. Kennet, p. 343'; compare *MPW* 2:373). Tindal also mistakenly cites AM among those who spoke against Clarendon leading to his impeachment (2:648n, see Echard 3:195); for the year 1678, he includes mention of the deaths of Oldenburg and AM (2:698). The same page references apply to Rapin De Thoyras, *The History of England*, trans. N. Tindal, 3rd edn, 5 vols (1743–45), which adds three volumes of continuation by Tindal. The first edition (1726–31, 15 vols quarto) does not include these. There are further editions and continuations (Smollett) of Rapin's *History* into the nineteenth century.

1735

The Craftsman, no. 449 (8 February): 'reprovingly assimilates the "modern [court] Whigs" to the "old Tories" and fights them with arguments out of *The Rehearsal Transpros'd*' (Legouis 1968, 228) – republished in *The Gentleman's Magazine* 5 (February), 69–71.

The Craftsman, no. 482 (27 September), 114–22: presents 'a pastiche of the *Essay* on Councils really aimed at Walpole's prelates though nominally at those of Charles II' (Legouis 1968, 228) – republished in *The Gentleman's Magazine* 5 (September), 544–7.

Thomas Gent, *Annales Regioduni Hullini* (London and York, 1735), 37: describing epitaphs in Holy Trinity Church, Hull, Gent notes of Robert Nettleton, sometime mayor of Hull, that he 'married Lydia, daughter of Mr. James Blaydes, and Anne his Wife, Daughter to the Reverend Andrew Marvell, and Sister to Andrew Marvell, Esq;', for whom he adduces brief biographical mention from Echard; Gent also notes the drowning in 1640 of 'the Rev. Mr. Andrew Marvel, Lecturer of Hull, sailing over the Humber, in Company with Madam Skinner, of Thornton-College, and young beautiful Coupple, who were going to be wedded ... Nor were there any Remains of them, or the Vessel, ever after found, tho' earnestly sought for, on distant Shores!' (141–2, index [205]).

1736

A Dialogue Between two noted Horses (Dublin, 1736), octavo half-sheet: this satire, sometimes attributed to AM but not here, follows the text of *POAS* 1697 ('We read, in profane and sacred Records ...').

1737

Henry Baker, *Medulla Poetarum Romanorum*, 2 vols (1737), 2:93–5, includes with attribution AM's translation of chorus from Seneca's *Thyestes*, here under the heading 'Mediocrity'. In this volume, Latin texts printed verso are set facing English translations recto.

Quotation from AM's *RT* for discussion of John Hales in *General Dictionary, Historical and Critical*, 10 vols (1734–41, the much enlarged translation of Pierre Bayle's *Dictionaire*), 5:707–8: 'Mr Andrew Marvel very justly observes, that "it is not one of the least ignominies of that age, that so eminent a person should have been by the inquity of the times reduced to those necessities, under which he lived".' (*RT* '2nd edit. 1672, in 8vo, pag. 175', see *MPW* 1:130)

1738

General Dictionary, Historical and Critical, 10 vols (1734–41), 7:480–5: now includes an entry for AM in this much enlarged translation of Bayle's *Dictionaire*. The biography expands that of Cooke (1726), which it supplements with references chiefly to Wood and more incidentally *RT2*, *Mr. Smirke*, the *Account*, and the Trinity College (Cambridge) Register, and also adds the verdicts of Burnet and Swift in favour of *RT* and *RT2*.

Thomas Birch's biography of Milton in *A Complete Collection of the ... Works of John Milton*, 2 vols (1738) refers to AM as having at the Restoration 'acted vigorously in [Milton's] behalf, and made a considerable party for him' (1:xxxv) and attributes to AM or Milton the verses sent with Cromwell's picture to Christina, queen of Sweden, here quoted with translation (1:lxii–lxiii).

Writing 'In Praise of Frugality', 'R. Freeman' glories in the story of AM 'one of the most disinterested Patriots in the Reign of Charles II [who] by managing a very narrow Patrimony, kept himself above corruption': 'He dined usually at a great Ordinary in the Strand' where having eaten well for half a crown he rejoices in his independence. (Wilding 1970, 252; *London Journal*, 978 (13 May 1738), reprinted in *The Gentleman's Magazine*, 8 (May 1738), 255)

1739

Johann Heinrich Zedler, [*Grosses Vollständiges*] *Universal-Lexicon*, 62 vols (1732–50), 19:1888: AM entry follows that of the 2nd edn of Benthem (1732 above), which it cites.

General Dictionary, Historical and Critical, 10 vols (1734–41), 8:142–5, 147–8: the entry for Samuel Parker quotes from AM, sometimes at length (*RT2*), with some of the bibliography of the Parker–AM controversy.

1740

Roger North, *Examen: Or, An Enquiry into the Credit and Veracity of a Pretended Complete History* (1740). In decrying White Kennett's history (see 1706 above), North scorns its reliance on 'scandalous Libels' such as 'the *Growth of Popery*, first and second Parts', among others; he deplores Kennett's praises of AM's *Account* and observes AM 'was very well qualified for Mischief of that Kind; having been Oliver Cromwell's Secretary, and survived his Master to good Purpose'. (*Examen*, vi, 69, 138–42, 663–6, Index sig. 4U2ʳ)

George Vertue, *Vertue Note Books*: AM listed in Vertue's table of contents and now credited (as 'Miltons under Latin Secretary') with having penned 'Bellipotens virgo' ... (notebook dating 1736–41), which epigram Vertue had earlier attributed to Milton following Toland's 'Life of Milton' (4:105, 166; compare 1:45, 123).

Attribution to 'Andrew Marvell' junior of *Satirical and Panegyrical Instructions to Mr. William Hogarth, Painter, on Admiral Vernon's Taking Porto Bello With Six Ships of War Only* (1740), sold by the oppositional bookseller H. Goreham.

1742

The History and Proceedings of the House of Commons From the Restoration to the Present Time, 14 vols (1742–44): for the debates on the parliamentary address of 26 March 1677, this Patriot historian notes, 'We have this, and the following Debates, on the authority of the celebrated Mr. Andrew Marvell, then Member for Kingston upon Hull' (1:249, 249–72 *passim*).

1743

John Nickolls, ed., *Original Letters and Papers of State, Addressed to Oliver Cromwell; Concerning the Affairs of Great Britain. From the Year MDCXLIX to MDCLVIII. Found among the Political Collections of Mr. John Milton. Now first Published from the Originals* (1743): first publication of the letter from 'Mr Andrew Marvell, to the Lord General Cromwell' about William Dutton, dated from Windsor, 28 July 1653 (98–9, Index sig. xx1ʳ).

1744

John Wesley, *Collection of Moral and Sacred Poems From the most Celebrated English Authors*, 3 vols (Bristol, 1744), 3:B2ᵛ: 'There are never wanting Miscreants, ('tis an authorized Term,) who admire no part of Milton so much as his Political Prose, and who would prefer a Marvel to a Spencer.'

[James Ralph] *Of the Use and Abuse of Parliaments; In Two Historical Discourses* (1744), 104: in describing the subornation of members of parliament in the 1670s, the Patriot Ralph adds: 'Mr. Marvel, in one of his Letters, declares, that Apostate Patriots were bought off, (when the King's Debts were to be saddled on the People) some at Six, others at Ten, one at Fifteen Thousand Pounds in Money, besides Offices, Lands, and Reversions to others; so that it is a Mercy, says he, they gave not away the whole Land and Liberty of England.'

James Ralph, *The History of England During the Reigns of K. William, Q. Anne, and K. George I*, 2 vols (1744–46): the Patriot Ralph draws heavily on AM's *Account* and his letters for both points of fact and wider perspectives on political corruption under Charles II; to gain AM credit, Ralph also supplies a brief biography (1:180) warmly defending him against Samuel Parker's malicious characterization; and, again commending AM as an example of virtue (1:344), Ralph adds much more from Thomas Cooke's biography including William Popple's epitaph (1:171 [see 1688 above], 179–80, 181, 191–3, 195, 213, 230, 252n, 253, 267, 275, 276, 277, 280n, 293, 310, 312–14, 315, 318, 320–1, 323, 324, 325–30, 344, 346 and index). Ralph's work also much influences the annotation of Anchitell Grey, *Debates* (1769).

1745

Record on the MS 'Sermons &c. of the Rev. Andrew Marvell' once in the possession of 'John Warburton Somerset Herald 1720 D° 1745' (inner front board) who writes on flyleaf recto: 'Mr Andrew Marvel of Kingston Super Hull was the Writer of the within Sermons &c He was a Presbitrion Minister there and Father of Marvel the Poet.' (Hull Central Library)

Phrase 'Number, Weight, and Measure', which may derive from AM's poem 'On Mr. Milton's *Paradise Lost*' occurs in Edward Young, *Night Thoughts*, Night IX (1745), line 1081 (Cox; compare also the biblical Wisdom 11:20; Daniel 5:25–8).

1747

AM's 'Eyes and Tears' quoted with attribution and praised by James Parsons in the of the Crounian Lectures on Muscular Motion for 1746, as published in *Human Physiognomy Explain'd* (1747), 79–80, and index; republished in *The Gentleman's Magazine* 18 (1748), 555.

1749

AM celebrated as 'MARVELL, steadfast in his borough's pay' in an anonymous poem, 'The Patriot', with note recalling that 'being poor he received the wages appointed for service in parliament, and was proof against all ministerial attacks'. (*Westminster Journal* (19 August) reprinted in *The Gentleman's Magazine*, 19 (September), 422; Wilding 1970, 252)

1751

Jean Arckenholtz, *Mémoires concernant Christine, reine de Suède*, 4 vols (Amsterdam, 1751–60), vol. 2, appendix 38, 68–70: from a copy of the original letter then in the possession of Dr Bernard in Amsterdam, Arckenholtz publishes 'un Poëme latin, que le savant André Marwell, Secrétaire de Cromwell & ensuite Deputé au Parlement d'Angleterre envoia en Suède à son ami Angelo, où il expose joliment les belles qualités de Christine'; printed here is the first half of 'A Letter to Doctor Ingelo' as 'ANGELO SUO MARUELLIUS'. (Kelliher 1969, 50–7)

The Royal Manual. A Poem. Suppos'd to have been Written By Andrew Marvel. And now First Publish'd (1751): includes prefatory letter supposed to have been written by 'A.M.', 31 December 1658, in presenting a putative Greek original expressing royal devotions, now in paraphrase. A revealing mid-eighteenth-century invention, this long deist psalm favours limited monarchy free from courtly corruption; it claims to have been submitted to Milton for correction and comment, a Milton then contemplating an epic not in rhyme (A2^v–A3^r). It is the work of Samuel Croxall (1689–1752), with whose *The Fair Circassian* it was republished in 1765.

A Catalogue of the Entire and Valuable Library of the Honourable Bryan Fairfax, Esq; (1756 [the whole bought by Francis Child]): lists 'Lord Anglesey's Catalogue with large MSS. Additions' (22) and AM's poems in folio, 1681 (40).

1753

The Works of John Milton, ed. Thomas Birch (with Richard Baron), 2 vols (2nd edn, 1753), 1:xl: published for the first time in this 'enlarged and improved' edition is AM's letter to Milton (see also 2 June 1654 above), taken 'From a copy transcribed from the original by the reverend Mr. Owen of Rochdale, in Lancashire'. Cromwell is noted as the 'my lord' cited by AM here, rather than Bradshaw. AM is again cited for 'the famous Latin verses, sent with the protector's picture to Christina queen of Sweden' (1:xlii) and for having at the Restoration 'acted vigorously in [Milton's] behalf, and made a considerable party for him' (1:xliv), but also for his commendatory verses in the second edition of *Paradise Lost* (1:lix).

Edmund Carter, *History of the University of Cambridge* (1753), 323: among poets from Trinity 'Andrew Marvell Esq.: the Poet Laureat of the Dissenters; famed for his Wit, but foiled in his own Weapon by Divine Herbert'.

[Robert Sheils] Colley Cibber, *The Lives of the Poets of Great Britain and Ireland To the Time of Dean Swift*, 5 vols (1753), 4:124–45: A patriot's entry for AM drawing on the lives by Thomas Cooke and Anthony Wood, but including AM's letter to Cromwell (compare 1743 above), the mock royal speech, and reference to the poems, including the Blood epigram and the whole of 'A Dialogue between the Resolved Soul and Created Pleasure' ('one of the best pieces, in the serious way, of which he is author').

1754

William Warburton, *A View of Lord Bolingbroke's Philosophy; In Four Letters to a Friend* (1754), 6; makes reference to AM as malign but witty (in comparison to Bolingbroke, who was only the former). Later editions have the same reference (3rd edn, 1756, 5).

1755

Samuel Johnson, *A Dictionary of the English Language*, 2 vols (1755, with subsequent editions): quotes from AM's poetry to illustrate the words *distrain*, *excise*, *nor*, and *surcingle*.

1756

William Mason, *Odes* (Cambridge, 1756): 'To Independency' celebrates AM as a freedom-loving patriot, who praiseworthily moved from erotic lyric to political satire; their shared Hull connection affords Mason scope for imagining the young AM on Humberside before his later turn to battling 'Freedom's foes' and triumphing over Samuel Parker. Many further editions.

1758

January: As part of Thomas Hollis's promotion of English liberties, 'The drawings for the engraving of Sidney, Milton, Ludlow, Marvell, etc. were made in January this year'. Taken from the 'choicest originals then extant', the 13 'effigies modelled in wax' include AM, but this antedates Hollis's purchase of his portrait of AM. (Blackburne 1:490, 502; see 1760 below)

Horace Walpole, *A Catalogue of the Royal and Noble Authors of England*, 2 vols (Strawberry Hill, 1758), 2:39: in Rochester entry quotes AM's judgement 'That Rochester was the only Man in England that had the true vein of satire' only to determine this 'A very wrong judgment: Indelicacy does not spoil flattery more than it does satire' (Collins, 24). Further editions include one of 1759 (2:45).

The Centinel, 2nd edn (Dublin, 1758) no. 29, 140: cites AM in review of Mason.

1760

9 July: Having advertised in the *York Courant*, the ardent republican Thomas Hollis (1720–74) buys 'of Mr. F. Billam of Leeds, by the means of Mr. Boydel the engraver, an original picture of Andrew Marvell, in oil, which was formerly in the possession of Mr. Ralph Thoresby' (Blackburne 1:97). Hollis then has Giovanni Battista Cipriani engrave the portrait, which process includes a drawing in pencil highlighted with white, on tinted paper (Harvard, Houghton, MS Typ 576 [44]). The engraving features AM with oak and laurel and a Phrygian liberty cap below, and in epigraphic capitals 'Andrew Marvell Member for Kingston upon Hull in the Parliaments which began April xxv MDCLX and May viii MDCLXI[.] The last commoner who received allowance from his constituents and the friend and protector of John Milton ...

> But whether fate or art untwin'd his thread
> Remains in doubt, fame's lasting register
> Shall leave his name inroll'd as great as those
> Who at Philippi for their country fell.' (Blackburne 1:96b)

The verses are from 'On his Excellent Friend Mr Andrew Marvell' (see 1697 above). This is one of Hollis's 'liberty prints', which he 'generously distributed with others to his friends and fellow-patriots; and to some, perhaps, who were neither'. Hollis also gave large numbers of books by his favourite republican, anticlerical, and patriot writers to collections near and far, conspicuously his great gifts to Harvard Library and Christ's College, Cambridge; these may be distinguished by their 'liberty' bindings, in fine morocco adorned with coded stamps of Athenian owls, Phrygian caps, figures of Britannia and the like (Bond). A number of such bindings of AM's works survive in disparate libraries, often with patriot inscriptions by Hollis.

ca. 25 December: Hollis writes: 'The picture of the incomparable John Milton hangs on one side of me in my apartment, and that of the incorruptible Andrew Marvell on the other. Surely, in the midst of such examples, I must at least avoid evil, if not do something positively good and noble.' To which his correspondent answers: 'With a Milton and an Andrew Marvell, not only before your eyes in picture, nor only in your library in print, but deeply engraved in your excellent mind and heart, what wonder if all your deeds are stamped with so eminent characters; and if you not only cease doing evil, but delight in doing good in the most diffusive manner a mortal ever did? I hate flattery ...' (Blackburne 1:104)

Biographia Britannica: Or, The Lives of the Most eminent Persons Who have flourished in Great Britain and Ireland ... digested in the Manner of Mr Bayle's Historical and Critical Dictionary, 7 vols (1747–66 [1760]), 5:3052–8: entry for AM is indebted to biography in 1738 *General Dictionary* through and through, which it for the most part just rewrites. In the Milton entry is included the letter to Milton from AM at Eton, 2 June 1654, not included in AM article because that had been 'wrote before this letter appeared in print' (3113), which was first in 1753. The life of Samuel Parker in this volume quotes from *RT2* on Parker's family background, which account 'mixed with a great deal of satire and ill-nature' supplies notice of Parker's education and early writings; Parker's 'sharp contest with Andrew Marvell' is described at length out of Wood and Burnet (5:3299–300, 3302).

1761

In this year Laurence Sterne publishes volumes 3 and 4 of *Tristram Shandy*, which with Uncle Toby's garden campaigns begin what has been seen as that novel's transposition of AM's 'Upon Appleton House' into an eighteenth-century setting, coloured by the present preoccupations of the Seven Years War. Sterne's Yorkshire associations and his acquaintance with Thomas Hollis may well have informed a regard for AM and many of Sterne's friends will appear in Thompson's subscription list for *The Works of Andrew Marvell, Esq* (1776). (Keymer 2002, 191–211; Keymer 1993)

Republication of John Toland, *The Life of John Milton*, ed. Thomas Hollis (1761), 110–11: includes the laudatory reference to AM as Milton's most frequent visitor in the Protectorate and as possible author of the epigram sent with Cromwell's portrait to Queen Christina, which is quoted in Latin and English.

1762

Christopher Smart refers to AM in a Hull passage from *Jubilate Agno*, Fragm. D, sect. 78–9:

> Let Marvel, house of Marvel rejoice with Brya a little shrub like birch.
> Let Hull, house of Hull rejoice with Subis a bird called the Spight which breaks the Eagle's eggs.
> Let Mason, house of Mason rejoice with Suberies the Capitol Cork Tree. Lord be merciful to William Mason. (Smart, I.xxiii, 115; Duncan-Jones 1967)

William Harris, *An Historical and Critical Account of the Life of Oliver Cromwell, Lord Protector of the Commonwealth of England, Scotland and Ireland. After the Manner of Mr. Bayle* (1762), 305–6n: in discussion of writers under Cromwell, 'Andrew Marvel is, I know, commonly said to have been employed, under Milton, by the commonwealth. But I apprehend this to be a mistake, as will appear from his own account' and quotes from *RT2* on AM's employment in the Protectorate only in 1657 (see also 428n).

The British Plutarch, 12 vols (1762), 6:220: in life of Milton, cites AM's defence of him at the Restoration, and notes AM's verses prefixed to *Paradise Lost*.

1763

Anchitell Grey, *Debates of the House of Commons*, 10 vols (1763): in addition to Grey's reports of AM's speeches in parliament (see above at the dates in question), the editor now supplies a biographical note on 'the famous Andrew Marvell' (based on Cooke, 1726) citing his 'strict integrity and fidelity' and his receipt of 'wages from his Constituents (1:14, 70); moreover, the notes on the House of Commons in the 1670s draw on AM's *Account* and quote it at length for the stormy adjournment of 28 May 1677 (4:262, 324, 326, 391).

Charles Churchill, *The Author* (1763): without here naming AM, Churchill (a friend of Wilkes and liberty) inveighs against ministerial corruption, and wonders:

> Is this the land, where, in those worst of times,
> The hardy Poet rais'd his honest rimes
> To dread rebuke, and bade controulment speak
> In guilty blushes on the villain's cheek,
> Bade Pow'r turn pale, kept mighty rogues in awe,
> And made them fear the Muse, who fear'd not Law?

But that this paragon is AM appears when Thompson later gives further lines putatively from his friend Churchill's *Rosciad*, though not there preserved, in which AM's incorruptible service to Hull and nation is memorialized. (Legouis 1965, 229; *The Poetical Works of Charles Churchill*, ed. D. Grant, Oxford, 1956, 249; Thompson 3:487)

Algernon Sidney, *Discourses concerning Government*, ed. T. Hollis (1763): the works of 'Marvell' are very useful to Hollis in illustrating the iniquities of the Restoration, quoting from 'An historical poem by A. Marvell' (28); 'Britannia and Raleigh; a poem by A. Marvell' (30); and other such state poems (2nd pagination 60, 103); also the *Account* (2nd pagination 68 and especially 196–8–see Patterson 1999, 42) and *A Seasonable Argument* (29, 2nd pagination 172, 174; hence its inclusion as AM's in Thompson's collection, 1776).

1764

Robert Nettleton raises monument in St Giles in the Fields to his great-uncle AM, following Popple's text (see 1688 above). This year too Nettleton gives the portrait of AM to the British Museum that now hangs in the National Portrait Gallery (see September 1657 above).

Edward Thompson, *The Soldier. A Poem. Inscribed to The Honourable General Conway* (1764), 20–1:

> There liv'd a Man, by HULL a Member chose;
> His name was Andrew Marvel, known to those

278 Andrew Marvell Chronology

> Who durst unfold their souls as Patriots shou'd,
> When vicious men would thirst for Patriot blood.
> An honest Member, but in days of yore,
> When Members had much truth, and yet were poor:
> When Members durst refuse a *venal vote*,
> And serv'd their Country in a thread-bare coat.
> Thus was our MARVEL, when his Country's good,
> Call'd him to serve her as a Member shou'd:
> Serve her he did (as Englishmen should do)
> Her good he voted, and, resolv'd, withdrew.
> Kept his integrity, in spite of want,
> In spite of *gold*, and Ministerial *cant*.
> In spite of menaces, in spite of *lies*,
> In spite of Scaffolds, and in spite of spies,
> Proud of his Honour, which was MARVEL'S pride,
> And, rather than he'd pawn it – starv'd – and died.
> Thus, MARVEL greatly stood to public view;
> If such my fate, be such my spirit too.
>
> In these rare days, such Men you rarely know,
> What ANDREW MARVEL was, is METHAM now. [The END]

1765

9 February: 'Dr. Mayhew [Boston] wrote to Mr Hollis an account of his receiving a very valuable present of books from him, several of which he had not seen before; particularly, "Marvel's Rehearsal transprosed," divers tracts in a new edition of Milton's prose-works [Baron's], etc.' (Blackburne 1:276)

June: Hollis donation to Harvard of *The Works of Andrew Marvell Esq.* (1726), the binding improved with a liberty cap and with lyres. Perhaps now too came Harvard's Hollis copy of *Mr. Smirke*, which he inscribed 'By Andrew Marvell. the incorruptible', having separated this from a bound volume that included Nedham's *Honesty's Best Policy*; Harvard's copy of Herbert Croft's *Naked Truth* also features Hollis annotation, with his cross-reference to Marvell's encomium of Croft's work in *Mr. Smirke* (3), which is there underscored.

3 September: Thomas Hollis busies himself 'in the morning looking over Andrew Marvell's works, and papers relating thereto, preparatory to a conversation with Mr. Bowyer [the publisher], concerning the new edition of them'. (Blackburne 1:361)

4 September: Hollis records that he was: 'With Mr. Bowyer, with whom I had a full conversation relating to the new edition of Andrew Marvell's works, to the printing of which he seemed reluctant, from the difficulties

that will attend it; animated him all I could to that end; and we are to talk farther concerning it.' After this, 'Mr. Bowyer very frequently turned his thoughts on the subject of Marvel's works. It is certain, that he consulted Dr. [Thomas] Birch concerning various parts of them; and communicated some particulars to Mr. Hollis.' (Blackburne 1:361)

21 September: *The Constitutional Courant: Containing Matters Interesting to Liberty and No Wise Repugnant to Loyalty* (Woodbridge, New Jersey): a manifesto against the Stamp Act, printed by William Goddard using the name 'Andrew Marvel' ('at the Sign of the Bribe Refused, on Constitution Hill, North America'), distributed in large numbers in New York and beyond; reprinted in Boston and Philadelphia. Another abridged edition (same title, but now has *Repugnant*) has the prefatory remarks 'To the Public' signed 'Andrew Marvel'. (See also *Pennsylvania Chronicle*, 30 September 1771, and 1773 below)

1767

23 April: Thomas Hollis meets with Richard Baron 'concerning the part Mr. Baron should take in a new edition of Andrew Marvell's works.... The result was, that the new edition was to be in one volume quarto, to be printed by Millar and Cadell; Mr. Baron to correct the press for the prose, and Mr. Bowyer for the poetical and Latin parts.' (Blackburne 1:362)

29 April: Hollis and Baron have 'a long conversation on the subject [of publishing AM]; when it appeared in the end, that Baron, not thinking himself equal to the task, for want of anecdotes, did not seem inclined to undertake it'. Bowyer too abandons the project, apparently owing to his fear of its poor sale. 'The want of two such able cooperators as Baron and Bowyer put an end to Mr. Hollis's project of republishing Marvell's works.' (Blackburne 1:362)

1768

In the year of Laurence Sterne's death appears his *A Sentimental Journey through France and Italy*, which reworks elements of AM's 'The Nymph complaining for the death of her Faun' where Sterne's Maria laments her abandonment by lover and by goat, and hangs on to her lapdog. (Keymer 1993)

James Robertson has the Muse celebrate Hull's 'favour'd Soil whence Marvel sprung / Where, Heav'n-inspir'd, her native Mason sung', in 'A Prologue Spoken at the Opening the New Theatre in Hull, October 3, 1768'. (Robertson, *Poems on Several Occasions*' 1773, 272).

1769

James Granger, *Biographical History of England*, 2 vols (1769): 'Andrew Marvel, &c. drawn and etched by J.B Cipriani, a Florentine, from a portrait

painted in the year 1660, now in the possession of Thomas Hollis of
Lincoln's Inn' cited under 'Commoners in great Employments' and noted
'a merry, and yet an indignant satirist, an able statesman, and an uncorrupt
patriot', with brief description of appearance and character quoted from
Cooke (vol. 2, pt 1, 256–7). Again noted under 'Men of Genius and
Learning', AM's portrait from *1681* is catalogued with the duodecimo copy
from Cooke's edition, 1726: here his probity as a satirist is commended
above his poetry; 'Flecknoe' is praised by name and linked to Dryden's
Mac Flecknoe; AM's death by poisoning 'generally believed' (vol. 2, pt 2,
339–40). Republished in 1775.

1771

Catherine Macaulay, *The History of England From the Accession of James I,
to that of the Brunswick Line*, 8 vols (1763–83 [vol. 5 1771]): draws on 'An
Historical Poem', attributed to AM, for its scathing view of Restoration
debaucheries (5:379), amidst which national servitude 'enlightened citizens' of the present can nonetheless discern the virtues of Milton, Henry
Neville, Algernon Sidney, and James Harrington, and 'In the character of
Andrew Marvel are allowed to be united in an exalted degree the wit, the
patriot, and the legislator' (5:382–3, [= 390–1]). In her history of the 1670s
in later volumes (1781–83), Macaulay often draws on AM's *Account* for its
parliamentary and political history sometimes citing it, sometimes not
(6:310, 327–9, 331, 334, 416; 7:26, 44–5, 47–8, 52–8, 69–70).

1772

Republication of Thomas Cooke's edition of *The Works of Andrew Marvell,
Esq.*, again in two volumes, now in small octavo, for T. Davies in Covent
Garden. This uncritically follows Cooke throughout, including his dedica-
tions long after their subjects had died. The republication seems to have
been designed to anticipate Thompson's much fuller edition of 1776,
among which booksellers Davies would again feature.

1773

10 June: Again signing himself 'Andrew Marvell' (see 21 September 1765
above), William Goddard prints three tracts this year using this persona.
Addressing his 'fellow citizens, friends to liberty, and enemies to despot-
ism', this energetic promoter of colonial rights now opposes the market-
houses that had been proposed by 'A Philadelphian' (*No. I. Philadelphia,
June 10th, 1773*). See also *Andrew Marvell's Second Address to the Inhabitants
of Ppiladelphia [sic]* (Philadelphia, 1773), where Goddard instead promotes a
public central market in Philadelphia.

1774

Francis Blackburne, *Reflections on the Fate of a Petition for Relief in the Matter of Subscription, Offered to the Honourable House of Commons, February 6th, 1772* (Second edition, first printed 1774; *The Works Theological and Miscellaneous ... of Francis Blackburne*, ed. Francis Blackburne, jr, 7 vols, Cambridge, 1805, vol. 7, 195): against claims for the king's sacerdotal power, is pleased to quote from AM's *Rehearsal Transpros'd* against Parker's like claim, 'On which Andrew Marvel, with his usual pleasantry, thus remarks; "Now this indeed is surprising; but this only troubles me, how his Majesty would look in all the sacerdotal habiliments, and ... the Pontifical Wardrobe .... But one thing I doubt, Mr. Bayes did not well consider; that if the King may discharge the function of the priesthood, he may too, (and its all the reason in the world) assume the revenue. It would be the best subsidy that ever was voluntarily given by the clergy." Rehearsal Transprosed, p. i. iii.'

1775

Edmund Calamy, *The Nonconformist's Memorial*, abridged by Samuel Palmer, 2 vols (1775), 1:211: Marvell's 'nephew' Thomas More cited as witty 'like his uncle Mr. Andrew Marvel', and of 'principles very moderate.' (Burdon 1982, 43; a second edition of Palmer's abridgement appears in 1778)

1776

The Works of Andrew Marvell, Esq. Poetical, Controversial, and Political, Containing Many Original Letters, Poems, and Tracts, never before printed. With a new life of the author, by Capt. Edward Thompson, 3 vols (1776). The first complete works of AM, this is an imposing large quarto edition, the volumes a legacy of the republican Thomas Hollis's projected edition of the previous decade, enhanced by Thompson's access to fresh materials from his native Hull, including most notably his belated access to the Popple MS (now Bodl. MS Eng. poet. d. 49). Celebrating AM as 'this illustrious Patriot,' the political thrust of this publication emerges already in the frontispiece portrait with inscription, in the title-page's eight-line epigraph from Thomson's *Liberty*, the subscription list (including Burke and Wilkes), and the dedication of the work to Hull and its Trinity House, applauding Hotham and the town's contribution to overthrowing 'the tyrant Stuarts' (1:A2^r–4^v, 1; Patterson 2002, 139–62). The portrait exists in two versions, one looking left (with the whole page framed square), one right (without the frame). By turns credulous and tendentious in his inclusion of verse and prose not likely AM's, Thompson aims to win 'strenuous and sincere friends to our Constitution', and so in the first volume he foregrounds AM's constituency correspondence in addition to other personal letters, followed by the *Account*, thus promoting the publication of parliamentary debates (1:lvi, 1–437, 439–648); in the second volume to add to *RT* and *RT2* two 1670s tracts attacking placemen and not otherwise known to be AM's (2:523–83: *A Seasonable Question, and an Usefull Answer; A Seasonable Argument To perswade all the Grand Juries in England, to petition for A New Parliament*); and in the final volume to present *Mr. Smirke* and the *Short Historical Essay* before including AM's poems (in Cooke's order) with a final 'Life of that most excellent citizen, and uncorrupted member of parliament, Andrew Marvell', much expanding on Cooke, if not always reliably, and including testimonies to AM's character and wit from a number of writers (3:433–93). The belated receipt of the Popple MS leads Thompson to include as addenda the 'Horatian Ode', 'First Anniversary', and 'A Poem upon the Death of his Late Highnesse the Lord Protector,' of which he notes 'The English language does not boast a more elegant elegiack poem, than this to the memory of the magnanimous and noble Cromwell'; he also adds the *Parliamenti Angliae Declaratio* [1648] as 'By Andrew Marvell', so eager is he to make AM a more Wilkes-like parliamentarian.

Thompson presented a copy of his edition, also with a print of AM, to the City of Hull (Bagguley and Shepherd 9). Trinity College, Cambridge, has a majestic 'Hollis' copy, which red morocco bindings feature Phrygian caps, Athenian owls, and Britannia among their marks of liberty; the portrait is the unframed image of AM looking right and some additional subscribers are noted in an extra leaf before the subscription list (shelfmark RW.14.2–4). Edmund Burke, one of the subscribers writes to Thompson thanking him 'for the obliging communication of Marvell Letters', although 'as these Letters were originally of a publick Nature, and wrote with extraordinary Caution, they are rather less agreeable than if they were private, and contain Marvells free opinion' (Burke 9:411; Patterson 2002, 139).

1 July: advertisement for the Thompson edition of AM's *Works* in *The Public Advertiser*, and no doubt in other like publications.

James Barry, *The Phoenix; or, The Resurrection of Freedom* (1776): with Locke, Milton and Algernon Sidney, AM is portrayed in this engraving as mourning British freedom, while American liberty beckons in the distance. (Frontispiece in Chernaik and Dzelzainis)

Francis Maseres, *The Canadian Freeholder: A Dialogue, Shewing, The Sentiments of the Bulk of the Freeholders of Canada concerning the late Quebeck-Act* (1776), 224–5: favouring parliamentary salaries, cites AM as 'that inflexible honest man and a faithful and diligent member of parliament'. Advises repeal of Quebec and the Boston Charter Act, 'as a Ground for a Reconciliation with the United Colonies in America' (t.-p.).

Thomas Mortimer, *The British Plutarch*, 6 vols (1776), 4:126–36: life of AM follows Cooke's and the dictionary biographies of yesteryear, and notes that 'An elegent new edition of the works of Andrew Marvell, has been lately published.' Also refers to AM's stalwart defence of Milton at the Restoration (4:227).

1777

Thomas Mortimer, *The Student's Pocket Dictonary; or, Compendium...* (1777), under 'Marvell' has patriot entry for AM.

The Beauties of Biography, 2 vols (1777), 1:225–41: uses Sheils's biography for AM (see 1753 above).

The Laughing Philosopher (Dublin, 1777), no. 26, 160: excerpt from 'Andrew Marvell's Coy Mistress' quotes passage 'Now, therefore, while the youthful hue ... yet we will make run.'

1779

John Campbell, *Lives of the British Admirals*, 4 vols (1779), 2:148, 282: cites *Account* in folio for history at time of the Test Act during 3rd Anglo-Dutch War.

1780

Francis Blackburne, *Memoirs of Thomas Hollis, Esq.* 2 vols (1780): frequent reference to Hollis's promotion of AM as an exemplary MP, defender of English liberties, and witness to monarchical corruption, for which dated entries see 1758– above (1:103, 104, 166, 251, 276, 353, 356, 361–3, 366, 367–71, 375, 490, 502; 2:619, 777, [840]).

Thomas Davies, *Memoirs of the Life of David Garrick*, 2 vols ([London and] Dublin, 1780), 2:23: attributes to Mallet the ballad 'William and Margaret', mistakenly ascribed to AM by Capt. Thompson on the strength of its inclusion in the Popple volume, but 'English poetry, in Marvell's time, was certainly not arrived at the elegence and harmony'. AM's name 'deserves to be revered by every sincere lover of his country'.

AM cited among 'Mr. Hollis's favourites' in a biography of the latter included in *British Biography*, 10 vols (Sherborne, 1778–80), 10:455.

Richard Gough, *British Topography*, 2 vols (1780), 2:466: under Yorkshire, notes 'Andrew Marvell's poems on Nun-Appleton house, and the hill and grove at Bilbrough, are in the editions of his works.'

William Cole's notes from Ely Cathedral registers feature references to the Marvells' presence in Meldreth and Shepreth, Cambridgeshire, from the early 1500s; with reference to one such he observes: 'Andrew Marvell the Republican Poet, probably descended from one of these.' (BL, Add MS 5861, 18ᵛ, 93ʳ, 105ᵛ, 111ᵛ; Ellis; Legouis 1928, 1)

Bibliography

This list supplies fuller author, title and publication details of works cited in brief in the entries above. Also cited are some publications that less directly inform my inferences above. Place of publication is London unless otherwise stated.

Editions of Marvell

Poetry and Prose

Cooke: *The Works of Andrew Marvell Esq.* Ed. Thomas Cooke. 2 vols. 1726.
Grosart: *The Complete Works of Andrew Marvell.* Ed. Alexander B. Grosart. 4 vols. 1872–5.
PL: *The Poems and Letters of Andrew Marvell.* H.M. Margoliouth revised by Pierre Legouis with E.E. Duncan-Jones. 3rd edn, Oxford, 1971.
Thompson: *The Works of Andrew Marvell, Esq. Poetical, Controversial, and Political, Containing Many Original Letters, Poems, and Tracts, never before printed. With a new life of the author.* Ed. Edward Thompson. 3 vols. 1776.

Poetry

Donno: *Andrew Marvell: The Complete Poems.* Ed. Elizabeth Story Donno. Harmondsworth, 1972.
The Latin Poetry of Andrew Marvell. Eds William A. McQueen and Kiffin A. Rockwell. Chapel Hill, North Carolina, 1964.
Marvell, Andrew. *Complete Poetry.* Ed. George deF. Lord. New York, 1968.
Marvell, Andrew. *Pastoral and Lyric Poems, 1681.* Eds David Ormerod and Christopher Wortham. Nedlands, Western Australia, 2000.
Smith: *The Poems of Andrew Marvell.* Ed. Nigel Smith. 2003.

Prose

MPW: *The Prose Works of Andrew Marvell.* Eds Annabel Patterson, Martin Dzelzainis, Nicholas von Maltzahn and Neil Keeble. 2 vols. New Haven, 2003.

Guide to manuscripts cited

Italy: Genoa, Archivio di Stato di Genova / Archivio Segreto, inserto 1. (AM letter of 20 Nov. 1658)
Russia: Moscow, Rossiiskii Arkhiv Drevnikh Aktov, Angliiskie dela, 35/1/208. (English affairs)
Sweden: Stockholm, Kungl. biblioteket, D 757. (Transcripts of documents relating to the reign of Karl XI)
United Kingdom:
Beverley, Yorkshire: Yorks. East Riding RO, PE 85/1, Flamborough Parish Register;Yorks. East Riding RO, PE69/1, Cherry Burton Parish Register; Yorks. East Riding RO, PE125/1, Winestead Parish Register.

Cambridge, Cambridge University Archive. Matr. 6 (CUR 101.2) (Matriculations); Subscriptiones II (Subscriptions to articles).

Cambridge University Library. MS Nn.4.12. (MS gift to Ann Sadleir)

Cambridge, Trinity College. Senior Bursar's Audit Book, 1637–59; Admissions and Admonitions, 1560–1759; MS R.5.5 (Anne Sadleir letterbook).

Claydon House letters. (Microfilm at Bodleian Library)

Edinburgh, National Library of Scotland. Advocates MS 19.1.12. (Miscellany of poems on affairs of state)

Hertford, Hertfordshire RO. MSS D/EP F.36 (Lady Sarah Cowper 'Poems Collected at Several Times from the year 1670'); D/EP F.37 (Lady Sarah Cowper 'The Medley'); D/EP F.81 (Cowper family correspondence); D/EP F.83 (Lady Sarah Cowper miscellany of political verse).

Hull Central Library. MS 'Sermons &c. of the Rev. Andrew Marvell'; Andrew Marvell Meldreth deed; Wills.

Hull City Archives. BRB 3–5 (Bench Books); BRD (Borough deeds); BRF (Borough finances: account books); BRL (Borough letters, especially the Marvell and the Stockdale letters to Hull Corporation, BRL/1194); BRM (Borough records, miscellaneous); DMX/132 (copy of Abraham de la Pryme MS, history of Hull).

Hull Trinity House (TH). ATH 1/3 (Third Order Book, 1665–1703); ATH47/1 (Miscellaneous In-Letters 1614–1720); FTH1/5 (Accounts 1656–91); NTH52/1 (Navigational, lights file, 1638–78); NTH57/1 (Navigational, duties file).

Hull University. DDFA39/26–29 (Escrick papers); DDMM28/1 (Kenneth Macmahon papers for photocopy of AM letter 29 Dec. 1675).

Leeds, University of Leeds, Brotherton Collection. MSS Lt 55 (Okeover miscellany); Misc. Letters 2 Marvell (17 Dec. 1670, 9 Dec. 1675).

Leeds, Yorkshire Archaeological Society, MS 13.44. (York edition of *The Character of Holland*, 1665)

Leicester, Leicestershire Record Office. Finch Papers.

London, British Library (BL). Add. MSS 4292 (Thomas Birch collections); 4459 (Thomas Birch miscellaneous); 5846, 5861 (William Cole collections); 7315, 7317 (Harley papers, poems on affairs of state); 8888 (William Popple writings); 15858 (Sir Richard Browne correspondence); 18220 (John Watson verse miscellany); 21427 (Adam Baynes papers); 22919 (letters to Sir George Downing); 31432 (William Lawes music book); 32555 (Daniel Defoe, 'The Compleat English Gentleman'); 33413 (John Milward Commons diary); 34362 (Danvers miscellany of poems on affairs of state); 35865 (Hardwicke papers); 50117 (Longueville commonplace book); 70012 (Portland [Harley] papers); 70120 (Portland papers, Harley correspondence); 70949 (Charnwood autographs); 71446 (Political and religious miscellany); 72603 (Trumbull papers, parliamentary); 72850 (Petty papers, correspondence); 73540 (Restoration miscellany); 78684 (Evelyn papers).

MSS Egerton 203 (copy of *Paradise Lost*, 1674); 3345 (Danby papers).

MSS Harl. 4218 (translation of Samuel Parker, *De Rebus sui Temporis*); 6584 (Gilbert Burnet 'Secret History')

MSS Lansdowne 95 (includes George Dethick, King at Arms, plan of Cromwell's funeral); 891 (Collections relating to Kingston-upon-Hull); Lansdowne 937 (White Kennett diary).

RP 3791. (photocopy, AM letter of 4 Apr. 1660)

MS Stowe 182. (transcripts of state papers)

London, Guildhall. MSS 30004, vol. 4 (Deptford Trinity House, Court Minutes, 1670–76); 30004, vol. 5 (Deptford Trinity House, Court Minutes, 1676–80); 30032, vol. 2 (Deptford Trinity House, Cash Book, 1661–95); 30051, vol. 1 (Deptford Trinity House, Select Entries, 1670–76); 30051, vol. 2 (Select Entries, 1677–81).

London, Inner Temple Library. MS 531C. (Rev. Andrew Marvell sermon)

London, Lambeth Palace. Z999: *Bibliotheca Angleseiana*, 1686 (much annotated); MS 933, no. 88.

London, Post Office Archives. Post Class 94, items 12 and 13. (Postal documents and copy)

London, Public Record Office:

    C6 (Court of Chancery pleadings, Collins)

    C7 (Court of Chancery pleadings, Hamilton)

    C8 (Court of Chancery pleadings, Mitford)

    C10 (Court of Chancery pleadings, Whittington)

    C24 (Court of Chancery, town depositions)

    C33 (Chancery, entry books of decrees and orders)

    C38 (Chancery, reports and certificates)

    C78 (Chancery, decree rolls)

    C181 (Crown office: entry books of commissioners)

    CO1/13 (Colonial papers, America and West Indies, 1656–59)

    PC2 (Privy Council, registers)

    PROB6 (Prerogative Court of Canterbury, Administration Act Books)

    SP16 (State Papers Domestic, Charles I)

    SP18 (State Papers Domestic, Interregnum)

    SP25 (Council of State, books and accounts)

    SP29 (State Papers Domestic, Charles II)

    SP31/17/33 (Council of State order book, Sept. 1658–Jan. 1658/99, copy)

    SP44 (State Papers, entry books)

    SP75 (State Papers Foreign, Denmark)

    SP78 (State Papers Foreign, France)

    SP82 (State Papers Foreign, Hamburg and Hanse towns)

    SP84 (State Papers Foreign, Holland)

    SP91 (State Papers Foreign, Russia)

    SP95 (State Papers Foreign, Sweden)

    SP105/222 (Journal of Sir Joseph Williamson, Cologne 1674)

London, Royal Society. MS 32 (George Ent commonplace book)

London, Society of Antiquaries. MS 138. (The 'Milton' State Papers.)

London, Stationers' Company. Microfilm *Wardens' Accounts 1663–1728, Records of the Worshipful Company of Stationers*. Ed. Robin Myers. Cambridge, 1985.

London, Victoria and Albert Museum. Forster Collection, Cat. No. 5895, Pressmark F. 48. D. 51 (AM letter of 5 Nov. 1674).

Longleat, The Marquess of Bath's Collection. [Sir Bulstrode] Whitelocke Papers, MS 124a (journal of Swedish embassy, 1653–54); Whitelocke Papers, Parcel 5, 'Verses'; Coventry papers, vol. 11.

Manchester, University of Manchester. Rylands English MS 347/200 (AM letter 19 Dec. 1674).

Matlock, Derbyshire RO. D239 M/01068 (Treby papers).

Oxford, All Souls. MSS 167 (Narcissus Luttrell, Political Miscellany); 171 (Narcissus Luttrell, 'State Affairs From Jan. 1678/79 unto Feb. 1680/81...'); 174 (Narcissus Luttrell, verse miscellany).

Oxford, Bodleian Library, MSS Ashm. 1506 (bound volume of Popish Plot pamphlets); Aubrey 6, 8 (John Aubrey's 'Brief Lives'); Ballard 11 (includes letters to Dr Arthur Charlett); Barlow 52 (Tsar's complaint against Carlisle, see 19 July 1664);

Bodleian facs. d. 119 (AM letter ca. 28 Jan. 1675); Bodleian Library Records, e. 533 (Liber Admissorum); Carte 35 (Ormonde correspondence); Carte 72 (newsletters to Ormonde); Carte 81, 103 (Wharton papers); Clarendon 57, 80–1 (Clarendon state papers); Dep.f.9 (Seymour Bowman parliamentary diary); Don.b.8 (Sir William Haward miscellany); Douce 357 (seventeenth-century English political verse); Eng. poet. d. 49 (the 'Popple' manuscript of Marvell's *Miscellaneous Poems*, 1681); Gough London 14 (includes corrected copy of *Directions*, 1667); Rawl. A34–66 (Thurloe state papers); Rawl. A176 (Pepys papers); Rawl. A245 (Anthony Hammond papers); Rawl. C179 (Council of State order book); Rawl. C983 (Bishop Henry Compton papers); Rawl. letters 50–1 (Wharton correspondence); Rawl. poet. 199 (seventeenth-century English poetry); Rawl. Q.c.3 (John Baron annotations on Fuller, *History of the Worthies*); Sancroft 146 (Sancroft notebook, including 'A Catalogue of my Bookes'); Tanner 57 (English historical papers); Wood Diaries (Anthony Wood's annotated almanacs); Wood F39–41 (Wood letterbooks); Wood F.46–7 (Anthony Wood, notes for *Athenae Oxonienses*).

Oxford, Corpus Christi College. MSS 310, (William Fulman collection), 332 (Christopher Wase papers).

Oxford, Queen's College. MS 284 (Barlow papers, includes the first pages of a draft translation of Bodl. MS Barlow 52).

Petworth House Archives, Orrery Papers 13187 ('R.F.' on Blake's victory).

Sheffield, Sheffield University, Hartlib Papers, 29/5 (Hartlib Ephemerides 1655–6); 55/15 ('A Poem to the Protector').

York, University of York, Borthwick Institute. Prob. Reg. 39–42 (Wills); Original wills, 1633–42.

United States:

Cambridge, Mass., Harvard University, Houghton Library. MS Typ 576 (Giovanni Battista Cipriani, drawings and etchings).

Colorado Springs, Colorado College, Tutt Library. Alice Bemer Taylor Collection, MS 0145 (AM note, 5 Jan. 1670/71): http://www2.coloradocollege.edu/Library/SpecialCollections/Manuscript/Taylor/MarvellA02.html [24 June 2004]

Haverford, Pennsylvania, Haverford College Library. Special Collections, MS 115. (AM constituency letter, 22 Oct. 1665)

New Haven, Yale University, Beinecke Rare Book and Manuscript Library. James Marshall and Marie-Louise Osborn Collection, MSS b. 54 ('A Collection of Witt and Learning ... to this present year 1677'); b. 136 (Copy of *Directions to a Painter*, appends copy of Trott letter); PB VII/15 ('Last Instructions'); Osborn files, 9986 (AM letter 24 Oct. 1674); Osborn files, 9987 (AM letter 4 Feb. 1675).

New York, Pierpont Morgan Library. LHMS, Misc. English. (AM letters of 29 May 1660, 24 Jan. 1673/74)

Philadelphia, Historical Society of Pennsylvania. Simon Gratz Collection: British Poets, Case 11, Box 1 (AM letter, 5 Jan. 1670/71).

Philadelphia, Library Company of Philadelphia. 'Folio Accessions 1–4999'; 'A Numerical Catalogue of the Books in Quarto'.

Princeton, N.J., Princeton University Library. Robert H. Taylor Collection, Box M (AM letter, 2 Dec. 1676); MS Taylor 5 (Restoration miscellany).

San Marino, California, Henry E. Huntington Library. MSS HA13634 (Hastings papers); HM 21813 (materials touching on Virginia rebellion of Nathaniel Bacon).

Washington, D.C., Folger Library. MSS L.c. 850; L.c. 1381–2; L.c. 1429–30. (Newdigate letters)

Print

Adelung, Friedrich von. *Kritisch-Literärische Übersicht der Reisenden in Russland bis 1700.* 2 vols. St Petersburg, 1846.

Allison, A.F. *Four Metaphysical Poets.* Pall Mall Bibliographies no. 3. Folkestone, 1973.

Anderson, P.B. 'Anonymous Critic of Milton: Richard Leigh? or Samuel Butler?' *Studies in Philology*, 44 (1947), 504–18.

Anselment, Raymond. '*A Tale of a Tub*: Swift and the "Men of Tast"', *Huntingdon Library Quarterly*, 37 (1974), 265–82.

Arber, Edward, ed. *The Term Catalogues, 1668–1709.* 3 vols. 1903.

Ashley, Maurice. *The Greatness of Oliver Cromwell.* 1957.

Aubrey, John. *Brief Lives.* Ed. Andrew Clark. 2 vols. Oxford, 1898.

Bagguley, William H. and Thomas Shepherd. *Andrew Marvell Tercentenary Celebration: Descriptive Catalogue of Exhibits at the Wilberforce Museum, High Street, Hull, March 31st to April 7th, 1921.* Hull, 1921.

Bailey, J.E. 'Andrew Marvell and Valentine Greatraks, The Stroker'. *Notes and Queries*, 6th ser. 9 (26 Jan. 1884), 61–3.

Bain, Carl E. 'The Latin Poetry of Andrew Marvell'. *Philological Quarterly*, 38 (1959), 436–49.

Barnard, John. 'The 1665 York and London Editions of Marvell's *The Character of Holland*'. *Publications of the Bibliographical Society of America*, 81 (1987), 459–64.

Beal, Peter (1993). 'Andrew Marvell, 1621–78'. In *Index of English Literary Manuscripts, Volume II (1625–1700), Part 2, Lee –Wycherley* (1993), 17–67.

Beal, Peter (1998). *In Praise of Scribes.* Oxford, 1998.

Birch, Thomas, ed. *A Collection of the State Papers of John Thurloe.* 7 vols. 1742.

Birrell, Augustine. *Andrew Marvell.* 1905.

Blackburn, Holly and Leofranc Holford-Strevens. *The Oxford Companion to the Year.* Oxford, 1999.

Blackburne, Francis. *Memoirs of Thomas Hollis.* 2 vols. 1780.

Blakiston, Noel. 'Andrew Marvell at Eton'. *TLS*, 8 Feb. 1952, 109.

Blaydes, F.A. 'Pedigree of Marvell'. *Notes and Queries*, 6th ser., 1 (April 1880), 271–2.

Bond, W.H. *Thomas Hollis of Lincoln's Inn.* Cambridge, 1990.

Bohun, Edmund. *The Diary and Autobiography.* Ed. S. Wilton Rex. Beccles, 1853.

Bongaerts, Theo, ed. *The Correspondence of Thomas Blount (1618–1679).* Amsterdam, 1978.

Boyce, Benjamin. 'An Annotated Volume from Pope's Library'. *Notes and Queries*, 202 (Feb. 1958), 55–7.

Boyle, Robert. *Works.* Ed. Thomas Birch. 5 vols. 1744.

Briscoe Eyre, G.E., ed. *A Transcript of the Registers of the Worshipful Company of Stationers: From 1640–1708 A.D.* 3 vols. 1913–14.

Brogan, Hugh and Elizabeth Donno. 'Marvell's Epitaph on —'. *Renaissance Quarterly*, 32 (1979), 197–9.

Brooks, F.W., ed. *The First Order Book of the Hull Trinity House 1632–1665.* Yorkshire Archaeological Society, Record Series, 105 (1942).

Brower, Reuben. 'Lady Winchilsea and the Poetic Tradition of the Seventeenth Century'. *Studies in Philology*, 42 (1945), 61–80.

Bühler, Curt F. 'A Letter by Andrew Marvell'. *Notes and Queries*, 197 (Oct. 1952), 451

Burdon, Pauline (1972). 'Andrew Marvell and Richard Flecknoe in Rome'. *Notes and Queries*, 217 (Jan. 1972), 16–18.

Burdon, Pauline (1978). 'Marvell after Cambridge'. *British Library Journal*, 4 (1978), 42–8.

Burdon, Pauline (1982). 'The Second Mrs Marvell'. *Notes and Queries*, 227 (Feb. 1982), 33–44.

Burdon, Pauline (1984). 'Marvell and his Kindred'. *Notes and Queries*, 229 (Sept. 1984), 379–85.

Burke, Edmund. *The Correspondence of Edmund Burke*. Gen. ed. Thomas W. Copeland. 10 vols. Cambridge, 1958–78.

Burton, Thomas. *Diary of Thomas Burton*. Ed. J.T. Rutt. 4 vols. 1828.

Cameron, W.J. 'Pope's Annotations on "State Affairs" Poems'. *Notes and Queries*, 203 (July 1958), 291–3

Campbell, Gordon. *A Milton Chronology*. Basingstoke, 1997.

Catalogus Librorum In Quavis Lingua & Facultate insignium Instructissimarum Bibliothecarum Tum Clarissimi Doctissimique Viri D. Doctoris Benjaminis Worsley, Tum Duorum Aliorum Doctrina Praestantium. 1678.

Chaney, Edward. *The Grand Tour and the Great Rebellion: Richard Lassels and 'The Voyage of Italy' in the Seventeenth Century*. Geneva, 1985.

Cheney, C.R., ed. *Handbook of Dates for Students of English History*. 2nd edn, Cambridge, 2000.

Chernaik, Warren. *The Poet's Time: Politics and Religion in the Work of Andrew Marvell*. Cambridge, 1983.

Chernaik, Warren and Martin Dzelzainis, eds. *Marvell and Liberty*. Basingstoke, 1999.

Christie, W.D., ed. *Letters Addressed from London to Sir Joseph Williamson while Plenipotentiary at the Congress of Cologne in the Years 1673 and 1674*. 2 vols. Camden Society, n.s. 8–9. 1874.

Cobbett, William and John Wright. *Parliamentary History of England*. 36 vols. 1806–20.

Collins, Dan S. *Andrew Marvell: A Reference Guide*. Boston, 1981.

Collins-Baker, C.H. *Lely and the Stuart Portrait Painters*. 2 vols. 1912.

A Compleat Catalogue of all the Stitch'd Books and Single Sheets Printed since the First Discovery of The Popish Plot... 1680.

Cook, John. *The History of God's House of Hull, Commonly Called the Charterhouse*. Hull, 1882.

Cox, Philip. 'Blake, Marvell, Milton and Young: A Further Possible Source for a "Proverb of Hell"'. *Notes and Queries*, 238 (Mar. 1993), 37–8.

Craze, Michael. *The Life and Lyrics of Andrew Marvell*. 1979.

Crino, Anna Maria. *Il Popish Plot: Nella Relazioni Inedite dei Residenti Granducali alla Corte di Londra (1678–81)*. Rome, 1954.

Crist, Timothy J. 'Francis Smith and the Opposition Press in England, 1660–1688'. Ph.D., Cambridge, 1977.

Crist, Timothy J. 'Government Control of the Press after the Expiration of the Printing Act in 1679'. *Publishing History*, 5 (1978), 49–78.

Cross, Claire. *Urban Magistrates and Ministers: Religion in Hull and Leeds from the Reformation to the Civil War*. University of York, Borthwick Papers 67 (1985).

Cutts, John P. 'British Museum Additional MS 31432: William Lawes' Writing for the Theatre and the Court'. *The Library*, 5th ser. 7 (1952), 225–34.

Darbishire, Helen. *Early Lives of Milton*. 1932.

Davidson, Peter. 'An Early Echo of Poems by Marvell'. *Notes and Queries*, 231 (Mar. 1986), 41.

Davidson, Peter. 'Green Thoughts. Marvell's Gardens: clues to two curious puzzles', *TLS*, 3 Dec. 1999, 14–15.

Davies, L.A. 'An Unpublished Poem About Andrew Marvell'. *Year in English Studies*, 1 (1971), 100–1.

Davison, Dennis. 'A Marvell Allusion in Ward's Diary'. *Notes and Queries*, 200 (Jan. 1955), 22.

Donno, Elizabeth Story. *Andrew Marvell: The Critical Heritage*. 1978.

Dryden, John. *Works*. Ed. Vinton Dearing, Edward N. Hooker, Alan Roper, H.T. Swedenberg Jr., *et al*. 20 vols. Berkeley, 1956–2000.

Dryden, John. *The Poems of John Dryden*. Eds Paul Hammond and Paul Hopkins. 5 vols. London, 1995– .

Duncan-Jones, E.E. 'Marvell in 1656'. *TLS*, 2 Dec. 1949, 791.

Duncan-Jones, E.E. 'Milton and Marvell'. *TLS*, 31 July 1953, 493.

Duncan-Jones, E.E. 'Marvell's "Friend in Persia" '. *Notes and Queries*, 202 (Nov. 1957), 466–7.

Duncan-Jones, E.E. 'Marvell's Letter to Sir John Trott'. *Notes and Queries*, 211 (Jan. 1966), 26–7.

Duncan-Jones, E.E. 'Smart and Marvell'. *Notes and Queries*, 212 (May, 1967), 182.

Duncan-Jones, E.E. 'J.W. and a Lost Portrait of Marvell by Lely'. *Notes and Queries*, 213 (Nov. 1968), 430–1.

Duncan-Jones, E.E. 'Marvell, R.F. and the Authorship of "Blake's Victory"'. *English Manuscript Studies 1100–1700*, 5 (1995), 107–26.

Duncan-Jones, E.E. 'Two Notes on Marvell'. *Review of English Studies*, 52 (2001), 192–4.

Dvortsovye Razriady. 3 vols. St Petersburg, 1850–54.

Dzelzainis, Martin. 'Marvell and the Earl of Castlemaine'. In *Marvell and Liberty*, eds Warren Chernaik and Martin Dzelzainis. Basingstoke, 1999, 290–312.

Ehrenpreis, Irvin. 'Four of Swift's Horses', *Modern Language Notes*, 70 (1955), 95–100.

Ellis, A.S. 'Pedigree of Marvell'. *Notes and Queries*, 6th ser., 1 (April 1880), 319.

Evelyn, John. *Diary*. Ed. E.S. de Beer. 6 vols. Oxford, 1955.

Finch, Ann. *The Poems of Anne Countess of Winchilsea*. Ed. Myra Reynolds. Chicago, 1903.

Fogel, Ephim G. 'Salmons in Both, or Some Caveats for Canonical Scholars'. *Bulletin of the New York Public Library*, 63 (1959), 223–36, 292–308.

Foxcroft, H.C., ed. *Supplement to Burnet's History of My Own Time*. Oxford, 1902.

Francis, F.C., ed. *Narcissus Luttrell's Popish Plot Catalogues. Luttrell Society Reprints*, 15 (1956).

Franklin, Benjamin. *The Autobiography of Benjamin Franklin*. Eds Leonard W. Labaree, Ralph L. Ketcham, Helen C. Boatfield, and Helene H. Fineman. New Haven: 1964.

French, J. Milton. *The Life Records of John Milton*. 5 vols. New Brunswick, New Jersey, 1949–58.

Fryde, E.B. and D.E. Greenway, S. Porter and I. Roy. *Handbook of British Chronology*. 3rd edn, 1986.

Fuller, Thomas Fuller. *The History of the Worthies of England*. 1662.

Gordon, Patrick. *Tagebuch des Generals Patrick Gordon*. Trans. Johann Stritter. Eds M.A. Obolenski and M.C. Posselt. 3 vols. Leipzig, 1849–51.

Gordon, Patrick. *Passages from the Diary of General Patrick Gordon of Auchleuchries*. Ed. Joseph Robertson. Aberdeen, 1859.

Green, James. *Poor Richard's Books*. Philadelphia, 1990.

Grey, Anchitell. *Debates of the House of Commons, From the Year 1667 to the Year 1694*. 10 vols. 1769.

Griffin, Patsy. *The Modest Ambition of Andrew Marvell*. Newark, Delaware, 1995.

Haan, Estelle. *Andrew Marvell's Latin Poetry: From Text to Context*. Brussels, 2003.

Haley, K.H.D. *William of Orange and the English Opposition 1672–4*. Oxford, 1953.

Haley, K.H.D. 'The Anglo-Dutch Rapprochement of 1677', *English Historical Review*, 43 (1958), 614–48.

Haley, K.H.D. 'Shaftesbury's List of the Lay Peers and members of the Commons, 1677–8'. *Bulletin of the Institute of Historical Research*, 43 (1970), 86–105.

Hammond, Paul. 'Marvell's Sexuality'. *The Seventeenth Century*, 11 (1996), 87–123

Hammond, Paul. 'Marvell's Coy Mistresses'. In *Re-constructing the Book: Literary Texts in Transmission*. Ed. Maureen Bell, *et al*. Aldershot, 2001, 22–33.

Hammond, Paul. *Figuring Sex between Men from Shakespeare to Rochester*. Oxford, 2002.

Hammond, Paul. 'Allusions to Milton, Marvell, and Dryden in an Unpublished Cambridge Prologue'. *Notes and Queries*, 248 (June 2003), 193–4.

Harrison, John and Peter Laslett, eds. *The Library of John Locke*. Oxford Bibliographical Society, n.s. 13. Oxford, 1965.

Hasler, P.W. *The History of Parliament. The House of Commons 1558–1603*. 3 vols. London, 1981.

[Hatton] *Correspondence of the Family of Hatton*. Ed. E.M. Thompson. 2 vols. Camden Society, n.s. 22–23. London, 1878.

Heawood, Edward. *Watermarks, Mainly of the 17th and 18th Centuries. Monumenta Chartae Papyraceae*, 1. Hilversum, The Netherlands, 1950.

Henning, Basil. *The House of Commons 1660–1690*. 3 vols. London, 1983.

Hetet, John S.T. 'The Wardens' Accounts of the Stationers' Company, 1663–79', in *Economics of the British Booktrade 1605–1939*. Eds Robin Myers and Michael Harris. Cambridge, 1985, 32–59.

Hetet, John S.T. 'A Literary Underground in Restoration England: Printers and Dissenters in the Context of Constraints, 1660–1680'. Ph.D., Cambridge, 1987.

Hine, Reginald L. *Confessions of an Un-Common Attorney*. 1945.

Hirst, Derek. '"That Sober Liberty": Marvell's Cromwell in 1654'. In *The Golden and the Brazen World*. Ed. John M. Wallace. Berkeley, 1985, 17–53.

Hirst, Derek and Steven N. Zwicker. 'High Summer at Nun Appleton, 1651: Andrew Marvell and The Lord Fairfax's Occasions'. *Historical Journal* 36 (1993), 247–69.

Hirst, Derek and Steven N. Zwicker. 'Andrew Marvell and the Toils of Patriarchy: Fatherhood, Longing, and the Body Politic'. *English Literary History*, 66 (1999), 629–54.

Hobbs, Mary. 'Early Seventeenth Century Verse Miscellanies and Their Value for Textual Editors'. *English Manuscript Studies 1100–1700*, 1 (1989), 182–210.

Hodge, R.I.V. 'Marvell's Fairfax Poems: Some Considerations Concerning Dates'. *Modern Philology* 71 (1974), 347–55.

Holberton, Edward. 'The Textual Transmission of Andrew Marvell's "A Letter to Dr Ingelo": The Longleat Manuscript'. *English Manuscript Studies*, 12 (2005, forthcoming).

Hume Brown, P., ed. *The Register of the Privy Council of Scotland*. 3rd ser. 16 vols. Edinburgh, 1908– .

Hunt, Arnold. 'The Books, Manuscripts and Literary Patronage of Mrs Anne Sadleir'. In *Early Modern Women's Manuscript Writing*. Eds Victoria Burke and Jonathan Gibson. Aldershot, 2004, 205–36.

Hunt, John Dixon. *Andrew Marvell: His Life and Writings*. 1978.

Hunter, Joseph, ed. *Letters of Eminent Men, Addressed to Ralph Thoresby*. 2 vols. 1832.

Isham, Gyles. 'Abram van den Bempde'. *Notes and Queries*, 202 (Nov. 1957), 461–3.

Kavanagh, Art. 'Andrew Marvell "in want of money": The Evidence in *John Farrington v. Mary Marvell*'. *The Seventeenth Century*, 17 (2002), 206–12.

Kavanagh, Art. 'Andrew Marvell and the Duttons of Sherborne in 1657'. *Notes and Queries*, 248 (June 2003), 183–8.

Kelliher, Hilton. 'Marvell's "A Letter to Doctor Ingelo"'. *Review of English Studies*, 20 (1969), 50–7.

Kelliher, Hilton. 'A New Text of Marvell's "To His Coy Mistress"'. *Notes and Queries*, 215 (July 1970), 254–6.

Kelliher, Hilton. *Andrew Marvell: Poet & Politician*. 1978a.

Kelliher, Hilton. 'Some Notes on Andrew Marvell'. *British Library Journal*, 4 (1978b), 122–44.

Kelliher, Hilton. 'Some Uncollected Letters of Andrew Marvell'. *British Library Journal*, 5 (1979), 145–50.

Kelliher, Hilton. 'Marvell, Andrew (1584–1641)', in *The Oxford Dictionary of National Biography*. Oxford, 2004a, vol. 37, 43–4.

Kelliher, Hilton. 'Marvell, Andrew (1621–78),' in *The Oxford Dictionary of National Biography*. Oxford, 2004b, vol. 37, 44–51.

Keymer, Thomas (1993). 'Marvell, Thomas Hollis, and Sterne's Maria: Parody in *A Sentimental Journey*'. *Shandean*, 5 (1993), 9–31.

Keymer, Thomas. *Sterne, the Moderns, and the Novel*. Oxford, 2002.

Klinkenborg, Verlyn. *British Literary Manuscripts, Series I: from 800 to 1800*. Pierpont Morgan Library. New York, 1981.

Konovalov, S. 'England and Russia: Three Embassies, 1662–5'. *Oxford Slavonic Papers*, o.s. 10 (1962), 60–104

Kyle, Chris R. '"It will be a scandal to show what we have done with such a number": House of Commons Committee Attendance Lists, 1606–1628'. In *Parliament, Politics and Elections 1604–1648*. Ed. Chris R. Kyle. Camden 5th ser., 17 (2001), 179–235.

Lawson, John. *A Town Grammar School Through Six Centuries*. Oxford, 1963.

Legouis, Pierre. 'Andrew Marvell: Further Biographical Points'. *Modern Language Review*, 18 (1923), 416–26.

Legouis, Pierre. 'Marvell's Maniban'. *Review of English Studies*, 2 (1926), 328–35.

Legouis, Pierre. *André Marvell: poète, puritain, patriote 1621–1678*. Paris, 1928.

Legouis, Pierre. 'Marvell and Addison: A Note to No. 89 of *The Spectator*'. *Review of English Studies*, 10 (1934), 447–50.

Legouis, Pierre. 'La Purge de Gargantua ou Marvell et Tallemant des Réaux'. *Études Anglaises*, 6 (1953), 236–8.

Legouis, Pierre. 'Marvell and "the two learned brothers of St. Marthe"'. *Philological Quarterly*, 38 (1959), 450–8.

Legouis, Pierre. *Andrew Marvell: Poet, Puritan, Patriot*. 2nd edn, Oxford, 1968 [1st edn 1965].

Leishman, J.B. *The Art of Marvell's Poetry*. 2nd edn 1968.

Locke, John. *Correspondence*. Gen. ed. P.H. Nidditch. 8 vols. Oxford, 1976.

Lord, George deForest. 'Two New Poems by Marvell?' *Bulletin of the New York Public Library*, 62 (1958), 551–70.

Lord, George deForest. 'Comments on the Canonical Caveat'. *Bulletin of the New York Public Library*, 63 (1959), 355–66.

Lord, George deForest, gen. ed. *Poems on Affairs of State: Augustan Satirical Verse 1660–1714*. [POAS] 7 vols. New Haven, 1963–75.

Love, Harold. 'Two Rochester Manuscripts Circulated from the Charterhouse'. *The Library* 6:16 (1994), 225–9.

Love, Harold (1997). 'How personal is a personal miscellany? Sarah Cowper, Martin Clifford and the Buckingham Commonplace Book'. In *Order and Connexion: Studies in Bibliography and Book History*. Ed. R.C. Alston. Cambridge, 1997, 111–26.

Lovelace, Richard. *Poems*. Ed. C.H. Wilkinson. Oxford, 1930.

Loxley, James. 'Marvell, Villiers and Royalist Verse'. *Notes and Queries*, 239 (June 1994), 170–2.

Loxley, James. 'Prepar'd at Last to Strike in with the Tyde? Andrew Marvell and Royalist Verse'. *Seventeenth Century*, 10 (1995), 39–62.

Ludlow, Edmund. *Memoirs*. Ed. C.H. Firth. 2 vols. Oxford, 1894.

Luttrell, Narcissus. *A Brief Historical Relation of State Affairs from September 1678 to April 1714*. 6 vols. Oxford, 1857.

Lynch, Beth. '*Mr Smirke* and "Mr Filth": A Bibliographic Case Study in Nonconformist Printing'. *The Library*, 7th ser. 1 (2000), 46–71.

Macdonald, Hugh. *John Dryden: A Bibliography of Early Editions and of Drydeniana*. Oxford, 1939.

Mandelbrote, Giles. 'The Organization of Book Auctions in late Seventeenth-Century London'. In *Under the Hammer: Book Auctions Since the Seventeenth Century*. Eds Robin Myers, Michael Harris and Giles Mandelbrote. New Castle, Delaware, 2001, 15–50.

Marchant, Ronald A. *The Puritans and the Church Courts in the Diocese of York, 1560–1642*. 1960.

Margoliouth, H.M. 'Andrew Marvell: Some Biographical Points'. *Modern Language Review*, 17 (1922), 351–61.

Marshall, Alan. 'Colonel Thomas Blood and the Restoration Political Scene'. *Historical Journal*, 32 (1989), 561–82.

Mathole, Paul. 'Marvell and Violence'. Ph.D., University of London, 2004.

Matthews, A.G. *Calamy Revised*. Oxford, 1934.

Miège, Guy. *A Relation Of Three Embassies From his Sacred Majestie Charles II to the Great Duke of Muscovie, The King of Sweden, and The King of Denmark*. 1669.

Miège, Guy. *La Relation de Trois Embassades...* Amsterdam, 1672.

Miller, Norman J., ed. *The Registers of Winestead, in Holderness, Co. York. 1578–1812*. Leeds: Yorkshire Parish Register Society, 1900.

Milton, John. *Complete Prose Works of John Milton*. Gen. ed. D.M. Wolfe. 8 vols. New Haven, 1953–82. [*CPW*]

Milton, John. *The Works of John Milton*. Gen. ed. F.A. Patterson. 20 vols. New York, 1931–40.

Milward, John. *The Diary of John Milward, Esq*. Ed. Caroline Robbins. Cambridge, 1938.

Moody, E. 'Chronology of Ann Finch's Poems'. http://www.jimandellen.org/finch/emafchr2.htm [28 April 2004].

Morgan, Blacker. *Historical and Genealogical Memoirs of the Dutton Family, of Sherborne, in Gloucestershire*. Privately printed, 1899.

Morton, Richard. *Pyretologia* [Gr.]. 1692.

Murray, Nicholas. *World Enough and Time: The Life of Andrew Marvell*. 1999.

Noble, Mark. *Memoirs of the Protectorate-House of Cromwell*. 2 vols. 1787 (first edn 1784).

Ogg, David. *England in the Reign of Charles II*. 2nd edn, Oxford, 1956.

Oldham, John. *The Poems of John Oldham*. Eds Harold F. Brooks and Raman Selden. Oxford, 1987.

Parker, Samuel. *A Reproof to the Rehearsal Transprosed*. 1673.

Parkin, Jon. 'Liberty Transpros'd: Andrew Marvell and Samuel Parker'. In *Marvell and Liberty*. Eds Warren Chernaik and Martin Dzelzainis. Basingstoke, 1999, 269–89.

Parks, Stephen. *The Luttrell File: Narcissus Luttrell's Dates On Contemporary Pamphlets 1678–1730*. New Haven, 1999.

Patterson, Annabel. 'The *Second* and *Third Advices-to-the-Painter*'. *Publications of the Bibliographical Society of America*, 71 (1977), 473–86.

Patterson, Annabel. *Marvell and the Civic Crown*. Princeton, 1978.

Patterson, Annabel. 'A Character of Marvell?'. *English Language Notes*, 17 (Dec. 1979), 113–19.

Patterson, Annabel (1999). 'Marvell and Secret History'. In *Marvell and Liberty*. Eds Warren Chernaik and Martin Dzelzainis. Basingstoke, 1999, 23–49.

Patterson, Annabel. *Marvell: the Writer in Public Life*. Harlow, Essex, 2000a.

Patterson, Annabel. 'A Restoration Suetonius: A New Marvell Text?' *Modern Language Quarterly*, 61 (2000b), 463–80.

Patterson, Annabel. 'Lady State's First Two Sittings: Marvell's Satiric Canon'. *Studies in English Literature*, 40 (2000c), 395–411.

Patterson, Annabel. *Nobody's Perfect: A New Whig Interpretation of History*. New Haven, 2002.

Patterson, Annabel and Martin Dzelzainis. 'Marvell and the Earl of Anglesey: A Chapter in the History of Reading'. *Historical Journal*, 44 (2001), 703–26.

Paulson, Ronald. *Theme and Structure in Swift's Tale of a Tub*. New Haven. 1960.

Pett, Peter. *The Happy Future State of England: or, A Discourse by way of Letter to the late Earl of Anglesey*. 1688.

Phillips, John. *The Secret History of the Reigns of K. Charles II. and K. James II.* 1690.

Phipps, Geraldine M. 'Britons in Seventeenth-Century Russia: A Study in the Origins of Modernization'. Ph.D., University of Pennsylvania, 1971.

Poetical Recreations Consisting of Original Poems, Songs, Odes, etc. 1688.

Poole, William. 'Two Early Readers of Milton: John Beale and Abraham Hill'. *Milton Quarterly*, 38 (2004), 76–99.

Pope, Alexander. *The Rape of the Lock and Other Poems*. Ed. Geoffrey Tillotson (Twickenham edition of *The Poems of Alexander Pope*, vol. 2). 3rd edn, 1962.

Povey, K. 'On the Diagnosis of Half-sheet Impositions'. *The Library*, 5th ser. 11 (1956), 268–72.

Pritchard, Allan. 'Marvell's "The Garden": A Restoration Poem?' *Studies in English Literature*, 23 (1983), 371–88.

Pritchard, Allan. 'The Houyhnhnms: Swift, Sentonius, and Marvell'. *Notes and Queries*, 235 (Sept. 1990), 350–6.

Raylor, Timothy. 'Reading Machiavelli; Writing Cromwell'. *The Turnbull Library Record*, 35 (2002), 9–32.

Raymond, Joad. 'Framing Liberty: Marvell's *First Anniversary* and the Instrument of Government'. *Huntington Library Quarterly*, 62 (2001), 313–50.

Raymond, Joad *Pamphlets and Pamphleteering in Early Modern Britain*. Cambridge, 2003.

Real, Hermann. 'The Authorship of some Anonymous Recommendatory Poems of Creech's Translation of Lucretius'. *Notes and Queries*, 213 (Oct. 1968), 377–8.

Reedy, Gerard. '"An Horatian Ode" and "Tom May's Death"'. *Studies in English Literature*, 20 (1980), 137–52.

Rees, Christine. '"Tom May's Death" and Ben Jonson's Ghost: A Study of Marvell's Satiric Method'. *Modern Language Review*, 71 (1976), 481–8.

Reresby, John. *Memoirs*. Ed. Andrew Browning; 2nd edn Mary K. Geiter and W.A. Speck. 1991.

Rivington, C.R. *A Brief Account of the Worshipful Company of Stationers*. 1921.

Robbins, Caroline (1957). 'Carlisle and Marvell in Russia, Sweden, and Denmark, 1663–1664.' *History of Ideas Newsletter*, 3 (1957), 8–17.

Robbins, Caroline. 'Six Letters by Andrew Marvell'. *Études Anglaises* 17 (1964), 47–55.

Robbins, Caroline. *Absolute Liberty*. Hamden, Connecticut, 1982.

Roberts, David. 'Two Shakespearian Allusions and the Date of Marvell's "The Nymph Complaining for the Death of her Faun"'. *Notes and Queries*, 247 (Sept. 2002), 338–43.

Roberts, William. *The Earlier History of English Bookselling*. 1889.

Rochester, John Wilmot, Earl of. *Works*. Ed. Harold Love. Oxford, 1999.

Savile, George, Marquis of Halifax. *Works*. Ed. Mark N. Brown. 3 vols. Oxford, 1989.

Savile Correspondence. Ed. W. D. Cooper. Camden Society, 71 (1858).

Scott, David. '"Particular Businesses" in the Long Parliament: The Hull Letters 1644–1648'. In *Parliament, Politics and Elections 1604–1648*. Ed. Chris R. Kyle. Camden 5th ser., 17 (2001), 273–341.

Scouten, Arthur H. and Herman Teerink. *A Bibliography of the Works of Jonathan Swift*. Rev. edn. Philadelphia, 1963.

Shaw, John. 'The Life of Master John Shaw'. In *Yorkshire Diaries and Autobiographies*. Ed. Charles Jackson. Surtees Society, 65 (1877), 119–62, 358–444.

Shawcross, John T. *Milton: A Bibliography for the Years 1624–1700*. Binghamton, 1984.

Silver, Victoria. 'The Obscure Script of Regicide: Ambivalence and Little Girls in Marvell's Pastorals'. *English Literary History*, 68 (2001), 29–55.

Smart, Christopher. *The Poetical Works*. Eds Karina Williamson and Marcus Walsh. 7 vols. Oxford, 1980–96.

Smith, Francis. *An Account of the Injurious Proceedings...* 1681.

Smith, Nigel and Maureen Bell. 'Andrew Marvell and the "femina periculosa"'. *TLS*, 26 Jan. 2001, 14–15.

Spence, Joseph. *Literary Anecdotes*. Ed. James Osborn. 2 vols. Oxford, 1966.

Stanewell, L.M., ed. *Calendar of the Ancient Deeds, Letters, Miscellaneous Old Documents, etc., in the Archives of the Corporation*. Hull, 1951.

The Statutes of the Realm ... From Original Records and Authentic Manuscripts. Ed. Alexander Luders, and others. 12 vols. 1810–28.

Stocker, Margarita and Timothy Raylor. 'A New Marvell Manuscript: Cromwellian Patronage and Politics'. *English Literary Renaissance*, 20 (1990), 106–62.

Swift, Jonathan. *A Tale of a Tub*. Ed. A.C. Guthkelch and D. Nichol Smith. 2nd edn. Oxford, 1958.

Swift, Jonathan. *The Prose Works*. Ed. Herbert Davis. 14 vols. Oxford, 1939–68.

Sykes, John. 'St Mary's, Hull'. *The Yorkshire Archaeological Journal*, 12 (1893), 464–80.

Sykes, John. 'Extracts from the Registers of the Church of Holy Trinity, Hull'. *The Yorkshire Archaeological Journal*, 14 (1896), 185–219.

Thane, John. *British Autography. A Collection of Fac-similies*. 3 vols. 1788–93. Vol. 2.

[Thoresby] *The Diary of Ralph Thoresby ... (1677–1724)*. Ed. Joseph Hunter. 2 vols. 1830.

Tickell, John. *The History of the Town and County of Kingston upon Hull*. Hull, 1798.

Tomlinson, E.M. *A History of the Minories, London*. 1907.

Toynbee, M.R. 'The Date of the Visit of King Charles I to Hull in 1639'. *Yorkshire Archaeological Journal*, 38 (1955), 1–2.

Treadwell, Michael. 'London Trade Publishers 1675–1750'. *The Library*, 4 (1982), 99–134.

A True and Faithful Account of the Several Informations Exhibited To the Honourable Committee appointed by the Parliament To Inquire into the late Dreadful Burning Of the City of London (1667, in 3 editions).

Tupper, F.S. 'Mary Palmer, Alias Mrs. Andrew Marvell'. *Publications of the Modern Language Association*, 53 (1938), 367–92.

Turner, W.A. 'Milton, Marvell and "Dradon" at Cromwell's Funeral'. *Philological Quarterly*, 28 (1949), 320–3.

Tyacke, Nicholas, ed. *The History of the University of Oxford. Volume IV. Seventeenth-Century Oxford*. Oxford, 1997.

Unkovskaya, Maria V. 'Anglo-Russian diplomatic relations 1580–1696'. D.Phil., Oxford, 1992.

Van Lennep, William. *The London State 1660–1800 ... Part I: 1660–1700*. Carbondale, Illinois, 1965.

Vertue, George. *Vertue Note Books*. 7 vols. Walpole Society, nos. 18, 20, 22, 24, 26, 29, 30. Oxford, 1930–55.

von Maltzahn, Nicholas. 'Samuel Butler's Milton'. *Studies in Philology*, 92 (1995a), 482–495.

von Maltzahn, Nicholas. '"I admird Thee": Samuel Barrow, Doctor and Poet'. *Milton Quarterly*, 29 (1995b), 25–8.

von Maltzahn, Nicholas (1996). 'The First Reception of *Paradise Lost* (1667)'. *Review of English Studies* 47 (1996), 479–99.

von Maltzahn, Nicholas. 'Marvell's Ghost'. In *Marvell and Liberty*. Ed. Warren Chernaik and Martin Dzelzainis. Basingstoke, 1999, 50–74.

von Maltzahn, Nicholas. 'Marvell's Constant Mind'. *TLS*, 21 June 2002, 14–15.

von Maltzahn, Nicholas. 'Marvell and the Lord Wharton'. *The Seventeenth Century*, 18 (2003), 252–65.

von Maltzahn, Nicholas (2005). 'Andrew Marvell and the Prehistory of Whiggism'. In *The Cultures of Whiggism*. Eds Abigail Williams and David Womersley. Newark, Delaware, 2004.

Wall, L.N. 'Marvell and the Third Dutch War'. *Notes and Queries*, 202 (July 1957), 296–7.

Wall, L.N. 'A Note on Marvell's Letters'. *Notes and Queries*, 202 (Mar. 1958a), 110–11.

Wall, L.N. 'Andrew Marvell of Meldreth'. *Notes and Queries*, 202 (Sept. 1958b), 399–400.

Wall, L.N. 'Marvell's Friends in the City'. *Notes and Queries*, 204 (June 1959), 204–7.

Wall, L.N. 'Marvell and the Skinners'. *Notes and Queries*, 207 (June 1962), 219.

Waller, Edmund. *The Poems of Edmund Waller*. Ed. G. Thorn-Drury. 1893.

Whitelocke, Bulstrode. *The Diary of Bulstrode Whitelocke 1605–1675*. Ed. Ruth Spalding. *Records of Social and Economic History*, n.s. 13. Oxford, 1990.

Wilding, Michael. 'Marvell's Reputation for Patriotism and Probity'. *Notes and Queries*, 215 (July 1970), 252–4.

Wildridge, T. Tindall, ed. *The Hull Letters ... 1625–1646*. Hull, 1887.

Williams, Harold. *Dean Swift's Library*. Cambridge, 1932.

Withington, Philip. *The Politics of Commonwealth. Citizens and Freemen in Early Modern England*. Cambridge, forthcoming.

Wood, Anthony. *Athenae Oxonienses ... To which are added, the Fasti*. 2 vols. 1691–92.

Wood, Anthony. *Athenae Oxonienses ... to which are added the Fasti*. Ed. Philip Bliss. 4 vols. 1813–20.

Wood, Anthony. *Life and Times of Anthony Wood*. Ed. A. Clark. 5 vols. Oxford, 1891–1900.

Worden, Blair. *The Rump Parliament*. Cambridge, 1974.

Worden, Blair. 'The Politics of Marvell's Horatian Ode'. *Historical Journal*, 27 (1984), 525–47.

Yardley, Bruce. 'The Political Career of George Villiers, 2nd Duke of Buckingham (1628–87)'. D.Phil., Oxford, 1989.

Yonge, James. *The Journal of James Yonge*. Ed. F.N.L. Poynter. 1963.

Index

Titled persons are listed under their titular names (Arlington, Buckingham), with some exceptions made for those whose fame derives from a time before their ennoblement (Monck). Inclusive as this index is, London, Westminster (also Whitehall), Hull (also its Corporation) and Yorkshire are so persistently the stages on which Marvell acted his life, or the places to or from which he wrote (or was written to or about), that to list references to them is impractical.

297

Printed in the United States
46526LVS00001B/8

9 780333 928882